THE TURNING POINT

THE TURNING POINT

1851—A Year That Changed Charles Dickens and the World

ROBERT
DOUGLAS-FAIRHURST

ALFRED A. KNOPF
NEW YORK 2022

THIS IS A BORZOI BOOK PUBLISHED BY ALFRED A. KNOPF

Copyright © 2021 by Robert Douglas-Fairhurst

All rights reserved. Published in the United States by Alfred A. Knopf, a division of Penguin Random House LLC, New York, and distributed in Canada by Penguin Random House Canada Limited, Toronto. Originally published in hardcover in Great Britain by Jonathan Cape, an imprint of Vintage Publishing, a division of Penguin Random House Ltd., London, in 2021.

www.aaknopf.com

Knopf, Borzoi Books, and the colophon are registered trademarks of Penguin Random House LLC.

Library of Congress Cataloging-in-Publication Data
Names: Douglas-Fairhurst, Robert, author.
Title: The turning point : 1851—a year that changed Charles Dickens and the world / Robert Douglas-Fairhurst.
Description: First United States edition. | New York : Alfred A. Knopf, 2022. | Includes bibliographical references and index.
Identifiers: LCCN 2021021682 (print) | LCCN 2021021683 (ebook) | ISBN 9780525655947 (hardcover) | ISBN 9780525655954 (ebook)
Subjects: LCSH: Dickens, Charles, 1812–1870. | Novelists, English— 19th century—Biography.
Classification: LCC PR4582 .D68 2022 (print) | LCC PR4582 (ebook) | DDC 823/.8 [B]—dc23
LC record available at https://lccn.loc.gov/2021021682
LC ebook record available at https://lccn.loc.gov/2021021683

Front-of-jacket photographs: Charles Dickens by Antoine A. Claudet, courtesy of Library Company of Philadelphia; engraving of the Crystal Palace, London, at the time of the Great Exhibition of 1851 © Photo 12/Alamy

Jacket design by Jenny Carrow

Manufactured in the United States of America

First American Edition

For Mac

The novelist demolishes the house of his life and uses its bricks to construct another house: that of his novel.

Milan Kundera, *The Art of the Novel*

Contents

PROLOGUE

Supposing

THE GREAT EXHIBITION BUILDING.—VIEW, SHOWING THE RIBS OF THE TRANSEPT.—(SEE PAGE 26.)

L ondon. December 1850. So far it has been an unusually mild winter—in Kensington there are reports that a tree is already sending out the first green shoots of spring. Not that everyone can see them. In fact some people can scarcely see past their own feet. Fog. Its dirty fingers probe and stroke the buildings, and make a ghost of anyone who ventures outside. It muffles the sounds of everyday life: the distant cries of street sellers, the clockwork chime of church bells, the steady rattle of horse-drawn cabs punctuated by the curses of foot passengers slipping on wet pavements. It is beautiful: in some places it is pale yellow or green in colour, creating halos around the hissing gas jets and turning every street scene into an impromptu stage set. It is also dangerous: on the evening of 23 December there is a collision in "dense fog" between two trains near Brick Lane, causing many passenger injuries after a carriage is "shattered in all directions." Fog everywhere.

Approaching the end of one year and the start of the next, the nation is getting used to seeing life as a series of pivots between the old and the new. Joseph Paxton's Crystal Palace—a nickname coined that summer by the playwright and wit Douglas Jerrold—is rapidly being assembled in Hyde Park, and already it is one of the most remarkable sights in London: a giant glass bubble wrapped around a cast-iron skeleton, like an experimental skyscraper gathering its strength for a final push upwards. On the ground there is a steady bustle of activity, as girders are bolted together and glass panels are slotted into place. Excitement about the forthcoming Great Exhibition of the Works of Industry of All Nations is also building. The *Illustrated London News* is carrying advertisements for sheet music featuring

"The Great Exhibition Polka," and it is also possible to buy a "Grand Authentic View" of the Crystal Palace engraved on steel "nearly Two Feet in Length"—although that is a mere doll's house design compared to the real building, which when completed will be 1,848 feet long by 456 feet wide, or roughly three times the size of St. Paul's Cathedral.

Elsewhere things are not progressing nearly so fast. Although mortality rates are falling, the latest official statistics show that they remain considerably higher in cities like London than elsewhere in the country, largely because of the diseases spread by contaminated water and overflowing graveyards. (A recent outbreak of cholera in Jamaica has given a terrible warning of what can happen when a city is gripped by infectious disease: in Kingston more than two hundred people have been dying every day, and with no more coffins left their bodies have been rotting in heaps under the tropical sun.) In December a young servant hired from the local workhouse achieves an unhappy kind of fame when it is revealed that she has been so badly mistreated by her employers—who have starved her, beaten her, and forced her to eat her own excrement—that when she is rescued the hospital surgeon who examines her declares that she is "the most perfect living skeleton I have ever seen." The newspapers are also full of reports describing how the convict George Hacket has recently escaped from Pentonville Prison, after levering up a part of the chapel floor and hauling himself down the prison wall using a rope made from knotted sheets; the next evening he sends a letter to the prison governor, in which he presents his compliments and announces that he is "in excellent spirits" and "in a few days intends to proceed to the continent to recruit his health." For all the visible signs of progress—everywhere ambitious modern buildings are rising out of the rubble of construction sites, and the streets are full of fresh scars as new sewers and gas pipes are laid—in some ways not much appears to have changed since the notorious thief Jack Sheppard achieved folk-hero status by repeatedly escaping from prison more than a century earlier.

The literary world is also caught between the old and the new. At her house in Chester Square, Mary Shelley is suffering from the brain tumour that will kill her in a matter of weeks; in her writing desk is a copy of

Shelley's poem "Adonais," wrapped around a silk parcel containing the charred remains of his heart and some of the ashes from his cremation on an Italian beach in 1822. Leigh Hunt, formerly a political radical and Keats's literary mentor, has recently celebrated his sixty-sixth birthday with the publication of a three-volume autobiography, in which he boasts that over a career spanning more than four decades he has somehow managed to avoid ever growing up: accused of being the "spoiled child of the public," he claims this is a title he is "proud to possess." At the same time there are signs the Romantic age is finally giving way to a more modern alternative. Alfred Tennyson has recently become Poet Laureate, following Wordsworth's death in April and the 86-year-old Samuel Rogers declining the office on account of his "great age," with Tennyson only deciding to accept after Prince Albert came to him in a dream and kissed him on the cheek. ("I said, in my dream, 'Very kind, but very German.'") The same month a revised edition of Elizabeth Barrett Browning's *Poems* is published, which now includes her *Sonnets from the Portuguese*, written during her courtship by Robert Browning a few years earlier; one sonnet begins "How do I love thee? Let me count the ways," a line that will later be reprinted in dozens of anthologies and borrowed by thousands of tongue-tied lovers, grateful that someone else had found a way to articulate their most intimate thoughts. "The old order changeth, yielding place to new," Tennyson had written in his 1842 poem "Morte d'Arthur." For younger writers this has started to sound less like an elegy than a manifesto.

It is at this historical juncture that Charles Dickens, one of the busiest men in London and currently the most famous writer in the English-speaking world, agrees to sit for a new portrait by the painter William Boxall. The portrait is never completed, after Dickens notices that it appears to be turning into someone else. First it is the notoriously ugly boxer Ben Caunt, a resemblance that probably occurred to Dickens because of the pun lurking in the artist's surname: at the end of December, he writes that Boxall paints like someone sparring with the canvas, repeatedly dancing backwards from it "with great nimbleness" before returning to make "little digs at it with his pencil." Then it is the murderer James Greenacre, whose wife's head had been found bobbing about in Regent's Canal in 1837, and whose waxwork effigy had subsequently been displayed at Madame Tussaud's. Finally, Dickens told the artist William Powell Frith, "I found that *I was growing like it!*—I thought it time to retire, and that picture will never be finished if it depends upon any more sittings from me."

It wasn't the only time Dickens would decide that a portrait hadn't truly captured his likeness. In 1856 he told his friend John Forster that a painting soon to be finished by Ary Scheffer showed "a fine spirited head . . . with a very easy and natural appearance to it," but "it does not look to me at all like, nor does it strike me that if I saw it in a gallery I should suppose myself to be the original." A few years later he was equally suspicious of the latest engraving of a photograph taken of him. "I do not pretend to know my own face," he told the artist. "I *do* pretend to know the faces of my friends and fellow creatures, but not my own." There

seems to be more going on here than the usual worry that other people cannot see us in quite the same way we see ourselves. For Dickens it was as if no artistic representation could ever depict someone with his famously fidgety energy. Kate Field, who attended Dickens's American public readings towards the end of his career, observed that even in photographs it looked as if his soul had been "pumped out of him."

Other images that survive from this period are no more successful. A daguerreotype probably taken in 1850 by the London photographer Antoine Claudet, still protected by its battered red leather and gilt case, shows Dickens trying to adopt a jaunty pose, with his left hand resting lightly on a side table and his right hand thrust into his trouser pocket, but he looks decidedly awkward, like an actor playing a role he doesn't quite believe in. A drawing made the previous year by the journalist George Sala affectionately retains Dickens's earlier pen name in depicting " 'Boz' in his Study," as the author reclines in his favourite armchair next to neat shelves

"Boz" in his Study

of books. Yet while his legs are comfortably crossed, and his eyes gaze off thoughtfully into the distance, his right hand—his writing hand—is again hidden from view, reaching inside an embroidered dressing gown as if trying to keep a secret.

Later images would attempt to make up for Dickens's personal elusiveness by showing him surrounded by his characters: a version of "Charles Dickens" that deliberately muddled together the man and the author who had used his fiction to scatter his personality in many different directions. By the end of his career Dickens had created around a thousand named characters; even his incomplete final novel, *The Mystery of Edwin Drood*, contained at least forty, including such human oddities as Deputy, a mysterious urchin who is paid a halfpenny by another character to throw rocks at him if he ventures out after 10 p.m. And never before in the history of fiction had so many characters seemed somehow bigger than their stories. Showing them hovering around Dickens was therefore more than just a way of imagining what might have been happening inside his head. It captured the feelings of many readers that these figures seemed on the point of walking off the page and entering real life.

Contemporary verbal portraits of Dickens aren't much better. "What a face is his to meet in a drawing-room!" wrote Leigh Hunt. "It has the life and soul in it of fifty human beings." Other witnesses quickly realised that trying to pin Dickens down in a single description would be like grabbing hold of a handful of smoke. Surviving anecdotes from this period reveal many different versions of him: the dandy who combed his hair "a hundred times in a day"; the actor who gestured with "nervous and powerful hands" while telling a story; the stickler for accuracy who devoted his life to the creation of elaborate fictions, and yet savagely beat his son in public when he discovered that "He has told *me* a lie! . . . He has told *his own father a lie!*"

Perhaps this is why Dickens's only surviving suit of clothes, the official court dress he bought to wear for a reception hosted by the Prince of Wales at St. James's Palace on 6 April 1870, just two months before his death, seems curiously empty of personality without Dickens himself being present to strut about in what he humorously described as his

"Fancy Dress"; set up on a stand in London's Dickens Museum, his hand-stitched wool tailcoat with gold trim looks more like a snake's shed skin. Nor are reports of Dickens's usual appearance any more helpful, perhaps because he always seems to have dressed as if he was on display. Caricatures of him published during his lifetime show a man gaudily encrusted with jewellery, making him look like a real-life Jacob Marley, whose ghost enters *A Christmas Carol* weighed down with chains and padlocks, while in 1851 Dickens appeared at a banquet "in a blue dress-coat, faced with silver and aflame with gorgeous brass buttons; a vest of black satin, with a white satin collar and a wonderfully embroidered shirt." "The beggar is as beautiful as a butterfly," sniffed Thackeray, "especially about the shirt-front."

Yet the same clothes that allowed Dickens to stand out from the crowd were also an elaborate shield he could hide behind. While his contemporaries busied themselves describing his "crimson velvet waistcoats," "multi-coloured neckties with two breast pins joined by a little gold chain" and "yellow kid gloves," the real Dickens could quietly slip away. Even the colour of his eyes was hard to be sure about: some people said green; others hazel, or grey, or *"dark slatey blue,"* or black, or a muddy combination of them all. In effect, by the end of 1850 Dickens had established himself in the public mind as something more than just another writer. He was an escape artist. Novelist, playwright, actor, social campaigner, journalist, editor, philanthropist, amateur conjuror, hypnotist: he was like a bundle of different people who happened to share one skin. Every time his contemporaries thought they'd worked out who he was, he managed to wriggle free.

Dickens sometimes enjoyed playing up to the idea that his name was a plural noun. He created multiple nicknames for himself, which in addition to "Boz" included "Revolver," "The Inimitable" and "The Sparkler of Albion." In the late 1840s, after making himself responsible for the stage lighting in some amateur dramatic performances, he added "Young Gas" and "Gas-Light Boy" to his growing repertoire of alter egos. He later sent a letter to one of the cast signed by all the characters he had played, including "Robert Flexible" in James Kenney's farce *Love, Law, and Physic* and "Charles Coldstream" in Dion Boucicault's comedy *Used Up*, with each signature being written in a distinct style of handwriting. The fact that "Charles" came directly after "Flexible" seems more than just a happy coincidence.

At the same time, he was wary of his literary identity being diluted by the work of other writers. In March 1850 he launched *Household Words*, a weekly journal that aimed to tackle some of the most pressing issues of the day. "All social evils, and all home affections and associations, I am particularly anxious to deal with," he had told a possible contributor in February. In practice this meant commissioning articles that would treat even weighty subjects like poverty or sanitation reform with a light touch, combining instruction and entertainment in a way that would appeal to readers who enjoyed this mixture in Dickens's own writing, where it formed the characteristic double helix of his style. "Brighten it, brighten it, brighten it!" he once instructed his subeditor W. H. Wills, after reading an article that was insufficiently "Dickensian"—a word that would soon be used to refer to any piece of writing that combined hard-hitting satire with sentiment and humour, whether or not Dickens himself was responsible for it. (Other coinages included "Dickensish," "Dickensesque" and "Dickensy.") Nonetheless he was wary of contributors who tried to flatter him by writing articles that offered little more than bad impressions of his style, like a form of literary karaoke: in one letter that summer he grumbled about the "drone of imitations of myself."

This problem was compounded by the sheer number of "Dickensian" plagiarisms and parodies clogging up the booksellers' shelves. The early flood of literary rip-offs and knock-offs that had accompanied Dickens's rise to fame—*Oliver Twiss*, *Nicholas Nickleberry*, and many more—might have abated, but there was still a steady trickle of publications that treated his style as a collection of narrative tricks that could be copied by anyone, rather than one that was as unique as a set of fingerprints. As early as 1845, George Cruikshank's *Comic Almanack* had printed "Hints to Novelists" that included advice on how to write in a style of "Weak Boz-and-Water," offering an example that began with a description of a tumbledown building full of cobwebs and memories of "broken hearts and ruined fortunes," in a part of London that is choked by fog: "It was a miserable November evening . . ." Clearly one challenge of writing *as* Dickens was to offer readers something more than those who spent their time merely writing *like* Dickens.

His audience already stretched from the highest to the humblest. The Queen once pressed a copy of *Oliver Twist* on the Prime Minister, Lord Melbourne, after confiding to her diary that she found Dickens's novel "excessively interesting"; at the other end of the social scale, his work was also appreciated by people like the elderly charwoman who every month attended a snuff shop where she listened to the latest instalment of *Dombey and Son* being read aloud. When she was told that Dickens had been spotted visiting some lodgings she cleaned, she was astonished that just one person had been responsible for a story so full of life. "Lawk ma'am! I thought that three or four men must have put together *Dombey!*" She was hardly an isolated case. Thanks to the influence of his fiction on popular culture—so far it had generated theatrical adaptations, songs, catchphrases, and even items of merchandise like Pickwick pastries and Fat Boy sweets—Dickens had become one of the few writers known by members of the public who couldn't even read.

This created problems: in 1850 Dickens published an article on begging letters in which he confessed that those who had contacted him so far included one man who wanted "a great coat, to go to India in," and another who asked him for "a pound, to set him up in life for ever." It also generated confusion. In a period where the lives of writers were attracting more attention than ever before, as could be seen in the revelation at the end of 1850 of the true identities of the three mysterious novelists who had published under the pseudonyms Currer, Ellis and Acton Bell (Charlotte, Emily and Anne Brontë), Dickens had so far managed to achieve a remarkable level of fame while letting the public know very little about him. Already he had resisted the attempts of some early biographers to slip underneath his guard, telling one American editor with thin-lipped irony in 1842 that the "Life of 'Boz'" he had published was "the most remarkable invention I ever met with."

Yet despite his fame Dickens's reputation was still surprisingly unstable. It wasn't just that he was personally elusive; his work was in danger of slipping out of his control. While a number of critics continued to praise his originality and humour, others were starting to wonder if he was a busted flush. Published in America the previous year, a book written by Thomas Powell had praised his former friend with one hand ("a man of genius . . . Mr. Dickens tells a story remarkably well") while using the other to deliver some jabs at his coarse over-writing; whereas his earliest works were "undoubtedly his best," Powell concluded, Dickens's talent was "fast fading away." Powell was a forger and thief who had only avoided prosecution in January 1849 after a court in London heard that he "was in a lunatic asylum, raving mad," so it is unlikely that Dickens took his criticisms very seriously. But they were only one version of an argument that had trailed his writing for a number of years, namely that he had been a far better novelist as the funny and original Boz than he could ever hope to be as the more serious and socially committed Dickens. As one journalist recalled, an "ancient female relative" of his who had thoroughly enjoyed Dickens's early works, which "could tickle her into ringing laughter, or melt her into passionate tears," used to warn him as a boy that "he has overworked himself—he has written himself out. *Mark my words, my dear, Boz has written himself out.*" Even Forster, whose biography of Dickens would later make every year sound like another step on the path to success, found himself cautiously returning to the word "perhaps" when looking back at this period of his friend's life. The idea that Dickens's most recent novel, *David Copperfield*, was driven forward by its characters "is to be said perhaps more truly of this than of any other of Dickens's novels"; the author's personal favourites were the Peggottys, "and perhaps he was not far wrong." Perhaps, perhaps.

Other writers were quick to recognise that, even after he had confirmed his early reputation with popular works like *A Christmas Carol*, the trajectory of Dickens's career continued to be far more wavering and uncertain than Forster later tried to make out. A short, strange book published under a pseudonym in 1849, which used the sketch of " 'Boz' in his Study" as its frontispiece, *The Battle of London Life; or, Boz and his Secretary*, made Dickens a literary character in order to imagine his doubts over what his next novel should be. In the first chapter he is seen "lolling in his favourite crimson-coloured library chair" with his lips pursed and his eyes fixed on the ceiling; three hours pass in silence, while his amanuensis waits patiently for some sparkling *bon mots* to be thrown his way, but when "Boz" finally opens his mouth it is only to say "What next? what next?"

At the end of 1850 most of the country was asking itself the same question. Although the revolutions that had convulsed mainland Europe in 1848 had never fully ignited in Britain, disenchantment with political radicalism was becoming ever more ingrained in the public mood. It was generally accepted that the great Chartist demonstration held on 10 April 1848 at Kennington Common, just across the river from the Houses of Parliament, had been something of a damp squib, with only 20,000 of the expected 200,000 demonstrators assembling in the rain to call for universal suffrage, and the delivery of a petition that was later revealed to have contained the signatures of "Mr. Punch" and "Pugnose." Yet major questions remained.

For many people the only revolutions that mattered now were those involving industry and transport, and neither of these could be influenced by the addition of a few funny names to a petition. There were now more than three thousand textile factories in England and Wales, altogether employing nearly half a million people, while over the past twenty years horse-drawn omnibuses and steamships had been introduced into an increasingly sophisticated *net-work* of communications. (The *Oxford English Dictionary* traces this sense of the word back to *Household Words* in August 1850.) However, by far the most visible signs of both industry and transport were the steam trains that had started to grind and whistle their way across the country. Here the statistics were startling. In 1830, when the first intercity railway line opened in Britain, there were less than a hundred miles of track. By 1850 that figure had grown to more than six thousand miles, linking London to Birmingham (1838), Bristol (1841) and Glasgow (1848) in a giant spider's web manufactured from iron and timber. Its effects on ordinary life were profound, altering everything from the physical appearance of the country—millions of tons of earth had to be gouged out of the landscape to create railway cuttings and level the ground for tracks to be laid—to the measurement of time, particularly after the nation's clocks were synchronised in the 1840s to ensure that all trains ran to the same timetable. It changed the way people saw the world, dissolving the view out of their carriage windows into a blur of movement, and even what they read on their journey: the first railway station bookstalls had been launched in 1848 by the entrepreneur W. H. Smith, selling two-shilling editions of popular novels.

New travel networks also changed how people thought. In an 1850 treatise on the likely prospects of the country, an opening chapter on the "Influence of Improved Transport on Civilisation" had pointed out that "The art by which the products of labour and thought, and the persons who labour and think, are transferred from place to place, is, more than any other, essential to social advancement." This was an idea Dickens strongly supported, and he saw his writing as part of the same project. He had long enjoyed comparing the act of composition to travelling by train, as if there were a natural connection between arranging words into lines of print and moving carriages along a set of tracks. As early as 1835, he explained that in order to "get on" with his writing he had to build up a head of steam: "my composition is peculiar; I can never write with effect— especially in the serious way—until I have got my steam up," and in a later letter he described the imagination as a "powerful Locomotive." Now he started to wonder if a novel could be turned into a vehicle for progress in a more meaningful way than simply moving its characters from A to B. What next?

"Now, what I want is, Facts," urges Mr. Gradgrind at the start of Dickens's *Hard Times*, emphasising the point with a jab of his square fore-finger. The 1851 census would certainly give Britain's other Gradgrinds much to ponder. The total population was now more than 21,000,000, or nearly double what it had been fifty years earlier, which one statistician calculated would take up an area of seven square miles, "allowing a square yard to each person," or three months for everyone to march briskly through London four abreast. Roughly a million women worked as ser-vants, including a third of all those aged between fifteen and twenty-five who lived in London. On 30 March, the date the census was taken, almost twice as many people were kept in lunatic asylums (21,004) as were being treated in hospitals (11,647), and there were also four times as many work-house inmates (131,582) as prisoners (30,959).

Some other aspects of life continued to slip through the statistical net. Rapid advances in science and technology had not wholly extinguished older ways of making sense of the world: the folklorist Thomas Sternberg reported that even in 1851 many Northamptonshire peasants continued to wear "lucky bones" to protect themselves against witchcraft, or made themselves amulets from the kneecaps of sheep or lambs to ward off cramps. And while the world was being woven together ever more tightly through networks of transport and communication, occasionally there were reminders that it remained full of mysterious gaps. The captain's map in Lewis Carroll's 1876 poem *The Hunting of the Snark*, which is praised by his crew for being "A perfect and absolute blank," was only a slight exaggeration of the truth when it came to parts of the world like the inaccessible regions of snow and ice that lay to the north of Canada. As far as most of the population was concerned (other than the indigenous people who actually lived there, who were rarely consulted) these regions were a blank sheet of paper just waiting to be written on. Anyone who set off to make his mark on them—like the polar explorer John Franklin, who had sailed with a company of 128 men aboard the HMS *Erebus* and HMS *Terror* in May 1845 to discover the fabled Northwest Passage, and by the following autumn had been swallowed up by the region's pack ice—was likely to vanish into a world of speculation and folklore.

Those who were alive at the time of the 1851 census could still be lost in other ways. Most of the working poor continued to live largely anonymous lives, with nothing but a marriage or criminal conviction in the public records to flesh out the bare facts of their births and deaths. Reflecting on *Hard Times* in 1854, Dickens explained that his satire in that novel was directed against "those who see figures and averages and nothing else—the representatives of the wickedest and most enormous vice of the time," who would try to comfort a labourer travelling twelve miles to and from his workplace every day "by informing him that the average distance of one inhabited place to another in the whole area of England, is not more than four miles. Bah!" Writing a decade after *A Christmas Carol*, he still saw himself surrounded by humbug. In response, his fiction took the other "figures" he saw every day—the ordinary people who were usually hidden in the grand sweep of statistics—and revealed that they too were extraordinary if looked at closely enough. Even a minor character like the Orfling in *David Copperfield*, who arrives from the workhouse and immediately distinguishes herself in David's eyes with her "habit of snorting," could be given the kind of attention that was far removed from the fate of individuals like the real servant who in 1850 had been subjected to a life of starvation and beatings. Dickens gave his readers history on a human scale.

This had been a particular challenge in the previous decade, when rising food prices had coincided with a series of bad harvests, and a potato blight had led to many crops rotting in the fields. The so-called Hungry Forties were experienced with particular savagery in Ireland, where a million people were estimated to have died of starvation between 1846 and 1851, with another 350,000 dying from typhus in 1846–47, and a further million emigrating to America or elsewhere. But the repeal of the Corn Laws in 1846, together with a sustained period of economic recovery, meant that by the end of 1850 even the statisticians were starting to feel more confident about the future. The forthcoming Great Exhibition, in particular, was leading many people to hope that it would inaugurate a new age of national prosperity and international cooperation, in which Great Britain would finally measure up to its name.

It was not only politicians and economists who found themselves looking forward to what the new year might bring. *Punch* was just one of many publications that found itself trying to make sense of events by making up stories about them. In "A Vision of the New Year," a poem published in the 1850 Christmas issue, the writer imagined the "newborn Year" in the traditional form of a child. "I am all the Future's own," it explains, "These favoured hands shall bring / The Dove-eyed Peace and Commerce, grown / A giant 'neath her wing." A later article, "Visions in the Crystal," was more playful, imagining Joseph Paxton's building as a giant crystal ball in which the whole of humankind could be seen "shaking hands together, with JOHN BULL in their midst, instructing them in that only genuine mode of fraternisation." Like most jokes it was poking fun at an idea some people took far more seriously. The *Illustrated London News* also imagined a bright new future, this time by employing a vaguely prophetic style. In an article on "The Old and the New Year," published on 21 December, it recalled Europe's grim recent history and trumpeted the idea that "We have left behind us the Plain of Terrors and journey with glad heart toward the Land of Promise." In fact wherever readers looked there was widespread agreement that whatever happened in the coming months, and however many

unforeseen plot twists there were, the new year had all the ingredients
to be a successful comedy: a story with a happy ending.

Dickens was far less certain. Already he had published two short articles in *Household Words* under the general heading "Supposing," which
pushed this type of thought experiment in a different direction. In both
articles he offered a number of alternatives to the current situation,
introducing each one with the same modest hypothetical, such as
"Supposing, we were all of us to come off our pedestals and mix a little
more with those below us . . . I wonder whether we should lower ourselves beyond retrieval!," or, with an eye on reforming the honours
system so that it recognised individual merit rather than inherited privi-
lege, "Supposing, we had at this day . . . an Earl Stephenson, or a
Marquess of Brunel, or a dormant Shakespeare peerage, or a Hogarth
baronetcy, I wonder whether it would be cruelly disgraceful to our old
nobility!" Another pair of "Supposings" would appear in 1851: in one he
asked his readers to imagine how they would feel if a "gentleman of
good family" convicted of assaulting a police officer were treated like the
host of a social salon during his week in prison, and in the other he contrasted the case of one woman who had died "in a most deplorable and
abject condition, neglected and unassisted by the parish authorities"
with that of a "drunken and profligate" prisoner, who had been "presented with a large gratuity for her excellent conduct." All four articles
played on the idea that some aspects of contemporary British life were
still far stranger than the "just suppose" of fiction.

Then, on 7 December, Dickens visited Hyde Park to see for himself
what progress had been made towards the Great Exhibition. Shortly after
his visit he decided to let his house for six months in 1851, convinced that
he would be swamped by visitors if he remained in London, but what
particularly unsettled him was the suspicion that the Crystal Palace was
merely a giant glass bauble that would distract people's attention from far
more important matters such as political reform and social justice. In one
letter he told the American academic Dr. Elisha Bartlett that "We are grad-

ually getting mad here, on account of the Great Exhibition," before asking in the next sentence whether New York had yet recovered from the public sensation of Jenny Lind, the soprano who had recently embarked upon a wildly successful tour of America, and also "whether Mr. [P. T.] Barnum will ever be President." The implication was that the forthcoming Exhibition could end up being just another triumph of spectacle over substance.

Even Dickens's famous sense of humour appeared to be under threat. On 14 December, *Household Words* included "A December Vision," in which Dickens imagined death passing through the world, turning every living thing to dust, and listed the many social wrongs in Britain that needed to be put right: thousands of children in London "hunted, flogged, imprisoned, but not taught"; crowds of people "fore-doomed to darkness and dirt, pestilence, obscenity, misery, and early death"; a legal system so tied up in knots it created "mad people babbling in hospitals" and "orphans robbed of their inheritance." Set against these problems were the politicians who endlessly delayed coming up with any solutions; but just as the weak and poor found themselves being struck down by death, Dickens warns, the same "mighty Spirit" would eventually take these individuals too, "turning its face hither and thither as it passed along on its ceaseless work, and blighting all on whom it looked." Like winter's fogs, death was inescapable.

By the start of the new year he was feeling slightly more optimistic. In "The Last Words of the Old Year," published in *Household Words* on 4 January 1851, he depicted a penitent 1850 on its deathbed admitting that "a Year of Ruin" had "smashed the country," leaving it almost as ignorant and backward as before, with scenes that included two starving seven-year-olds "whose heads scarcely reached the top of the dock" being sentenced to a whipping for stealing a loaf of bread. Dickens looked forward to 1851 as an opportunity for the country to do things differently. "I have seen a wonderful structure, reared in glass, by the energy and skill of great natural genius," the dying year remarks. Now it asks itself if the world is ready to unite for "another Exhibition—for a great display of England's sins and negligences, to be, by a steady contemplation of all eyes, and steady union of all hearts and hands, set right?"

Dickens's question came at a pivotal moment in his life. In the special Christmas edition of *Household Words* published at the end of 1850, he had written about "the branches of the Christmas Tree of our own young Christmas days, by which we climbed to real life." One of the presents he vividly remembered playing with as a boy was his sister's doll's house: "a stone-fronted mansion with real glass windows, and door-steps, and a real balcony," containing "elegantly furnished" rooms and a miniature set of blue crockery. Now the adult Dickens lived in the real thing. Number 1 Devonshire Terrace was a substantial house with a grand stone entrance located near to the gates of Regent's Park. He had rented it since the end of 1839, filling it not only with full-sized crockery but also a full-sized family: Charley (b. 1837), Mary (b. 1838), Katey (b. 1839), Walter (b. 1841), Francis (b. 1844), Alfred (b. 1845), Sydney (b. 1847), Henry (b. 1849) and baby Dora (b. 1850), together with his loving but understandably exhausted wife Catherine. Her portrait was on the wall alongside his, both of them painted by Dickens's friend Daniel Maclise, but anyone who compared the paintings would have been in no doubt as to how their marriage appeared to other people. Whereas Dickens is pictured in 1839 sitting by the study window in his earlier home of 48 Doughty Street, his hand resting on a book and his glittering eyes caught in a shaft of sunlight, Catherine's hands are occupied with a fiddly piece of embroidery, her eyes cast downwards. This second work has been described as "a pendant" to Maclise's earlier portrait, although when it was first exhibited in 1848 some viewers went even further. A misprint in the catalogue meant that it was labelled "Mr. Charles Dickens," and two visitors were overheard trying to make sense of what they were looking at. "Why," said one of them, "it is a portrait of a lady; it can't be *Mr.* Charles Dickens!" "Oh yes it is," replied her friend. "You know he is a great actor, as well as writer; and the picture represents him in some female character." If you were Catherine Dickens—Mrs.

Charles Dickens—living alongside a famous writer meant living in his shadow; sometimes you could disappear in plain sight.

Much else had changed since Dickens's childhood. The time when his family had fallen into debt, and he had been sent to work at Jonathan Warren's tumbledown blacking warehouse on Old Hungerford Stairs, near what is now Charing Cross railway station, was one scab in his memory he could never resist picking. At Warren's he was paid six shillings a week to paste labels onto small earthenware bottles of shoe polish, while the rats rustled in the shadows and the twelve-year-old Dickens felt his ambitions crumbling around him. "My whole nature was so penetrated with the grief and humiliation" that life was slipping away, he later wrote in an autobiographical fragment, "that even now, famous and caressed and happy, I often forget in my dreams that I have a dear wife and children; even that I am a man; and wander desolately back to that time of my life." Sometimes this wandering took on a physical form. In his first book, *Sketches by Boz*, Dickens had described, as one of London's early-morning sights, small office lads in large hats "who are made men before they are boys" struggling not to buy "the stale tarts so temptingly exposed in dusty tins at the pastry cooks' doors." That had also been his own experience, writing in the autobiographical fragment that "in going to Hungerford Stairs of a morning, I could not resist the stale pastry put out at half-price on trays at the confectioners' doors in Tottenham-Court Road; and I often spent on that the money I should have kept for my dinner." In *David Copperfield* he returned to the same scene once more, describing the "stale pastry put out for sale at half-price at the pastrycooks' doors": evidence that no matter how successful he was as a writer there were sinkholes in his memory that continued to exert a gravitational pull. Wherever he went physically, his "wandering fancy" often ended up in the same place.

While the young David Copperfield enjoys a "small collection of books" that open up his imagination and keep alive his "hope of something beyond that place and time," the adult Dickens now had a well-stocked library in his ground-floor study, including shelves of his own publications. His imagination also spilled over into the rest of the house, where the pictures on display included a painting of *The Old Curiosity Shop*'s Little Nell by Fanny McIan, and specially commissioned portraits of *Barnaby Rudge*'s Dolly Varden and *Nicholas Nickleby*'s Kate Nickleby by William Powell Frith, which Dickens hung on the walls like honorary family members. A few months earlier, he had written that he was busy with "my various children—real and imaginary," and his own children were painfully aware that their father sometimes confused them with his paper-and-ink offspring. "I am certain that the children of my father's brain were much more real to him at times than we were," confessed his eldest son Charley, who had returned to Eton College by train after Christmas at the start of 1851, and was greeted at the railway station by forty or so friends "with their heads out o' the coach winders . . . a hallooing 'Dickens!' all over the Station!" So Dickens recounted his servant's report, evidently proud that in this story his namesake was turning out to be the hero. Whether or not Charley really was this popular was far less important than his father's ability to reshape real life until it had the reassuring outlines of a piece of fiction.

Dickens also remained keenly aware of how easily his own life could have gone in a different direction. "Pause you," Pip later urges the reader in *Great Expectations*, "and think for a moment of the long chain of iron or gold, of thorns or flowers, that would never have bound you, but for the formation of the first link on one memorable day." It is an idea that had long haunted Dickens. "I wear the chain I forged in life," Marley tells Scrooge. "I made it link by link, and yard by yard; I girded it on of my own free will, and of my own free will I wore it." But at the end of 1850 Dickens knew that many of his readers still did not have this kind of freedom. That was one of the reasons for his commitment to social reform: it was a way of allowing more people to choose the direction of their lives, even if—like Marley—they ended up choosing badly. "Whether I shall turn out to be the hero of my own life . . . these pages must show," is the opening line of *David Copperfield*. One reason Dickens needed a novel to express this idea was that for too many people it was still a question that was out of their hands. If you were a domestic servant shivering in a garret, or a factory worker in danger of having your limbs mangled by the latest piece of machinery, the idea that you could be the hero of your own life was usually restricted to the parallel world of fiction.

The final number of *David Copperfield* was published in November 1850, bringing to a close a novel that had started off as an exercise in imaginative time-travelling, after Dickens chose to model parts of his hero's childhood on his own early life. Yet by the end of this year many of the questions raised in the novel—how do we become the people we are? can the past ever be escaped? is it possible to write a happier future for ourselves?—were not only pressing for Dickens. They also reflected the national mood.

The idea that a novelist could be viewed as a representative figure or a cultural spokesman sounds absurdly ambitious now, but at the time it was a natural extension of Dickens's all-embracing popularity. In 1844, Richard Horne's *A New Spirit of the Age* had declared that "Dickens is manifestly the product of his age," a living embodiment of its energy and ambition, and a few years later Harriet Martineau, in the second volume of her entertain-ingly opinionated *History of England During the Thirty Years' Peace: 1816–1846*, had saluted Dickens as "a man of genius who cannot but mark the time, and accelerate or retard its tendencies." Over the next two de-cades this view would be widely shared, as "Dickensian" slowly became a loose synonym for "Victorian," and increasingly the "Dickensian" would not be identified with early works like *The Pickwick Papers* but with some-thing new. Starting in 1851, Dickens would produce a number of what the critic Lionel Stevenson later described as his "dark" novels—not because they were gloomy (in some ways they were the funniest novels Dickens ever wrote) but because they reflected his growing sense of a serious social mission, and his understanding of the kind of narrative that would be required to do it justice. Over time they would come to resemble a perma-nent shadow cast by—and on—the age.

The first of these "dark" novels was *Bleak House*. On modern book-shelves it looks as solid as a brick, but as originally published it was a far riskier affair. Although Dickens's decision to issue it in monthly instal-ments, between March 1852 and September 1853, followed the same pattern of publication he had used for most of his earlier novels, in other ways it was the greatest fictional experiment of his career. Dickens's "dark" novels would later include *Hard Times* (1854) and *Little Dorrit* (1856), both of which examined the state of the nation in relentless close-up: north and south, city and country, rich and poor; but this was an approach that could not have been adopted if Dickens had not already developed it in the writ-ing of *Bleak House*. In terms of its subject matter and technique alike, this novel was a signpost towards the future. Yet Dickens's progress towards the first instalment in March 1852 was far from straightforward. Like Esther, the character in *Bleak House* who shares storytelling duties with an anonymous narrator, he had "a great deal of difficulty in beginning to write . . . these pages," and to trace his stuttering progress through the previous year reveals more than his sense of a country that was "going to pieces," as Sir Leicester Dedlock complains halfway through the novel. It shows that *Bleak House* was Dickens's attempt to reassemble Britain on the page, as he pieced together fragments of contemporary life to reflect the world his readers knew, while at the same time offering them a model of the fairer, kinder world they could enjoy if they accepted the need for reform.

The novel hints at how challenging this process could be when Esther visits the chaotic home of philanthropist Mrs. Jellyby. Having already met her son, who has "tumbled downstairs" and bumped his head, and her daughter, whose hair is also "tumbled" about, it isn't any great surprise when Esther opens some cupboards and piles of household rubbish come "tumbling out":

> . . . bits of mouldy pie, sour bottles, Mrs. Jellyby's caps, letters, tea, forks, odd boots and shoes of children, firewood, wafers, saucepan-lids, damp sugar in odds and ends of paper bags, footstools, blacklead brushes, bread, Mrs. Jellyby's bonnets, books with butter sticking to the binding, guttered candle ends put out by being turned upside down in broken candlesticks, nutshells, heads and tails of shrimps, dinner-mats, gloves, coffee-grounds, umbrellas . . .

It is a deftly choreographed piece of narrative slapstick, as Dickens parodies a catalogue entry by piling up chaotically unrelated items that happen to begin with the same letter ("boots . . . bags . . . blacklead brushes, bread . . . bonnets, books with butter sticking to the binding . . ."), but also a curious insight into his own methods of composition. As the critic Robert Newsom has pointed out, "Revealing the way Dickens puts together his novels is rather like opening one of Mrs. Jellyby's closets": all kinds of unexpected materials tumble out.

Dickens himself was fully aware that a set of written fragments might not add up to a coherent whole. Towards the end of *Bleak House* he describes a still night in London, as the streets are slowly drained of people and "every noise is merged, this moonlight night, into a distant ringing hum, as if the city were a vast glass, vibrating." By the time this instalment was published in 1853, the Crystal Palace had long since shut its doors to the paying public, but Dickens's metaphor retains an echo of the crowds who had patiently filed along its walkways to view the beautiful, bizarre and at times baffling objects on display: a sheet of paper 2,500 feet long, an inlaid mosaic table containing two million pieces of wood, a canister of boiled mutton produced for a polar expedition, an artificial silver nose, an early version of Braille, an expanding hearse, a set of fruit stones carved into complicated shapes by Prince Albert's brother, a bouquet of flowers made from the wings of birds and beetles, a dressing table that doubled as a fire escape . . . Such objects served as a good warning of what William James would refer to later in the century as the "blooming, buzzing confusion" of life that assaults the senses until it is organised in some way. What a novel like *Bleak House* could do was to transform this confusion into something more coherent. Simultaneous events could be turned into sequences; the babble of a crowd could be concentrated into conversations between identifiable individuals; the seemingly random events of life could be rearranged into a plot. And in doing this Dickens would not only alter the direction of his own career as a novelist, he would change the future of the novel.

If there is one phrase that gathers together all these ideas it is a *turning point*: "a point at which a decisive change of any kind takes place; a critical point, crisis." Developing earlier ideas in geometry of an object being moved until it points in a different direction, this figurative application is now "the usual sense," according to the *Oxford English Dictionary*. Some nineteenth-century examples show the two parts of this phrase being yoked together by a hyphen ("turning-point" rather than "turning point"), creating a little pivot around which the idea could revolve; but far more important than any minor variants in printing was its range of possible applications. For in a period when the English-speaking world was altering dramatically in terms of technology and trade, with "turning point" it had found a phrase that could be used to investigate the relationship between changes of global importance and the smaller kinks and swerves of individual lives.

As Frederick Arnold explained the idea in his 1873 book *Turning-Points in Life*, "There are, unquestionably, 'turning-points' both in the history of the race and in the history of the individual. Such are the great battles, the great revolutions, the great discoveries of history. Each art, each science, has its 'turning-points,' its moments. Such are evermore to be found in the lives of individuals." Arnold's preferred explanation for these moments was providence, arguing that God interferes at the critical junctures of our lives "to favour the ends which He designed." Many of his contemporaries agreed, and "turning point" was often used to describe the experience of religious conversion. Just as original sin was sometimes explained as a single decision that had far-reaching consequences ("Was temptation not the turning point in Adam's life?" asks one sermon from 1858), so books including George Eliel Sargent's *The Turning Point: A Book for Thinking Boys and Girls* (1849), Mary Elizabeth Beck's *Turning-Points, and Their Results in the Lives of Eminent Christians* (1881) and Louisa C. Silke's *Turning-Points; or, Two Years in Maud Vernon's Life* (1885) all celebrate characters recoiling from sin and moving towards a supposedly bright future. All present their stories as joyful evidence that our lives are primed by providence.

Other writers spun the same language in less religious directions. For Samuel Smiles, in *Self-Help* (1859), his bestselling book of biographical sketches, the key moment in anyone's life arrived when they tried to change the kind of story they were in. One of Smiles's examples is Hugh Miller, the self-taught Scottish geologist and folklorist, who saves himself from a life of drunkenness after he sees the words of Bacon's *Essays* dancing on the page before him, and immediately takes a pledge of abstinence. "It is such decisions as this that often form the turning points in a man's life," Smiles concludes, "and furnish the foundation of his future character." By 1909, when Mark Twain was asked to contribute to a series of articles in *Harper's Bazaar* on "The Turning Point of My Life," the idea had become so familiar he could enjoy mocking it as just another piece of high-flown rhetoric that needed to be brought down to earth. "I know we have a fashion of saying 'such and such an event was the turning-point of his life'," he explains, "but we shouldn't say it," because if we think of life as a chain of events there is no logical reason to believe one link in the chain will be weighted with any more significance than the rest. To talk of turning points also assumes that we are free to change direction, whereas in Twain's view our ingrained temperament and circumstances beyond our control are far more likely to keep us trudging along the same path forever.

The other main area of disagreement lay in whether a turning point had to involve just one moment in a life—either a Damascene conversion or a secular Eureka! For William M. Thayer, in his 1895 book *Turning Points in Successful Careers*, while there might be a steady accumulation of factors leading to a change of direction, the change itself was likely to be rapid and decisive. Thayer even includes a chapter on Dickens, and sees the pivotal period in his life as one when he gave up his early work as a legal clerk and tried to carve out a career as a professional writer. It was a decision Dickens himself later narrowed down to a single moment in 1833, when he carried a package containing his first story, "Mr. Minns and his Cousin" (later published as "A Dinner at Poplar Walk"), down Fleet Street, entered a dark alley known as Johnson's Court, and stealthily dropped it into the letter box of the *New Monthly Magazine*—a physical turning away from the crowd that also marked a potentially decisive turning point in his career. Possibly for this reason, Dickens was drawn to describing equally significant moments in his fiction. In *David Copperfield*, Micawber holds on to David as "a young but valued friend . . . who is connected with the most eventful period of my life; I may say, with the turning-point of my existence." Pip in *Great Expectations* is equally confident that his life would have turned out very differently had the escaped convict Magwitch not returned to visit him in London: "A great event in my life, the turning point of my life, now opens on my view."

However, at other times Dickens appears to have thought that, for anyone who did not believe the future was already written by an invisible hand, every moment was potentially a key moment; undertaking life's journey meant travelling on a path that bristled with fingerposts. And the most significant turns in a life could take far longer to complete than his own decision to enter Johnson's Court. That much is clear from numerous articles published in his journals *Household Words* and its successor *All the Year Round*. A leading article on Dickens's old friend Douglas Jerrold sees the "turning-point of his career" as the period when "he rose steadily towards the distinguished place which was his due among the writers of his time"; in another piece, the nine years of the English Civil War are summarised as "the great turning-point in English History." Such examples suggest that Dickens and his contemporaries did not only think of a turning point as a sudden crisis or unexpected twist of fate. It could also be a period that led to slower, more far-reaching changes.

This book identifies 1851 as a turning point for Dickens, for his contemporaries and for the novel as a form that created important lines of communication between them. Roughly a third of the way through *Bleak House*, Dickens asks his readers a series of questions. Most will be solved by the end of the novel, but the final one has no simple answer:

> What connexion can there be between the place in Lincolnshire, the house in town, the Mercury in powder, and the whereabout of Jo the outlaw with the broom, who had that distant ray of light upon him when he swept the churchyard-step? What connexion can there have been between many people in the innumerable histories of this world who from opposite sides of great gulfs, have, nevertheless, been very curiously brought together!

"What connexion can there be . . ." is a question that always intrigued Dickens. It underlies his stories about fragmented families and the unpredictable recoil of human memory; it helps to explain his attraction to railways, telegrams and all the other new ways in which people were starting to be linked together; it is sunk deeply into the texture of his writing, with its snagging repetitions and catchphrases whereby one thing does not always lead on to another but can just as easily get stuck in a loop. It also underlies many of the other questions his contemporaries were asking themselves and each other at the start of 1851. Did the rich and the poor live together in one nation or in two separate nations? What was—what should be—the relationship between Britain and the rest of the world? If the Great Exhibition had the potential to be a significant turning point in history, what would have happened without it, and how far was the country going to deliver on its promises? The events of the coming year would provide plenty of opportunities to answer these questions, but the fullest and most imaginative answer to "What connexion can there be . . ." would be *Bleak House* itself, a novel that creates a "web of very different lives" and shows how intimately they are connected.

Bleak House has been accurately described by one critic as "a novel quite unlike any which Dickens—or anyone else—had written before," and to see how it emerged from its surroundings it is necessary to write a different kind of biography. Dickens once characterised the proofs of an edition of *Household Words* as an "inky fishing-net," alluding to his many editorial interventions in the form of handwritten corrections and crossings-out. Most biographies are also inky fishing nets—not only because they try to capture their subjects using lines of print, but because so much of what a life includes inevitably falls between the cracks. The problem is recognised by Julian Barnes in his 1984 novel *Flaubert's Parrot*. "You can define a net two ways, depending on your point of view," his narrator observes. "Normally you would say it is a meshed instrument designed to catch fish. But you could, with no great injury to logic, reverse the image and define the net as a jocular lexicographer once did: he called it a collection of holes tied together with string." However, a biography that restricts its scope can sift events with a finer mesh; to borrow Virginia Woolf's description of the modern novel, it can "record the atoms as they fall." In this book I follow the twists and turns of a single year in the life of Charles Dickens to reveal what happened to him in this crucial period, and how these events influenced the writing of his greatest novel. My aim is not only to record the atoms as they fell, but to reveal the patterns they made as they settled. The usual term for this approach is *microhistory*, but when it comes to the shape of someone's life it would be equally accurate to describe it as *slow biography*. Whereas most biographies speed up the events of their subjects' lives until they resemble the actors in a jerky black-and-white film—years pass in pages; events follow one another without any hesitation or brooding—this book tries to slow a life down until it returns to something closer to the texture of ordinary experience.

1851 is a year that would alter Dickens both personally and creatively. He would have to cope with the trauma of a double bereavement and a home life that was in danger of falling apart. He would also launch a campaign to change how writers were perceived, using his own fiction and journalism to demonstrate that writing was not only shaped by the world, but could press back against its surroundings and try to mould them into something new. And by the start of the year he was ready to face the challenge. As he told another writer, who had sent him a story about the social reforms that might knit a divided country back together again, "I am on the tip toe of expectation."

WINTER

Stages

D ickens opened his bright green front door after breakfast on Saturday 25 January and stepped out into another mild day. It was partially cloudy with a gentle breeze, but there was no sign of frost or snow: perfect weather to walk to work despite the stinking cold he was suffering from. (Later that day he would send a letter complaining that "everybody seems to be ill, more or less, all along of the late unseasonable weather.") It was a publication day for *Household Words*, and Dickens set off to travel the distance of just under two miles to his office, a fine-boned and dapperly dressed 38-year-old with a "light step and jaunty air." Three weeks earlier the *Morning Post* had reminded its readers that the new year was "the birthday of new undertakings, social, literary, and commercial—a turning point in all men's careers," and Dickens too was keen to get on. A later caricature would depict him walking with almost comical determination in a foot race (he completed the twelve-mile course in three hours), and his usual pace was equally impressive: "striding along with his regular four-miles-an-hour swing," according to his son Charley, "his lips slightly working" as he thought of something or someone he might later try to turn into a piece of writing.

Almost all this writing required close daily contact with the city where he lived. London was "a vile place," he had increasingly come to believe, telling the novelist Edward Bulwer Lytton in February that whenever he came back from abroad and saw "that great heavy canopy" of smoke sinking over the rooftops, "I wonder what on earth I do there." The short answer was that he needed it to think about and to think with: in many ways it was the most important relationship of his life. "For a week or a fortnight I can write prodigiously in a retired place (as at Broadstairs), and

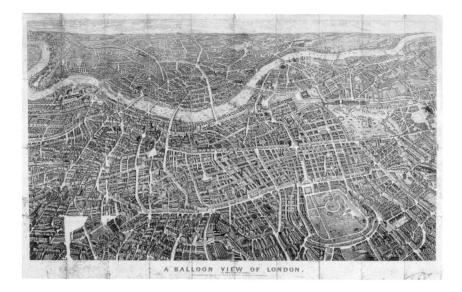

A BALLOON VIEW OF LONDON.

a day in London sets me up again and starts me," he had written to John Forster from Switzerland in 1846 while trying to begin *Dombey and Son*. "But the toil and labour of writing, day after day, without that magic lantern, is IMMENSE!! . . . *My* figures seem disposed to stagnate without crowds about them." He needed to be surrounded by life in order to recreate it on the page.

Dickens told an American visitor the following year that "he had trained his eye and ear to let nothing escape him," and he had already given the same skill to David Copperfield, who boasts when he visits his friend Traddles that "I looked at nothing, that I know of, but I saw everything," including the odd detail that "his blacking-brushes and blacking were among his books—on the top shelf, behind a dictionary." In 1867, Dickens would explain his tactics in more detail to the Methodist pastor G. D. Carrow:

> When in the worst parts of the city my invariable precaution was to seem not to notice any person or thing in particular. I would walk along slowly, preserving an air of preoccupation, and affecting as nearly as possible the ways of a collector of house rents or of a physician going his rounds. When any scene of especial interest attracted

my notice I usually halted at a crossing as if waiting for a conveyance
or as if undecided which way to go. Or else I would stop and purchase some trifle, chatting with the vendor and taking my time for
making a selection, or would order a glass of half-and-half [a mixture
of ale and bitter], wait for the froth to subside, and then consume an
hour in sipping it to the bottom . . . I suppose, sir, that I know London
better than any one other man of all its millions.

Even walking to work could produce a tempting sideways glimpse of
something that might lodge in his mind, and this type of first-hand research
was especially important at a time when the country as a whole appeared
undecided about which way to go.

If Dickens had wanted a bird's-eye view of his route in January, he
could have looked at a giant map such as *A Balloon View of London*, published that year, which unfolded to reveal the higgledy-piggledy appearance
of the city as seen from an airborne vantage point over Hampstead, and
in which the tangled lines of streets and splotches of parkland looked
barely able to contain the thousands of tiny brown smudges representing
London's buildings. Alternatively, for a three-dimensional map he could
have visited the Colosseum, a pleasure dome in Marylebone that first
opened its doors in 1832, and featured a vast panorama of London viewed
from a 112-foot-high rotunda that was reached by an "ascending platform." (Dickens had reported on the relaunch of this attraction in 1835,
when he was impressed by the Colosseum itself—"a perfect scene of
enchantment"—but was far less enthusiastic about the other visitors, a
boringly respectable crowd of "match-making mammas," "sleepy papas"
and "marriageable daughters in scores.") Inevitably these overviews gave
the impression that London was little more than a giant container for its
most famous landmarks. So did many guidebooks published this year,
such as *Knight's Pictorial London*, in which the reader was taken on a rapid
tour of the Tower of London, Westminster Abbey and other historic
sights, as if everything else in the city were merely a set of obstacles liable
to get in their way.

The London that Dickens knew wasn't this static. Instead it was an enormously complicated puzzle where the pieces kept changing shape. New buildings announced themselves with plate-glass windows and ostentatious gas jets, like the gin palaces Dickens had written about in *Sketches by Boz*, with their "stone balustrades, rosewood fittings, immense lamps, and illuminated clocks, at the corner of every street." Fires broke out, like the one that destroyed a public house in St. Martin's Lane on 10 January 1851, killing three members of the same family. Even hidden parts of the city were being dug up and replaced, like the sewers at the bottom of Northumberland Street, a short walk from the *Household Words* offices, which had flooded just before Christmas the previous year, drowning two workmen who were unable to get out in time.

There was a part of Dickens that loved this evidence of the city renewing itself. In "A Preliminary Word" to the first issue of *Household Words* in March 1850, he had told his readers that he intended to reveal "the many social wonders" that could be seen in "the stirring world about us," and at the time nowhere was stirring more dramatically than London. With railway lines slicing through old neighbourhoods, and rows of houses creeping ever further outwards from the centre, it was a city on the move. Usually this idea pleased Dickens: when the Phantom in *The Chimes* announces that "The voice of Time . . . cries to man, Advance!" he also offers a brisk summary of Dickens's own faith in progress. Dickens had expressed his views more bluntly when he reacted to the first exhibition of paintings by the Pre-Raphaelite Brotherhood in 1850, complaining that their desire to return to the visual style of the Middle Ages was backward-looking in more than just an aesthetic sense. If these artists were serious about "cancelling all the advances of nearly four hundred years and reverting to one of the most disagreeable periods of English History," Dickens argued in a scornful *Household Words* article, there might as well be a Pre-Newtonian Brotherhood for those objecting to the laws of gravity, or a Pre-Galileo Brotherhood for those still refusing to believe that the earth revolves around the sun.

Yet even Dickens was sometimes alarmed at the speed of change. In *The Old Curiosity Shop*, Kit becomes confused about exactly where the shop itself stood after it was pulled down to make way for a "fine broad road," and in *Little Dorrit* Mrs. Clennam's house doesn't even wait for a demolition crew, collapsing at the end of the novel into a pile of rubble and a cloud of choking dust. Dickens also worried about large-scale urban projects like the creation of New Oxford Street, which was completed in 1847 after a thoroughfare had been driven through St. Giles, a district of squalid poverty south of Bloomsbury that stretched roughly from Soho in the west to Seven Dials in the east. The new thoroughfare joined Oxford Street with Holborn and resulted in the eviction of some five thousand slum dwellers; none of them was rehoused, and later in 1851 Dickens would point out that this only shifted the problem elsewhere. "Thus, we make our New Oxford Streets, and our other new streets," he wrote, "never heeding, never asking, where the wretches whom we clear out, crowd." Unsurprisingly, many ended up squeezing themselves back into whichever parts of the old slum still remained. In 1849, *The Times* had published a letter from fifty-four people whose dwellings were adjacent to Tottenham Court Road, complaining that "We live in muck and filthe. We aint got no priviz, no dust bins, no water-splies, and no drain or suer in the hole place." When a *Times* journalist followed up this communication he discovered a woman suffering from cholera, a "strange boy" who had eaten nothing for two days other than a solitary crust of bread, and a child wearing a sack who was being consumed by fever while his parents looked helplessly on. They were all living in just one room.

Other writers were sometimes more concerned about the flattened buildings themselves; faced with the disappearance of those parts of London that Dickens had known, the poet Matthew Arnold claimed that "I should like to see them all placed carefully under glass." But for Dickens nothing in London was more important than its endlessly shifting population. In his early sketch "The Streets—Morning," he had tried to capture the experience of being surrounded by people who drifted in and out of his consciousness from one sentence to the next: the "last drunken man" staggering home before sunrise; a bricklayer's labourer "with the day's dinner tied up in a handkerchief" walking briskly to work; middle-aged clerks plodding onwards to their counting houses, knowing almost all their fellow commuters by sight "but speaking to no one." This fascination with London's anonymous crowds never left him, and when he was walking through London his attention was repeatedly snagged by the people he passed on the street. Usually they behaved like theatrical extras, but occasionally one stepped into the spotlight to deliver a line Dickens could file away in his memory or jot down in his memorandum book. "Well Sir, your clothes is all shabby, and your boots is all burst," or "Then I'll give up snuff." It meant that each time a character like Scrooge or Fagin opened his mouth he revealed himself to be living with one foot in the world of fiction and another in the world of Dickens's readers. As Sir Arthur Helps would later explain in an obituary of Dickens, "We can hardly call them characters, for they are persons with whom we have lived," and "the reality of whose existence" even the most literal-minded people "refuse to entertain any historic doubts." Through Dickens's writing, imaginary beings took on the solidity of physical facts.

In January 1851, London's anonymous crowds included several individuals who would later be singled out by fame. To take just one example, an ambitious young writer named Marian Evans had recently moved into a chaotically bohemian household at 142 Strand, where she would spend the next couple of months living alongside the radical publisher John Chapman. She would also become caught up in a lopsided love triangle with Chapman and his wife, a triangle that later revealed itself to be more like a badly drawn square when it became clear that the couple also shared their home with Chapman's mistress, an arrangement that suited nobody apart from Chapman himself. In March, Evans would leave 142 Strand, fleeing an atmosphere that had started to crackle with unhappy erotic tensions; six months later she would return to take charge of Chapman's latest publishing venture, the high-minded *Westminster Review*, a journal she would go on to edit (despite only being credited as the "assistant editor") until 1854. But on 25 January all that was to come, and less than three weeks after she had first moved to London she was still at the stage of settling into her new rooms and exploring the city.

On 4 May the following year, Dickens would visit 142 Strand to chair a meeting held in opposition to the price-fixing policy of the Booksellers' Association, and in January 1858 he would write to Marian Evans—who by now had adopted the pseudonym of George Eliot—to congratulate her on the publication of her first work of fiction, the two-volume collection *Scenes of Clerical Life*. "My Dear Sir," his letter begins, indicating that he hadn't yet made the connection back to the fiercely intellectual young woman he had first encountered nearly six years earlier in Chapman's house. (It wasn't a memorable meeting for Eliot either, who wrote that Dickens was "disappointing . . . not distinguished looking in any way—neither handsome nor ugly, neither fat nor thin, neither tall nor short.") But had he caught sight of her years earlier as he walked to work? He probably wouldn't have been surprised if he had. "The world, he would say, was so much smaller than we thought it," Forster reported, "we were all so connected by fate without knowing it; people supposed to be far apart were so constantly elbowing each other; and to-morrow bore so close a resemblance to nothing half so much as to yesterday."

The city that Dickens and Eliot shared wasn't only a place for seeing and being seen. It assaulted the other senses too. On Saturday morning the air was full of the cries of street sellers and the steady rumble of traffic, not to mention the smells of horses and light industry. In 1851, the approach of London could be tasted in the air long before the city itself came into view, and a whiff of smoke "could always distinguish a London letter . . . on putting it to the nose." It is sometimes said that smell is relative, and perhaps Victorian noses weren't as sensitive as our own to some of these odours, just as we aren't usually aware of the petrol fumes being belched out in a modern city. On the other hand, Dickens's office boy noticed that he was "a man who lived a lot by his nose," and on the evidence of Dickens's letters it was just as alert as the rest of his senses; in 1838 he had written to his landlord that the drains servicing the two water closets of 48 Doughty Street "have been a serious annoyance to us . . . although we have had the plumbers in the house half a dozen times." By 1851, despite moving to Devonshire Terrace, he couldn't escape similarly unpleasant smells simply by leaving his house. The Thames was now so polluted its banks were caked with raw sewage being slopped around by the tides, while the river itself was a thick ribbon of smells winding its way through the city. The closer Dickens got to the *Household Words* offices, located just a couple of hundred yards from the river, the worse the stench became, and an article he had already accepted for the issue of the journal to be published on 1 February showed that he didn't expect his readers simply to take such unpleasant facts for granted. In "Father Thames" Richard Horne imagined the river jovially offering him a cup of tea made with Thames water, which is revealed to be a rich stew of industrial waste, sewage, rotting vegetables, dead dogs, and an "inky flood" of liquid pouring out of urban graveyards. It is only after travelling a considerable distance upriver that Horne discovers a more pleasant alternative: a series of "bright spouting springs" pouring out 50 million gallons of new river water every day. "I breathe fresh life," Father Thames announces solemnly, looking forward to a time when a pollution-free river "shall be himself again."

Horne's article was closely modelled on Dickens's own habit of asking his readers to look at familiar surroundings in a new way. And as Dickens's readers learned to see London through his eyes, its imaginative shape started to change alongside its physical fabric. A cartoon published in 1890 that showed a fictitious "Charles Dickens Street," in which the buildings were twisted into some of Dickens's most famous characters—in Sikes Court a carriage entrance is formed from a mouth stretching open in an angry grimace—was only a literal version of what mid-century readers had long experienced for themselves. London was becoming Dickensian. Even when he was walking to work, Dickens's route took him past many of the places he had already described in his fiction, and many more he would go on to re-create in later works. If he chose to walk down Portland Place and the grand neoclassical sweep of the recently completed Regent Street, for example, he would pass the Dombeys' house at the corner with Bryanston Square, the shop in *The Pickwick Papers* where Sam Weller spies a Valentine's card, and the "handsome suite of private apartments" in

Nicholas Nickleby where Sir Mulberry Hawk and Lord Frederick Verisopht are discovered "reclining listlessly on a couple of sofas" while nursing hangovers from "last night's gentlemanly frolics"; he could then cut across to Leicester Square, where Sir George Saville's house is pulled down by rioters in *Barnaby Rudge*, and finally pass through Covent Garden, renamed

"Common Garden" in *Oliver Twist* by Bill Sikes, who boasts that it is where fifty boys sleep rough every night if Fagin wants a fresh selection of thieves to "pick and choose from." Alternatively, on leaving Devonshire Terrace, Dickens could walk across to the highly respectable Fitzroy Square, which the narrator in *Nicholas Nickleby* dismisses for its "dowager barrenness and frigidity," continue down Tottenham Court Road, where Traddles ventures in *David Copperfield* to recover a table and vase from a pawnbroker's shop, pass through Seven Dials, where Nicholas Nickleby and his sister get lost in a labyrinth of streets, and finally make his way down Bow Street, where the Artful Dodger and Barnaby Rudge both appear before magistrates in their respective novels. And that is only a small selection of the fictional echoes that surrounded him on his way to work. In fact, whichever route he took, Dickens would have found himself in a situation similar to Scrooge's when he is visited by three spirits on Christmas Eve. Walking to Wellington Street North on Saturday 25 January, Dickens was surrounded by the ghosts of stories past, stories present and stories yet to be.

He was also committed to making the country as a whole more "Dickensian" by using *Household Words* to champion social and political reform. After launching the journal in March 1850, within a month he had published "A Tale of the Good Old Times," an article by Percival Leigh that poked fun at people who sentimentalised the recent past, when a mother could be "dragged to the gallows with her child at her breast, for shop-lifting, to the value of a shilling," and also pointed out that the age of Shakespeare wasn't altogether one of hey nonny no and begone dull care. "Would Everybody, would Anybody, would *you* wish to have lived in these days, whose emblems are cropped ears, pillory, stocks, thumbscrews, gibbet, axe, [and] chopping-block?" Less than two months later Dickens published "Press On," a poem by Richard Horne about a stream that is forever moving forward while murmuring what turns out to be a piece of general advice for life: "Press on!"

By the end of November Dickens's attitudes had hardened, and he had written a fiercely partisan piece on the Pope's recent declaration restoring the Catholic hierarchy in England—a decision that had unleashed a wave of anti-Catholic propaganda across the country—in which he expressed his long-held view that, as he told Forster in 1846, Protestantism was a progressive religion of "neatness; cheerfulness; industry; education; continual aspiration," whereas Catholicism was characterised by "dirt, disease, ignorance, squalor, and misery." That sort of judgement was hardly a model of Christian charity, but Dickens found it impossible to regard the Catholic Church's rituals as anything other than pieces of bad theatre. In his article everything is made to support the view that Catholicism was rooted in the kinds of superstitions that modern Christians ought to have outgrown. Even the weather seems to be on his side, as he describes a scene that takes place "one November evening at dusk, when all was mud, mist and darkness, out of doors, and a good deal of fog had even got its way into the family parlour." As John Bull's family grope about in the fog, so the mud outside their door threatens to become an emblem of the muddle within.

Dickens's suspicion of the idea that Britain had proved itself a progressive modern nation latched on to equally large targets elsewhere. The law, in particular, had continued to resist attempts to reform its more archaic practices since the period when, at the age of fifteen, Dickens had spent around eighteen months working as a legal clerk for Ellis and Blackmore solicitors in Gray's Inn. In an article on "The Martyrs of Chancery," published in *Household Words* on 7 December 1850, a young lawyer named Alfred Whaley Cole had outlined some of the recent cases heard by the Court of Chancery (which had jurisdiction over matters such as trusts, estates, land law and the guardianship of orphans), producing outcomes that were technically legal but scarcely met most people's definitions of justice. One involved a man with "pinched features" and a "weak starved voice" who had been imprisoned for twenty-eight years after spending a legacy and then learning that another relative intended to dispute the will; a second described a man who had been jailed "by mistake," but because "The Court of Chancery, like all dignified bodies, is never in a hurry," he was then forced to wait a further seventeen years for his release. In

February 1851, Dickens would publish a second instalment, this time in response to a letter in *The Times* that had claimed the Court of Chancery was "blameless," and if some individuals spent a long time in prison that was because they had acquired a taste for it. That certainly didn't match Dickens's assessment, although anyone who had followed his career from the start might have wondered if his fixation on the law was evidence that he had secretly developed what Forster once described as an "attraction of repulsion." It was a phrase he originally used to refer to Dickens's appalled fascination with the squalor of St. Giles, but it would not have been much of a stretch—conceptually as well as geographically—for it also to have been applied to this particular institution.

Dickens had first written about the Court of Chancery in *The Pickwick Papers*, where Mr. Pickwick rents a room in the Fleet Prison from a gaunt "Chancery prisoner" who has lived there "long enough to have lost his friends, fortune, home, and happiness." (Later Mr. Pickwick learns that the prisoner has "obtained his release at last" by dying.) Dickens himself became snarled up in Chancery red tape in 1844, after suing the publishers of a plagiarism of *A Christmas Carol*. Initially he was successful, writing to Forster that "The pirates are beaten flat. They are bruised, bloody, battered, smashed, squelched and utterly undone." But he was then forced to enter into a further six Chancery suits against the publishers, printers, booksellers and pseudonymous author, after which he discovered that not only would he fail to receive any damages, he would also have to pay nearly all his own costs. Altogether the proceedings ended up costing him around £700: a huge sum at the time, and an outcome that in Dickens's view was typical of a legal system that all too often appeared to distribute rewards and punishments the wrong way round. As he told Forster, "I shall not easily forget the expense, and anxiety, and horrible injustice of the Carol case, wherein, in asserting the plainest right on earth, I was really treated as if I were the robber instead of the robbed."

At the start of 1851, the political world seemed equally resistant to change. On 21 February, less than three weeks after the official state opening of Parliament, Lord John Russell's government would resign following growing criticism over the recently announced budget, but just ten days later Russell—"damaged, weak and unpopular" according to the contemporary diarist Charles Greville—would pick up his office exactly where he had left it, after nobody else could form an administration. His ministry would eventually fall a year later, following a vote of no confidence led by the headstrong former Foreign Secretary Lord Palmerston, but in the meantime the fact that a government could resign yet carry on regardless seemed emblematic of a democracy that worked rather better for those making the rules than it did for those governed by them. It was a crisis that would apparently change nothing.

Dickens's own political views had mellowed somewhat since his days as a young shorthand reporter for the radical newspaper *The True Sun*, but more than a decade after leaving the reporters' gallery in Parliament he still found it impossible to think about "that great Dust Heap down at Westminster" without being gripped by anger and despair. "Night after night," David Copperfield explains of his own stint as a gallery reporter, "I record predictions that never come to pass, professions that are never fulfilled, explanations that are only meant to mystify. I wallow in words." Forster put it more bluntly, explaining that when it came to the ability of politicians to stretch the truth to breaking point, Dickens "omitted no opportunity of declaring his contempt at every part of his life." No doubt some of this can be put down to his suspicion of empty rhetoric—a favourite motto was "Don't talk about it—do it!"—together with his hatred of any kind of suspense. "The interval between the accomplishment of anything, and 'its first motion,' Dickens never could endure," Forster reported, "and he was too ready to make any sacrifice to abridge or end it." But at the start of 1851 it wouldn't have taken an unusually impatient observer to conclude that Britain's political machinery was rusting to a halt.

In 1850, Dickens's friend and literary hero Thomas Carlyle had published *Latter-Day Pamphlets*, a survey of the country's current state that at times resembled a dystopian novel in disguise. While most people in Britain were relieved that they had managed to avoid similar recent political upheavals to their European neighbours, Carlyle's gloomy assessment was that unless decisive measures were taken an even worse outcome was only a matter of time. The events of 1848 were proof that society rested on a "powder-mine of most flammable mutinous chaotic elements," he argued, and the spark most likely to set them off was not revolution but democracy. That is because democracy was "forever impossible," according to Carlyle, as it went against the natural tendency of the strong to dominate the weak and the educated to rule the ignorant. In this context, all talk of "enfranchisement, emancipation, freedom, suffrage, civil and religious liberty" was nothing but "fatal infinite nonsense." Giving the poor a vote would be particularly wrong-headed, Carlyle reasoned, because they had already demonstrated that they couldn't cope with such responsibility after a lifetime spent "doing too little work and drinking too much beer." Carlyle's authoritarian tendencies are on full display here, as he laments the fact that the ballot box is merely a test of popularity, so that elections reward those who are most electable rather than those who are fittest to lead. What comes next is even more disturbing, as he offers a grim vision of Britain being overwhelmed by "floods of beggars," untreated sewage, and acres of paper generated by useless parliamentary debates. His conclusion is that what the country needs isn't more democracy. What it needs is stronger leaders.

Although Carlyle was photographed in 1851 displaying a firmly clenched jaw and a distant, long-suffering stare, not everyone took him seriously; according to the poet and translator Edward FitzGerald, books like *Latter-Day Pamphlets* "make the world laugh, and his friends rather sorry for him." But in wondering whether the European revolutions of 1848 had really achieved anything, Carlyle was tapping a current of thought that remained live. Tennyson's most recent poem, his great elegy *In Memoriam*, offered a similarly conservative view of progress:

> Ring out old shapes of foul disease;
>   Ring out the narrowing lust of gold;
>   Ring out the thousand wars of old,
> Ring in the thousand years of peace.

If there's a suggestion here that such improvements might be harder to achieve than someone ringing a bell (when you read the lines aloud, "ring out" sounds identical to "wring out"), Tennyson's stanza goes around in a circle of its own; following an ABBA rhyme scheme, it is a ring that ends up more or less where it started. Appearing in 1850, the publication of *In Memoriam* was perfectly timed for readers who wanted some stability and harmony after years of uncertainty, and increasingly it seemed that time itself was on their side. As the historian G. M. Trevelyan once observed, with Europe's underlying political structures remaining largely unaffected by the threat of revolution, as these events began to fade into memory and anecdote it was hard to escape the conclusion that 1848 had been "the turning point at which modern history failed to turn."

Dickens arrived at the *Household Words* office promptly at 8 a.m. According to Percy Fitzgerald, who worked alongside him as an editorial assistant for nearly fifteen years, local tradesmen "noted regularly his lithe figure briskly flitting past as the clock struck, his little bag in his hand." That small detail of Dickens appearing like the mechanical figure on a clock rings true; one friend noticed that from the time he chose to eat his breakfast onwards, "order and regularity followed him throughout the day," so that whether he was walking or writing "he was governed by rules laid down for himself by himself, rules well studied beforehand, and rarely departed from." Someone else who worked for a time as Dickens's amanuensis observed that combing his hair was "invariably the first thing he did on entering the office," and then he would get to work.

Located on the eastern side of a busy thoroughfare leading onto the Strand, 16 Wellington Street North was a "graceful, *dainty* little structure," Fitzgerald recalled, with a shop on the ground floor where sales of *Household Words* could be made direct to the public, a narrow staircase up to an editorial office on the first floor, with a bow window "giving a flood of light, quite necessary for literary work," and living apartments on the upper floors where Dickens could bivouac if he needed to stay overnight. The building had local legend as well as convenience to recommend it.

According to Dickens, his own office was located on the same spot that William Hogarth had chosen for the final tableau of his sequence of six engravings *A Harlot's Progress*, which would undoubtedly have appealed to a writer who had chosen "The Parish Boy's Progress" as the subtitle for *Oliver Twist*. Apparently, Dickens used to tell contributors that "he had often sat in that first-floor front, conjuring up mind-pictures of Kate Hackabout [the woman whose fall from grace Hogarth vividly depicts] lying dead in her coffin." It meant that each time he picked up his pen in that room he was part of a story that was still developing.

One entry in Dickens's memorandum book reads " 'The office'[.] The life of the office. The men in it." In January 1851 the most regular presence in the *Household Words* office besides himself was W. H. Wills. Known to his friends as Harry, he was a former staff writer at *Punch*, and in 1850 he had been recruited to serve as Dickens's subeditor on this new journal, a job that required him to be both a rudder in terms of its future direction and a brake when it came to some of Dickens's more fanciful ideas. The other permanent member of staff was Richard Horne, although he would shortly leave *Household Words* after clashing with Wills, who complained that his colleague was not giving five guineas' worth of service for his five-guinea weekly salary; in June he would be replaced by Henry Morley, the only member of staff with a university degree, who had attracted Dickens's attention with some papers on sanitation reform that had recently been reprinted in the liberal *Examiner*. Other contributors came and went on a less regular basis, together with numerous would-be journalists who, according to a rueful article written by Dickens and Morley in 1853, used to turn up uninvited in Wellington Street clutching bundles of papers, and then return "red-faced and ireful" demanding a personal interview with the editor after their contributions were rejected.

Also present at the weekly editorial meetings, which usually began late on Thursday afternoon and continued over dinner in the office, was Dickens's literary adviser John Forster. Their first encounter had taken place at Christmas 1836 in the house of the novelist William Harrison Ainsworth. Dickens had read Forster's critical review of his early play *The*

Village Coquettes in the *Examiner*, noting that it was *"rather* depreciatory"
but "so well done that I cannot help laughing at it," and long after they had
met Forster still remembered the impression made upon him by Dickens's
cheerful eyes, waves of glossy chestnut hair, and an alert expression "that
seemed to tell so little of a student or writer of books, and so much of a
man of action and business in the world." Their friendship developed
quickly, and as early as 1837 Dickens was signing himself "Yours always."
Before long Forster had become an unofficial member of Dickens's
extended family, "a part, and an essential part, of our home," and for many
years the two men spent Christmas Day together, celebrating the anniversary of a relationship that was no less meaningful than Dickens's marriage
and in the end would last considerably longer.

To Dickens's other friends Forster could be overwhelming, a man
whose stocky build and booming voice added to his larger-than-life personality. "As I look back," wrote Percy Fitzgerald, "I can never call up the
image of Dickens without seeing Forster beside him; Forster seems always

to interpose his bulky form. He was ever bustling about his friend interpreting him and explaining him." Such busy ministrations continued long after Dickens's death, as Forster set about writing a biography (published in 1872–4) in which his own figure would continue to blot out all potential rivals. One reviewer complained that the book "should not be called the Life of Dickens but the History of Dickens' Relations to Mr. Forster," and it is true that occasionally it reads like an autobiography that has accidentally got tangled up with Dickens's life. Yet however easy it is to mock Forster for attempting to hitch a ride on Dickens's fame, overall it was Dickens who was the chief beneficiary of their friendship, and not only because the version of him loyally promoted in *The Life of Charles Dickens*— generous, pure-minded, faithful—was one he might have chosen for himself. It is also because for many years Forster was Dickens's first reader and unofficial editor. Sending him the proofs of *The Battle of Life* in 1846, Dickens encouraged him to "knock out a word's brains here and there" if the writing started to drift into blank verse, as it often did when he was straining for sentimental effect, but Forster's editorial duties went far beyond the occasional verbal cull. They included cutting instalments to length, regularising punctuation and, crucially, offering suggestions that were intended to tighten Dickens's grip on his readers. "Don't fail to erase anything that seems to you too strong," Dickens urged him when forwarding some chapters of *Barnaby Rudge* in 1841, and Forster obliged by chipping away at a number of places where the writing bulged melodramatically. In effect he was Dickens's critical conscience.

Forster's promotion of Dickens was also part of a much larger project. The son of a Newcastle butcher, as a young man Forster had rejected a university education in favour of the literary hurly-burly of London, and in his first published review he offered a powerful defence of the role played by writers in modern culture. Later his bookplate included the motto "Follow Me," and nobody could have worked harder to put it into practice. Whether he was encouraging ailing talents such as Charles Lamb—sad, lonely, often drunk—who came to treat his "dear boy" as a flattering hybrid of fan and apprentice, or helping contemporaries such as

Bulwer Lytton and Thackeray ("Whenever anybody is in a scrape we all fly to him for critical refuge"), over the years Forster turned himself from an ambitious young journalist into something more like a one-man literary agency.

Ultimately Forster's aim was to do more than help individual writers. Convinced that literature was as important to a developing nation as "services done by professors of arms, law, divinity, and diplomacy," every deal he brokered and introduction he made was another step towards turning it into the moral compass of a potentially directionless age. (In 1850 he had pointed out that on the government pension list writers were grouped together with royal coachmen.) Of particular relevance to Dickens was Forster's stress on the idea that good writing and popular writing should not be thought of as mutually exclusive categories. Milton's hope that *Paradise Lost* would "fit audience find, though few" had often been skewed into the assumption that the fit *were* the few, and that only averagely talented writers could therefore have a genuinely broad appeal. It took a writer like Dickens to prove that the same novel could please servants and cabmen as well as readers of *Paradise Lost*, but it took a tireless campaigner like Forster to persuade them that reading fiction could be more than just a guilty private pleasure.

Forster's obsession with dignity was firmly rooted in personal experience. Scorned by some of his colleagues as a "low scribbler . . . totally unused to the Society of Gentlemen," his anxiety about his own social origins produced a hair-trigger responsiveness to real or imagined slights. (It was reported that his butler was so cowed by him that, after hearing that his own house was on fire, he finished serving dinner in nervous silence before asking for permission to leave.) Indeed, although at times Forster displayed the hide of a rhinoceros, battering his friends with pomposity and condescension, at other times he seemed to have been born without a skin at all. His perceptive description of Dickens as "often uneasy, shrinking, and over-sensitive" underneath his "hard and aggressive" demeanour was also close to being a secret confession.

For London's gossips Forster was a particular gift. Stories about him trying to dance in shoes that were too big for him, or losing his temper with a hapless servant—a muttered "Biscuits," followed by a louder "BIScuits," and finally a roar of "*BIS*cuits"—swiftly passed from anecdote into legend. According to another friend, Dickens "revelled" in these stories, and he could not resist laughing at the man he nicknamed "The Mogul": his clumsy jokes, his foghorn attempts at whispering (a noise which, Dickens recalled, "seems to go in at your ear and come out at the sole of your boot"), his sudden explosions of "Monstrous!," "Incredible!," "*In-tol*-erable!" One of the most enjoyable aspects of teasing him was that he was apparently oblivious to the possibility that anyone might treat him as a figure of fun. When he later appeared in *Our Mutual Friend* only thinly disguised as Podsnap, whose "question about everything was, would it bring a blush into the cheek of the young person," it was characteristic of Forster to have been practically alone among Dickens's friends in not working out who the model was, despite the fact that in his first published review he had warned that certain passages "would be apt to raise a blush on the cheek of a young English female."

But for all his bluff and bluster, Forster was a keen observer of the literary world, other than the large blind spot that covered his own place in it, and he had especially sharp eyes when it came to his famous friend. It was Forster who later recalled Dickens tracing shorthand notes on a tablecloth ("quite an ordinary habit with him"), and made the connection back to Dickens's earlier life as a parliamentary reporter. The key difference was that in the *Household Words* office, unlike in the Houses of Parliament, there was no attempt to pretend that this was a democracy. According to the partnership agreement under which the journal had been established a year earlier, Dickens had a half share in the business, while the rest was divided up among the publishers Bradbury & Evans (a quarter share), Wills (an eighth), and Forster (an eighth), and although everyone was expected to contribute to the journal's success there was never any doubt as to who was in charge.

A humorous drawing later printed in *The Queen* newspaper showed a meeting of the writers involved in producing the special Christmas edition of *Household Words*, with each contributing a different chapter to a ghost story Dickens had planned in advance. (The joke seems to be that the only "spirits" present—despite the terrified faces of the writers clustered around that table—are those contained in the large glass bottles being carried in by a cheerful-looking waiter.) In some ways the picture was also a microcosm of Wellington Street as a whole, because this was an environment in which literary collaboration and competition were thickly intertwined.

Few places were better suited than Wellington Street North, Upper Wellington Street and Wellington Street South to demonstrate Dickens's notion that people supposed to be far apart—in this case literary rivals—were constantly elbowing each other. Between 1843 and 1853, more than twenty newspapers or periodicals and thirteen booksellers or publishers scratched out a precarious living on this three-part street, from premises containing "great splashes and dried-up pools of ink" and ceilings that were "darkened with the smoke of innumerable candles." At No. 5 Wellington Street South could be found the editorial offices of the *Examiner*, whose literary editor was Forster, and at No. 13 were the former offices of *Punch*, the satirical magazine that in its first issue (published in 1841) had included a spoof of *Oliver Twist* among its "Literary Recipes." *Punch*'s earliest editor, Henry Mayhew, had more recently been employed by the *Morning Chronicle*, where he had published a series of startling reports on the hand-to-mouth lives of the poor; it was also where in 1836 Dickens had published his early sketch "Our Next-Door Neighbour," in which he pointed out how enjoyable it was when walking through a street to speculate "on the character and pursuits of the people who inhabit it." Dickens already knew Mayhew as a charming, somewhat rackety journalist with an unruly mop of hair and a mind brimming with get-rich-quick schemes, including the unsuccessful manufacture of artificial diamonds. In 1844 Mayhew had married the daughter of Dickens's friend Douglas Jerrold, and in the following year Dickens had cast him as Knowell in a charity performance at St. James's Theatre of *Every Man in His Humour*. Having quarrelled with the *Morning Chronicle* in 1850, and established his own magazine to print further revelations, Mayhew would shortly become one of Dickens's literary neighbours, moving the office of *London Labour and the London Poor* from 69 Fleet Street to 16 Upper Wellington Street. Also within shouting distance of the *Household Words* office was G. M. W. Reynolds, one of Dickens's most hostile critics, who lived at 7 Wellington Street North, and edited his radical journal *Reynolds's Weekly Newspaper* from the same address.

The opposite side of the street was dominated by the grand portico of the Lyceum Theatre, where a stage adaptation of *David Copperfield* in three acts by John Brougham had opened on 6 January that year. Looking out from his office window in the evening, Dickens could spot "young ladies with peculiarly limp bonnets, and of a yellow or drab style of beauty, making for the stage-door of the Lyceum theatre, in the dirty little fog-choked street over the way," who would shortly transform themselves into "beautiful fairies" through the magic of gaslight and greasepaint. They too were part of this central artery running through literary London, which every day encouraged the circulation of ideas from early in the morning until late at night.

A more accurate representation of the number of writers involved in *Household Words* would have needed to be a lot larger than the drawing published in *The Queen*. The list of ambitious young journalists who owed their later success to Dickens's ability to spot talent and give it a push into print included G. (George) A. Sala, who in this drawing is pictured looking quizzically at the viewer, like a silent-film comedian mugging to the camera, Charles Kent, John Hollingshead, and many more. Yet while different writers dipped in and out of the pages of *Household Words*, only one name really mattered. Among the possible titles that Dickens originally considered for his journal (*The Cricket . . . The Shadow . . . The Comrade . . . The Microscope . . . The Highway of Life . . . The Lever . . . The Rolling Years . . . The Holly Tree . . . Everything*) one had been *Charles Dickens*, and even after he chose *Household Words* it was made abundantly clear to his readers that his hand would be guiding everything they read. The title page of each issue announced that this was "A WEEKLY JOURNAL. CONDUCTED BY CHARLES DICKENS," and at the top of each double-page spread came another reminder in smaller but equally insistent type: "[Conducted by Charles Dickens]." It was the sort of complicated pun Dickens loved, allowing him to present himself as an electrical conductor, an orchestral conductor, a conductor of mysterious mesmeric forces, and even an omnibus conductor who invited a crowd of strangers to clamber on board every week and rattle away on a set of new adventures.

The other contributors quickly discovered that this form of control extended to matters of style. Even if they didn't set out to imitate Dickens, when their contributions appeared anonymously in print his voice was always in the background, and frequently pushed its way further forwards after he edited their words to make them consistent with his own views and a relentlessly buoyant house style. Dickens had various metaphors for these changes: in February 1851, he wrote to Mary Boyle, an author and amateur actress with whom he carried on a flirtatious friendship for many years, comparing his editorial methods to "disciplining one's thoughts like a regiment . . . putting each soldier into its right place," and to careful "use of the pruning-knife." But whether he was reordering an article or trimming it into shape, Dickens prided himself on his ability to smooth over these changes so that readers would not notice anything. (Towards the end of his life, he offered a prize of six pairs of gloves to his daughter if she could identify which part of another writer's story he had added.) And other than in exceptional cases, such as Elizabeth Gaskell's stubborn resistance to Dickens's editorial suggestions, these changes were not a matter for negotiation. In submitting their articles to his careful attention, the journal's other contributors also had to submit to his will. Every page they wrote was conducted by Charles Dickens, and picking up an issue of *Household Words* was supposed to make his readers feel that it was him they were shaking by the hand.

One of his central aims was familiarity. Beneath the title of every issue was a slightly altered quotation from Shakespeare's *Henry V*: "Familiar in their mouths as Household Words." The original line is "Familiar in his mouth as household words": by shifting the emphasis from an individual to a group, Dickens underlined his hope that in becoming a friendly presence in his readers' homes, *Household Words* would allow him to promote ideas that were close to his own heart, from the need for sanitation reform and better education to the transformative power of the imagination. This stress on familiarity was also supported by his journal's physical appearance: printed in two columns of tiny type on twenty-four pages, the design was closely modelled on the slightly smaller and cheaper *Chambers's Edinburgh Journal*, despite Dickens's claim that "There is nothing I am more desirous to avoid than imitation." This was a highly successful family magazine, owned by the Edinburgh publishers Robert and William Chambers, on which Wills had previously spent three years as subeditor, and which Dickens had criticised for its drab utilitarianism, complaining that it was "as congenial to me, generally, as the brown paper packages in which Ironmongers keep Nails." Adapting its design for a new purpose allowed him to fill the same plain packages with something different: the journalistic equivalent of sweets and fireworks.

Dickens had used the "Preliminary Word" to *Household Words* to remind his readers that "in all familiar things, even in those that are repellent on the surface, there is Romance enough, if we will find it out," and in the articles that followed he tried to show what he meant. The first instalment of a two-part report on "The Amusements of the People" recounts the rollicking melodrama enjoyed by working-class spectators at a London theatre, and proves that Dickens is fully sympathetic to its power to transfigure everyday life by trying to do something similar in his writing, as he describes the curtain rising on "a very large castle" sparsely furnished with a single table and two chairs, and a villain who reveals his true character by wearing a pair of boots "apparently made of sticking-plaister." "Valentine's Day at the Post Office," co-written with Wills, is similarly dedicated to taking fragments of ordinary experience and giving them a more imaginative gloss, as it describes sheepskin bags of letters arriving to be sorted on 14 February and a postal worker who "rapidly cut their throats, dived into their insides, abstracted their contents, and finally skinned them" by turning the bags inside out.

In his final contribution to the opening issue, "A Bundle of Emigrants' Letters," Dickens tackles some individual human dramas that were usually hidden inside the raw statistics about emigration to Australia. This was a significant issue at the time. Australia was still a penal colony, with four convict ships arriving in Western Australia this year alone: the *Mermaid* on 13 June, the *Pyrenees* on 28 June, the *Minden* on 14 October and the *Marion* on 2 November, altogether carrying more than a thousand criminals who had been sentenced to transportation, often for relatively minor offences such as pickpocketing. Officially the hope was that these criminals could be rehabilitated once they had been removed from the scene of their temptation, rather as modern waste is sometimes shipped overseas to be recycled. Growing doubts that penal transportation could be thought of as either just or merciful (the last convict ship sailed in 1867) were compounded by the recognition that, as a rapidly developing country, what

Australia really needed was skilled labour rather than reluctant muscle; posters in Britain that promised "FREE PASSAGE!" to South Australia specified carpenters, blacksmiths, stonemasons and builders as those among "the classes of persons now in requisition." Others emigrated in the hope of finding opportunities to get rich quickly, particularly after the well-publicised discovery of gold fields in New South Wales and Victoria in 1851, but for many people the long sea voyage to Australia in cramped, unsanitary conditions was not a free choice. It was a matter of simple economic necessity. A number of paintings showed new emigrants looking unhappily resigned to their fate—as in *The Last of England*, begun by Ford Madox Brown in 1852, which depicts a grim-faced middle-class couple staring ahead and being buffeted by sea spray as the white cliffs of Dover slowly recede behind them. There are few signs that their lives are about to change for the better.

Dickens was far more optimistic. "It is unquestionably melancholy that thousands upon thousands of people, ready and willing to labour, should be wearing away life hopelessly in this island," he wrote in "A Bundle of Emigrants' Letters," "while within a few months' sail (within a few weeks' when steam communication with Australia shall be established) there are vast tracts of country where no man who is willing to work hard . . . can ever know want." This was an idea he continued to promote in the pages of *Household Words*. On 5 April 1851, he would co-write with Wills an article on "Small Beginnings," describing a number of juvenile offenders who had been given some training in a Ragged School before emigrating to Australia; the boys were said to have expressed the view that "no words could convey an idea of the gratitude they felt for what had been done for them." Recently Dickens had granted a similar opportunity for self-reinvention in *David Copperfield* to Mr. Micawber, who transforms himself from peripatetic bankrupt to successful magistrate after he emigrates to a storybook version of Australia, and in "A Bundle of Emigrants' Letters" Dickens gave some glimpses of the lives of those who had travelled to the real thing. A joiner in Melbourne writes an unpunctuated gush of love to his wife still living in Britain, telling her "Oh that I could see you here then you would spend the happiest days you have ever spent there is not the care and trouble on your mind here as there is at home," while a poor woman who has emigrated to Sydney confesses that her recently arrived children have left their box of clothes in Plymouth, "but as *they* arrived safe I do not care to trouble any one to enquire for this."

All three articles published in the opening instalment of *Household Words*—"The Amusements of the People," "Valentine's Day at the Post Office" and "A Bundle of Emigrants' Letters"—demonstrate in pin-sharp detail Dickens's conviction that if he wanted to introduce his readers to fresh ways of thinking, it would not be enough to describe the world in conventional terms. Instead he would have to unpeel it until it looked raw and new. And by the start of 1851 he had come to realise that the same principle applied to his fiction. Writing late at night, in the letter to Mary Boyle in which he had boasted of drilling his contributors' thoughts like soldiers on parade, he explained that although the fire in his study was going out, he saw "the first shadows of a new story hovering in a ghostly way about me." *Bleak House* was beginning to stir into life.

If Dickens was looking around him for inspiration, there was one London building that promised to take his own guiding principles as a writer—finding romance in the familiar, making the ordinary seem extraordinary—and bring them to sparkling life: the Crystal Palace.

Harry Wills's article "The Private History of the Palace of Glass," published in *Household Words* on 18 January 1851, explained how Joseph Paxton had come to design his "tremendous pile of transparency." The fact that Paxton had already gained fame and fortune despite an extremely limited formal education was seen by some as an equally important sign of the times. Made head gardener of the Duke of Devonshire's Chatsworth estate when he was just twenty-two years old, Paxton embodied the Victorian ideal of self-cultivation with every prize orchid he grew. By 1851 he had also launched several successful horticultural magazines including the long-running *Gardener's Chronicle*, made a small fortune by speculating in railway shares, met Dickens, Thackeray, Douglas Jerrold and other authors who attended the regular Wednesday-night dinners hosted by his publishers Bradbury & Evans, and invested the huge sum of £25,000 in a new liberal newspaper, the *Daily News*, which briefly featured Dickens as its editor and Harry Wills as assistant editor when it was launched in January 1846. Not that everything Paxton created was a success: his only son George turned out to be a pompous drunk with an embarrassing fondness for gambling, womanising and "exposing his private parts to make water in the most disgusting way." But otherwise Paxton was a remarkable example of a Victorian success story, someone who had risen to the top through a combination of talent and unrelenting hard work.

By 1851, he had already achieved fame as the architect of several large cast-iron-and-glass buildings that were primarily designed as display cases for eye-catching exotic contents. Indeed, the decision to preserve some elm trees in Hyde Park, by enclosing them in the Crystal Palace's main structure, was a striking reminder that Paxton's original plan for the Great Exhibition building, rapidly sketched on a piece of pink blotting paper, was based on the modular construction methods he had previously employed for the "Great Stove" (i.e., Conservatory) in the grounds of Chatsworth House in 1836, which covered around 28,000 square feet and at the time was the largest glass building in the world.

Although Wills's *Household Words* article confidently anticipated that the Crystal Palace would eventually be seen as a modern wonder of the world, at a time when Hyde Park was still a muddy building site many visitors found themselves wondering in a rather different sense. On 1 February, *The Times* reported that part of the glass had given way in a strong wind, and in response to fears that Paxton's whole experimental structure was unsafe, on 18 February a sample gallery was tested in the presence of the Queen and Prince Albert, during which soldiers of the Royal Sappers and Miners (today's Royal Engineers) were ordered to run on the spot and mark time in unison, before eight heavy wooden frames containing lead shot were rolled around the floor on castors. The structure held firm. As Dickens wrote two days later, "I am beginning to think by the way, that if the Crystal Palace don't begin to fall down very soon, one or two of the C[ivil] E[ngineer]s will look a little dim in the sight of the public before long." Once Dickens had enjoyed a joke he rarely let it go: in the 31 May issue of *Household Words* he returned to the same theme, adding to Henry Morley's scientific piece "The Wind and the Rain" a remark that "the wind has got into some little notoriety of late, for not having blown down Mr. Paxton's Crystal Palace . . . which, it appears, it was bound to do, and ought by all means to have done"; and again in a speech delivered on 9 June he scoffed that this "wonderful building . . . ought to have fallen down, but . . . it refused to do so."

Dickens's interest reflected more than the fact that the Crystal Palace was being built in sections, like one of his own novels. He had long been fascinated by conservatories. That partly reflected his love of light-filled architecture: on 15 February he published an article ("Red Tape") attacking the window tax, which had the effect of forcing many poor people into gloomy living conditions without proper access to sunlight or fresh air. By contrast, a conservatory was a building made almost entirely out of windows, and Dickens loved the sudden physical contrasts it produced. On 14 December 1850, a *Household Words* article by Wills and Nathaniel Ward on "Back Street Conservatories" had described how to build a "miniature conservatory," which could be placed on a windowsill and used to block views of the city with artfully arranged greenery, and Dickens had already revealed his attraction to the larger variety. In his early farce *Is She His Wife?* a cheerful bachelor numbers a conservatory among the many improvements he has made to his tiny cottage (others include Grecian balconies, Gothic parapets and a thatched roof), while Dickens himself would later build a conservatory onto Gad's Hill Place, a "charming addition to the house" that opened into the drawing room and dining room, and was filled with hothouse plants. He proudly showed it off to his daughter Katey just a few days before his death. Nor was it only conservatories that attracted his attention. He also recognised the enchantment of large industrial buildings with glass windows when they were viewed from a distance: in *Hard Times*, travellers on the express train think that Coketown's factories resemble "Fairy palaces" that are illuminated at night, although this turns out to be a cruel trick of the light when we are introduced to the grim working conditions inside.

The Crystal Palace may have looked more attractive than a smoke-blackened factory, but Dickens worried that it had a similar potential to reveal the growing gulf between rich and poor. The pages of *Household Words* were filled with articles describing industrial processes, reflecting Dickens's fascination with how one thing became another, and the excited language of these articles sometimes made the manufacture of candles or pottery sound far more enchanting than the noisy, smelly business it usually was. But as the area of construction in Hyde Park, located almost exactly halfway between his home and his editorial workplace, continued to hum with activity, Dickens found himself wondering what was really going on behind the scenes. "What a thing it is, that we can't always be innocently merry, and happy with those we like best," he wrote to a friend towards the end of January, "without looking out of the back windows of life!" And while most people who visited the site of the Crystal Palace saw a forward-looking building—one made entirely from front windows, as it were—Dickens was increasingly drawn to its more backward-facing aspects.

In "Plate Glass," co-written with Wills and published in the 1 February issue of *Household Words*, there is much evidence of his excitement at visiting the Thames Plate Glass Company, viewing the sheets of newly cast glass that sparkled "like innumerable diamonds," and the channels into which glowing embers dropped "like a long Egyptian street on a dark night, with a fiery rain falling." Yet this article also touches on the darker side of glass manufacture, including an accident in which one worker's shoes were "filled with white-hot glass," and the sight of a foul creek "so horribly slimy that a crocodile, or an alligator, or any scaly monster of the Saurian period, seemed much more likely to be encountered in such a neighbourhood than the beautiful substance that makes our modern rooms so glittering and bright; our streets so dazzling, and our windows at once so radiant and so strong." Even as the final pieces of Paxton's building were being slotted into place, Dickens remained aware that such shiny feats of engineering could have a hidden human cost.

His fears were sharpened by the demise of a short-lived committee set up to represent working-class interests at the Great Exhibition. The first public gathering held to publicise the Exhibition had included a celebrated speech by the Bishop of Oxford on the "Dignity of Labour," in which he promised that the exhibits would uphold "the dignity of the working classes" while also making "other people feel the dignity which attaches to the producers of these things." Similarly, at a grand dinner given by the Lord Mayor of London for Prince Albert in March 1850, the toast proposed by the Earl of Carlisle had been "The Working Men of England." At the time, Dickens was one of a number of prominent writers and politicians who had been asked to join a Central Committee of the Working Classes, intended to encourage visits, distribute information and recommend cheap accommodation in London, but when it asked the Royal

Commission for official recognition it met with a blank refusal, and after just five meetings Dickens moved a resolution to dissolve the committee with immediate effect. Apparently the Exhibition organisers preferred to toast the working classes rather than include them in their planning. Dickens's original letter accepting the Bishop of Oxford's invitation had claimed that he was "very happy to become a member of the Committee . . . and to do all in my power to advance its objects," but he is unlikely to have been surprised when they met with equally powerful objections. The fears that Chartist agitators had stirred up in 1848 were still simmering away in the background, and as a number of other articles published recently in *Household Words* had indicated, such as "A Walk in the Workhouse" and "London Pauper Children," the gleaming surfaces of modern life could not disguise the fact that for many people life was still nasty, brutish and pathetically short.

The Parish Soup Kitchen, a painting by George Elgar Hicks that was completed this year and exhibited at the Royal Academy in 1852, offered a sentimental version of the same idea, depicting a crowd of surprisingly plump beggars queuing up to fill their jugs with soup underneath signs piously warning them not to expect anything more from life: "Having Food and Raiment let us be Therewith Content." As Dickens already knew from first-hand experience, the truth about such lives was usually much less picturesque. The *Household Narrative*, a monthly supplement of news and commentary partly compiled by Forster, had included in its January 1850 issue the following courtroom cross-examination, which Dickens had witnessed in the Guildhall, after a fourteen-year-old crossing sweeper named George Ruby was asked to give evidence in an assault case, and appeared confused when handed a Bible to take the oath:

> Alderman Humphery: Well, do you know what you are about? Do you know what an oath is? Boy: No. Alderman: Can you read? Boy: No. Alderman: Do you ever say your prayers? Boy: No, never. Alderman: Do you know what prayers are? Boy: No. Alderman: Do you know what God is? Boy: No. Alderman: Do you know what the devil is? Boy: I've heard of the devil, but I don't know him. Alderman: What do you know? Boy: I knows how to sweep the crossings. Alderman: And that's all? Boy: That's all. I sweeps a crossing.

When the report goes on to say that the Alderman "had never met with anything like the deplorable ignorance of the poor unfortunate child in the witness-box," there may be a touch of Dickens's hand in the choice of wording. For the crossing sweeper is not just a poor unfortunate because he is deserving of the reader's pity; he is unfortunate because he is poor. The exchange was another burr that stuck in Dickens's memory.

The issue of *Household Words* that was published on Saturday 25 January 1851 featured, as its leading article, the first instalment of a new book by Dickens that would continue to be serialised until December 1853. *A Child's History of England* was not presented as a work of fiction, although if some of its characters and incidents had slipped into one of Dickens's novels it is unlikely many readers would have noticed. Its origins can be traced back to 1843, when Dickens told Douglas Jerrold, "I am writing a little history of England for my boy . . . for I don't know what I should do if he were to get hold of any Conservative or High Church notions; and the best way of guarding against any such horrible result is, I take it, to wring the parrots' necks in his very cradle." By the end of 1850, the recent "Papal aggression" scare had made this concern seem even more urgent, and Dickens decided to ransack some popular books including Thomas Keightley's *History of England* (1837–9) and Charles Knight's *Pictorial History of England* (1837–40) to tell the story of England from *c.*50 BC to the Glorious Revolution of 1688, when "the Protestant religion was established" in the country.

In historical terms, the result was an uneven mixture of broad brush-strokes and picturesque details. Dickens's first instalment, which describes the country before and after Julius Caesar's invasion, gave readers a good sense of what they could expect in the coming months. There are blood-thirsty accounts of human sacrifice by the Druids, and little bursts of patriotism ("Still, the Britons *would not* yield") that occasionally verge on jingoism; the focus throughout is on rulers rather than ordinary people; and Dickens adopts a tone that is generally light but largely free from humour. Later instalments continued in a similar vein, although increasingly Dickens's title disclosed an unexpected ambiguity. For this is not just a history written *for* a child. At times it reads more like one written *by* a child, in which Dickens refuses to take the past for granted, and instead regards it with the wide eyes of an innocent set adrift among its many absurdities.

As *A Child's History of England* developed, Dickens's patience with his material grew increasingly thin. Henry VIII is dismissed as "a most intolerable ruffian, a disgrace to human nature, and a blot of blood and grease upon the History of England," while James I attracts a whole thesaurus of opprobrium: "cunning, covetous, wasteful, idle, drunken, greedy, dirty, cowardly, a great Swearer, and the most conceited man on earth." At the same time, Dickens started to recognise that it was still far too soon to celebrate escaping from the clutches of the past, because many of the characters and events he found himself describing were more like the shadowy twins of current affairs than their distant ancestors. His examples stretched from Oliver Cromwell's rejection of the House of Lords when it refused to do his bidding, which prompts Dickens to interject, "I wish this had been a warning to Parliaments to avoid long speeches, and do more work," to the buildings that arose from the ruins created by the Great Fire of London, about which Dickens gloomily observes that "there are some people in [the city] still—even now, at this time, nearly two hundred years later—so selfish, so pig-headed, and so ignorant, that I doubt if even another Great Fire would warm them up to do their duty." In effect, Dickens's history lessons were also an account of how England had come to be in the state it was at the time he was writing. Occasionally this took on a personal dimension, because some passages read suspiciously like another set of autobiographical fragments in disguise. "Every day he divided into certain portions," Dickens writes of King Alfred, "and in each portion devoted himself to a certain pursuit," which was also a good summary of how Dickens himself tried to spend his time.

Most of the book was dictated to his sister-in-law Georgina Hogarth, who lived with the family in Devonshire Terrace. This mode of composition may have encouraged Dickens to adopt a style that was distinctly theatrical in places. Several passages are reminiscent of the stage directions in a Victorian melodrama ("[Henry II's] passion was so furious that he tore his clothes, and rolled like a madman on his bed of straw and rushes"), while others fall into a form of accidental blank verse that makes it sound as if these historical figures are delivering their lines in a spotlight. ("'No?' cried the King. 'No, by the Lord!' said Leof.") Such theatricality underlined Dickens's long-held suspicion that political life was itself a kind of performance, in which the people involved were merely playing roles. But perhaps everyone else was too.

In February, Dickens travelled to Paris "for a Household Words purpose" to look around its new cattle market and abattoir—both of which he admired for their cleanliness and efficiency, in stark contrast to the

unhygienic misery of Smithfield Market in London—and at the same time
he arranged to visit the celebrated dandy Count d'Orsay. Formerly the
host of London's most fashionable salon at Gore House, which he had run
alongside his partner Lady Blessington, d'Orsay had fled the country following his bankruptcy in 1849. Now he was leading a much quieter life in
his "atelier" at 49 Rue de la Ville l'Évêque: a large room with a loft he had
transformed into "a bedroom, a salon, a smoking-room, a studio, a conservatory, a museum, which all Paris ran to see." Despite his modest living
conditions d'Orsay still retained much of his former glamour. Lord and
Lady Holland's physician, who met him for the first time in October 1850,
described him as "a man of striking appearance, with a head of Jove and
Apollo combined, tall and graceful, elaborately dressed, and full of wit and
humour." D'Orsay had earlier been one of the most glittering stars in
Dickens's social universe, becoming godfather to Dickens's son Alfred and
sketching the writer in 1841 and again in 1842, with the second sketch
making Dickens look rather like d'Orsay himself, as he poses in a tailored
jacket with his left hand resting nonchalantly upon his hip. D'Orsay's current lifestyle involved even more elaborate forms of disguise. With his
splendid costumes and refined conversation, he was like a character from
a play who had escaped from the stage and entered real life. And on his
return to London, Dickens found himself wondering if this sort of theatricality might be more than just the relic of a bygone age. Perhaps it was
another sign of the times.

Dickens's own fascination with the theatre had started early and
never stopped. As a child he had acted out the stories he read, treating
their characters like a set of ghosts he could flesh out and bring to life,
and throughout his career he was drawn to the bright lights of the theatre. As a young legal clerk in London he had attended hundreds of
productions, and may even have paid a fee to perform in one of the city's
private theatres, later recalling the experience in his early sketch "Making
a Night of It," where a fellow clerk calmly receives insults such as "Give
that dog a bone!" and "Throw him O-VER!" while he cocks his hat and
stands "with his arms akimbo, expressing defiance melodramatically."

At one point Dickens had considered becoming a professional actor, writing in 1832 to George Bartley, the stage manager of Covent Garden Theatre, to introduce himself as someone with "a strong perception of character and oddity, and a natural power of reproducing in his own person what he observed in others." Despite rehearsing for up to six hours a day, a sore throat meant that he missed his audition, and he never tried again, telling one friend that he "gradually left off turning my thoughts that way . . . See how near I may have been to another sort of life."

Although this was a turning point that hadn't occurred in his life, Dickens often found himself "turning [his] thoughts that way" in his writing. In several novels he dangled plotlines that imagined how this rival career might have developed: perhaps as successfully as Nicholas Nickleby's, who joins Mr. Vincent Crummles's touring company as the juvenile lead and wows provincial audiences with his Romeo; or perhaps as pathetically as Mr. Wopsle's in *Great Expectations*, who ends up sporting a dodgy wig in a ramshackle production of *Hamlet*, where "on the question whether 'twas nobler in the mind to suffer, some roared yes, and some no, and some inclining to both opinions said 'Toss up for it.'" Yet the fact that Dickens could imagine such different outcomes with equal gusto indicates that he did not simply abandon his theatrical ambitions when he became a full-time writer. Instead he absorbed them into his daily routine. His eldest daughter Mary (known in the family as Mamie) once observed him in the process of composition:

> . . . my father wrote busily and rapidly at his desk, when he suddenly jumped up from his chair and rushed to a mirror which hung near, and in which I could see the reflection of some extraordinary facial contortions which he was making. He returned rapidly to his desk, wrote furiously for a few moments, and then went again to the mirror. The facial pantomime was resumed, and then turning toward, but evidently not seeing, me, he began talking rapidly in a low voice.

It was like a private version of the "monopolylogues" he had enjoyed watching as a young man: farces at Covent Garden and the Adelphi Theatre in which the virtuoso actor Charles Mathews took on all the parts himself, swapping facial expressions and voices like a series of hats. For Dickens, the blank page had become a stage on which he could perform his own inimitable one-man show. Repeatedly he borrowed his plots from successful plays and created a style that was streaked with melodrama. He was fully aware of these theatrical tendencies in his writing, and in common with many of the things he took most seriously his fingers itched to poke fun at them. As early as *Sketches by Boz*, he had included one sketch ("Mrs. Joseph Porter") in which amateur theatricals disintegrate into chaos, and another ("Horatio Sparkins") in which a flash shop assistant named Horatio tries out gnomic one-liners such as "I say, what is man?," like a minor character in *Hamlet* secretly auditioning for the role of the hero.

Dickens also maintained close links with the professional theatre through his friendship with the great Shakespearean actor William Macready. This involved their families too: Dickens was godfather to Macready's son Henry, and in turn Macready was godfather to the writer's daughter Kate Macready Dickens. Nineteen years older than Dickens, Macready was determined to change acting's reputation as a bohemian but rather disreputable profession, and Dickens responded with gratitude, not least because Macready's campaign paralleled his own efforts to improve the social standing of writers like himself. Macready too had an outsider's sensitivity to matters of class and status, and Dickens quickly recognised how much they had in common. Having learned while touring America in 1844 that Macready was attracting hostile reviews as the new manager of Drury Lane Theatre, he wrote to express his outrage that a man like him could "fret, and fume, and chafe himself for such lice of literature as these! . . . I speak to you, as I would to myself." (In the same letter he also warned Macready about the dangers of his careless eating habits, and prescribed sherry with an egg beaten into it—precisely the same backstage pick-me-up he would rely on during his own reading tours.) Later he would see Macready as a warning about the dangers of early retirement, telling Forster that "However strange it is to be never at rest, and never satisfied, and ever trying after something that is never reached, and to be always laden with plot and care and worry, how clear it is that it must be, and that one is driven by an irresistible might until the journey is worked out!"

In the opening months of 1851, Dickens was more concerned to celebrate the destination that Macready had already reached, attending his final performances of *King Lear* at the Haymarket on 3 February and *Macbeth* at Drury Lane on 26 February. On the 27th he wrote to Macready, confessing that as "a mere boy" he had been one of his "faithful and devoted adherents in the pit," and commemorating the moment when "the great vision to which I am beholden . . . faded so nobly from my bodily eyes last night." (Dickens's use of vaguely Shakespearean language was a flattering way of indicating to Macready that he remained fully present to his mind's eye.) The following Saturday, Dickens spoke at a farewell banquet held at the Hall of Commerce, again praising Macready's final appearance as a "great vision" that had for many years "improved and charmed us." Within a few months he had visited Macready at his country home, Sherborne House in Dorset, where according to family reports he helped the old actor to decorate a four-panel dressing-room screen with more than five hundred prints, a scrapbook creation that included the lovers from *Romeo and Juliet* and the death of Falstaff from *Henry V*. It was another good example of how theatre could seep into everyday life, and this was something Dickens already knew plenty about, not only through the bright clothes he enjoyed wearing, but also through his way of editing *Household Words*, which at times resembled an actor-manager urging each member of his company to perform their roles while he worked to combine them into a single coherent production.

Yet in acting out his stories in front of the mirror, Dickens was demonstrating how easily a writer's life could become a series of soliloquies without an audience. If he had come close to leading "another sort of life" as a professional actor, he was also aware that for many writers the alternative to scratching out a living was something far worse: a life that ended in the workhouse. On 1 January 1851, Dickens opened the year by thanking an aspiring author for sending him her latest manuscript. "I have read it with great pleasure," he told her, "as the reflection of a young, earnest, and truthful heart." So far so encouraging. "But," he went on, "I am bound in honesty to advise you, not to dream of venturing (except for pleasure-voyages) on the great sea of literature . . . I fear you may be shipwrecked." It is likely that his memory was still raw from the previous year, when he had visited the once-popular author John Poole, creator of the nosy comic character Paul Pry and his catchphrase "I hope I don't intrude," and had seen up close what could happen to writers who failed to live up to their early promise. Two weeks before he sent this letter, on 18 December 1850, he told the Prime Minister Lord John Russell that the 64-year-old Poole was "in a prematurely shattered state, and perfectly unable to write." Currently he was living on the fifth floor of a house in Paris, where Dickens had seen him looking "very shakey" the previous June, surviving on a small pension Dickens had created for him from the proceeds of some theatrical benefit performances three years earlier. "In the sunny time of the day, he puts a melancholy little hat on one side of his head," Dickens wrote, "and, with a little stick under his arm, goes hitching himself about the Boulevards; but for any power he has of earning a livelihood he might as well be dead."

Nor was he an isolated case. In February 1851, Dickens joined a committee of nearly seventy writers, scientists and artists to create a public testimonial for William Jerdan, the former owner and editor of the *Literary Gazette*, in recognition of "the constant and great services he has rendered to the literature, science, and art of this country," after Jerdan had been forced into bankruptcy and found himself without a guaranteed income. The committee eventually raised over £900, of which ten guineas came from Dickens—a substantial contribution from someone who was hardly a close friend. Yet in Dickens's eyes such unfortunate cases were symptoms of a far wider problem, which was the basic insecurity of a profession in which reputations could be quickly made (as his own had been with the publication of *The Pickwick Papers*) and just as quickly fade if the eyes of the public turned elsewhere.

The career of William Harrison Ainsworth provided another cautionary tale. If he had died soon after his early success with novels like *Jack Sheppard*, a bestselling romp through the life of a notorious highwayman that overlapped with *Oliver Twist* when it was first serialised in *Bentley's Miscellany* between 1839 and 1840, Ainsworth might now be thought of as a writer like Byron: a literary star who shone briefly but brightly, and left his readers wanting more. Instead, with each novel he ground out (some forty altogether), he left them wanting less. He outlived his fame. In the 1860s, Robert Browning told Forster that he had just met "a sad, forlorn-looking being" who "reminded me of old times." Slowly this shabby figure "resolved himself into—whom do you think?—Harrison Ainsworth!" To which Forster replied, "Good heavens! Is he still alive?" In 1851 Ainsworth was still in touch with his former protégé Dickens—the previous year they had arranged a dinner to talk about forming a small club of "about a dozen—literary men, artists, and maybe a Doctor or so"—and his journal *Ainsworth's Magazine* was still being printed by Dickens's publishers Chapman & Hall. But already his reputation had begun to slide downhill, and the slope was getting steeper every year.

With such examples before him, Dickens was far more sympathetic to writers who had fallen on hard times than he was to those who merely wanted to piggyback on his own success. His father had been especially quick to capitalise in the early days, selling off individual handwritten pages of Dickens's farce *O'Thello*, complete with a certificate of authenticity, and cadging several "loans" from Chapman & Hall. At the start of 1851, it was his younger brother who was "rasping my very heart" by "trading on my name," Dickens complained, after Fred had attempted to buy more than £150 of goods from an upholsterer and draper in January on Dickens's credit. (Fred's own story didn't have a happy ending: George Sala saw him in Boulogne shortly before his premature death in 1868, and reported that he spent his days playing cards and living off a diet that was "mainly gin.") Such unpredictable demands further underlined how risky a writer's life could be. While the Literary Fund, established in 1790 to give financial aid to impoverished authors, was only one of several organisations that aimed to enhance the security and status of professional writers, there was clearly a long way to go.

This was especially true for novelists. "The Victorian has been peculiarly the age of the triumph of fiction," Edmund Gosse argued in 1892, but earlier in the century things were far less certain, and writers who set out to explore the form of the novel still tended to view themselves as pioneers rather than settlers. In 1851 it was less than two decades since an article entitled "The Influence of the Press" had tucked "novels" into a list of "those lighter productions which attract and are alone read by the multitude—newspapers, magazines, reviews, novels, superficial travels," although since then there had been some attempts to defend the novel as a more serious form. Most influentially, in his collection of lectures *On Heroes, Hero-Worship, and the Heroic in History*, published in 1841, Thomas Carlyle had urged his readers to think of the modern author as a hero rather than a hack. The fifth lecture reprinted in his book, "The Hero as Man of Letters," pointed out that a great writer might still "be taken for some idle nondescript," someone who was expected to amuse people in return for "a few coins and applauses," but in the future this notion would appear absurd. Until then, Carlyle noted, the "unrecognized" and "unregulated" world of authorship needed protection through a system of mutual support, although "the organization of [a] Literary Guild is still a long way off, encumbered with all manner of complexities." On the other hand, he concluded, "there can be no doubt that it is coming . . . For so soon as men get to discern the importance of a thing, they do infallibly set about arranging it, facilitating, forwarding it; and rest not till, in some approximate degree, they have accomplished that."

It was a call to which Dickens willingly responded. In 1848 he had written to Thackeray that he was conscious of the "honour and dignity" he had so far achieved in his own career, and was "possessed with the hope of leaving the position of literary men in England, something better and more independent than I found it." Now he decided to launch a scheme that he hoped would "entirely change the status of the Literary Man in England."

At the start of 1851, Dickens was working on a prospectus that he would announce on 10 May in *Household Words*. In it he outlined his plans for a proposed "Guild of Literature and Art," the latest version of an organisation he had been trying to set up for some time. (Four years earlier he had got as far as writing a draft prospectus for a Provident Union of Literature, Science, and Art, though ultimately this plan had come to nothing.) Members of a newly formed Society of Authors and Artists would be expected to take out life insurance, thereby encouraging "the duties of prudence and foresight" in those whose income depended upon a "precarious" profession. Benefits of the scheme would include the ability to apply to a specially endowed institute for a salary, which would be established at a higher rate for "Members" (who would be "of established reputation" and elected for life) and a lower rate for "Associates" (younger writers or artists in need of temporary financial help), and there might also be the possibility of living in one of "a limited number of free residences . . . sufficiently small to be adapted to a very moderate income." In return, each beneficiary would be expected to give three public lectures per year in literature or art, and as the institute developed they could look forward to "co-operating towards works of national interest and importance" on more popular subjects than "those which usually emanate from professed academies." It was a hugely ambitious scheme, and the vagueness of Dickens's phrasing indicated that at this stage much of it was based on loosely sketched-out hopes rather than clearly defined plans.

Perhaps surprisingly, some of the fiercest opposition to this fledgling Guild came not from rival organisations but from other writers. Thackeray had already voiced his scepticism about the need to support authors through charity. In *The History of Pendennis* (1849–50) he described his hero rapidly completing a novel, after digging the manuscript out of "a long-neglected chest, containing old shooting jackets, old Oxbridge scribbling-books, his old surplice, and battered cap and gown, and other memorials of youth, school, and home." The manuscript is so dull Pendennis falls asleep while reading it in bed, but after sprucing it up and appealing to a publisher's snobbery by leaving some invitation cards sent by a Marchioness and "another lady of distinction" carefully-carelessly lying around in his apartments, he sells it for a handsome sum and gains "a quick and considerable popularity." Thackeray's conclusion wasn't hard to spot: to anyone with any sense, writing was a potentially lucrative hobby rather than a serious profession, and only the marketplace could judge who deserved to make a living by their pen.

Similar ideas had also been put forward in non-fictional writings. On 3 January 1850, an editorial in the *Morning Chronicle* urged the government to discontinue literary pensions, arguing that the same laws of supply and demand operated in publishing as in any other industry, and it was necessary for bad writers to sink in order for the better ones to rise. Two days later, Forster once again demonstrated his sensitivity to questions of reputation and status by responding in an *Examiner* article on the "Encouragement of Literature by the State." Here he wondered if the *Morning Chronicle's* stated desire to remove support from "authors of the middling and lower order" was in fact a covert attack on authors who came from the "middling and lower orders," i.e., the wrong social class. Perhaps, Forster grumbled, a writer like Thackeray should not be so quick "to pay court to the non-literary class," in other words his aristocratic friends, "by disparaging his literary fellow-labourers." On 12 January, Thackeray continued his attack in a letter to the *Morning Chronicle* on "The Dignity of Literature," arguing that far from the literary profession being held in disrepute, "the pen gives a place in the world to men who had none before, a fair place, fairly achieved by their genius." And so the controversy rumbled on.

Dickens decided not to add his public voice to the "Dignity of Literature" debate. But he had already outlined his position in the earlier private letter to Thackeray, when he had pointed out that works like Thackeray's collection of parodies, "Punch's Prize Novelists," were hardly dignified productions. It was a great pity, Dickens told him, that writers should "take advantage of the means our calling gives us with such accursed readiness, of at all depreciating or vulgarizing each other."

Probably some of Dickens's prickliness was the result of their growing rivalry. As early as January 1848, during the successful serialisation of

Vanity Fair, Thackeray had boasted to his mother that he was "all but at the top of the tree—indeed there if the truth be known & having a great fight up there with Dickens." That claim was more firmly rooted in Thackeray's competitive instincts than it was in commercial fact—Dickens's sales would always outstrip his own—but the idea that they were engaged in a tussle for supremacy was one that some critics were also keen to promote. "THACKERAY and DICKENS, Dickens and Thackeray—the two names now almost necessarily go together," wrote the critic David Masson in an 1851 article comparing *The History of Pendennis* and *David Copperfield*. Their rivalry also seeped into everyday life: Thackeray's daughters Annie and Minnie named their cats after characters in Dickens's novels, and later it was observed at the Garrick Club "that if either entered a room where the other was talking or reading, the newcomer would look embarrassed, as if he were searching for something he had mislaid or someone he wanted to see." However, Dickens's decision to champion the Guild of Literature and Art reflected his sense that increasingly modern writers were going to be people like him—fizzing with ambition but located outside the traditional class system—rather than figures like the socially refined Thackeray.

That didn't stop many of these writers from being suspicious of the Guild's principles. According to Carlyle, poverty demonstrated a writer's seriousness of purpose. "He must pass through the ordeal and prove himself. This ordeal; this wild welter of a chaos which is called Literary Life: this too is a kind of ordeal!" The historian and Whig politician Thomas Macaulay was blunter still, replying to a request for his support by warning that Dickens's scheme would "give encouragement, not to good writers, but to bad, or at best, middling writers." There was even a surprising reluctance to support the Guild from permanently cash-strapped figures like Leigh Hunt, who tended to spend money as freely as if it belonged to someone else, not least because it usually did. Whereas Dickens insisted that writers were as capable of looking after their own affairs as bankers or shopkeepers, Hunt sadly insisted that he was not. "Supposing us to be in want of patronage and in possession of talent enough to make it an honour to notice us," he had written in the *Tatler* in 1831, "we would much rather have some great and comparatively private friend, rich enough to assist us, and amiable enough to render obligation delightful, than become the public property of any man, or of any government." Not that this principled stance later prevented him from accepting an annual Civil List pension of £200, or applying to the Literary Fund, or twice angling to be Poet Laureate, or happily receiving a cheque for £900 from Dickens following two charitable performances of Ben Jonson's *Every Man in His Humour* in 1847. But it did suggest some of the muddled thinking that the Guild faced in its attempts to encourage financial self-reliance among writers.

In 1851 the Guild had an official address: 10 Lancaster Place, just off the Strand, a two-minute walk from the *Household Words* offices. Yet the conclusion to Dickens's journal article announcing the Guild's establishment, during which he referred to "the secret experience of his daily life, and of the calling to which he belongs," again indicated that for him this enterprise was far more than just another civic duty. It was personal. Those who ended up in one of the Guild's houses would not be objects of charity, Dickens assured his readers, but the residents of homes that were "completed with due regard to the ordinary habits and necessary comforts of gentlemen." That made it sound as if Dickens assumed they would all be male, although the Guild's official prospectus, printed and distributed in April, explicitly pointed out that the proposed Branch Insurance and Provident Society would be for "all writers, of either sex." But Dickens's choice of the word "gentlemen" involved more than just sexual politics.

Towards the end of the century, Lady Emily Lytton observed in a letter to the Reverend Whitwell Elwin that Dickens was "dreadfully vulgar," and his characters fell far short of being "real ladies and gentlemen." This was evident, she concluded, from the fact that they generally "seem to do nothing but drink." Her comments were hardly significant as literary criticism, but they did reflect a more widely held prejudice about Dickens, which had less to do with what he wrote than where he came from. "Like the perpetual drinking," her correspondent pointed out, "the vulgarity belonged to the class from which Dickens sprung and was deeply ingrained in him. He never got rid of it. He could not even relish the company of gentlemen." This might have come as a surprise to Lady Lytton's grandfather, Edward Bulwer Lytton, who had become one of Dickens's closest literary advisers, and in whose grand stately home, Knebworth, Dickens had discussed the conclusion to *Great Expectations*, his novel about gentlemanly qualities such as honesty, humility, politeness, courage and self-respect being available to everyone regardless of the accident of birth. In 1851 this sort of idea was closely bound up with plans for the Guild, an enterprise that Dickens hoped would turn writers into members of a professional association, like doctors or solicitors, rather than spending their entire careers living from hand to mouth. The paradox was that in planning for this future of literary self-help, Dickens was relying on the

MAYER BROTHERS

aristocratic Bulwer Lytton alongside figures like the self-made Forster. This may have been partly strategic, because when Dickens referred to the "free residences" planned for writers and artists he was aware that Bulwer Lytton had already agreed to have them built on his Knebworth estate, but probably a more important reason was their unexpectedly close friendship at the time.

In many ways Dickens and Bulwer Lytton were the odd couple of Victorian literature, and anyone who met them together in 1851 might have been puzzled at the thought that they could have had anything in common. Politically they were misaligned. Although Bulwer Lytton had started as a Radical MP, making his maiden speech in the House of Commons on 5 July 1831 during the second reading of the Reform Bill, by the start of 1851 he had decided that his preferred model for society, which involved an enlightened aristocracy leading the rest of the community by example, left him only one political home: "good old Toryism." Perhaps more significantly, it is hard to imagine someone who made fun of his friends as much as Dickens did being fully at ease in the company of a man who was so exquisitely sensitive to criticism that a family friend once described him as being "like a man who has been flayed alive and is sore all over." It is equally hard to imagine Dickens's commitment to family life not being unsettled by the scandalous breakdown of Bulwer Lytton's marriage eighteen years earlier, which had demonstrated in painful detail that the union of two unhappy people was far less likely to solve their problems than it was to double them.

Bulwer Lytton would later look back on his proposal to Rosina Doyle Wheeler in 1827 as the worst decision of his life. The daughter of an Anglo-Irish landowner and a women's rights advocate, Rosina was beautiful and witty, with a sharp mind and an equally sharp tongue. She was also a perceptive critic of her husband, a man she had enjoyed teasing while he was courting her, and took even greater pleasure in finding new ways to provoke once their marriage had fallen apart, amid accusations of cruelty and neglect on her side and infidelity on both sides. Anyone who read their gooey early love letters might have concluded that their relationship was

doomed from the start. In 1826, for example, signing himself "Zoo own Puppy," Bulwer Lytton told Rosina that "if oo does not love me, and feels that me cannot make oo happy, why me will leave oo and try to live as I have lived, wretched and isolated, *but alone.*" Within a few years this had become an unwitting prophecy. However, while other separated couples of the period chose to live quietly at a polite distance from each other, Rosina—who felt herself to be financially punished as well as personally slighted by her husband—dedicated her life to revenge. By 1851 she had become a skeleton in Bulwer Lytton's closet who was determined to rattle as loudly as she could, whether she was bitterly annotating his old letters with reminiscences of the day when "I was married to the man . . . and *marred* as the Irish pronounce it for the rest of my life," or writing books like the fictional autobiography *Miriam Sedley*, published in the spring, which began "It was a dark and stormy night at the end of August": a playful reminder of the famously melodramatic opening to Bulwer Lytton's 1830 novel *Paul Clifford*. "Exposure is the only thing that complex monster dreads, and consequently the only check I have on him," she told one correspondent. Accordingly she became an expert in humiliation.

In the years to come, as Dickens's own marriage started to crumble, Bulwer Lytton's private life would become a dreadful warning of what the future might hold. One note in Dickens's memorandum book, "WE—fettered together," was in some respects a sad summary of the situation Bulwer Lytton already found himself in, as he was unwilling to divorce a wife who would have gleefully used an appearance in court to expose his affairs and his attempts to spy on her. Rosina would announce on the eve of her wedding anniversary in 1854 that she was "fettered yet forsaken." In this respect at least Bulwer Lytton agreed with her, telling a friend that "I despair of my release," his choice of language indicating that although he and his estranged wife no longer met in person, they continued to echo each other in their writing, where they could bicker and denounce each other to their hearts' content. During his speech at Macready's farewell banquet, Dickens had quoted Bulwer Lytton's lines about the struggle against "those twin gaolers of the human heart / Low birth and iron fortune," but if his friend's marriage had proved anything, it was that there were worse fates than poverty. Edward and Rosina Bulwer Lytton had become the twin gaolers of each other's hearts.

Even the prose styles of Dickens and Bulwer Lytton were at odds: Dickens's was heartfelt but crackling with mischief; Bulwer Lytton's was elaborately formal and cloudy with abstractions. Dickens ranged across the whole of society from high to low; Bulwer Lytton, according to a waspish essay published in *A New Spirit of the Age*, was "a great writer," but one whose aristocratic tastes meant that he had "no true sympathy with humanity until it is refined and polished." On the other hand, he shared Dickens's ability to alternate quiet periods of writing with bouts of furious energy, and he too had learned how to disguise an essentially shy personality with noisy bursts of sociability. Even his critics were forced to admit that he was good company: "very frank, easy, careless (sometimes, perhaps, studiously so), good-natured, pleasant, conversable."

If Bulwer Lytton sometimes appeared to be putting on an act, that is probably not a coincidence. As well as being a supporter of theatrical reform (during his first period as an MP he had championed the 1833 Dramatic Copyright Act), he too enjoyed the theatre of everyday life: someone who spotted him at the Athenaeum private members' club in 1838 reported that he was wearing "high-heel boots, a white great coat, and a flaming blue cravat," while his horror of ageing meant that those who met him later in life strongly suspected that his rich chestnut curls were dyed and noted that "his face looked as if art had been called in aid to rejuvenate it." (One of Dickens's nicknames for him was "The Hirsute," a mocking tribute to his magnificent whiskers; when Bulwer Lytton cut them off at Rosina's insistence in 1827, he mourned them like the fall of an empire: "O Glory and Vanity of this world, where is Rome? Where is Babylon? Where are my whiskers?") He also shared Dickens's commitment to good works, especially if they involved an element of showmanship: when Dickens spoke at Macready's farewell banquet, Bulwer Lytton was in the chair, and Dickens provoked cheers in the audience by connecting him to "the romantic passions of the stage."

Above all, what united these two writers was a fierce determination to elevate the professional status of writing itself. As early as 1832, Bulwer Lytton had proposed the organisation of a "Society of Literary Men" that would publish works of quality and come to the aid of writers in financial distress, while his fiction had gravitated towards scenes that pointed out "the vast debt which the world owes to authors," and lamented that those who did not succeed were "the most pitiable, the most heart-sickening object in the world." Now that he was comfortably settled in the faux-medieval splendour of Knebworth House, remodelled six years earlier to include a jagged new roofline of spires and battlements, he intended to join Dickens by using his social position to help those who had been unable to write their way out of low birth or iron fortune. 1851 was the year in which they would try to change the direction of these writers' lives.

In answering Carlyle's appeal for a "Literary Guild," it was natural that Dickens would draw upon his theatrical experience, because the theatre offered a perfect example of individuals working together towards a common goal. In the right hands it was also a good fundraising tool. Having abandoned his early plans to be a professional actor, Dickens told Forster that after he began to write he "didn't want money" and "had never thought of the stage but as a means of getting it." He had already used the theatre to support individual writers: not only John Poole and Leigh Hunt, but also the bankrupt Irish dramatist and actor Sheridan Knowles, who was given a lump sum of £575 19s 7d in 1848 after a benefit performance. (Dickens settled this account on the same day he replied to another begging letter from his brother Fred, which once again revealed a sharp contrast between helping deserving cases and throwing good money after bad.) Now Dickens set about applying the same principle to the Guild as a whole.

As a boy Dickens had enjoyed staging plays in a home-made toy theatre, and the thrill of pushing wobbly cardboard characters around on the stage was one he had never fully outgrown. During a conversation towards the end of his life with the journalist Charles Kent, as they walked near Poets' Corner in Westminster Abbey, he asked Kent, "What do you think would be the realisation of one of my most cherished daydreams?" The answer was to "hold supreme authority in the direction of a great theatre, with a skilled and noble company," where the plays would be "touched up here and there in obedience to my own judgement; the players as well as the plays being absolutely under my command." Those who met him earlier had already detected the glint of a budding actor-manager in his eye. In 1843 he was visited in Devonshire Terrace by the French journalists Amédée Pichot and Paul Forgues, who wrote later that Dickens's appearance, with his "rather untidy hair [falling] over the forehead of an unhealthy pallor" and "bright, restless eyes," could easily have led to him being mistaken for "the manager of a troupe of strolling players." (Among the other possible identities they considered were "the secret agent of a diplomatic intrigue" and "a lucky gambler.") Of course, by then Dickens had already learned how to manage the troupe of actors living inside his head, which is why his spoof of a band of travelling players in *Nicholas Nickleby* (a novel he dedicated to Macready) had all the intimacy of someone teasing an old friend. Yet the appeal of directing flesh-and-blood actors never fully left him—later he would adopt "Crummles" as his nickname when stage-managing amateur theatricals. Nor did the prospect of taking a troupe onto the open road. "Blow domestic hearth!" he had written to the author Mary Cowden Clarke in 1848, following a successful run in Glasgow with his Amateur Company—a group of journalists, former professional actors and other friends Dickens had organised into an ad hoc touring company. "I should like to be going all over the country and acting everywhere. There is nothing in the world equal to seeing the house rise at you, one sea of delighted faces, one hurrah of applause."

In the opening months of 1851, he was still happily reflecting on some performances by the Amateur Company that Bulwer Lytton had hosted at Knebworth on 18–20 November the previous year. Through the clever use of a portable stage and lighting hired from a firm in London, the Banqueting Hall had been converted into a theatre holding around 170 people: tenants and other local people on the first night, followed by two performances for the nobility and county gentry. On the last night, Bulwer Lytton announced that he intended to write a new play for the Amateur Company to perform, in order to raise money for those writers' houses on his estate—the first public mention of the Guild of Literature and Art—and after returning to London Dickens expressed his satisfaction that "everything has gone off in a whirl of triumph." That was also a modest way of patting himself on the back. When F. P. Delmé Radcliffe added an epilogue to the play performed at Knebworth, Ben Jonson's *Every Man in His Humour*, he singled out Dickens by noting that he played far more parts

in the evening's entertainment than his official role of the swaggering
Captain Bobadil:

> Amongst the party there *are* pretty pickin's!
> But say, can newspaper describe Charles Dickens?
> Author and actor; manager, the soul
> Of all who read or hear him! on the whole
> A very *Household Word*.

The connection back to his journal reminded the audience how tightly
linked these activities were in Dickens's mind. In *Nicholas Nickleby*, his hero
had expressed pity for anyone who had "no relish for theatrical entertainment, properly conducted," and while it is hard to imagine anyone having
more relish for theatrical minutiae than Dickens—one witness claimed to
have seen a list of demands for a particular performance that included "a
nail for hanging a coat on, and the position it should occupy"—in some
ways it was another extension of his work as the "Conductor" of *Household
Words*. Both involved him treading, and frequently smudging, the line
between collaboration and being in charge.

What was it like being in Dickens's Amateur Company? According to
Mary Cowden Clarke, who joined in 1848 to play Mistress Quickly in a
production of *The Merry Wives of Windsor*, it was like an enhanced version
of being in his company more generally—an unpredictable mixture of the
energising and the exhausting. While rehearsals were "strictly devoted to
work—serious earnest work," she recalled, with everyone involved being
issued with a printed list of rules, there was also plenty of time allotted to
various kinds of fun, from convivial suppers to games of Twenty
Questions. Such equal commitment to rehearsal and relaxation was
entirely typical of Dickens. Forster observed that his friend had two selves,
the serious and the playful, which took turns according to the needs of the
moment; the stage was somewhere they could play equally important
roles, like the weeping and smiling masks of Greek theatre.

On New Year's Eve Dickens had hosted the Amateur Company at Devonshire Terrace for a country dance "of the wildest description, and the most appalling duration." The next morning he was exhausted, or possibly suffering from a hangover, telling the Hon. Mrs. Richard Watson (who was one half of a "spirited and enlightened" couple with liberal political views to whom he had dedicated *David Copperfield*), "I write this on my back on the floor." A week later his company travelled up to Rockingham Castle, the historic family home of the Watsons, with a simplified version of the "beautiful and complete little Theatre" he had previously hired for Knebworth. Even this was a bit of a squeeze: the venue chosen for their performances was a narrow picture gallery with elaborate Venetian glass chandeliers dangling overhead. One alcove with a newly added bay window provided a suitable stage area, which Dickens had previously measured out, although his sketch of the set showing where he wanted the various sofas, tables and chairs to be placed suggested a degree of optimism over just how much space he and his company would have to play in. Otherwise the surviving prompt copy for one of the dramas performed there, Boucicault's *Used Up*, reveals Dickens's characteristically thorough preparation, including detailed instructions on the props needed for each scene. (One example is "Bowl of hot soup, spoon, and bread. Ready L."; a painting of this scene by Augustus Egg duly shows Dickens as Sir Charles Coldstream dipping his spoon into the soup with a hunk of bread on the side.) He also arranged to have a poster printed, despite the fact that no paying members of the public were to be admitted, announcing that "The Theatre will be opened at a QUARTER BEFORE EIGHT, and the Performances will commence at EIGHT O'CLOCK. GOD SAVE THE QUEEN!" Like the toy theatre of his boyhood, Dickens wanted this "little Theatre" to resemble the real thing as closely as possible.

It was now that fundraising efforts for the Guild started to speed up. Over Christmas Bulwer Lytton had written the first draft of his new play, *Not So Bad As We Seem, or Many Sides to a Character*, and in January he sent it to Dickens. It turns on a decision made by Mr. David Fallen, an impoverished author devoted to "the glory of Letters," not to sell the memoirs of a profligate nobleman after they fall into his hands—a manuscript that seems likely to contain the sort of spicy revelations that would embarrass the nobleman's friends but get an excellent price from the booksellers. Eventually morality wins out over greed: the starving author surrenders the manuscript to Lord Wilmot, one of the nobleman's friends, even though Wilmot enjoys pretending to be a heartless rake, and soon it is revealed that nobody else is quite so bad as they seem either: the memoirs are far more generous than anyone expected them to be, the rake is secretly a soft-hearted philanthropist, and the author is handsomely rewarded with an annual pension. Privately earmarking the plum role of Wilmot for himself, Dickens reported back to Bulwer Lytton that the play was "Full of character, strong in interest, rich in capital situations, and *certain to go nobly.*"

That last phrase included a hidden pun, because in an attempt to use the publicity surrounding the Great Exhibition to boost his own scheme, Dickens had decided to ask the Duke of Devonshire for permission to borrow his grand London residence, Devonshire House in Piccadilly, as the venue for a royal charity premiere, to be followed by further perfor-mances in London and a tour of other towns and cities. Dickens already knew the Duke's gardener, Joseph Paxton, through their earlier work on the *Daily News*, and clearly saw him as another refracted self-image: in a speech for the General Theatrical Fund on 14 April, Dickens would praise the "wonderful achievement of my ingenious friend Mr. Paxton," and in another speech to the Gardeners' Benevolent Association on 9 June he would use him as evidence that "This is a great age . . . when a man by the power of his own genius and good sense can scale such a daring height as Mr. Paxton has reached, and composedly place his form on the top." Despite this personal connection, he approached his task circumspectly. His letter to the Duke on 4 March drips with flattery, reminding him of his "generosity," delicately asking for his "kindest consideration," and elabo-rately signing off "With every apology for the trouble I give your Grace, and every sincere assurance of the respect which seems to justify me to myself in doing so." Fortunately, the Duke was already flattered by the fact that he had been contacted by one of his favourite writers ("I have made a friendship with Charles Dickens," he wrote in his diary on the day he received this letter. "I worship him"), and he happily gave permission for the Amateur Company to use Devonshire House for a gala performance of *Not So Bad As We Seem* on 30 April, the evening before the official opening of the Great Exhibition.

The preparations for this occasion are meticulously catalogued in a scrapbook compiled by the Duke. A fat volume bound in brown leather, its detailed paper trail includes letters from Dickens, the official prospectus of the Guild, negotiations with Buckingham Palace, a list of subscribers, and in pride of place at the front of the volume a gilded ticket for five guineas, announcing a performance of "SIR EDWARD BULWER LYTTON'S NEW COMEDY, IN THE PRESENCE OF HER MAJESTY AND HIS ROYAL HIGHNESS THE PRINCE ALBERT." What isn't included is the key detail that the stage in Devonshire House would be erected under Paxton's personal supervision. The designer of the Crystal Palace was also to be Dickens's "stage architect."

SPRING

Disappearances

The Times.

N°. 20,739.

LONDON, MONDAY, MARCH 3, 1851.

PRICE, WITH A SUPPLEMENT, 5d.

On Saturday 1 March, tucked away among all the other advertisements jostling for attention on the front page of *The Times*, there was an appeal to "P. P. P.":

> Pray WRITE to your unhappy parents, to whom the uncertainty of your fate is most agonizing: there has not been one letter or inquiry for you since that dreadful day you left us, so you might have remained in that home your absence has made so miserable. We cannot remove until we hear from you—

A tiny sliver of print on a crowded page, it was the advertising equivalent of putting a message in a bottle and dropping it into the ocean. Not that P. P. P.'s unhappy parents would have lacked alternative ways of finding their wayward offspring. Three months later, in a *Household Words* article on "Disappearances," Elizabeth Gaskell would express a breezy confidence in the power of the newly established detective branch of the London Metropolitan Police to track down such individuals. Supported by the "vast organized machinery" of the police, Gaskell claimed, it was no longer necessary to be "haunted by the possibility of mysterious disappearances." Anyone who tried to dodge his proper responsibilities by leaving his old life behind would soon be "overtaken by the electric telegraph, and clutched back to his fate by a Detective policeman."

Yet still the *Times* advertisements came. Two days later, on Monday 3 March: "MISSING, since Wednesday last, R. W. D., a man, 53 years of age, 5 feet 9 high, marked with Small-pox, dark eyes, hair grey: was last seen in Goswell-street, St. Luke's: had on brown trousers, flannel jacket," and also

"WILLIAM STRAPPS, age 48, born at Donington, in Lincolnshire" who "has not been heard of the last four years; his trade a weaver." Such advertisements were like detective stories in capsule form. In fact some of them now look oddly like sketches for Dickens's unfinished novel *The Mystery of Edwin Drood*, in which the leading character disappears on Christmas Eve, and the decision is taken that "placards and advertisements should be widely circulated" imploring him to get in touch. "MISSING, a YOUNG MAN" reads another advertisement published in *The Times* on Friday 7 March, before going on to explain that the man's "disconsolate friends" were offering a reward for information. What happened next is not known: like Edwin Drood's fate, the end of this story remains lost in the vast empty regions of the unwritten.

In 1851 there was a new term for such individuals: "missing person *n.* (frequently in *plural*) a person whose whereabouts are unknown and who has not been traced or confirmed to be alive." The earliest example in the *Oxford English Dictionary* dates from August 1850, filling a gap in the language that was increasingly needed to make sense of all these other gaps that seemed to be opening up in the world. Two years later Dickens would publish the nostalgic essay "Gone Astray," in which he recalled how as a child he had once become lost in the swarming streets of London. What these *Times* advertisements revealed was how easily adults could also vanish, especially at a time when so many were unmooring themselves from their old lives in villages and small towns and setting themselves adrift in the largest city in the world.

This spring the interest in "missing persons" wasn't limited to individuals like P. P. P. or R. W. D. The whereabouts of Sir John Franklin's Arctic expedition was still a mystery, following a last sighting of his ships in July 1845 in northern Baffin Bay. Not until October 1854 would their fate finally be revealed. That is when Dr. John Rae, the Chief Factor of the Hudson's Bay Company, informed the Admiralty that some Eskimos (Inuit) had recently told him of meeting with a party of about forty white men in a starving condition, who were attempting to make their way south in the spring of 1850, and who had bought some seal meat from them; returning later to the same area, the Inuit found the men's remains, including some bones that had apparently been gnawed on by human teeth. According to a scribbled note left in a cairn on the remote north-west corner of King William Island, Franklin had died on 11 June 1847, after his ships had been trapped in the pack ice for nine months. On 22 April 1848, with no prospect of a thaw, the surviving officers decided to abandon their giant wooden coffins and lead more than a hundred men on a march towards the distant Great Fish River. Weakened by hunger and scurvy, they may have known there was no realistic prospect of reaching it. Even dragging sledges weighing up to 1,400 pounds, they could only carry enough supplies to last around forty days, less than half of what they needed to survive, and as the men marched along they left a sad trail of objects behind them, including a chronometer, four teaspoons, a copy of *The Vicar of Wakefield*, and some still-loaded guns.

But in the spring of 1851 this information had not yet come to light, and a much better reflection of the national mood at the time could be found in works like Stephen Pearce's *The Arctic Council Planning a Search for Sir John Franklin*, a painting on a suitably heroic scale completed this year, which depicted members of the Admiralty studying charts and gazing off thoughtfully into the distance; only time would tell whether their expressions should be interpreted as signs of hope or dread. Currently the public was still digesting news from the previous autumn that 124 objects from Franklin's winter camp of 1845–6 had been discovered on the coast of Baffin Island: "coal bags, empty canisters for preserved meats . . . pieces of clothing, wood, casks, iron." Within a few years, people would piously start to refer to these physical odds and ends as "relics" (the word chosen by Dickens in the first of his three *Household Words* articles on "The Lost Arctic Voyagers," published in 1854), lending them the hazy glamour usually associated with a saint's bones, but in 1851 they could still be treated as a collection of clues, turning every reader into an armchair detective hoping to solve The Mysterious Case of Sir John Franklin and the Missing Polar Expedition.

Similar challenges on a much smaller scale were posed by many of the other advertisements that appeared in *The Times* this week. On Monday 3 March, a reward of two pounds was offered for a small gold chain lost between Hammersmith and Islington, and an unspecified amount for "an IVORY DOUBLE OPERA-GLASS, with plain gilt mounting and focus screw" left in a Paddington omnibus near the Princess's Theatre. On Friday that week, next to the advertisement about a missing "YOUNG MAN" was one about a missing King Charles spaniel with a grey muzzle answering to the name of Duchess (reward for safe return: one sovereign). If these advertisements revealed something about the lifestyles of selected individuals, they revealed far more about urban life in general. Increasingly people were on the move, and wherever they travelled they tended to leave behind them the human equivalent of a snail's trail.

It was a modern phenomenon that had recently been noticed in the pages of *Household Words*. In "Railway Waifs and Strays," published in the final issue of 1850, Harry Wills and Christopher Hill took their readers on a guided tour of the lost property warehouse attached to a London railway terminus, pointing out that a visitor "might readily guess at the owners from the articles—they are so perfectly characteristic," such as a silk handkerchief formed into a bundle containing "A pair of hair-brushes; a chart and tariff of fares of the Austrian Lloyd's Steam-Boats Company; a small jar of preserved meat beside a pot of bear's-grease, to give it a flavour; a play-bill of the San [sic] Scala Theatre, where the owner had, it would seem, the pleasure of hearing Donizetti's new opera of 'La Regna de Golconda [sic]'; a case of tooth-picks, a Prussian bill for post-horses, a comb, a half nibbled pipe of macaroni, and a screw of tobacco." Such items made the railway lost property office sound like a parody of the Victorian middle-class living room, with its lovingly assembled knick-knacks and carefully curated clutter. However, putting these miscellaneous objects into a list meant that they could reflect the ramshackle unpredict-ability of life while also being kept safely under control. It was a narrative trick Dickens had enjoyed playing from the start of his career. A sketch like "Brokers' and Marine-store Shops," first published in 1834, is full of lists that attempt to capture the visual chaos of a junk shop ("twenty books— all odd volumes; and as many wine-glasses—all different patterns; several locks, an old earthenware pan, full of rusty keys; two or three gaudy chimney-ornaments—cracked, of course; the remains of a lustre, without any drops; a round frame like a capital O, which has once held a mirror; a flute, complete with the exception of the middle joint; a pair of curling-irons; and a tinder-box"), while in *The Old Curiosity Shop* Dickens provides a detailed inventory of the shop itself, which is full of "rusty weapons of various kinds," "fantastic carvings" and "strange furniture," before "curi-osity" is revealed to be the driving motor of his plot—the desire to know what will happen next—in addition to describing what Nell and her grand-father are forced to abandon when they leave their home behind.

It was hard to avoid lists of objects in the spring of 1851, because for many observers they were the only way to make sense of the sheer scale of preparations for the Great Exhibition. An article published in the *Illustrated London News* on 1 March provided a typically breathless update on the "wagon-loads of goods" that were arriving in Hyde Park: "pillars of polished granite—fountains—colossal statues—gigantic masses of coal—a contribution of spermaceti [a waxy substance extracted from the heads of whales], which will cost £1000 in its preparation—models of the Britannia and Dnieper Bridges—a monster telescope—the hydraulic press from the Menai Straits, whose lifting power exceeds 2620 tons—displays of feathers, furs, and Spitalfields silk manufactures . . ." Such is the journalist's excitement about these "treasures of industry and art" that the dashes in his administrative checklist look more like a series of gasps. Currently the interior of the Crystal Palace resembled another lost property office, but just as the items listed in "Railway Waifs and Strays" offered little glimpses into the lives of their owners, so these statues and pillars and other items were starting to be viewed as telltale physical traces of the countries they had left behind. They were also the ingredients for a much bigger story, because in gathering together so many different objects from around the world, the organisers of the Great Exhibition wanted it to be something other than a giant version of the Old Curiosity Shop. Instead their hope was that it would usher in a new age of global harmony, forming what one journalist sceptically referred to as "the turning point of [the world's] future destinies."

Two poems published in *Household Words* at the end of the first week in March showed that Dickens was fully aware of the scale of this ambition. Mrs. Bradburn's "A World at Peace" confidently anticipated a time when "Man may enjoy unbroken peace and rest / 'Ere this fair globe has grown a century older," while in "The Congress of Nations" George Meredith celebrated global brotherhood in a poem that rose to a final exclamation mark like someone letting off a firework:

> A glorious epoch brightens history's page,
>   Shedding upon the Future dazzling lustre;
> How proud the thought that England is the stage,
>   Which shall re-echo with the Nations' muster!

More ambitious still was a series of articles on "Three May-Days in London," published in subsequent issues on 19 and 26 April and 3 May, in which Charles Knight offered a rapid history lesson dealing with various events that had happened in London on 1 May in different years. Moving grasshopper-like from the apprentice riots in 1517, through the various entertainments (including thimble-riggers, a tame elephant and a scale model of Amsterdam carved in wood) that were on show in the 1701 May Fair, and finally arriving at the official opening of the 1851 Great Exhibition, these articles were an attempt to show just how much progress had been made in the country as a whole over the previous 350 years. "Look upon it reverently," Knight concludes his survey of the Crystal Palace and its groundbreaking, mind-expanding contents. "Do homage to the promoters of it, in all love and loyalty . . . in this goodly work there is hope beyond performance—hope of 'Peace on earth, good-will towards men.'"

Inevitably such wide-eyed enthusiasm was ripe for satire. Indeed several writers had already recognised that the sheer scale of the Great Exhibition threatened to make people lose all sense of proportion in other ways too. The previous year, George Sala had produced a hand-drawn booklet that promised to show *"Wot is to Be"* in 1851, depicting various national stereotypes: an effete French dancing master, a whiskery German carrying a giant sausage on his head, and several others. There is no happy mingling of nations here: each set of characters remains strictly confined to their own section of the booklet, like a collection of beetles arranged in a display cabinet.

The hope that the Great Exhibition would usher in a new era of peace and harmony had also attracted less comic forms of suspicion. On 22 March, Richard Horne's *Household Words* article "A Time for All Things" pointed out that although modern Britain did some things very well ("A tunnel under the Thames is called for—and it is accomplished . . . An enormous Exhibition Palace for the Industry of all Nations is called for— and it is accomplished"), other important goals were no closer to being achieved in 1851 than they had been for many years. Overcrowded burial grounds, the stinking Thames and all the other familiar urban miseries continued to "stick fast in the mud of obstinacy and imbecility," and the biblical echo in the title Dickens chose for this article ("To every thing there is a season, and a time to every purpose under the heaven") indicated just how long he thought they had been hanging around. Two weeks later his journal included another poem touching on the Great Exhibition, although this one was considerably more realistic about the human cost of all these impressive industrial artefacts. In John Critchley Prince's "A Voice from the Factory," a weaver dutifully echoes some standard lines about the Exhibition's mission "to inform and dignify the age" and bind quarrelling nations in "new, but friendly bonds," yet he goes on to point out that as the "slave, not servant" of his workplace, "I shall not see our Babel's summer wonder," other than by reading about it on his only day off each week. Such a tiny reward for being one of the workers whose labour the Exhibition was supposed to be celebrating makes his final burst of praise sound understandably hollow. "Hail to the time that makes all nations brothers!" he cries, having already pointed out that this is a party to which he has not been invited. "Hail to the advent of the coming May!"

The presence of "A Voice from the Factory" in *Household Words* accurately reflected Dickens's own ambivalence about class. On the one hand, he was keen to promote the interests of ordinary workers, as his earlier membership of the relevant Exhibition committee had shown, and he was also happy to use pieces like this one to invite his middle-class readers to climb inside the heads of working-class individuals and have a look around. Such activities were fully in line with his "Preliminary Word" to the first issue of *Household Words*, which emphasised his desire to bring together "the greater and the lesser in degree . . . and mutually dispose them to a better acquaintance and a kinder understanding." On the other hand, even after he had put Prince's poem through his inky fishing net, there was no suggestion that the speaker should criticise an economic system that made it impossible for him to take a proper holiday. And that isn't altogether surprising.

Dickens's attitude towards class was always complicated, not least because as a former child labourer who now worked with his hands as a bestselling author he was unusually hard to locate within the traditional class system. This could produce some awkward contradictions. The previous year, for example, he had visited the Westminster Ragged School, telling Miss Coutts that it was "an awful place, in a maze of filth and squalor," but also noting proudly that "some people to whom I talked, took occasion to admire my diamond ring." (Whether they were approving its workmanship or trying to decide how to steal it is a question he does not go into.) His attitude towards individual workers was equally ambiguous. Some years earlier he had become friendly with a cabinetmaker named John Overs, to whom he lent a copy of Carlyle's *Chartism*, encouraging him in his studies and writing a preface for Overs's 1844 book *Evenings of a Working Man*. However, when the man shared some unflattering views on Macready, Dickens was quick to put him in his place. "You have lost sight of your true position in regard to that gentleman," Dickens warned him in a stinging letter of rebuke, "and all other gentlemen with whom you have come in contact." There was no attempt to pretend that a cabinetmaker's opinions were of equal value to those of his social superiors.

Working-class crowds were an even more troubling phenomenon for Dickens. When he was in the right mood, he enjoyed sharing their lively sense of fun: some of the happiest scenes in *Sketches by Boz* involve him walking around popular leisure attractions like Greenwich Fair, where the boisterous energy of "an extremely dense crowd" bubbles over into his writing, as he describes how "the screams of women, the shouts of boys, the clanging of gongs, the firing of pistols, the ringing of bells . . . the hallooing of showmen, and an occasional roar from the wild beast shows" all compete for the visitor's attention, just as they tumble over each other in his prose. At the same time, Dickens was conscious of how quickly this energy could become a destructive force, from the "struggling current of angry faces" that hunts down Bill Sikes in *Oliver Twist*, to the howling mob that storms Newgate Prison in *Barnaby Rudge*.

These fears of a lively crowd becoming a destructive rabble were widely shared in 1851. The prospect of large groups of working-class visitors seeking admission to the Great Exhibition, in particular, had long been a cause of concern for the organisers. With memories of Chartist demonstrations still fresh, and rumours circulating of foreign anarchists being attracted to London to fan revolutionary embers back into life, many people found it hard to look at all those large sheets of glass in the Crystal Palace without feeling nervous. In *David Copperfield*, Dickens had depicted the eccentric Betsey Trotwood arriving at the home of her new great-nephew David and, instead of knocking on the front door, peering through a window and "pressing the end of her nose against the glass." It is a funny and touching scene, but if thousands of Betsey Trotwoods decided to assemble in Hyde Park the fear was that the "Great Unwashed," as Thackeray had recently dubbed them in his novel *The History of Pendennis*, wouldn't be content merely to press their noses against the glass.

Already the streets around Hyde Park had been widened, and although the official explanation was that they would provide easier access for members of the public, it was tacitly understood that they would also allow the cavalry to ride three abreast if they were needed to put down demonstrations. Nearly three years after the Chartist threat had collapsed, this remained a worrying possibility. And whether or not working people "almost to a man" were "red-hot proletarians, entertaining violent opinions," as Henry Mayhew would suggest this year, the structural vulnerability of the Crystal Palace was hard to miss. As the Duke of Wellington remarked, "Glass is damned thin stuff."

Most of this fear about working-class visitors was the result of ignorance rather than proper research. Put simply, for the majority of middle-class readers who bought copies of *David Copperfield* or *The History of Pendennis*, the lives of the poor were as mysterious as those of the Exhibition's anticipated foreign visitors. That is because for several years it had been evident that England was not one nation but two. These were nations "between whom there is no intercourse and no sympathy," as a radical journalist in the industrial north had explained in Disraeli's 1845 novel *Sybil; or The Two Nations*, and "who are as ignorant of each other's habits, thoughts, and feelings, as if they were dwellers in different zones, or inhabitants of different planets." They were, Disraeli concludes in urgent capital letters, "THE RICH AND THE POOR." But if this realisation that people who lived in the same country could inhabit different worlds was chastening enough when it came to the grim working conditions of the north, it was worse still in London. For as Dickens knew from years of careful observation, here the two nations of rich and poor could be found jostling each other in the same streets.

In the spring of 1851, this interest in the hidden world of the poor was central to the ongoing serialisation of Mayhew's investigation into London's beggars, street sellers, and all those other people whose lives usually passed unnoticed. Although by the middle of the century many thousands earned their living in the streets, in terms of cultural representation they were practically invisible. Their appearances in print tended to be restricted to cartoons in *Punch*, which whittled away their lives into a series of comic catchphrases, or novels in which they provided little more than splashes of local colour, as with Dickens's description in *Dombey and Son* of "the water-carts and the old-clothes men, and the people with geraniums, and the umbrella-mender, and the man who trilled the little bell of the Dutch clock as he went along." By contrast, Mayhew decided that these people would be central to his work rather than a set of footnotes to it. The background was thrust into the foreground, and for many readers the effect was as astonishing as it would have been if pieces of theatre scenery had come to the front of the stage and introduced themselves to the audience.

For his original *Morning Chronicle* articles, published from 1849 onwards, Mayhew's contributions as the paper's Metropolitan Correspondent had been advertised as part of "a full and detailed description of the moral, intellectual, material, and physical condition of the industrial poor throughout England," but by the time he set up the office for his new periodical in Wellington Street his investigations had long outgrown their original home. Instead of providing his readers with "descriptions" of the poor from a safe distance, much of each instalment of *London Labour and the London Poor* was taken up by first-hand interviews with the crossing-sweepers, Punch and Judy entertainers, sandwich sellers, rag-gatherers, rat-killers, doll's-eye makers, thieves, beggars, and all the other pieces of human flotsam and jetsam that had washed up in the capital. Here they were encouraged to tell their own stories in their own words, transcribed by Mayhew in shorthand and then lightly edited by him to remove any jarring examples of swearing or blasphemy. Soon many of them would face the prospect of being arrested or moved on in the area around Hyde Park, visible evidence of one of the "two nations" being especially unwelcome at a celebration of "the Works of Industry of All Nations," but in Mayhew's pages they found a permanent home. No work in the period did more to bring alive what his later magazine *The Great World of London* called "the riot, the struggle, and the scramble for a living."

While there were some strange omissions—Mayhew included nothing on domestic servants, for example—mostly he lived up to the billing he gave himself in the work's preface. Part pioneer and part anthropologist, he was a "traveller in the undiscovered country of the poor" who brought back stories about people "of whom the public has less knowledge than of the most distant tribes of the earth." They included "the poor half-witted and very persecuted harp-player" whose handwritten sign explained that "from the delapedated [sic] condition of my present instrument I only produce ridicule" (following the publication of this interview, readers sent in donations totalling £2 10s, which were enough to buy him a new harp), and the old showman who travelled with performing animals and told Mayhew that he "sometimes had trouble to get lodgings for the bear," even though "Bears is well-behaved enough if they ain't aggravated." Whenever Mayhew's writing threatened to descend into the period's usual responses of disdain or whimsy, his ear caught the unique accent of an ordinary voice and elevated it to the dignity of print. There was the realism of the Italian showman whose monkey had died: "I did cry!—I cry because I have no money to go and buy anoder monkey!" Or the humour of the man who hawked flypapers: "It ain't a purfession and it ain't a trade, I suppose it's a calling." Or the watercress girl shuffling along in carpet slippers that were far too big for her: "I ain't a child, and I shan't be a woman till I'm twenty, but I'm past eight, I am." Each week readers who bought the latest instalment of Mayhew's work could hear the unknown world that existed all around them being fleshed out and brought to life.

As well as being physical neighbours in Wellington Street, Mayhew and Dickens were imaginatively close. While Dickens's novels had shown Mayhew how to strike a balance between London's sprawl of contingent details and the promise of an underlying pattern, Mayhew's interviews gave factual support to ideas that Dickens had long been attempting to work through in his fiction. Indeed, Mayhew's account of a clown who cracks jokes even though he is starving echoes one of the interpolated stories in *The Pickwick Papers* so closely that one wonders if Mayhew sometimes deliberately chose figures who seemed to have stepped out of a work of fiction. Not that he was always complimentary about Dickens: he viewed the sentimental depictions of working-class life in *The Chimes* as "profound rubbish"—a description that teetered awkwardly between admiration and exasperation. But it is hard to avoid feeling, when we start to listen to Mayhew's speakers, that we have heard them somewhere before, or that the woodcuts that originally accompanied them in his journal (most of them engraved from daguerreotypes taken by Richard Beard, a London photographer who in 1841 opened the first portrait studio in Europe) are on the verge of twisting themselves into the illustrations of Cruikshank or Hablot Browne ("Phiz"). The rag-and-bottle shop owner who "can't read very much" is only one layer of grime away from becoming *Bleak House*'s illiterate Krook, while the "pure-finder" (i.e., collector of dog dung) who would "sooner die in the street" than go into the workhouse would later get her wish as Betty Higden in *Our Mutual Friend*, a novel that also contains the ballad seller Silas Wegg and scavenger Gaffer Hexam, both of whom have close relations in Mayhew. It is not that truth is stranger than fiction, but that in Mayhew's work, as in Dickens's, truth and fiction keep swapping places until, like Mrs. Flintwich in *Little Dorrit*, we "don't know which is which, or what is what."

Above all, what these connections show is that although Dickens and Mayhew were equally interested in the facts and figures underpinning modern life—one of the regular index entries for *Household Words* was

"Statistics," while the pages of *London Labour and the London Poor* are packed with sober tables of research punctuated by calculations of the strange-but-true variety: "Total quantity of rain falling yearly in the metropolis, 10,686,132,230,400 cubic inches"—both writers were strongly drawn to human stories that would usually be swallowed up by anonymous tables of data. The key difference is that Dickens was rarely content to describe people and events as they were, when he could instead imagine them as they might exist in a piece of fiction.

There are hints of this in an article on "Bill-Sticking" that Dickens contributed to *Household Words* at the end of March. Advertising posters were a familiar sight in London, and a "bill-sticking clause" in the 1839 (Metropolitan) Police Act that penalised "every person who, without the consent of the owner or occupier, shall affix any posting bill or other paper against or upon any building, wall, fence or pale" had done little to curb the activities of men who swarmed around fences and hoardings, armed with bulging bags of posters and extendable sticks. In some areas, practically every square foot of external space was covered by a tatty patchwork of posters, advertising everything from future theatre performances to the boastful claims made for popular beauty products like Rowland's Kalydor, "a most soothing, healing, and refreshing milk for the face, hands, and arms . . . soothes and heals all Irritation, Chaps, Chilblains, Cutaneous Eruptions, &c; and produces a beautiful and delicate complexion." Most of "Bill-Sticking" is taken up by Dickens's interview with the "King of the Bill Stickers," who claims to earn five shillings a day "including paste" slapping up his posters all around London, yet whereas Mayhew might have remained in the background when interviewing this kind of subject, here everything is filtered through Dickens's imagination. Whether Dickens is telling us that the bill-sticker sometimes dreams of turning his open-topped cart into an arbour by "training scarlet runners across it in the season," or facetiously noting a "slight tendency to repetition" that may also "have been observed in the conversation of His Majesty King George the Third," the facts are repeatedly animated by little flickers of fancy.

Three of Dickens's articles in the previous year, all of them supposedly "From the Raven in the Happy Family," had pushed this technique further still. Dickens had successively owned three pet ravens in the 1840s, the first of which he had arranged to be stuffed after it died in 1841 with a final croak of "Halloa old girl!" Now it perched stiffly in an elaborate glass case in his study. By contrast, "Happy Families" were groups of different animals exhibited living in uneasy intimacy, or at least without eating each other, in the same enclosure; the "Happy Family Exhibitor" interviewed by Mayhew had an impressive total of fifty-four animals living in one cage, including three cats, two dogs, two monkeys, two hawks, ten starlings, five white rats and a screech owl, which he displayed for money near Waterloo Bridge or the National Gallery. The release in 1851 of the card game still known as Happy Families, in which contestants have to reunite the families of Mr. Bones the Butcher, Mr. Pots the Painter and other similarly named professions, added a competitive element to this idea, and soon current events would nudge it in a more satirical direction. On 19 July, *Punch* included a cartoon by John Tenniel ("The Happy Family in Hyde Park") as part of its response to the Great Exhibition, depicting a model of the Crystal Palace that is full of tiny foreign visitors, whose capering antics are being pointed out by a grave-looking Prince Albert, the joke being that expecting some nations to get along with each other required a leap of faith almost as large as putting a hawk into the same cage as five white rats. (Tenniel was probably the artist responsible for the design of the Happy Families cards, which added an extra in-joke to his *Punch* cartoon; this spring he would also join the team painting the scenery for *Not So Bad As We Seem*.) Yet nobody tackled this subject with quite the same comic brio as Dickens.

"I croak the croak of revolt, and call upon the Happy Family to rally round me," the Raven concludes his first long complaint about living in a cage with other animals. "You men have had it all your own way for a long time." His response is to point out that life outside the cage isn't so different to his own inside it. If people laugh at the parrot for saying the same things over and over again, "Did you ever hear, among yourselves, anything approaching to a parrot repetition of the words, Constitution, Country, Public Service, Self-Government, Centralisation, Un-English, Capital, Balance of Power, Vested Interests, Corn, Rights of Labour, Wages, or so forth?" As for the idea that ravens are notorious for taking away shiny coins and teaspoons to hide in secret places, that is nothing compared to the behaviour of gold prospectors in California, who were currently "turning up the ground with their bills, grubbing under the water, sickening, moulting, living in want and fear, starving, dying, tumbling over on their backs, murdering one another, and all for what? Pieces of money that they want to carry to their favourite holes. Ravens every one of 'em!" The other two articles use the same satirical technique to tackle an even broader range of targets: overdressed funerals, overstuffed graveyards, balloon ascents, statues to undeserving heroes and many more. Repeatedly, Dickens peers at familiar ideas through an unfamiliar lens; repeatedly, he takes the raw materials of life and reshapes them into teasing fragments of narrative. All that is missing is a plot where they can snap into place.

Dickens also enjoyed shuffling fragments of real life into stories through the charitable project that took up regular slices of his time this spring. "There is nothing in London that is *not* curious," he wrote to one correspondent on 22 March, the same day he published "Bill-Sticking" in *Household Words*, and few things excited his own curiosity more than Urania Cottage, the London refuge for "fallen women," most of them former prostitutes and thieves, he had opened in November 1847 with the aim of helping them turn their lives around. In *Oliver Twist*, the teenage prostitute Nancy briefly dreams of emigration and "a home in some foreign country where I could end my days in solitude and peace," and in *David Copperfield* Mr. Peggotty explains how he is going to save his seduced and abandoned niece Emily: "Theer's mighty countries, fur from heer. Our future life lays over the sea . . . No one can't reproach my darling in Australia. We will begin a new life over theer!" His plan succeeds: safe from scandal on the other side of the world, Emily devotes her life to repentant spinsterhood and good works, while the friend who accompanies her to Australia, the equally fallen Martha, marries a young farm labourer, a decision that is made somewhat easier by the fact that, as Mr. Peggotty admits with refreshing candour, "Wives is very scarce theer." In effect, both women are permitted to live out the dream that Dickens had spent the past three years plotting for his female charges. Unlike the stories of instant riches that were starting to trickle in from the Australian gold fields, such as a British metallurgist who was said to have made "a profit of a hundred thousand pounds in the course of a day or two," according to Frederick Arnold's *Turning-Points in Life*, the rewards Dickens sought for his Urania Cottage pioneers were chiefly moral. Their new lives in Australia were to be a form of slow-motion salvation—an opportunity to slough off past mistakes and start again.

This aim was closely connected to the subject of a speech Dickens made on 14 April. Returning again to the theme of the Guild of Literature and Art, he told those present that in contributing to the General Theatrical Fund they were not performing an act of charity; instead "you will be helping those who help themselves." That might seem an unusual justification for an operation such as Urania Cottage, which was entirely funded by Miss Coutts, but as he had told her in a long letter first outlining the scheme in 1846, a woman who truly wanted to change her life would have to do it herself. "It is explained to her that she is degraded and fallen, but not lost, having this shelter; and that the means of Return to Happiness are now about to be put into her own hands, and trusted to her own keeping." In effect, Urania Cottage was a mixture of a boarding school and a training centre, although the way that Dickens wrote about it in his letters suggests he also saw it as a moral sanctuary in which these fallen women (or girls, as he usually referred to them while they remained in the home) could be shown how to achieve their very own Paradise Regained.

The house was located in Shepherd's Bush, surrounded by fields and market gardens at a time when the area still lived up to the pastoral promise of its name, but it was close enough to the city to be reached by catching an omnibus in Oxford Street followed by a short walk. The more significant distance between Urania Cottage and other institutions for "fallen women" in London was not geographical but ideological. Most were run by Anglican nuns who treated the "penitents" in their care as lost souls in need of salvation. Accordingly the atmosphere inside these places was one of carefully nurtured shame. Days were spent doing work such as laundry, as if removing the stains from other people's clothes was a natural extension of trying to cleanse one's own soul, and this labour was punctuated by regular prayers and periods of silent reflection. "Pernicious and unnatural" was Dickens's summary verdict, dismissing the House of Mercy that a vicar had proposed to Miss Coutts as "but a kind of Nunnery." Of course, for many of the people who worked in these institutions, including the poet Christina Rossetti, who enrolled as an Associate Sister at the St. Mary Magdalen Penitentiary in Highgate, that was precisely the point.

Dickens wanted Urania Cottage to be different. Instead of being made to feel guilty and ashamed, the dozen or so girls who were resident at any one time would be treated as members of "an innocently Cheerful family" and "*tempted* to virtue." As the home was supposed to be a blank slate, their past lives would never be referred to. If they lasted the probationary period of "about a year" that Dickens thought necessary, they would learn how to run their own homes, and could then become domestic pioneers in the colonies. For this reason the girls were expected to do all their own washing and cleaning, empty their own chamber pots, bake their own bread and sew their own clothes. Such activities would be practical lessons in self-help, and also a series of rehearsals for their new roles in countries like Australia. Inevitably there were prayers in Urania Cottage, and Dickens marked a selection of passages in the prayer book for twice-daily services, but for these girls the emphasis was to be on the next stage of their lives on earth rather than preparing themselves for heaven.

If all this makes Dickens's scheme sound like an even more ambitious version of his much-loved amateur theatricals, that is probably not a coincidence. His friend Arthur Helps remembered how "he looked at all things and people dramatically. He assigned to all of us characters; and in his company we could not help playing our parts." In this respect Urania Cottage was like a giant version of the toy theatre Dickens had been fascinated by as a boy. The first thing the girls heard when they entered the house was a prologue written by him: an address that was read to them by the matron in charge introducing them to their new lives. Next they were ritually dressed in costumes he had chosen from a shop in Tottenham Court Road, plainly cut clothes in bright fabrics that were "as cheerful in appearance as they reasonably could be—at the same time very neat and modest." Some girls even acquired the names of pantomime-like characters as they underwent their very own transformation scenes: Dickens's letters to Miss Coutts are full of the latest antics of Stallion or the volatile little Fairy.

Once again Dickens's motto for the place was "Don't talk about it—do it!," and he led by example: everything went through his hands, including the choice of furniture and books for the home, interviewing the staff, using Miss Coutts's funds to pay the bills, organising lessons in choral singing, and selecting and hanging up suitable texts, such as "a little inscription of my own" in the living room "referring to the advantages of order, punctuality, and good temper." Each day ran in a groove that followed "the whole routine of household duties," and although the timetable Dickens drew up included some opportunities for leisure activities, it also gave precise instructions on everything else, from when the girls should get up (6 a.m.) to when they should go to bed (9 p.m.), including two hours of schoolwork every day (10:30 a.m.–12:30 p.m.) and a bath every Saturday. In exercising Dickens's particular style of "active management," nothing was left to chance. As Jenny Hartley has written, so tightly regulated was Urania Cottage that "when he was not there he could look at his watch and know what they were doing every half-hour of the day." On this stage set the inmates were expected to play their roles cheerfully and obediently. They were also given regular reviews: each day they were marked out of four by one of the matrons on a specially printed form, under nine separate headings of Truthfulness, Industry, Temper, Propriety of Conduct and Conversation, Temperance, Order, Punctuality, Economy and Cleanliness, and every Saturday evening their marks were totted up and entered into a large house book, which also served as a running tally of how much money they would be presented with—six shillings and sixpence per thousand marks—when they left the home.

According to the 1851 census, most of the inmates of Urania Cottage were in their late teens, with some being as young as fourteen. They included seventeen-year-old Ellen Glyn and fifteen-year-old Emma Spencer, both of whom had been in Clerkenwell Workhouse and attended Field Lane Ragged School, who looked "terribly destitute and wretched" when Dickens first met them, and tried to reassure him that they "in no sense belonged to the class from whom the greater part of our inmates have been taken," i.e., prostitutes; nineteen-year-old Mary Anne Wilson, "a desolate creature without father or mother" who "answered me plainly, and said that she had been about the streets for a year"; and Elizabeth Watts, who had been a prisoner in Tothill Fields, and in 1854 would send a letter from Australia with news of her marriage—an outcome that "tastes like a sweetmeat," Dickens crowed. Often their first contact with Dickens came through a four-page printed letter he arranged to be distributed in selected prisons and workhouses, addressed to one "who was born to be happy and has lived miserably," and promising her "a HOME" where she would be treated "with the greatest kindness."

After Dickens had accepted a girl into Urania Cottage, he continued to play a large part in her life. Official committee meetings were held once a month, when he and the other members he had recruited, who included a prison governor and two clergymen, would interview each inmate to check on her progress, and deal with any major incidents. At the start of June this year there was a "Tribunal" for what Dickens ironically described as "one and all the most innocent and deferential of girls"; although he did not go into any details of their supposed transgressions, he enjoyed recounting the scene for Miss Coutts, as one of them "spoke very low, with her arms hooked behind her, and her eyes on the ground—and all the others, one after the other, did exactly the same," as if all were following the same stage directions. But Dickens was also ready to bustle over to Shepherd's Bush whenever there was a matter he could resolve as a "Committee of One." This happened fairly often, and most of the time it was an administrative headache he welcomed. If the girls who came to him were a social problem, it was one to which he was confident he had a solution.

This spring Dickens was again actively recruiting for Urania Cottage: a letter probably sent on 7 March informed Miss Coutts that he was "going to see some young women proposed to us from the Magdalen," i.e., the Magdalen Hospital on Blackfriars Road, founded in 1758 "for the reception of penitent prostitutes." It is possible that his interest in their fate was sharpened by his own domestic situation, because soon he and his family would also have to move to a new home. In September 1847 he had learned that the lease on Devonshire Terrace, taken on 1 December 1839, would run out in 1851, and in March 1849 he had responded to news of his brother-in-law Henry Austin's latest house move by telling him "I suppose you have been washing in a cheese-plate this morning, and breakfasting out of a clothes-basket. Those agonies of moving, though two years off, afflict me already." Now that his time in Devonshire Terrace was coming to an end, his letters started to fill with news of the houses he intended to visit and the offers he was tempted to make. At the end of January, there was a property in Highgate he asked Austin, who was Secretary of the

General Board of Health, for his opinion of "in a sanitary and soft watery pint [*sic*] of view," and in another letter he told Miss Coutts that this house would be "well adapted to my young people," here meaning his own children, before using the next paragraph to tell her that he planned to "write a little account of the Home, in Household Words": an apparent switch of focus that was really a confirmation that he had viewed Urania Cottage as an extension of his own home all along.

Although Dickens made some awkward jokes in his letters about the prospect of becoming homeless, telling Austin that he had made an unsuccessful offer "with fear and trembling" on the Highgate property, his impending move tapped a much deeper source of anxiety. The word "houseless" had rippled uneasily through his earlier fiction. In *Oliver Twist*, when Mr. Sowerberry the undertaker leads Oliver down a street of mouldering tenements that are "the nightly haunts of some houseless wretches," it serves as a warning about where the boy too might end up if he does not behave himself, while in *The Old Curiosity Shop* the response of Nell's grandfather to her telling him gently that they must now "live among poor people" is to cry out "Ah! poor, houseless, wandering, motherless child!" And once David Copperfield is safely tucked up in bed after his flight to Aunt Betsey's, he relates how "I prayed that I might never be houseless any more, and never might forget the houseless."

No doubt some of this can be attributed to the number of times Dickens's family had been forced to move from one address to another when he was a child, always just one step ahead of the bailiffs. But his situation in 1851 hardly compared with that of the girls he was trying to help, and certainly not with the way it was portrayed more widely at the time. Representations of the "fallen woman" had tended to treat her supposed transgressions as moral crimes that deserved the harshest punishment. The widespread assumption was that she had chosen to place herself beyond the bounds of decent family life, and should be treated accordingly—hence paintings like Richard Redgrave's luridly melodramatic *The Outcast*, presented to the Royal Academy this year, which depicts a father angrily turning out his daughter and her illegitimate baby into the snow, while other members of his family cling to him imploringly or beat their fists against the wall. Even the efforts of charities and religious organisations to help these women were sometimes met with hostility or ribaldry, like the couplet Tennyson wrote in response to another planned home for fallen women: "Home is home, though never so homely, / And a harlot a harlot, though never so comely." Interestingly, Dickens tended to follow a similar line when dealing with fictional versions of girls like Ellen Glyn or Emma Spencer. Until this point in his career, whenever he wanted to introduce a prostitute into one of his novels, Dickens's usual tactic had been to manufacture a scene of tear-jerking pathos, from Nancy in *Oliver Twist* rejecting Rose Maylie's attempt to save her ("'Oh, lady! lady!' she said, clasping her hands passionately before her face, 'if there was more like you, there would be fewer like me, there would—there would!'"), to Alice Marwood in *Dombey and Son* dying repentant after hearing about Christ's ministry to "the blind lame palsied beggar, the criminal, the woman stained with shame, the shunned of all our dainty clay." Such examples closely matched cultural stereotypes of the "fallen woman": passionate, desperate, usually doomed.

Yet even as Dickens was using his fiction to write about such figures in conventionally melodramatic terms, he was adopting a far more realistic approach to their living counterparts. In *David Copperfield*, he gives Martha a speech in which she threatens to drown herself ("Oh, the river! . . . I know that I belong to it. I know it's the natural company of such as I am!"), before elevating her voice to an even more implausibly noble pitch: "It has been put into your hearts, perhaps, to save a wretched creature for repentance. I am afraid to think so; it seems too bold." That is very different from Dickens's attempts to capture the voices of the girls at Urania Cottage. On one occasion "Little Willis" was caught playing a game with the Bible, as she tried to discover her future husband's name by placing a key in the Book of Ruth and waiting for it to move while she recited the alphabet, and Dickens threatened to dock all her marks for a month.

> After a day or two I went out, and she requested to see me, and said—I wish you could have seen her come in diplomatically to make terms with the establishment—"O! Without her marks, she found she couldn't do her work agreeable to herself"—"If you do it agreeable to us," said I, "that'll do."—"O! But" she said "I could wish not to have my marks took away"—"Exactly so," said I. "That's quite right; and the only way to get them back again, is to do as well as you can."—"Ho! But if she didn't have 'em giv' up at once, she could wish fur to go."—"Very well," said I. "You shall go tomorrow morning."

In other respects Dickens's thinking about the home zigzagged unpredictably between fact and fiction. His original letter to Miss Coutts outlining the scheme has been described as "a short story, manifesto and sales brochure all rolled into one," and over the next few years he happily expanded on its narrative possibilities. Not only did his letters repeatedly turn the inmates into characters, and particular events into scenes, he also spent hours writing up the histories of each girl in a special case book. The book was later lost, but from the frequent references to it in his correspondence it appears that Dickens viewed the practice of putting their lives into writing—an experience he found "interesting and touching in the extreme"—to be as necessary as giving them new clothes and domestic skills.

No doubt part of this answered Dickens's own need to make sense out of life by making stories out of it. He certainly seems to have used some events at Urania Cottage as raw material for his fiction. At the start of November 1849, he had been forced to expel one inmate, the sparky but unruly Isabella Gordon, and he later passed her in the lane "going slowly away, and wiping her face with her shawl"; within days he was rewriting the scene for the eighth instalment of *David Copperfield*, in which the disgraced Martha leaves Yarmouth for London, "gathering her shawl about her, covering her face with it, and weeping aloud." But the chief appeal of Urania Cottage's inmates appears to have been that the endings of their stories were still unknown. Originally Dickens had planned that the history of each girl in his case book should have "a final blank headed its 'Subsequent History,' which will remain to be filled up, by degrees, as we shall hear of them, and from them, abroad." It is not recorded how successful he was in meeting this ambitious target, especially for girls like Isabella Gordon who disappeared from view, but whether or not he managed to trace the actual course of their lives he could certainly enjoy plotting possible narrative outcomes for them, as he did for their fictional counterparts in *David Copperfield*. On 21 March 1851 he told Miss Coutts, "It is most encouraging and delightful! Imagining backward to what these women were and might have been, and forward to what their children may be." The successful ones, like Elizabeth Watts, who not only married in Australia but went on to have thirteen children, would end up living out a kind of romance plot; the unsuccessful ones, like Isabella Gordon, would pass into a future that was all too likely to be a tragedy of wasted potential. In either case Dickens's narrative powers were exhausted; from now on it was the former inmates of Urania Cottage themselves who would determine what kind of story they were in.

As long as the girls remained in the home, Dickens had identified another genre of writing they could slip into: detective fiction. His letters to Miss

Coutts are packed with mysteries needing to be solved, including minor thefts, rule-breaking, criminal damage and possible romantic liaisons with young men spotted hanging around in the garden. Dickens prided himself on being the man who could solve them all. "I have narrowly investigated everything," he told Miss Coutts in November 1850 in relation to a "case" in which two inmates had absconded after stealing a cloak and other articles worth £7 from one of the matrons. His investigations into other offences at Urania Cottage were similarly meticulous. Whether he was interviewing the likely culprits, or engaging in undercover surveillance ("I have directed all the beds to be narrowly and secretly examined," he explained after learning that the two young thieves had also stolen a purse containing half a crown), Dickens had created a world in which hidden secrets would always be brought to light.

Dickens's amateur sleuthing at Urania Cottage was typical of his fascination with detective work, which would acquire a new focus in the first half of 1851. This had already spread into almost every area of his life. George Sala recalled that he had "a curious and almost morbid partiality for communing with and entertaining police officers . . . He seemed always at ease with these personages, and never tired of questioning them." In the 1840s Dickens had seriously entertained thoughts of becoming a magistrate, like one of his literary heroes Henry Fielding, and although he dropped this plan it did not prevent him from making several less official contributions to the justice system. On one occasion in London, he had a girl taken into custody for using bad language in the street, and insisted that she should be prosecuted, later arriving at the court with a copy of the Police Act in which he had helpfully marked the relevant passage for the presiding magistrate. In Paris, he handed a drunken coachman over to the authorities, and was surprised when the man later turned up at his lodgings with a police certificate for him to sign, confirming that he had begged Dickens's pardon and refunded the original one-and-a-half-franc fare. "Isn't this admirable?" gloated Dickens, noting that the coachman's remorse was somewhat compromised by the fact that he "WAS DRUNK WHEN HE CAME IN!!"

Dickens was equally scrupulous when it came to his own domestic security. On one occasion, Thomas Beard was sent round to Dickens's study in Devonshire Terrace on an errand, and was instructed to "twist round the rewolving [sic] table in the middle of the room, open all the drawers—there is alternately a real drawer and a sham, and the key is in one of them—until you find a half bound Diary for 1847, which bring unto me." Another letter explained to Georgina Hogarth in patient detail how his writing table at Gad's Hill should be opened, using a particular key he had enclosed. "In the left hand top-drawer is a bunch of keys, one of which has a bone-label attached to it. That key is the key of the nest of drawers on the top of the stand with the looking-glass door, between the new window and the large window. In one of those drawers (I think the second or third from the bottom) are several of the bound books of my Readings," two of which he wanted to be sent to him in London. "If you will copy these instructions for Matilda"—one of his domestic servants—"she cannot go wrong," he added reassuringly.

When it came to law and order more generally, Dickens took pride in his ability to perform the literary equivalent of an inside job. That wasn't only because of his earlier experience as a solicitor's clerk. He also ensured that he remained fully up to date with the latest innovations in solving crime, not least the methods of London's new Detective Police, who by 1851 worked in pairs in each of the city's seventeen divisions. Dickens's fascination with the figure of the detective had already been evident in his commissioning of *Household Words* articles such as Wills's "The Modern Science of Thief-Taking," which offered a glowing tribute to "the high amount of skill, intelligence, and knowledge, concentrated in the character of a clever Detective Policeman." What especially appealed to Dickens about detective work was that, unlike other branches of the law, particularly the go-slow absurdities of Chancery, those involved seemed equally keen on his personal rule of "Don't talk about it—do it!" That is one reason why he was so struck by Gaskell's "very curious and interesting" *Household Words* article on "Disappearances." Her main assertion, that if the detective police had been around at the time of these cases "there would be no doubt as to their success," articulated a fantasy that had been developing in his own mind for years.

Many of his early sketches had presented "Boz" as an urban detective who was capable of retrieving whole life stories from the tiniest clues. In "The New Year," someone who owns a house with green blinds is instantly identified as a publisher, while in "London Recreations," the history of a suburban couple whose only son died when he was five years old is obliquely revealed by the fact that they have grown an unusually large gooseberry, which they keep "carefully preserved under a wine-glass, on the sideboard, for the edification of visitors." Such sketches make Boz sound less like a literary *flâneur*, happy to wander the streets and describe whatever catches his eye, than a young Sherlock Holmes in training. More recently, Dickens's original plan for *Household Words* had been for him to adopt the persona of "a certain SHADOW which may go into any place . . . and be in all homes, and all nooks and corners, and be supposed to be cognisant of everything, and go everywhere, without the least diffi-culty . . . the thing at everybody's elbow and in everybody's footsteps." If that made his mouthpiece into a potent mixture of omniscient narrator and social busybody, it also gave him the air of a modern detective: some-one who was at home anywhere and capable of finding out anything.

This parallel between writing and detective work was one that Dickens enjoyed making. In "A Detective Police Party," a two-part article published in successive issues of *Household Words* in July and August 1850, he described meeting several members of the new detective force in his Wellington Street office, reporting that "Every man of them, in a glance, takes an inventory of the furniture and an accurate sketch of the editorial presence." That was also a skill Dickens prided himself on possessing. His Rockingham Castle friends the Watsons remembered "his marvellous quickness of vision, taking in everything at a passing glance," and Dickens gave the same keen eyes to sympathetic characters like Riah in *Our Mutual Friend*, who proves how perceptive he is when Eugene Wrayburn approaches Lizzie Hexam in the street and languidly starts flirting with her. "The Jew having taken in the whole of Eugene at one sharp glance," we are told, "cast his eyes upon the ground, and stood mute." As Dickens continues in "A Detective Police Party"—by making his own thumbnail sketches of the detectives, before revealing that they are fellow storytellers with a rich seam of anecdotes to mine—it becomes clear how much he felt he and the police had in common. Both were capable of seeing what other people had failed to notice, making connections that unexpectedly revealed seemingly random events to be fragments of the same story. In Dickens's eyes, the fact that detectives sometimes adopted disguises to infiltrate the criminal underworld also added an appealing touch of theatre to their work. In fact, one of the members of the Detective Police Party, Inspector Charles Field, thinly disguised by Dickens as "Inspector Wield," had "performed some of the leading characters" as a teenage actor at the Catherine Street Theatre, located next to Wellington Street, which may have encouraged Dickens to think of this Charles as another of his alter egos. What is beyond question is Dickens's admiration of Inspector Field's professional skill, which regularly toppled over into hero worship.

The most glaring example comes in another *Household Words* article written in the first half of 1851, "On Duty with Inspector Field," where the other Charles is now given his proper surname, and Dickens reveals the results of some on-the-ground research he had conducted with his namesake towards the end of spring. It is not an especially cheerful piece of writing, as Dickens describes the experience of accompanying Inspector Field on a "dull and wet" night when "the long lines of street-lamps are blurred, as if we saw them through tears." There are some brief encounters with local characters, who are observed for a sentence or two before Dickens's attention switches elsewhere: a lost boy, "extremely calm and small," who thinks he might remember how to get home if he is taken to a nearby street; a "raving drunken woman in the cells" who has screamed herself hoarse and is soothed with a drink of water. So far Dickens's account is fairly muted, as if the "dull" weather has somehow managed to infiltrate his style. However, what sparks Dickens's writing into life is his account of an "expedition" into Rats' Castle, one of several seamy corners of St. Giles that had still not been cleared away.

Inspector Field's colleague Mr. Rogers carries a bull's-eye lantern, which could direct its beam like a modern torch, and wherever he points this "flaming eye" we see what it sees, starting with a foul-smelling cellar full of thieves "in various conditions of dirt and raggedness," one of whom is asked to stand up and remove his cap so that Inspector Field can take a closer look at him. This lantern is merely an extension of the inspector's own "roving eye that searches every corner of the cellar while he talks." Nothing can escape it, and we are told that nobody can escape the inspector's hand either, "the well-known hand that has collared half the people here, and motioned their brothers, sisters, fathers, mothers, male and female friends, inexorably, to New South Wales" as convicts. No other part of Inspector Field's body is described in any detail (in "A Detective Police Party," Dickens mentions his "portly presence" and "husky voice," but again dwells on his "large, moist, knowing eye" and "corpulent forefinger"), but that is because for Dickens he is not really a human being at all. Instead he represents the long arm of the law in all its impersonal force. While he jokes with the thieves in their cellar, Inspector Field is presented as a *deus ex machina* who is simply biding his time.

The references to "we" in Dickens's article ("We are punctual. Where is Inspector Field?") may have been more than an editorial flourish. It is possible Dickens was accompanied by another young writer when he was poking around in "this compound of sickening smells, these heaps of filth, these tumbling houses, with all their vile contents, animate and inanimate, slimily overflowing into the black road." The first mention of Wilkie Collins in Dickens's correspondence comes on 8 March in a letter to their mutual friend Augustus Egg, who was about to take on the role of Mr. David Fallen in *Not So Bad As We Seem*. "I knew his father (William Collins, R. A., the painter) well," Dickens writes, "and should be very glad to know him." They met four days later, after Dickens left his card inviting Collins to attend a read-through of the play followed by a cast dinner. As a law student at Lincoln's Inn, Collins had been an enthusiastic participant in amateur theatricals, so for Dickens to ask him to play Smart the valet in *Not So Bad As We Seem* was a natural next step. So was their developing friendship, especially after Collins published "A Terribly Strange Bed" in *Household Words* the following April.

If Dickens admired the younger man's talent as a writer, he also enjoyed being comically exasperated by his shabby clothes and general air of untidiness, and in later years hearing about the secret, potentially sleazy aspects of his private life. During this period of his career, to the outside world Collins was a solid part of the Establishment, a member of the Garrick Club with a taste for champagne and cigars, who wrote thoughtful thrillers and smart pieces of journalism. When he went home, however, it was either to his bachelor apartment or to one of his two mistresses: a domestic arrangement that was spread across three households and several decades of unconventional family life. Dickens quickly recognised him as another potential rival self, even if he liked to pretend they were attracted to each other purely as opposites: the "Genius of Order" versus the "Genius of Disorder." Inviting him to explore the rookeries of St. Giles was exactly the sort of danger-flecked nocturnal adventure Collins would have relished.

However, none of his other activities this spring gave Dickens as many opportunities to demonstrate his genius for order as ongoing preparations for the production in which he and Collins would soon share a stage. Dickens was also keeping a careful eye on the playwright. "I have never known Bulwer so anxious about anything he has written, or so intensely interested in it," Dickens told the Duke of Devonshire on 20 March. "He hovers around the Comedy, whatever we are doing with it, as if he could not possibly detach himself from the—to an author—most disheartening preliminaries." That sounds as if he felt that Bulwer Lytton was intruding on his own territory, because during the rehearsal process nobody hovered more determinedly than Dickens. "Carpenters, scene painters, tailors, bootmakers, musicians, all kinds of people, require my constant attention," he boasted on 23 March, warning that although he had written a "very rapid and droll" first scene of the farce he had promised to contribute to the evening's entertainment, he was struggling to "get a meaning into it." At the start rehearsals were scheduled on Mondays and Tuesdays, with Dickens drilling his actors for up to five hours at a time, although by the end of March he was telling the Duke of Devonshire that they had already rehearsed "until far into the early morning" on three nights that week. "Everybody is working hard, and Bulwer flies to and fro continually, in energetic restlessness," he added, again partly projecting his own behaviour onto his friend.

The cast shared his enthusiasm, though perhaps not always his levels of commitment. Richard Horne, who played the bullying guardsman Colonel Flint, later recalled that nobody could have been as "assiduous and unwearying as Dickens," who appeared to be "almost ubiquitous and sleepless" at the time; even with a gap of twenty years to soften his memories, Horne's smile comes across as rather forced. Other evidence of Dickens's approach can be found in the Duke of Devonshire's scrapbook, where alongside a number of notes informing each actor when they would be needed for rehearsals, there is a later notice in Dickens's hand marked "IMPORTANT TO OBSERVE," reminding the cast that any conversation in Devonshire House's green room "unless in a very low voice, IS HEARD UPON THE STAGE." After spending so much time rehearsing Bulwer Lytton's dialogue, the last thing Dickens wanted was for the audience to be distracted by offstage chatter.

However, the most remarkable thing about Dickens's punishing rehearsal schedule is that it formed only one strand of a dense weave of activities this spring. His surviving correspondence from 25 April provides a representative sample. He returns some tickets for a forthcoming Literary Fund dinner, explaining that he will be unable to attend; he thanks Messrs Brookes & Sons of Sheffield, "Manufacturers of Fine Penknives, Razors, etc.," for their "elegant present" of a case of cutlery, telling them that the joke in his last novel about young David Copperfield being as sharp as "Brooks of Sheffield" was "one of those remarkable coincidences that defy all calculation"; he responds to the latest set of accounts sent to him by Bradbury & Evans; he writes to his former illustrator George Cruikshank, who had fallen out with him after becoming a fervent advocate for the temperance cause, reassuring him that "I have never felt the slightest coolness towards you, or regarded you with anything other than my old unvarying feeling of affectionate friendship"; he sends a long and chatty letter to his old Swiss friend Emile de la Rue in Genoa, describing how the forthcoming Exhibition meant that London was crowded to a "preposterous extent"; he thanks the opera director Frederick Gye for placing Covent Garden Theatre at his disposal for two nights of rehearsals; he confirms a naval officer's hunch that a particular article in *Household Words* "is not mine and was written by a lady"; he instructs his stage manager Thomas Coe to have a fresh copy of one part made from his prompt book, and sends another letter about the play to the manager of the Haymarket Theatre; he writes to Daniel Maclise, telling him that an engraver is offering to work unbidden on his proposed picture of the Amateur Company; finally, he informs the physician David Moir that he has no immediate plans to start another novel, but "reversing the order of vegetable things" he hopes that some new green covers will appear "about the dead of winter." Eleven letters written on one day (it is likely there were others that have not survived), all carefully tailored to their recipients, and all squeezed into the gaps between editing, rehearsals, charity work, family life and everything else Dickens had to do from one hour to the next. Viewed in this light, his timetable for the inmates of Urania Cottage starts to look positively thin by comparison.

As the scheduled performance date approached, other professionals started to get involved. The portable theatre that had recently been purchased for the Amateur Company, which a year later would be advertised for sale complete with "its unique stock of scenery" and "all its simple and ingenious Mechanism," was being assembled under Paxton's supervision in Devonshire House, assisted by the "Machinist" of the Lyceum Theatre (i.e., the person responsible for designing and constructing stage machinery), and Paxton was also contriving a new system of ventilation for the picture gallery. But at the heart of everything was Dickens, whether he was choosing scene painters, making a "long list" of the furniture required onstage, or advising on the details of particular costumes: "The figure should be slighter [with] Dress-coat, white cravat, gold double chain."

Two days before the dress rehearsal, he wrote to Wilkie Collins, explaining that it might be socially awkward if Collins's friend Charles Ward were to attend a planned cast supper at Devonshire House, as Dickens had already sent the Duke a list of who was to be invited. In the final sentence of the letter he could not hide his own excitement: "I have been there all day, and am covered in sawdust."

By then real life had proven to be far harder to control than its theatrical double. The 1851 census was taken on the evening of Sunday 30 March, and nobody was exempt from having their details written down on the official blue form. (The entry for Buckingham Palace began, "Name and Surname of each Person who abode in the house, on the Night of the 30th March, 1851: *Her Majesty Alexandrina Victoria*; Relation to Head of Family: *Wife*; Condition: *Mar[ried]*; Age: *31*; Rank, Profession, or Occupation: *The Queen.*") The census revealed that there were several other men named Charles Dickens currently living in England: a shoe-mender aged forty, an apprentice vellum binder aged twenty, a silk warehouseman aged seventeen, even a Charles John Dickens who was a 26-year-old linen draper, like a real-life Horatio Sparkins. Dickens's own return listed him as a 39-year-old "Author" but also as a "Visitor," because although he had spent the evening with his mother Elizabeth, younger brothers Alfred and Augustus, and sister Letitia, they weren't at Devonshire Terrace. Instead they had been the guests of Robert Davey, formerly Senior Surgeon to the Royal Infirmary for Children in Waterloo Bridge Road, who lived with his wife at 34 Keppel Street, off Russell Square in Bloomsbury. It is where Dickens had arranged for his parents to move in as boarders a few months earlier, after it became clear that John Dickens required ongoing medical care; according to Mrs. Davey, Dickens "called frequently and sometimes stayed to dinner." On 30 March he would stay considerably longer.

John Dickens was still recovering after an emergency operation performed in Davey's house five days earlier by Robert Wade, a surgeon who had been summoned after Davey examined his patient and discovered that his genitals were a deep purple colour and "fearfully swollen and disfigured." Wade later wrote about the case in a textbook on urology; although he did not identify John Dickens by name, he diagnosed the underlying problem as a stricture of the urethra, which had worsened over previous days and was now causing his patient "most intense" pain. Working quickly, he had to make a deep incision in the perineum, followed by further incisions in the penis, scrotum and groin, in order to insert a catheter and release some of the urine that had accumulated in the bladder. The patient was thought to be too weak for chloroform, so he remained conscious throughout the whole procedure; it was little wonder that Dickens described it as "the most terrible operation known in surgery," adding that afterwards the room was "a slaughter house of blood."

Wade's rather optimistic memory of events was that afterwards his patient experienced only "a little occasional smarting," but soon Dickens's letters started to fill with anxious medical bulletins. The next day he wrote to Catherine with the news that John Dickens was "very weak and low, but not worse, I hope, than might be expected," and on 27 March he told Forster that his father was "as well as anyone in such a situation could be." His real fears could still be glimpsed through the cracks of other letters. On 29 March, he warned Wills that Bulwer Lytton was in "sudden agonies" with some minor revisions to Not So Bad As We Seem, a title that had taken on an unhappy new association in the circumstances, and the day before he had written to the Duke of Devonshire wishing him the best of luck in his battle with a common cold (the "enemy"): "I hope this glorious morning will be the death of him." He also found himself thinking back to the time when he had first confronted his father's personal failings, that period in his childhood when the family had repeatedly been forced to move from one set of cheap lodgings to the next, telling Catherine the day after John Dickens's operation that it was raining incessantly and "A van containing the goods of some unfortunate family, moving, has broken down outside—and the whole scene is a picture of dreariness."

The end came just a few hours after the census form for 34 Keppel Street was filled in. Dickens had been with his father for some time, according to Mrs. Davey's much later recollections, "standing or sitting by the bedside, and holding his hand," and at five o'clock in the morning John Dickens died "with little or no pain." Dickens's first thoughts were for his mother. "I remember he took her in his arms, and they both wept bitterly together," Mrs. Davey wrote, before Dickens took decisive action to comfort her in a more practical way. "He immediately paid whatever his father owed, and relieved his mother's mind on that score," telling her that "she must rely upon him for the future"—a gesture that provoked a mixture of gratitude and prickly defensiveness from his brother Alfred, who told their mother that "It is something to know how nobly Charles has behaved in this trial . . . although we are not all in a position to shew such substantial proofs of affection for the memory of our dear father." John Dickens was buried in Highgate Cemetery on 5 April, with the gravestone inscription chosen by Dickens paying tribute to his "zealous, useful, cheerful spirit." A handful of fellow journalists also did their best to burnish his memory: one obituary in the *Gentleman's Magazine* outlined his career from working as a clerk in the Navy Pay Department to being "one of [the] most efficient, and most respected, members of the Press," adding that his character combined "a naturally generous disposition and a kind heart" with "thorough business habits."

It is hard to imagine Dickens reading that last comment without wincing. In the coming days, one phrase he kept returning to in his letters was "my poor father," where a glum joke hovered, especially after it was discovered that John Dickens's effects were valued at less than £40. In his most recent novel, Dickens had poked gentle fun at his father in the shape of Wilkins Micawber, the middle-aged clerk who scrapes by with a mixture of sunny optimism and a leech-like ability to borrow money from his friends. Despite being incarcerated in the King's Bench Prison for his debts, he remains resolutely confident that something will "turn up," which thanks to the loyalty of his wife in sticking by him, and the generosity of Dickens in providing him with narrative solutions, it always does. In John Dickens's case, the something was also a someone: his son, who for many years had reliably turned up to bail his parents out of their latest financial scrape. Conjuring up Micawber was therefore the perfect way for him to express his exasperation while dissolving it in laughter. "The longer I live, the better man I think him," Dickens told Forster, and it is probably true to say that his judgement of his father softened considerably when the only demands he could make were on his memory. But Micawber, with his "rhetorical exuberance" and quicksilver changes of mood, was just one of a whole rogue's gallery of irresponsible fathers through whom, over many years, Dickens had attempted to work out their relationship in his fiction, from *Dombey and Son*'s chilly Mr. Dombey to *David Copperfield*'s alcoholic Mr. Wickfield. Nor did John Dickens's death resolve the issue.

The rehearsals for Dickens's Devonshire House theatricals were suspended for a week while he made the funeral arrangements, and he was also hit by a period of insomnia, telling Catherine on 4 April that he was "so worried and worn" he had been up for three nights in a row. The following year he wrote about his experiences in "Lying Awake," a *Household Words* article that tried to capture the thoughts that pinball around inside an insomniac's head as he lies "saucer-eyed" in bed. These thoughts bounce off in various directions, but they always return to the same place: the inescapable full stop of death. They include Dickens's memories of a relative who once saw "a man with his throat cut" dashing past him one foggy London night, Christmas pantomimes that provoke fits of mirth in the audience "when the baby is boiled or sat upon," and a swollen drowned body that he had spotted during a tour of the Paris morgue, where it lay in a corner "like a heap of crushed over-ripe figs." By the time Dickens's narrator starts to list some of the punishments that criminals used to suffer in Britain ("the rack, and the branding iron, and the chains and gibbet . . . and the weights that pressed men to death in the cells of Newgate"), he discovers that "I had been lying awake so long that the very dead began to wake too, and to crowd into my thoughts most sorrowfully." His solution is "to lie awake no more, but to get up and go out for a night walk." And at the start of April that was Dickens's solution too.

"It was among Mr. Dickens's maxims that a given amount of mental exertion should be counteracted by a commensurate amount of bodily fatigue," according to George Sala, "and for a length of years his physical labours were measured exactly by the duration of his intellectual work." Usually this meant long walks after his scheduled writing hours, following a "mentally-measured route" that allowed him to shake off his old stories and pursue scraps of thought that might turn into new ones. But at the start of April, what had previously been a habit suddenly acquired the air of a physical compulsion. His experiences would eventually produce "Night Walks," one of the "Uncommercial Traveller" articles he wrote some years later for *All the Year Round*, in which he describes wandering through London on a "damp, cloudy and cold" night when the city is brimming with mystery and stirring with a vague sense of threat. Much of this atmosphere is generated by Dickens's encounters with the poor, the lonely, and all the other "houseless" figures whose lives appear to be out of sync with the city's usual rhythms. They include a "beetle-browed hair-lipped youth of twenty" he sees sleeping rough outside St. Martin's Church, who whines and snaps at Dickens "like a worried dog" before twisting out of his grasp and leaving him "standing alone with its rags in my hand," and a mysterious red-faced man who enters a coffee house and takes a cold meat pudding out of his hat, which he stabs with his knife "like a mortal enemy" before tearing it apart with his fingers and devouring every scrap. The strangeness of these descriptions partly reflects the unconventional lifestyles of the people involved. As Virginia Woolf would later reflect in her 1930 essay "Street Haunting," to be in the streets when we have no real business there allows us to evade the usual rules of life; because "we are no longer quite ourselves," we can explore who else we might want to be, or who we fear we might become. But if the night allowed Dickens to experience the city's shadowy secret self, it also provided him with an alibi to exaggerate his own characteristic style. In an empty theatre, he contemplates the orchestra pit, "like a great grave dug for a time of pestilence," and "a strong serpent of engine-hose, watchfully lying in wait for the serpent Fire, and ready to fly at it"; passing through a railway station, he pictures a recently arrived engine heaving and perspiring, as if "wiping its forehead and saying what a run it had had." Soon afterwards the dawn comes, and an exhausted Dickens returns home to bed, but his descriptions of night-time London had already revealed that someone who was unable to sleep could still have experiences that were as vivid and unpredictable as a dream.

Two weeks after the death of John Dickens, the family suffered another loss. On 14 April, while Dickens was speaking at the sixth annual dinner of the General Theatrical Fund at the London Tavern, his eight-month-old daughter Dora died suddenly in Devonshire Terrace after suffering convulsions. The news was brought by a servant, although Forster chose to let Dickens finish his speech before telling him; as he went on to talk about "actors having to come from scenes of sickness, of suffering, aye, even of death itself, to play their parts before us," Forster later recalled, "my part was very difficult." Dora's death left Dickens bewildered by grief. "I had been nursing her, before I went out," he told Henry Austin the next day, but she had died "in a moment." Returning home with his friend Mark Lemon, the editor of *Punch* and a fellow cast member of *Not So Bad As We Seem*, Dickens stayed with her body all night, with Mamie later remembering that her father did not break down until an evening or two later, when some beautiful flowers that had been sent to the house were brought into his study. He "was about to take them upstairs and place them on the little dead baby, when he suddenly gave way completely."

This was in stark contrast to the way his narrators had previously responded to the deaths of children in his fiction, which usually involved a mixture of tear-jerking pathos and reassuring spiritual uplift. *The Old Curiosity Shop*'s Little Nell dies to the sound of heavenly music, with Dickens's narrator firmly telling us "So shall we know the angels in their majesty, after death," while in *Dombey and Son* Paul Dombey clasps his hands in preparation for the "old, old fashion—Death!" as the narrative rises to a triumphant climax: "Oh thank GOD, all who see it, for that older fashion yet, of Immortality! And look upon us, angels of young children, with regards not quite estranged, when the swift river bears us to the ocean!" However, even at a time of high infant mortality (in London at this time roughly one in five died in their first year) the reality of losing a child was rather different.

On Easter Sunday, six days after Dora's death, Tennyson's first child was stillborn, and although he took refuge in poetry, the elegy he composed repeatedly flinched away from using a straightforward past tense, as if he still couldn't quite believe it himself.

> Little bosom not yet cold,
> Noble forehead made for thought,
> Little hands of mighty mould
> Clenched as in the fight which they had fought.

The fact that "fought" comes as the final syllable of a nine-syllable line makes it all the more heart-wrenching: it is like a miniature of the nine months of pregnancy, but one that ends with a death rather than a life. Three days later, Charles Darwin was mourning the loss of his beloved ten-year-old daughter Annie. She had been ill for some time, probably suffering from tuberculosis, and Darwin had recorded her symptoms daily in a special diary: "Poorly with cough and influenza," he had written on 13 March, followed by a string of dittos for eight days. A week after her death, he sat down to produce a twelve-page handwritten memorial, in which he tried to conjure up everything about her that he missed: "her eyes sparkled brightly; she often smiled; her step was elastic and firm; she held herself upright, and often threw her head a little backwards, as if she defied the world in her joyousness." His description of the dead Annie had the same loving precision as his notes on barnacles, the sea creatures that were the focus of his current research, and would soon be revealed as the tiny building blocks helping him to construct his grand theory of evolution. But despite the growing evidence in his research that nature created far more lives than it could possibly sustain, there was no suggestion that he should simply accept his daughter's death as a statistical necessity and move on.

Dickens's response to Dora's death was equally raw. Less than three weeks after losing his father, he found himself making a second set of funeral arrangements, this time choosing to lay her "little coffin" in a catacomb until a suitable plot in Highgate Cemetery became available. When he managed to secure one several years later, the gravestone inscription read simply: "Dora Annie, the ninth child of Charles and Catherine Dickens, died 14th April 1851, aged eight months." She had been named after the hero's doomed young wife in *David Copperfield*, and when Dickens tried to prepare Catherine for news of her death he treated his baby daughter much like a character on a fictional deathbed. Writing to his wife in Malvern, from where he had rushed to be with his father, he began by telling her that Dora had been taken ill: "I will not deceive you. I think her *very* ill." In the next paragraph he edged closer towards the truth without committing to it just yet: "There is nothing in her appearance but perfect rest. You would suppose her quietly asleep." Not until the final paragraph did he raise the possibility that Dora's rest might never be broken, telling Catherine that "if—*if*—when you come, I should even have to say to you 'our little baby is dead,' you are to do your duty to [our other children], and to shew yourself worthy of the great trust you hold in them." Dickens was trying to make the shock "as gradual as we could," he later told Miss Coutts; it was an attempt to break the news without causing his wife to break down. His strategy appears to have been successful ("she is quite resigned to what has happened and can speak of it tranquilly") but this remains one of the strangest letters he ever wrote. For "if—*if*—" was more than just a kindly thought experiment. It was a two-word summary of the storytelling impulse itself.

Dickens's caution was partly a response to Catherine's own fragile state of health. At the time she was staying at Knotsford Lodge in Malvern, where Dickens had taken her on 13 March to be subjected to "a rigorous discipline of air, exercise, and cold water." Whether her complaint was chiefly physical or psychological in origin is unclear. Dickens's letters at the time refer mysteriously to "an alarming disposition of blood to the head, attended with giddiness and dimness of sight," and his wife's "alarming confusion and nervousness at times," which he traced back "3 or 4 years." Catherine herself wrote on 11 March that she had been "suffering for some time from a fullness in the head" that produced "violent headaches," which suggests severe attacks of migraine, and it has also been speculated that she may have been suffering from post-natal depression and/or anaemia following the birth of Dora. However, the likeliest explanation is one that Dickens gave to another correspondent, which was that he had simply taken her there "for her health." That sort of vague aspiration perfectly matched the all-purpose claims being made at the time for the water cure, a set of quasi-medical procedures that ranged from being swaddled in wet sheets to drinking endless cups of spring water, and were advertised as an effective therapy for every imaginable kind of complaint: rheumatism, impotence, gout, liver disease, smallpox, syphilis, asthma, convulsions, suicidal feelings and many more. Malvern was a highly fashionable spa town: Annie Darwin was also there in March, undergoing her final unsuccessful round of treatments under Dr. Gully, and this summer Thomas Carlyle would try out the same practitioner, writing to Ralph Waldo Emerson: "It is a strange quasi-monastic—godless and yet devotional—way of life which human creatures have here, and useful to them beyond doubt."

It is likely that Dickens's decision was especially prompted by the lithographer R. J. Lane, who had dedicated the new edition of his book *Life at the Water Cure, or a Month at Malvern, a Diary* to Dickens, and had sent him a copy in February. This edition included Bulwer Lytton's *Confessions of a Water-Patient*, which reprinted some articles he had written for the *New Monthly Magazine* enthusiastically detailing the period he had spent in 1844 taking the water cure under another practitioner, Dr. James Wilson. Not everyone respected Bulwer Lytton's evangelical fervour for this branch of alternative medicine; after he claimed to have been rejuvenated in Malvern, one sceptical acquaintance reported that "Sir Edward Bulwer is young, blooming, and no longer deaf . . . All this was told me by the quite altered water-cured man. I expect to hear of him reunited to the wine-cured Lady B." Now Dickens wrote to Dr. Wilson to arrange some treatment for Catherine, telling him that he intended to rent a "cheerful cottage or house for us in your neighbourhood," and he was therefore sending Anne Brown, Catherine's long-serving maid, to make the practical arrangements.

Accompanied by her sister Georgina, with Dickens shuttling back and forth between Malvern and London, Catherine would end up staying at Knotsford Lodge for around a month. Dr. Wilson's 1844 book *The Practice of the Water Cure* would have warned her what to expect. The table of contents set out his treatments like an elaborate restaurant menu, beginning with an outline of "The sweating process," before going on to give an account of "The wet sheet" and various bathing options ("The douche bath," "The shallow bath," "The sitz [i.e., hip] bath," "The head bath," "The foot bath" and "The elbow bath"), and finally instructions for applying "The compresses." Some of the testimonials printed in this book and its predecessor, *The Dangers of the Water Cure and its Efficacy Examined* (1843), may have been especially encouraging to a woman in Catherine's position. One former patient had suffered symptoms that included "a tremendous headache which lasted generally twenty-four or thirty-six hours," while a case that came under the heading "Water Cure in Miscarriages, Debility, &c." (Catherine had also suffered a miscarriage in 1847) featured a female patient who told Dr. Wilson, "The elasticity and freshness of spirit, the joyous state of existence, which I thought gone for ever, have returned to me; my cheek has recovered its bloom, my eye its brightness, and surely you know enough of human nature to feel assured that no woman can be ungrateful for the restoration of her good looks." Dr. Wilson's conclusion to this case may also have encouraged Dickens: "It will be a grand thing and a blessing, when men get healthy wives, and women healthy husbands!"

Dickens's own attitude towards Malvern was reassuringly upbeat. In October, he published Harriet Martineau's article "Malvern Water" in *Household Words*, in which she provided an admiring sketch of the town as a holiday "play-ground." Among the invalids she encounters when she steps off the train are a "paralytic gentleman, pursuing his infirm walk between his wife's arm and his stick," an "ashy-pale lady" returning from one of the town's wells, and, viewed more apprehensively, "the emaciated girl who is resting, with her cheerful mother, under the tree in the church-yard." Martineau's emphasis on the other visitors is repeated in a letter

Dickens sent to Forster shortly after Catherine's arrival, in which he makes the town of Malvern sound like a giant theatrical set:

> It is a most beautiful place. O Heaven, to meet the Cold Waterers (as I did this morning when I went out for a shower-bath) dashing down the hills, with severe expressions on their countenances, like men doing matches and not exactly winning! Then, a young lady in a gray polka going *up* the hills, regardless of legs; and meeting a young gentleman (a bad case, I should say) with a light black silk cap on under his hat, and the pimples of I don't know how many douches under that. Likewise an old man who ran over a milk-child, rather than stop!—with no neckcloth, on principle; and with his mouth wide open, to catch the morning air.

As this letter suggests, Dickens was especially intrigued by the notorious douche bath, a thunderous deluge of mountain water that was rigged up to be used by patients in a series of little wooden huts. The journalist Joseph Leech explained what happened when an attendant pulled a string to release the water:

> . . . a momentary rush, like a thunderstorm, was heard above me, and the next second the water came roaring through the pipe like a lion upon his prey, and struck me on the shoulder with a merciless bang, spinning me about . . . For a minute and a half I remained under this water spout, buffeting fiercely, until the cold column had cudgelled me as hot as a coal—aye, black and blue too; but good gracious! What a glorious luxury—a nervous but still ecstatic luxury, that made you cry out at once in terror and rapture . . .

It was the ultimate power shower, and as someone who enjoyed similar shocks to the system (in the summer of 1849, he reported gleefully to Thomas Beard that he had discovered a waterfall near his lodgings on the Isle of Wight, "which I have driven a carpenter almost mad by changing into a—SHOWER BATH— with a fall of 150 feet!"), Dickens was quick to adopt a scaled-down version for private domestic use. His letters written later this year return to the subject with all the enthusiasm of a child playing with a new toy. He told Henry Austin, "I don't care for the possibility of a Tepid Shower. But what I want is, *a Cold Shower of the best quality, always charged to an unlimited extent*, so that I have but to pull the string, and take any shower of cold water I choose," and he enclosed a detailed sketch of what he meant, a design that featured a wooden panel to conceal the bath and "Light, cheerful-colored water proof curtains, extending the whole width of Warm Bath, and capable of being drawn close for shower."

Whether Catherine shared his excitement is not known, although it is unlikely she would have viewed Malvern's body-buffeting water treatments in quite the same holiday spirit as her husband. There were also signs that they had not yet managed to wash away some earlier tensions in their marriage. In an article entitled "A Few Facts About Matrimony," published in *Household Words* the previous year, Frederick Knight Hunt had offered a rich set of statistics regarding the personal circumstances of people who got married, but he introduced his data by referring to marriage itself as "that charming mystery of mysteries" and "that lode star of young maidens and gay bachelors," which made it sound more like a romantic fantasy than a practical domestic arrangement. A similar gap between rhetoric and reality also seems to have opened up in the marriage of Charles and Catherine (always "Kate" to him) Dickens over the years. In the early days of their courtship, Dickens treated this romance as a story he was determined to control in every way. His letters to her involved an awkward mixture of endearing baby talk (she is often described as "coss," i.e., cross) and stiff reserve. Many of them confused protectiveness with possessiveness, just as Dickens's desire to put things right when they quarrelled was not always easy to distinguish from a conviction that "whatever I do must be right." If he "improve[d] very much on acquaintance," as Catherine reported to her sister in February 1835, he left her in no doubt that she should seek to improve herself too. Any hint of petulance was swiftly crushed—"I *must* see you, and *will not be prevented*"—and although part of this may have been a private game, in which Dickens played the Petruchio to his Kate, and she giggled coquettishly as he sought to tame her, there are also many letters entirely free from humour, in which he writes to his "Dearest Girl" less like a wife-in-training than a child needing to be kept in line. "Mind you are punctual my dear"; "I perceive you have not yet subdued one part of your disposition."

Catherine was sweet-natured and compliant, but by the time she arrived in Malvern she had given birth to nine children in thirteen years, which meant that she had been pregnant for approximately half of her married life. It was little wonder if she sometimes felt overwhelmed. At the end of 1849, the former *Edinburgh Review* editor Francis Jeffrey received a letter from Dickens reporting that Catherine was expecting another baby to add to a family that already included Jeffrey's five-year-old godson Francis, nicknamed "Chickenstalker" by his father after a character in *The Chimes*. In his reply, Jeffrey advised Dickens that although "there can never

be too many Dickenses in the world," this latest addition to the family—
who would turn out to be the short-lived Dora—should perhaps be the
last. Like a fruit tree that suffers from *"overbearings,"* he gently suggested,
Catherine was in danger of being exhausted by the seemingly endless
crop of children she was producing. "Take 'em away to the Fondling [i.e.,
Foundling Hospital]," Dickens had joked to Macready six months after the
birth of Alfred in 1845, while seven years and four children later he rue-
fully suggested that he might ask the Bishop of London to hold "a little
service in Saint Paul's beseeching that I may be considered to have done
enough towards my country's population," as if divine intervention alone
could prevent his wife from becoming pregnant. His own part in these
events was treated more like a medical mystery or the inevitable consequence of him performing his marital duty; although various forms of
contraception such as douches and condoms made from sheep intestine
could be obtained by anyone determined enough, they were unreliable as
well as unpleasant, and highly unlikely to be used by a respectable married
couple.

But Dickens too could be "overbearing," albeit in less physical ways.
The *Household Words* journalist Henry Morley met Catherine later in 1851,
when he reported that she was "stout, with a round, very round, rather
pretty, very pleasant face, and ringlets on each side of it. One sees in five
minutes that she loves her husband and her children, and has a warm heart
for anybody who won't be satirical, but meet her on her own good-natured
footing." That was also Dickens's usual approach to his wife: most of his
letters to her crackle with mischief, while expressing a good deal of ten-
derness and warmth. But always there was the danger of him losing his
patience with someone who, like almost everyone else he knew, was incapable of keeping up with him. Choosing to sign some of his letters "Bully
and Meek" may have been another private joke, yet it had an uncomfortable truth at its heart—one that would take on a grim new life a few years
later during their marital separation, when Dickens's behaviour would
fully support his daughter Katey's view that "My father was a wicked
man—a very wicked man." Although there had been several earlier clues

that a man who was so warm-hearted with regard to strangers was capable of behaving in a far chillier fashion towards his own family, perhaps nothing signalled what was to come as clearly as his response to Catherine's grief at her baby's death. Although his letters frequently expressed his sympathy and loving concern, there was also a vein of hardness—or, as he might have described it, *firmness*—in his attitude, telling one friend that "this shock may even do her good." It was as if he thought that losing a child could be the emotional equivalent of an invigorating cold shower.

By the time Catherine returned home from Malvern in mid-April, any irritation Dickens may have felt at his own marital situation would have been tempered by his knowledge of what Bulwer Lytton was going through. As the new date for the first performance of *Not So Bad As We Seem* approached, and the Amateur Company's rehearsals switched to Devonshire House, Bulwer Lytton's estranged wife Rosina decided that a performance before the Queen was the perfect opportunity to step up her long-running campaign of public humiliation.

On 6 May she wrote to the Duke of Devonshire, threatening to "publicly expose that most contemptible wretch Sir E Bulwer Lytton" by appearing on the first night disguised as an orange seller and pelting the audience with rotten eggs, her rationale being that a corrupt enterprise deserved an equally corrupt physical display. On 15 May, the day before the rescheduled first performance, she wrote to the Duke again, this time perplexingly in French: "Monseigneur! Agréez mes profonds regrets de ce que vous vous êtes encanaillé de pareils gredins [Sir! Accept my sincere regrets that you have debased yourself with such scoundrels] . . ." Her fury was directed towards Dickens as well, writing a letter that was mistakenly forwarded by Catherine to Charley at Eton, in which she made the same threat to attend "the Fooleries at Devonshire House" and distribute a playbill denouncing the "swindle" of the Guild's scheme, "for verily, no one has contributed more blackly to the *Guilt* of Literature than Sir Liar coward Bulwer Lytton and his gang!" The letter continued with a stream of insults, characterising Dickens as a "ci-devant penny a-liner" who was about to make a fool of himself, and their guest of honour as "the little sensual selfish-Pigheaded Queen that goes to see such a set of disreputable charlatans." If the Queen were to have her thrown in the Tower as a result of her protests, "I should at least live rent free which would be a great saving to me," she noted with lopsided logic. Oddly, she also wondered if Dickens might help her to get some cheap copies of her playbill printed, which wasn't too likely given its contents: a series of angry jibes in which she insulted every part of the forthcoming play, from its supposed title of "EVEN WORSE THAN WE SEEM, OR THE REAL SIDE OF OUR CHARACTER," to the part played in it by "MR. CHARLES DICKENS, *who to act with the more life, has a dead child in one pocket, and a dead father in the other.*" Returning the letter to his mother on 11 May, Charley warned her, "It pitches into the Guild like anything . . . It is not cool at all, oh no."

Dickens's response was swift. In addition to formally acknowledging Rosina's letter (sadly the only part of this response to have survived is his signature), he decided to tighten the security around Devonshire House. "I have already sent for Inspector Field of the Detective Police (who is used in all sorts of delicate matters, and is quite devoted to me)," he wrote to Bulwer Lytton, explaining that the inspector would be in plain clothes and would remain in the Hall throughout to prevent any trouble. All he needed from Bulwer Lytton was someone who would point out Rosina if she tried to enter, and permission for Dickens to take charge of the whole operation. "Upon the least hint that this person coming in was not to go up," Dickens told him, "he would very respectfully shew the way in a wrong direction, and say not a word until he had conducted the lady out of all hearing." Exactly how Field would silently create this diversion in a crowded lobby is not clear, but Dickens's confidence in his plan was absolute. In his own head the end of this story had already been written.

Bulwer Lytton was far less certain about how some stories ended—not only because of his failed marriage, but also because of his dabbling in the occult. In 1842 he had published *Zanoni*, a novel that dealt with mystical themes in a respectfully serious way, and by 1851 his fascination with the idea that the dead might not stay dead was widely shared. This manifested itself in various ways, from mainstream collections like Sheridan Le Fanu's *Ghost Stories and Tales of Mystery*, which allowed even those readers who didn't believe in supernatural forces temporarily to imagine that they did, to more oddball publications like *The Celestial Telegraph; Or, Secrets of the Life to Come Revealed Through Magnetism*, which echoed some of Bulwer Lytton's ideas in making a case for mesmeric trances as a quasi-scientific way of communicating with the dead. Yet although Dickens was intrigued by "the unfathomed ties between man and man," which he enjoyed testing by mesmerising his wife and any friends who were willing to put themselves under his control, he had grave doubts that these ties extended beyond someone's death. Indeed, that sort of pun on "grave" was one of his standard responses to supposed evidence of the supernatural, as in *A Christmas Carol*, when Scrooge is confronted by the chained ghost of Marley and tells him, "You may be an undigested bit of beef, a blot of mustard, a crumb of cheese, a fragment of an underdone potato. There's more of gravy than of grave about you, whatever you are!" The narrator quickly notes that Scrooge's wisecrack is an attempt to mask his terror, "for the spectre's voice disturbed the very marrow in his bones," but in fact such hearty literalism mirrored Dickens's own usual approach to reports of the supernatural.

In February 1848, for example, he had written a review of Catherine Crowe's *The Night Side of Nature; or, Ghosts and Ghost Seers* for Forster's *Examiner*, in which he claimed that spectral apparitions "always elude us" when we try to confirm their existence, because they are either "delusions" caused by illness or the products of a hazy "middle state" of consciousness suspended between sleep and waking. On the other hand, although in public he scoffed at the claims of spiritualists as "humbug," ghosts continued to intrigue him in private, and the moment in "Lying Awake" when the dead begin to wake and "crowd into my thoughts" was just one of many occasions when he wondered if the dead might not be altogether gone, even if the only afterlife they could be sure of was their continued existence in the heads of those who survived them.

There were also plenty of reports at the time of the dead rising up and startling the living in more physical ways, because the scandal of over-crowded graveyards meant that bits of bodies were frequently seen poking out of the ground, like a piecemeal parody of Christian resurrection. In 1850, the passage of the Metropolitan Internments Act enabled the Board of Health to close graveyards that were full and supervise the creation of new cemeteries, but the situation evoked when Scrooge visits his own grave in a City churchyard and discovers that it is "choked up with too much burying" had still not been fully resolved. In December 1850, a poem in *Household Words* noted the appearance of London's "half-unburied dead" glinting through the fog:

> I saw from out the earth peep forth
> The white and glistening bones,
> With jagged ends of coffin-planks,
> That e'en the worm disowns;
> And once a smooth round skull rolled on,
> Like a football, on the stones.

Such ghoulish sights were still haunting Dickens a decade later. In *Great Expectations*, as Magwitch picks his way through the nettles and brambles of the graveyard where Pip's parents are buried, we are told that in the young boy's eyes he looks "as if he were eluding the hands of the dead people, stretching up cautiously out of their graves, to get a twist upon his ankle and pull him in." In some respects this is a straightforward revenge fantasy being inflicted on Magwitch, who has just made young Pip "[cling] to him with both hands" by tilting him backwards over a gravestone until he is giddy with fear. But it is also a memory that reaches back much fur-ther, because by the time this story is being told Magwitch is himself dead and buried, so the detail of dirty hands reaching up to pull him into the grave shows how powerful his grip remains on Pip's imagination. Such echoes worked to remind Dickens's readers that it was not necessary to believe in ghosts to acknowledge the threat of the past rising up and over-whelming the present.

As the revised date of 16 May approached for the Guild's royal perfor-mance at Devonshire House, Dickens set out to master this threat in a new piece of writing. It had been decided that his one-act farce would not follow *Not So Bad As We Seem* on the first night, as "the Queen gets very restless towards 12 o'Clock," but it would be played after the later public performances, and Dickens was keen that his contribution should send audiences back out into the world with a smile on their lips and generous thoughts in their hearts. Having enlisted the help of Mark Lemon to share writing duties, by 1 May he was feeling more confident about what they had produced. "I think it will be very good," he confided to Bulwer Lytton. "It is called Mr. Nightingale's Diary." The title was a reference to the fact that the main character is a hypochondriac who keeps a diary, "my only comfort," in which he records his daily symptoms, but it was also a clue about the play's relationship to Dickens's life. For although *Mr. Nightingale's Diary* is not a topical play, in the sense that it does not contain any direct references to current events, it does take many of Dickens's worries from the previous months and peep at them through a comic filter.

If it now seems even thinner than most farces (Richard Horne thought its plot "so very slight as scarcely to merit the name"), that is because it was little more than a vehicle for Dickens to produce a quick-fire series of comic turns. In this sense it was the ideal after-piece to *Not So Bad As We Seem*, releasing the full theatrical potential of Bulwer Lytton's subtitle "Many Sides to a Character" by reminding the audience that, unlike the fixed sides of a square or a pentagon, onstage these sides could multiply according to the needs of each moment. Dickens's main role was Mr. Gabblewig, a lawyer who schemes to win Mr. Nightingale's niece by dis-guising himself as five characters in quick succession. One by one they distract and befuddle poor Mr. Nightingale, until he is only too glad to give his blessing to the relatively sane Mr. Gabblewig and escape from the stage. As a piece of writing it is hardly sophisticated: the story is predictable, the dialogue inconsequential. Yet there are also moments when some of

Dickens's more serious recent concerns briefly rise to the surface, like the debris from a shipwreck.

The action takes place at a hotel in Malvern, where Mr. Gabblewig has come to take the cold-water cure in order to wash away "the tormenting remembrance" of Rosina, whose uncle, Mr. Nightingale, has refused her permission to marry. "You see he married a wife when he was very young," we are told by a servant. "And she was the plague of his life ever afterwards." Mr. Gabblewig's mock shocked response to this idea is "O Rosina, can such things be!," a line Dickens presumably delivered with a knowing wink in the direction of Bulwer Lytton. Of course the plague is exactly the sort of disease Mr. Nightingale would worry about catching, even though the landlord points out that "Of all the invalids that come down here, the invalids that have nothing the matter with them are the hopeless cases." (Here Dickens's love of puns briefly flickers into life: a fake invalid is also medically in-valid.) Next we are introduced to Slap, a con artist who writes begging letters and asks not to be associated with his father's name, just as in 1841 Dickens had responded to his own father's tendency to cadge loans and incur unpaid debts by instructing his solicitor Thomas Mitton to insert a notice in the newspapers disowning the bills of anyone "having or purporting to have the surname of our said client." (By then Dickens's brother Alfred had also started writing clandestine begging letters to Dickens's publishers Chapman & Hall, in one of which he requests "with the greatest reluctance possible" the loan of a £5 note.) And in performance, central to everything was Dickens himself, as he disappeared from view and then reappeared a few lines later as a former actor named Charley, followed by an energetic walker ("Walk in our sleep—sometimes—can't walk enough"), a deaf old sexton who has "Buried a many. They was strong, too,—once," and several other roles. It was more than just a tribute to the quick-change artistry of Charles Mathews. Slipping from one role to the next, Dickens was secretly inviting the audience to watch his own life unfold in a dizzying series of disguises.

SUMMER

Making an Exhibition

In Britain the first public glimpse came in July, when the *Preston Guardian* reported neutrally that "several young ladies [in Harrogate] have appeared recently in the Bloomer costume." The following month it was a mother and daughter in London, both of them allegedly vegetarians, who were spotted in Oxford Street dressed in baggy trousers and waistcoats, accompanied by "a crowd of ragged urchins and a number of the curious of both sexes"; when "the mob got troublesome" the pair escaped in a cab "amid shouts of laughter." Less than two weeks later a mother and two daughters were seen wearing similar clothing in Belfast; according to a local newspaper, some onlookers were puzzled by "the singular and theatrical-looking compound of the attire of both sexes which was paraded before them," while others "expressed an opinion the reverse of complimentary" in comparing them to "persons whose over-dressed gaiety of appearance in public stamps the class to which they belong," i.e., prostitutes. On all three occasions the women wore variations on an outfit consisting of a belted knee-length tunic and pantaloons gathered at the ankle, known as a "Bloomer costume" after the American journalist Amelia Bloomer, with the women being referred to as "Bloomers." (It would be several more years before this word started to be applied to the clothing itself.) Celebrated by its supporters as a more sensible alternative to the full skirts that could trip the wearer up or be dragged along in the mud, and whalebone corsets that cramped women's ambitions along with their bodies, for others the Bloomer costume was not just a fashion choice that was—to borrow a fairly new expression—*the rage*. It provoked outrage.

The decision to experiment with a new style of clothing in ordinary towns and cities has been described as "the turning point in . . . nineteenth-century dress reform—the moment when woman's rights leaders took it out of private spaces and into the public arena." Not that this was quite what Amelia Bloomer had intended. As her husband looked back over the year's events, he acknowledged that the "reform-dress movement was simply an episode in Mrs. Bloomer's life and work" and she "never dreamed of the wonderful celebrity which it brought to her name." The original call for a more rational form of dress, which would also significantly reduce the risks to women carrying children or lighted candles, had appeared in Amelia Bloomer's *The Lily*, a New York–based newspaper that described itself as "DEVOTED TO THE INTERESTS OF WOMEN," with a particular focus on temperance matters and a modest circulation of around five hundred copies a month. In "Our Costume," published in the April issue, Elizabeth Cady Stanton argued that a shorter skirt and "Turkish trowsers," similar to the outfits worn in some European spas, would offer women far greater freedom of movement, and she urged her readers to ignore the comments of "men and boys [who] laugh at us." But it was Bloomer's later defences of the costume that were reprinted in the *New York Tribune* and elsewhere, complete with illustrations, sewing instructions, and inspiring accounts of the women who had chosen to wear it in place of the "ball and chain" of heavy skirts, and as a result it was her name that became linked to this new fashion as securely as a label sewn into a shirt collar.

Over the course of the summer, as supporters and satirists alike considered what it meant for a woman to wear trousers in public, Bloomer's celebrity slowly toppled over into notoriety. She later recalled her first article defending female pantaloons as "half-serious, half-playful," and that also neatly summarised public reactions to the Bloomer outfit as a whole. For those who enjoyed contemporary farces like *Bloomerism; or the Follies of the Day*, a one-act play by John Henry Nightingale that Dickens judged "very good," or comic songs like Henry Abraham's "I want to be a Bloomer," the sight of women wearing trousers was like a modern version of a Shakespearean comedy in which new clothes playfully muddled up old identities. For others, like the *Times* journalist who described this type of cross-dressing as "aggression . . . most daringly manifested," it represented a dangerous breach in the social order.

Most of *Punch*'s coverage shuttled between these position by treating Bloomerism as a joke though with an unusually flinty edge. As early as 28 June it printed a cartoon of a woman wearing plus fours and smoking, alongside a satirical letter on "Women's Emancipation" supposedly written by "a strong-minded American Woman." Many later cartoons played thumping variations on the same form of role reversal, by pretending to catch "Bloomers" in the act of bossing their husbands around, or asking strange men to dance, or otherwise suggesting that it wasn't only in their choice of attire that these women wanted to wear the trousers. On the other hand, a spoof address from "Mrs. Bloomer to the Female Race" was also seamed with a few moments of genuine wonder. "Yes: I see Woman rise from her Petticoats, as *the long imprisoned Butterfly* rises from its crippling and *confining sheath!*" declares Mrs. Bloomer, as if a whole new species was magically emerging before her eyes.

Such jokes were rather less funny for the women who every day had to wrestle with the alternative. At one point this year, the young Jane Ellen Panton noticed two women wearing Bloomer costumes at the end of her crescent. "They had hats and feathers and soft grey boots with shiny leather toes," she later wrote, "and were altogether awesome specimens of humanity." Inevitably they were being followed by "the ubiquitous street-boy making use of all possible opprobrious terms," but for Panton their importance lay in the fact that they were "the first persons who ever made women aware that they possessed legs, and that they should use them more than they did in those days." While they offered an inviting glimpse of the future, their attire would continue to be viewed as provocatively eccentric for many years to come. As late as 1876, a *New York Times* editorial identified a "curious nervous disorder peculiar to women," of which the most visible symptom was "an abnormal and unconquerable thirst for trousers," with the author recommending a form of aversion therapy that involved dressing the woman "exclusively in trousers" and confining her to a room where the walls, floor and even the windows would be "covered with trousers of the brightest patterns." In the eyes of this journalist, such women were an affront to masculinity and a threat to civilisation as a whole, but at least they were visible enough to be taken seriously. By contrast, to a young girl in 1851, unless she had been poring over recent press reports, a woman in trousers would have seemed as unlikely as a centaur.

Back in Seneca Falls, New York, Amelia Bloomer continued to wear the new fashion "on all occasions, at home and abroad, at church and on the lecture platform, at fashionable parties and in my business office," later claiming that in all her travels "I met with nothing disagreeable or unpleasant, but was universally treated with respect and attention by both press and people wherever I appeared." That wasn't always the experience of her British followers. Over the summer a backlash against the public visibility of Bloomers quickly gathered momentum, and although by the autumn there were five Bloomer waxworks on display in Madame Tussaud's, one speaker at Miss Kelly's Theatre in Soho (built under the Duke of Devonshire's patronage, and sometimes used by Dickens for his rehearsals) was met by "several outbreaks of laughter and discordant noises." Another speaker was forced to abandon her planned lecture at the Royal Institution in Finsbury because an "unusually violent" mob had gathered to hoot their derision. Indeed, by the time Dickens decided to join in the debate, Bloomerism was being viewed as something far more worrying than a few items of innovative clothing.

Perhaps that helps to explain the tetchiness of his response in "Sucking Pigs," first published in *Household Words* on 8 November, because few of his articles are written so baldly or have dated so badly. His criticisms fall under two main headings. In the first place, he dislikes the idea of women delivering lectures at all, confessing that his mind would be "disturbed" if his own wife decided "to entrench herself behind a small table ornamented with a water-bottle and tumbler, and from that fortified position to hold forth to the public," just as he would doubt the usefulness of her "serving on a Grand Jury for Middlesex" or "taking the chair at a Meeting on the subject of the Income-Tax." (There are parallels here with "Bloomeriana: A Dream," published in *Punch* on the same day, a cartoon by John Leech that conjures up a topsy-turvy world in which women race horses, work as soldiers and drive cabs, while men scrub floors and look on perplexedly.) Nor would Dickens love his wife any more if she were to enter into another branch of public life, he declares, because her proper place is at home, safely tucked away in a "haven of refuge" where her children await.

The notion that a wife who seeks fulfilment outside the home must be a rival rather than an equal is something Dickens had already gestured towards in the first of his "From the Raven in the Happy Family" articles, where the raven observes that the owner's wife "has made the discovery that she has no business to be the comfort of [his] life . . . but is quite ill-used in being the solace of his home, and wants to go out speechifying." This leads to Dickens's second criticism in "Sucking Pigs," which is the lack of moderation in reforming women that accompanies their rejection of sartorial modesty. "Mrs. Bellows cannot come out of a pair of stays without instantly going into a waistcoat," he argues, overdoing things in his own right. In fact, not even becoming a fully-fledged Bloomer would satisfy her. "She must agitate, agitate, agitate." Instead of preserving "a quiet little avenue of her own in the world, begirt with her own influences and duties," Dickens complains, "She must go in to be a public character . . . She must work away at a Mission." Clearly it is not the fictitious Mrs. Bellows who is most agitated here. Although Dickens's use of the editorial "we" in his article allows him to present himself as the impartial voice of reason, on several occasions his attack becomes far more personal in tone. He refers to his wife as "Julia" rather than Catherine, but he also mentions that they have nine children, just like his own family until very recently, and his final assessment that the behaviour of women like Amelia Bloomer is "unreasonable and groundlessly antagonistic" amounts to little more than the fact that he disagrees with it and it annoys him. Ultimately his conclusion applies far better to himself than it does to them.

As Dickens's introduction points out, "Sucking Pigs" was the "offspring" of his earlier piece "Whole Hogs," published in August, in which he criticised what he considered to be the unhealthy extremism of many reforming campaigns, such as those supporting teetotalism and vegetarianism. His assessment in "Sucking Pigs" was that such all-or-nothing arguments "never can be profitable." However, that wasn't entirely true in his own case, because he continued to use his irritation as a rich source of inspiration over the coming months. For example, in 1852 he returned to the spectacle of women dressing in men's clothes when he came to write about Joan of Arc in *A Child's History of England*. She had already been enlisted in the debate over Bloomerism: in an article published in the July 1851 issue of *Harper's New Monthly Magazine*, the women who had discarded their trailing skirts and adopted "the far more convenient, equally chaste, and more elegant dresses of Oriental women" were celebrated for being "as bold as Joan d'Arc." Dickens strongly disagreed. How much happier Joan of Arc would have been, he suggests, if she had ignored the call to enter public life and had instead "resumed her rustic dress that day, and had gone home . . . and had been a good man's wife, and had heard no stranger voices than the voices of little children!" The link to modern women like Amelia Bloomer is unspoken but unmistakable.

Even in 1851, the idea that do-gooders would do better to work for improvements closer to home was not a new one for Dickens. The previous year he had visited Caroline Chisholm, who had established the Family Colonisation Loan Society to help the poor emigrate, and had supplied Dickens with the raw material for "A Bundle of Emigrants' Letters" in the first issue of *Household Words*. There were five children in her house, including a sickly newborn baby, and almost no domestic help, but it was the other new arrivals—a postbag of around three hundred letters every day—that chiefly occupied their mother's attention. As an early biographer noted, the house bustled with activity from morning to evening: "the pen hands of the Chisholms seemed never to cease moving, except when relieved in order to shake hands with their numerous unknown friends. Callers came, asked their questions, and departed; the door was always on the swing." Yet what Dickens particularly noticed was the fact that Mrs. Chisholm seemed much more interested in these strangers than she was in her own family. A week after his visit, he told Miss Coutts that "I dream of Mrs. Chisholm, and her housekeeping. The dirty faces of her children are my continual companions." Here was another case in which apparently charity did not begin at home. Instead Mrs. Chisholm had chosen to look at the world in a way Dickens had previously satirised in *The Mudfog Papers*, where one of the new inventions presented to an imaginary gathering of scientists is a pair of spectacles "which enabled the wearer to discern, in very bright colours, objects at a great distance, and rendered him wholly blind to those immediately before him." Mrs. Chisholm might have been far-sighted as a philanthropist, but when it came to what was happening under her own nose, Dickens concluded, she was about as perceptive as a rock.

This leads to another reason for the suspicion that had started to gather around British Bloomers. They were promoting an idea that was an American import, and although it was perfectly acceptable to wear Paris fashions, that was hardly the same thing as adopting an outfit that had originated in the cultural backwaters of Seneca Falls, New York. The problem was especially acute this summer, when people from around the world were supposed to be flocking to the Crystal Palace to take their lead from British culture rather than their American cousins. The growing rivalry of these two nations could be detected not only in assessments of the American exhibits that were arriving in Hyde Park, such as Elias Howe's sewing machine and Samuel Colt's revolver, both of which attracted widespread though somewhat grudging admiration, but also in press coverage of the visit to the Crystal Palace in September of Mrs. Caroline Dexter. A mesmerist and clairvoyant who had been christened "the apostle of Bloomerism" by *The Times*, she was accompanied by several disciples in full costume who handed out leaflets advertising forthcoming lectures on dress reform, and were said to have "secured to themselves all the attention which could be spared from the miracles of art and industry around them." The strong implication was that such missionaries were a distraction from what was really important, as if worrying about a problem that had been identified in America was as misguided as dwelling on anything else that could be discerned only at a great distance.

Nor was it only American visitors who faced this type of suspicion. In *Little Dorrit*, the Italian Cavalletto discovers that it is "uphill work for a foreigner" to make his way in a down-at-heel part of London known as Bleeding Heart Yard, despite being an "easy, hopeful little fellow," because his neighbours consider it "a sound constitutional national axiom that he ought to go home to his own country." In 1851 such attitudes were not confined to small pockets of urban poverty, nor were their targets restricted to immigrants like Cavalletto. In October, almost exactly a year after he had published *"Wot is to Be,"* George Sala contributed to *Household Words* an article on "The Foreign Invasion," recalling how fearful people had been at the start of the summer concerning what—and more particularly who—was expected to arrive in the coming months. "The nasty, dirty, greasy, wicked, plundering, devastating, murdering, frog-eating, atheistical foreigners! . . . pantheism, polytheism, deism, Mahommedanism, Buddhism, everywhere. England, of course, nowhere. The foreigners in London! Fire, famine, and slaughter; Popery, brass money, and wooden shoes!" Now that these predictions had not come to pass he could look back and smile at their absurdity, but the joke would only have been funny if his readers had recognised the basic truth of what he was satirising.

A similar set of ideas ran through an earlier article in *Punch* that reflected on the build-up to the Great Exhibition by asking "Where Are The Foreigners?" Here too the writer presents a pantomime version of London being overrun by "foreigners in sledges—foreigners on camels," even an elephant stuck in the narrow opening of Temple Bar, and expresses his mock disappointment that such visions have not materialised. Other than a few more beards and moustaches being visible on the streets, "London is nearly the same as at any other season." Yet just a few days before the grand opening on 1 May, there were still people who were reluctant to let the facts get in the way of a bad joke. The previous issue of *Punch* had featured a half-page cartoon that purported to show a group of foreign visitors preparing to sleep overnight in Hyde Park. It is a

BIVOUAC IN THE PARK THE NIGHT BEFORE THE EXHIBITION.

huddle of national stereotypes, who smoke long German pipes, slumber in tents on which small Tricolours flutter Frenchly, or, in the case of a group of Native Americans, dance around a fire that throws the feathers of their headdresses into silhouette like giant pointing fingers. The overall mood is relaxed and friendly, rather like a modern pop festival, but the title of the cartoon, "Bivouac in the Park the Night before the Exhibition," together with the smudged outlines of hundreds more tents, suggests something far more menacing: an army camping out before a battle. It neatly captured the national mood in the days preceding the Crystal Palace finally opening its doors on Thursday 1 May: eager anticipation mixed with a faint lurking dread.

In the end it was a triumph, one of those chapters in the nation's story that later seemed to improve with each telling. From early in the morning, reported *The Times*, London's veins "beat full and strong under the pressure of a great and hitherto unknown excitement" as thick crowds of spectators made their way to Hyde Park for the opening ceremony. The band played, speeches were made, hats and handkerchiefs were waved, the artillery boomed, and at noon the waiting spectators hurrahed as Queen Victoria's

diminutive figure arrived by carriage and was swallowed up by the Crystal Palace, followed by faint strains of "God Save the Queen" leaking out through its glass walls. As the day continued, different witnesses noticed different things: the cheers that greeted the arrival of the Duke of Wellington on what was his eighty-second birthday; a smiling Chinese visitor dressed in an embroidered silk robe who managed to sneak in among the foreign ambassadors and prostrate himself before the Queen (it later transpired that this was a publicity stunt for the Chinese junk *Keying*, a tourist attraction moored at Blackwall); the "busy hum" generated by 25,000 members of the public who had secured tickets for the opening day. What nobody could miss was the Crystal Palace itself, as it glittered impressively in the sunshine following a sharp early-morning shower, at once a container for the Great Exhibition and its own greatest exhibit.

"Nothing more completely represents a nation than a public building," Disraeli had claimed in his 1847 novel *Tancred*, where he criticised London for being architecturally "very monotonous." By contrast, the Crystal Palace was a giant architectural exclamation mark, and it included enough variety to satisfy even the shortest attention span, from the calico roof coverings that diffused light onto the exhibits below, to the glass fountain weighing four tonnes that stood gently pulsing at the heart of the building. What had also become increasingly obvious was that the Crystal Palace was far more than just a piece of striking architecture. It was a prism that refracted the hopes and fears of an entire nation. Even its method of construction was being held up as a lesson for the future; when a writer in *Punch* suggested that the new Houses of Parliament, located two miles away and still nowhere near completion after a decade of fiddly neo-Gothic building work, might be replaced by a "Crystal Parliament," it wasn't altogether a joke. The underlying assumption was that some of the country's other institutions might benefit from similar levels of speed and transparency to those enabled by Paxton's design. A new catchphrase celebrated his ability to solve seemingly intractable problems: "Ask Paxton."

Of course not everyone was convinced. Though the Crystal Palace was often compared to a modern cathedral, the Gothic re-created in glass, Ruskin thought it a miserable failure. The first volume of his great prose hymn to Gothic architecture, *The Stones of Venice*, had been published on 3 March (Dickens received a signed presentation copy bound in crimson morocco), and it centred on the idea that Venice's finest buildings could be viewed as cultural touchstones, evidence of the qualities that could be "easily applicable to all possible architectural inventions of the human mind." However, after visiting the Crystal Palace, Ruskin concluded that it did not demonstrate anything like the same levels of creativity or skill. Whereas Gothic architects "out of fragments full of imperfection, and betraying that imperfection in every touch, indulgently raise up a stately and unaccusable whole," Paxton's building had been bolted together like a battleship or bridge. When compared to a real cathedral, it was a mere simulacrum of the sublime. Uniform and predictable, it lacked the quirky decorative details and other traces of individuality that proved it had been made by human hands; ultimately it lacked life. As Ruskin went on to explain in an essay published three years later, what truly depressed him was the idea that after hundreds of years of architectural experiment involving a "lofty search after the ideal," in the middle of the nineteenth century "we suppose ourselves to have invented a new style of architecture, when we have magnified a conservatory!"

Yet while Ruskin dismissed the Crystal Palace as nothing more than a giant greenhouse, there were far more people who saw it instead as a fairy-tale vision brought to life, and they competed with each other to find the best way of reassembling it in words. Thackeray composed a poem for the opening day in which his usual layered irony was replaced by simple awe: "As though 'twere by a wizard's rod / A blazing arch of lucid glass / Leaps like a fountain from the grass / To meet the sun." Charlotte Brontë drew on similar vocabulary, writing that the Exhibition was "such a bazaar or fair as Eastern genii might have created. It seems as if only magic could have gathered this mass of wealth from all the ends of the earth—as if none but supernatural hands could have arranged it thus, with such a blaze and contrast of colours and marvellous power of effect." Charles Dodgson, fresh from his first year at Oxford and still some time away from adopting the pseudonym Lewis Carroll, also considered the Crystal Palace more unreal than real. Writing to his sister Elizabeth, he confessed that his first impression on entering the building was "bewilderment" because it looked like "a sort of fairyland"; he especially admired a tree that featured some mechanical birds "chirping and hopping from branch to branch exactly like life," although he was unconvinced by one bird that stood at the foot of the tree trying to eat a beetle, as "it never succeeds in getting its head more than a quarter of an inch down, and that in uncomfortable little jerks, as if it was choking." Charles Kingsley wept when he first saw the Exhibition, declaring in a sermon preached four days later that it was one of the "proofs of the Kingdom of God." Another visitor was overwhelmed in a rather different way: William Morris, then aged seventeen, was so appalled by the Exhibition's vulgar materialism that he staggered from the building and was sick in the bushes.

"As you do not say that you are coming to see the great exhibition," Dickens wrote to the American author G. W. Curtis, "I conclude that you intend to be *the* man, memorable through future ages, who didn't see it."

The scanty references in his letters suggest that Dickens remained unenthusiastic even after he had seen it. "I don't say 'there's nothing in it'—there's too much," he told Mrs. Richard Watson on 11 July. By then he had made at least two visits, although he confessed that he had been "bewildered" by the experience, and couldn't be sure that he'd seen anything apart from the glass fountain and August Kiss's sculpture of an Amazon warrior slaying a panther. "I have a natural horror of sights, and the fusion of so many sights in one has not decreased it." The paradox is that among the sights of the Great Exhibition was Dickens himself, because the seventy-two daguerreotypes displayed by John Mayall, the photographer who in 1860 would take the first *carte de visite* photographs of Queen Victoria, included a 12-inch-by-10-inch image of the novelist. He was also joined in the building by two of his most famous creations interpreted in stone: a statue by Robert Ball Hughes that depicted Oliver Twist slumped on the floor after he has been shot, and another by the same sculptor of Little Nell wistfully sitting in a churchyard with a book on her lap, a fitting tribute to a character who joins Mrs. Jarley's waxwork show in *The Old Curiosity Shop* after hearing about its "constantly unchanging air of coldness and gentility." Such items meant that even when Dickens wasn't there in person he was capable of drawing the crowds.

Several other exhibits may already have been familiar to him, including the elaborately detailed architectural ornaments made out of papier mâché that were manufactured by Charles Bielefeld, one of his neighbours in Wellington Street North. (In November, Richard Horne produced an article for *Household Words* describing how the company could use "mashed rags" of paper to make anything from delicate picture frames to slabs of imitation marble.) By contrast, the foreign displays contained a number of surprises, ranging from India's giant Koh-i-Noor diamond to the sax-horns, sax-trumpets and saxophones manufactured by Adolphe Sax of Paris. In one of its earlier spoof articles on the Great Exhibition, *Punch* had suggested that instead of a new building the organisers should instead "put London under a glass cover," like a giant version of the cloches that protected arrangements of stuffed birds or wax fruit in some middle-class living rooms, but the real Crystal Palace went much further than this. It invited visitors to travel the world in half a day.

Many of them approached the Great Exhibition less like a modern trade fair than an old-fashioned cabinet of curiosities, a collection of objects that was designed to show off the owner's informed but eclectic taste. Whether visitors were marvelling at a steam-powered envelope-making machine, or William Jenkins's "Expanding and Collapsing Pianoforte for gentlemen's yachts, the saloons of steam-vessels, ladies' cabins, etc.," the glass surroundings of the Crystal Palace allowed everything to be examined in the same even light. "Just now we are an objective people," wrote a journalist in *The Times*. "We want to place everything we can lay our hands on under glass cases, and to stare our fill." In this setting even practical objects could acquire an additional sheen of glamour. Some of the most popular exhibits, attracting 827,000 visitors over the course of the Exhibition, turned out to be the flushing toilets in "retiring rooms" that could be used for the price of a penny. (This may be one source for the euphemism "to spend a penny.") Particularly in the context of ongoing debates over public sanitation, each pull of the chain felt like a small triumph of progress.

For many people the most interesting exhibits weren't collapsible pianos or diamonds the size of a bird's egg. They were the other visitors. A "crystal palace" had been a popular location in pantomimes for at least a decade, albeit one that was created using painted backdrops and gauzy lighting effects rather than real sheets of glass, while the idea of public life as a kind of performance had recently generated a phrase that took on a whole new meaning in the context of huge crowds arriving in Hyde Park: *making an exhibition of yourself*. The *OED*'s first example is taken from Dickens's *A Child's History of England* in 1854, although an earlier example can be found in an instalment published in October 1851, describing a notable day in Henry II's life as one "when the king made this curious exhibition of himself." It was a phrase that was in the air: the previous year Dickens had told Miss Coutts about one of the Urania House inmates, who had broken into the cellar where beer was kept and "made a very repulsive exhibition of herself." In all these examples, the underlying fear was of behaving in a way that was contemptible or laughable in the eyes of other people, like an actor performing in front of an unsympathetic audience, and this summer the inescapable visibility of visitors in the Crystal Palace made that an ever-present threat.

The idle rich were one source of comment, especially those who were more used to riding up and down Rotten Row, the broad track in Hyde Park where fashionable Londoners went to show off on horseback, and had now apparently replaced that exercise with walking up and down the building's nave. Working-class visitors were scrutinised even more closely, despite the fact that fears of "King Mob" taking the opportunity to riot had proven to be unfounded. Everything about them was discussed with a curiosity that bordered on distaste, from their supposedly dirty appearance to their habit of bringing packed lunches with them that smelled of "gin and oranges." As early as April 1850, *Punch* had included a cartoon of the forthcoming Exhibition that featured skinny specimens of the industrial working class being kept in bell jars, such as "An Industrious Needle Woman" and "A Distressed Shoemaker," and the depiction of working-class visitors in subsequent cartoons—a seemingly endless parade of rural smocks and other visual clichés—typically treated them as figures who were as alien as moustached Frenchmen.

Unsubtle though these cartoons were, they filled a space in the public imagination that had been opened up by the official classification scheme, because although the Bishop of Oxford had looked forward to the Exhibition as a celebration of "The Dignity of Labour," in 1851 that loose term "labour" included anyone who worked for a living, and so could refer to factory owners as well as the people they employed. Yet around three-quarters of the total number of visitors came from working-class backgrounds, travelling to Hyde Park from all over the country before paying the cheapest admission price of a shilling—not an insignificant amount to someone on modest wages (in *A Christmas Carol* Bob Cratchit earns fifteen shillings a week), as Dickens would have recognised, given that a shilling was also the price of each single paper-covered instalment of a novel like *David Copperfield*. In June, he wrote a letter of complaint to the Secretary of the South Eastern Railway pointing out that on a recent busy train to Gravesend, a woman with a second-class ticket had been placed in the first-class carriage alongside him, and had then been bullied into paying an extra fourpence for sitting there; the ticket inspector took a shilling from her but failed to return with any change. It was exactly the sort of minor injustice that always rankled with Dickens, and having published "A Biography of a Bad Shilling" in *Household Words* earlier that year, which followed a forged coin as it circulated through different hands, including as part-payment for the making of a dozen shirts that enabled it to "sustain an entire family who were on the verge of starvation," he was acutely conscious that to many people such a small sum of money could still mean a great deal.

In May he published "Cheap Pleasures," an article by Harry Wills and Eustace Murray that explored some of the other ways someone might choose to spend a shilling, or a penny, or perhaps nothing at all, in the pursuit of leisure. (The authors expressed a particular hope that the Crystal Palace might eventually be turned into a winter garden, thereby encouraging "a wide dissemination of cheap pleasures.") There was certainly no shortage of options this summer. At the Royal Academy Exhibition, held in May, the new paintings included Millais's *Mariana*, depicting Tennyson's character stretching out in front of a stained-glass window, the same artist's *The Woodman's Daughter*, and Charles Allston Collins's *Convent Thoughts*—works that marked a "turning point" in both artists' careers "from which they may either sink into nothingness or rise to a very real greatness," according to a letter by Ruskin on "The Pre-Raffaelites" that appeared in *The Times* on 13 May. (The *Annual Register* spoke for more sceptical critics in dismissing the paintings as "examples of talent strangely applied.") Alternatively, for heterosexual men in search of something other than elevated thoughts, *The Bachelor's Pocket Book for 1851*—bound in soft red leather and published by William Ward, who ran a "Parisian Depository" (i.e., sex shop) at 67 Strand, less than a hundred yards from Dickens's *Household Words* offices—featured a guide to the seedier aspects of London's nightlife, including advertisements for French letters ("also known by the term of French Gloves, Cumdums, etc.") and illustrated reviews of twenty "Cyprians," i.e., prostitutes, written in a style of relentlessly smirking innuendo. We are told, for example, that "Miss Alice Grey" of New Street, off Portland Road, "frequently performs the rites of the love-inspiring queen according to the *equestrian* order, in which style she is said to be perfect in her paces, having studied under a professed riding master," although as much of this guide reprinted older material from *The Swell's Night Guides* of the 1840s, it is impossible to know what would have happened if a whip-toting visitor had followed its advice and knocked on her door.

In any case the crowds were elsewhere: eating oysters in London's pleasure gardens, or marvelling at the daredevil horseback performances at the Royal Hippodrome, or catching up with the latest additions to the Zoological Gardens, which in 1851 included Obaysch, the first hippopotamus to be seen in Europe since the Roman Empire, after it had arrived in May 1850 as a gift from the Ottoman Viceroy of Egypt. (Dickens was a regular visitor to the zoo, where it was reported that he "chaffed with the monkeys, coaxed the tigers and bamboozled the snakes, with a dexterity unapproachable," exotic animals being just another challenge to his powers of imaginative sympathy.) There were also major sporting events like the Epsom Derby at the start of June, which a few years later would be celebrated in a panoramic painting by William Powell Frith, although his stiffly posed figures were very different to Dickens's energetic account of the 1851 occasion, added to a *Household Words* article by Harry Wills, in which canvas booths flutter, hampers fly open, everyone jumps to their feet to get a good view of the race, and pigeons fly off with news of the result.

For the journalist Blanchard Jerrold (son of Douglas), in his later book *London: A Pilgrimage* (1872), the Derby was a brief pastoral interlude in city life, a day when the peer and shoe-black alike could take aim at a coconut, three sticks for a penny, and "all classes are intermingled for a few hours on the happiest terms." But in 1851 the idea of different classes mingling continued to provoke far more uncertain responses. In a letter to the *Morning Chronicle* published in 1842, Dickens had pointed out that at a time when "so wide a gulf has opened between the rich and poor, which, instead of narrowing, as all good men would have it, grows broader daily," it was important to recognise that each of "these two great divisions of society" was "dependent on the other." Since then there had been some attempts to bridge this gulf, at least in fiction. In his popular novel *The History of St. Giles and St. James*, serialised in 1847–9 and reissued in two volumes in 1851, Douglas Jerrold dwelt on the idea that the lives of the rich boy, St. James, and the poor boy, St. Giles, were as intimately connected as a body and its shadow. In one scene, all the main characters emerge from Covent Garden Theatre, and Jem the linkman (the clue lies in his job title) bears witness to the fact that "[y]oung St. Giles was the robber of St. James." Dickens went even further in a speech to the Metropolitan Sanitary Association on 10 May, when he reminded his audience of the dangers of living in unsanitary conditions. "No one can estimate the amount of mischief which is grown in dirt," he warned, "[and say] here it stops, or there it stops," when "the air from Gin Lane will be carried, when the wind is Easterly, into Mayfair." Because of the speed with which infectious diseases could spread, districts like St. Giles and St. James were far closer than they might appear on a map. It meant that when Henry Morley contributed "The World of Water" to *Household Words*, in which he described the "great system" of circulation linking all the world's oceans together, his explanation that blocks of coral were "built by little members of the vast and industrious community which swarms within the crystal palace of the sea" was more than just a flash of poetic prose. Published on 24 May, two days before the first shilling visitors were admitted to the Exhibition, his article was also a celebration of the "vast and industrious community" that was making itself visible in another crystal palace, and potentially a warning about what else they might bring with them besides gin and oranges.

Other writers had already realised that the mingling of nations and classes could be a rich source of comedy. Never one to see a passing band-wagon without trying to climb on board, by the time the Exhibition had opened Henry Mayhew had started to serialise a novel that took a selection of comic stereotypes—greedy letting agents, gullible country bumpkins, and others drawn from recent press reports—and turned them into actors in a slapstick farce. Illustrated by George Cruikshank, *1851: or The Adventures of Mr. and Mrs. Sandboys and Family* does not have anything quite as sophisticated as a plot. Rather it is a series of narrative set pieces loosely connected by the title characters, who come down to London from the Lake District to see the Exhibition and "enjoy themselves," but are repeatedly frustrated in their efforts to reach Hyde Park, as they are swindled out of their money, lose their luggage, and then fall in the Serpentine. The unfortunate Mr. and Mrs. Cursty Sandboys turn out to be just as doomed as their name suggests. Most of the comedy depends on their close encounters with various cheats and other visitors who seem determined "to make an exhibition of themselves," but Mayhew's writing does not only bring together different social types. It also mixes up different literary styles, as comic dialogue mingles with a report on the opening ceremony originally written by Mayhew for the *Edinburgh News*, together with tales of London's lowlife drawn from the ongoing serialisation of *London Labour and the London Poor*. The result is a novel that isn't very good as a novel, but as a social document it gives a fascinating early glimpse of how writers might try to capture the year's events in narrative form. For in turning 1851 into *1851*, Mayhew did not attempt to choose among the many different ways these events were being written about at the time. Instead his novel was a babble of competing voices, an all-embracing narrative mess.

Mayhew's comic muddle was only one attempt to imagine what effect the Great Exhibition might have on ordinary people's lives. In a stirring speech at the Mansion House banquet held on 21 March 1850, during which he outlined his hopes for the following year, Prince Albert had offered a vision of global harmony:

> . . . we are living at a period of most wonderful transition, which tends rapidly to accomplish that great end, to which, indeed, all his-

tory points—*the realisation of the unity of mankind* . . . the Exhibition of 1851 is to give us a true test of the point of development at which the whole of mankind has arrived in this great task, and a new starting point from which all nations will be able to direct their further exertions.

It was a utopian dream—eagerly embraced by figures like the computer pioneer Charles Babbage, who anticipated that the Exhibition would promote "the interchange of kindly feelings between the inhabitants of foreign countries and our own," and also by publications like *The Parlour Magazine of the Literature of All Nations*, a twopenny periodical first published on 3 May 1851, which featured a "collection of intellectual treasures" selected from the editor's "foreign wanderings." The central aim of such publications was to allow the reader's eyes to mimic the movements of a tourist's legs, roaming here and there while occasionally pausing to enjoy the view. Yet although the experience of walking around the Crystal Palace promoted the fantasy of living in a world without borders—one that could even infiltrate the individual human body, with an eau de Cologne fountain in the Austrian section and a French manufacturer offering "Samples of chocolate and mustard, manufactured by steam"—the actual mixing of nationalities was approached far more warily.

George Sala's response in "The Foreign Invasion" not only satirised specific fears of what the expected influx of visitors might bring, from revolutionary ideas to unruly facial hair, but also targeted the way these fears had been whipped up by the popular press. The opening cartoon in *The Comic Almanack* for 1851, edited by Mayhew, was typical in muddling up foreign visitors and permanent immigrants, supposedly for comic effect, by depicting a crowd of grinning Black women "from the Savage Islands" who have just arrived on the English coast "in Consequence of *Exporting* all our own to Australia!!!!!" The racism of this cartoon was developed in a sketch later on in the book, which imagines the consequences of intermarriage. "Three quarters of a year of unexampled bliss have fled quickly by: I am the father of two raisin-coloured little heirs. I wish I could persuade my wife not to wear the kitchen poker suspended from her neck." Other attempts to make fun of foreigners relied on similarly clumsy stereotypes, which ignored what was really happening in London in order to create a fantasy parallel world in which the French never washed, and cannibals visited restaurants solely in order to smack their lips over the other diners. Many other songs, cartoons and sketches played variations on the same basic plot, in which international and national perspectives on the Great Exhibition awkwardly circled around each other and sometimes collided head-on.

In this context, the continued existence of American slavery was a source of particular tension. The ivory statue by American sculptor Hiram Powers of a Greek slave delicately shackled at the wrists was thought to be in especially bad taste. An American fugitive slave named William Wells Brown visited the Exhibition at the end of June, and although he was "pleased to see such a goodly sprinkling of my own countrymen in the Exhibition—I mean coloured men and women well-dressed, and moving about with their fairer brethren," he also noticed the "sneering looks" of some Virginian exhibitors, and concluded that if the United States was unable to produce any art better than this statue "it would have been more to their credit had they kept that at home." British responses included a poem by Elizabeth Barrett Browning published in *Household Words*, and a satirical cartoon by John Tenniel depicting a Virginian slave frozen in the same pose. "We have the Greek captive in dead stone," *Punch* pointed out at the start of June, "why not have the Virginian slave in living ivory. Let America hire a black or two to stand in manacles, as American manufacture."

Naturally such questions were being tackled with far greater urgency in America itself. Having run into financial difficulties with his abolitionist newspaper the *North Star*, in 1851 the social reformer and former slave Frederick Douglass merged this publication with the *Liberty Party Paper* to launch *Frederick Douglass' Paper*, a weekly periodical based in Rochester, New York, that focused on the anti-slavery movement and other attempts at social reform. Six years earlier his impassioned memoir *Narrative of the*

Life of Frederick Douglass, an American Slave, Written by Himself had become
a bestseller, with five English and seven American editions published by
1849, and during a lengthy speaking tour he had written from Dublin
astonished at how he was viewed outside his own country. "I go on stage
coaches, omnibuses, steamboats, into the first cabins, and in the first public
houses, without seeing the slightest manifestation of that hateful and
vulgar feeling against me. I find myself treated not as a *color*, but as a *man*."
1851 would prove to be a significant year in testing the strength and reach
of this idea on both sides of the Atlantic. In April, the *Household Narrative*
noted the growing unpopularity of the Fugitive Slave Act in large parts of
America, and starting on 5 June the serialisation in *The National Era* of
Harriet Beecher Stowe's *Uncle Tom's Cabin* gave this pressure for reform a
story to build itself around. Centred on the mistreatment of a slave at the
hands of a vicious plantation owner, on whose orders Tom is beaten to
death after he refuses to say where two other slaves have escaped to, it
quickly became one of the most popular novels of the age.

Dickens's response to this growing social movement was at best equiv-
ocal. In 1848 he had sent Macready a copy of Douglass's memoir, having
first torn out a "hideous and abominable portrait" of the author in case
it prejudiced his friend against the book, and in 1852 he would use a
Household Words article on "North American Slavery," co-written with
Henry Morley, to praise *Uncle Tom's Cabin* as "a noble work; full of high
power, lofty humanity; the gentlest, sweetest, and yet boldest, writing."
He had already declared his fierce opposition to slavery in *American Notes*,
while Catherine was one of the 560,000 British women who signed the
Stafford House Address, an anti-slavery petition presented to Stowe in
1853. Yet when Mary Webb, the Black actress for whom Stowe had written *The Christian Slave*, a one-woman reading version of the novel,
contacted Dickens in 1857 to ask if she might use the "little Theatre" in
his house for a performance, he briskly explained that it was "quite out
of the question," adding that he was "the meekest of men, and in abhor-
rence of Slavery yield to no human creature—and yet I don't admit the
sequence that I want Uncle Tom (or Aunt Tomasina) to expound King

Lear to me." Black lives were important to Dickens, but that did not mean
they could claim the same privileges as friends like Macready. According
to the American journalist Grace Greenwood, who dined with Dickens
in the summer of 1852, he was even more suspicious in private. " 'Mrs.
Stowe,' he said, 'hardly gives the Anglo-Saxon fair play. I liked what I saw
of the colored people in the States. I found them singularly polite and
amiable, and in some instances decidedly clever; but then,' he added with
a droll, half smile, and a peculiar comical arch of his eyebrows, 'I have no
prejudice against white people.' "

Dickens's ambivalence about race was compounded by an equally
complicated tangle of attitudes towards foreigners in *Household Words*. In
March 1851, Dickens's article "A Monument of French Folly" had repeated
popular clichés about the French, such as the assumption that they were
"extremely sallow, thin, long-faced, and lantern-jawed," and rarely ate anything but soup and onions, and had pointed out how ridiculous they were.
He would return to the same idea five years later, in an article on
"Insularities" that mocked the English tendency to sneer at things merely
because they weren't English, and noted that although patriotism was to
be encouraged it was "of paramount importance to every nation that its
boastfulness should not generate prejudice, conventionality, and a cherish-
ing of unreasonable ways of acting and thinking, which . . . are ridiculous
or wrong." Yet when it came to writing about countries that were less
familiar to him than France, Dickens was capable of embracing prejudice,
conventionality and unreasonableness to an alarming degree. In an article
on "The Great Exhibition and the Little One," co-authored with Richard
Horne and published at the start of July this year, he scornfully contrasted
England with China as two countries that displayed "the greatest degree
of progress, and the least . . . England, maintaining commercial intercourse with the whole world; China, shutting itself up, as far as possible,
within itself." In the galleries of the Crystal Palace, the first was characterised by massive steam locomotives and the thrum of industrial machinery,
whereas the second apparently contained little more than the tinkling tea-
cups and joss sticks of the "flowery Empire." Worse still was the "Chinese

Gallery" in Hyde Park Place, where visitors were invited to inspect "a lady of quality" from Canton, whose bound feet had been reduced to "lotus flowers" a mere two and a half inches long. Even the wooden junk moored on the Thames at Blackwall was interpreted by Dickens as a symbol of Chinese "stoppage." Never mind the fact that many of the so-called "Chinese" exhibits in the Crystal Palace were supplied by the East India Company, and so had been manufactured chiefly to satisfy Western tastes; so far as Dickens was concerned China was merely an exotic footnote to the story of "development" being championed by modern progressives like Prince Albert.

Yet Dickens was always interested in seeing both sides of a question, and even before the Exhibition had opened he recognised that for many visitors it was the English rather than themselves who were the foreigners—a fact that should probably encourage a little more humility in their hosts. At the end of the summer, George Sala observed that perhaps in future the editors of foreign newspapers "will no longer declare that we live on raw beef-steaks, and occasionally eat the winners of our Derbies . . . that we are in the daily habit of selling our wives in Smithfield market; and that during the month of November three-fourths of London commit suicide." It was building on a joke Dickens had already made in "Foreigners' Portraits of Englishmen," a co-written article published in September 1850, which pointed out that the character of "a true born Briton" dreamed up by European writers was a hash of "every unlikely extravagance it is possible to assemble in one character."

Another article, "A Pilgrimage to the Great Exhibition from Abroad," written by William Howitt and published in June 1851, ridiculed English complacency in a different way. Regardless of the fact that the Exhibition had "stamped an indelible feeling of the greatness of England in all nations," Howitt pointed out that the arrangements for welcoming foreign visitors to London were insultingly inadequate. After steaming up the Thames, passengers were marched off their ship and forced to wait for several hours in the Custom House, "cooped up like so many sheep," while their passports were examined and their luggage subjected to leisurely inspection. It was a "wretched stumbling-block" for new arrivals, he concluded, and it threatened to destroy the "sense of national greatness" this year was supposed to promote. When compared to mainstream celebrations of the Great Exhibition such articles formed the most minor of undercurrents, but they also underlined the principle Dickens was becoming increasingly committed to in his own writing: a willingness to look at the familiar world through the eyes of a stranger.

While the attention of the press this summer was mostly on large-scale transformations—the development of Hyde Park into the site of a world fair, the plan for Britain to emerge as the leading industrial power— Dickens was still focused on trying to bring about a smaller set of changes in the literary world. More than two weeks later than originally planned, the first performance of *Not So Bad As We Seem* took place on Friday 16 May in the Devonshire House rooms Paxton had altered to fit the Guild's "little moveable theatre." High ticket prices meant that it was far from being the sort of evening where you might rub shoulders with one of the struggling writers it was intended to support. Instead, besides the Queen, Prince Albert and the rest of the royal party, the audience featured what the *Illustrated London News* fawningly described as "all the highest representatives of the rank, beauty, and genius of this wonderful England, and her foreign Ambassadors." What isn't known is whether Rosina Bulwer Lytton was also present to carry out her threatened campaign of disruption, although her animosity towards Dickens after 1851 suggests his plans to have her escorted off the premises may have been put into effect. In 1854 she would refer to him as "that Dunghill divinity Mr. Charles Dickens" who had arranged for "hired Literary Assassins" to crush his rivals, while her 1866 autobiography *A Blighted Life* took aim at him as a "patent Humbug" whose "*every* bad passion has left the impress of its cloven hoof upon [his] fiendish lineaments."

Whether or not the evening was enlivened by her throwing rotten eggs, it didn't lack incidents of other kinds. Richard Horne recalled that one scene set in Will's Coffee House was rather spoiled by an actor who forgot he was wearing a sword, and as he turned round accidentally swept "Decanters, glasses, grapes, a pine-apple, a painted pound cake, and several fine wooden peaches" off the table, whereupon Dickens improvised a line in perfect blank verse: "Here, drawer [i.e., waiter]! come and clear away this wreck!" Another actor almost missed his cue, after getting lost backstage and finding himself in an empty gallery "wigged, powdered, buckled, ruffled, perspiring, maddened," and gasped out "Where— where's the stage" to a passing figure who fortunately turned out to be the Duke of Devonshire himself, and "who with a most delighted and delightful urbanity, at once put him upon his right course."

Afterwards the Queen's response was polite but measured, writing in her diary that the cast "acted on the whole well, Dickens (the celebrated author) admirably," while the play was "full of cleverness, though rather too long." Most of the official reviews also hedged their bets. The general consensus was that *Not So Bad As We Seem* was not as bad it might have been, which was hardly the ringing endorsement Dickens and Bulwer Lytton had hoped for. Only the *Illustrated London News* was thoroughly convinced, praising the play as "a triumph of dramatic skill" alongside a full-page illustration that showed the audience watching the Amateur Company perform, the central focus of the picture being not the stage but the temporary royal box, where another performance was in progress, one in which a young woman who had been christened Alexandrina played the role of Queen Victoria before her adoring public. The *Morning Chronicle* applauded the performances of the actors but criticised the plot as "perplexingly hazy," while the *Globe* also considered the plot to be "not particularly clear," and concluded that in seeking to put across a thesis about the treatment of writers it "abounds more in point than in wit." Perhaps the bluntest judgement came from Lord Broughton (John Cam Hobhouse), who confessed to his diary that the play, "so far as I could hear it, was below mediocrity." He escaped before the final act to go to a ball being held a few hundred yards away at Apsley House, where his host was the Duke of Wellington, who himself had sat through only two acts before leaving.

What they missed was a clumsy attempt by Bulwer Lytton to explain the moral of his play. "Oh, trust me," Wilmot/Dickens tells the garret-dwelling scribbler, "the day shall come, when men will feel that it is not charity we owe to the ennoblers of life—it is tribute!," and the final scene concludes with some doggerel toasting the future of the Guild: "SUCCESS TO THE SCHEME!" It was an appropriately awkward conclusion to a play that was supposed to be a celebration of mutual aid, yet viewed the solution to its hero's plight as aristocratic patronage. While this undoubtedly reflected Bulwer Lytton's own anomalous position in the world of letters, and perhaps also the fact that the staging of the play had depended on the support of the Duke of Devonshire, as a call to action it left some puzzled and others frankly annoyed. Two days earlier, in a speech to the Royal Literary Fund that was also attended by Forster, Thackeray had argued that in the modern age the figure of the "oppressed literary man" was as much a figment of the imagination as any other literary character, pointing out that "I have been in all sorts of society in this world, and I don't believe there has been a literary man of the slightest merit or of the slightest mark who did not greatly advance himself by his literary labours." Pitying writers was therefore both unnecessary and unhelpful, because what the literary world needed wasn't more charity; what it needed was better writing. To pretend otherwise, Thackeray wrote to Mrs. Carlyle afterwards, as Dickens and his friends were doing by "painting their faces and asking for your money," was to "make literature a chronic beggary." In any case, Thackeray warned his own audience, "Literary men are not by any means, at this present time, the most unfortunate and most degraded set of people whom they are sometimes represented to be." It was a witty reminder that the title of Bulwer Lytton's play could easily be spun back on the author and his friends after the glittering spectacle of their opening night. They too were not nearly as bad as they seemed— certainly not in terms of their social and financial position.

Thackeray followed this up with a letter to Forster, who in the play had taken on the role of Hardman: an MP who has "a hard life of it" like all "men who live for others." Thackeray reported that his letter was received "like a slap in the face," because it asked Forster "to tell Dickens and you his familiar friend, that I'm not his enemy" but "we're on different sides of the house . . . I don't believe in the Guild of Literature[,] I don't believe in the Theatrical scheme; I think *that* is against the dignity of our profession." In Thackeray's eyes this marked the end. "I can't ever be friends with him again. He is what he tried to fancy I am but knows better, a traitor and a sneak." And as Thackeray's friendship with Forster spluttered to a halt, so his opposition to Dickens grew: Devonshire House would mark the point at which their paths, after awkwardly overlapping for several years, finally diverged.

Further performances by the Amateur Company took place at Devonshire House on 27 May, when it was followed by *Mr. Nightingale's Diary*, and then at the Hanover Square Rooms on 18 June and 2 July. But although Dickens continued to take centre stage he was no longer living in London. Instead he had sublet Devonshire Terrace for the summer and decamped with his family to a clifftop house in Broadstairs, a small seaside town on the Kent coast, from where he wrote to Count d'Orsay on 18 May, in confident if occasionally clumsy French, that the Exhibition was making everyone "even madder than usual." He planned to stay in Broadstairs until the end of October, by which time the Great Exhibition would have closed and hopefully the nation's sanity restored. With London "filling to [a] preposterous extent," he viewed his temporary relocation in comically heroic terms. It was a daring escape before he was swallowed up by the approaching mob. "I must fly," he told his estate agent William Phillips, "to save myself."

In recent years Broadstairs had become something of a home away from home for Dickens. He first took his family there in 1837, staying in lodgings while he finished *The Pickwick Papers*, and again in 1839 when he rented a house near the Albion Hotel and hired a temporary cook who one day got "remarkably drunk . . . was removed by constables, lay down in front of the house and addressed the multitude for some hours." The following year the family returned to a different house in the same street, where Dickens settled down to write sections of *The Old Curiosity Shop*: "the writing table is set forth with a neatness peculiar to your estimable friend," he told Thomas Beard, "and the furniture in all the rooms has been entirely re-arranged by the same extraordinary character," after which he felt confident enough to start "the old man and the child on their Curiosity-Shop wanderings."

The holiday home he most yearned for was Fort House, which stood prominently on top of a breezy hill overlooking the town, with nothing but a cornfield to interrupt its wide sea views, and a private garden with reassuringly high walls. His first opportunity to rent it came in August 1850, and he arrived before the heavily pregnant Catherine to get it ready for a family holiday that ended up stretching into October. "The house is excellent," he wrote to her. "We were in mighty confusion last night and this morning getting it to rights, but it is now quite orderly and is full of sweet air, sea views and comfort." He continued to rhapsodise about it in other letters: it was an "airy nest" and a "Hermitage," a pastoral refuge in which he could recharge and reflect. The following year he was worried that the house might be harder to rent if "the Broadstairs people" were "made, Expositionally, more than usually sharkish," but fortunately he managed to secure it again at an affordable rent, telling Forster at the start of June that "It is more delightful here than I can express. Corn growing, larks singing, garden full of flowers, fresh air from the sea.—O it is wonderful!"

Early watercolours and photographs show a squat three-storey house originally built as a sea fort, with wide awnings stretched over its windows and two chimney stacks poking out of its roof. It was "bleakly situated," according to one early biographer, and in fact it was later renamed "Bleak House" in honour of its association with Dickens, although only after some substantial remodelling at the start of the twentieth century had almost doubled its size, with the addition of a set of faux crenulations around its skyline that made it look more like a child's illustration of a fort than the real thing. For a while it was run as a museum and then as a boutique hotel, and although it is now in private hands it remains full of Dickensian memorabilia: photographs, cigarette cards, theatre posters, even a sturdy wooden chair that is labelled as having been taken from Dickens's study in Gad's Hill Place. In her final novel *Eva Trout* (1969), Elizabeth Bowen recognised the historical "piety" that led to these effects being assembled, turning the house into a giant altar to fame, and the rest of modern Broadstairs isn't very different. In between the shops selling plastic spades and beady-eyed seagulls waiting to swoop on dropped chips, there are memories of Dickens around almost every corner. Inside the Charles Dickens seafront pub a blackboard promises "Dicken's [*sic*] Nibbles"; there is an Old Curiosity Shop tea room and a Marley's restaurant; a narrow street has been renamed Dickens Walk; and a dusty museum is located in "Dickens House," a seafront cottage that local historians loyally claim as the inspiration behind Betsey Trotwood's home in *David Copperfield*. (Sadly there is no longer any sign of the donkeys she attacks whenever she sees one wandering across the immaculate "patch of green" she has decided is her front garden.)

Broadstairs in 1851 was very different. A visitors' guide published in 1831 characterised the town as "a fashionable place of resort" that was "very deservedly frequented by many families of distinction, by whom it is enlivened in the summer months," but it didn't have much to describe beyond a pier and two libraries. In fact the book's title illustration, a carved panel representing *The Picturesque Pocket Companion to Margate, Ramsgate, Etc.*, offered a good summary of the place that Broadstairs occupied in the minds of its early tourists; compared to the flashy modern resorts located nearby it was merely a restrained afterthought, an *"Etc."* Since then little had changed. In a letter to the Harvard professor Cornelius Conway Felton in 1843, Dickens fleshed out his surroundings with some sketches of the people he had spotted recently—children who "assemble every morning and throw up impossible fortifications which the sea throws down again at high water," and old gentlemen who "look all day through telescopes and never see anything"—but he also acknowledged that the town was "intensely quiet."

For a writer that was probably its main attraction; the poet Samuel Rogers was another regular visitor, and after their first meeting in 1839 he and Dickens saw each other there most years. It was certainly something Dickens welcomed in 1851. "The invaders from all nations have terrified me out of London by their letters of introduction," he explained at the end of June, so he had fled to the coast "where there is a Crystal Palace not made with hands, in which are many wonderful inventions that I never tire of." The biblical allusion ("God dwelleth not in temples made with hands") quietly confirmed his preference for natural sublimity over man-made imitations like Paxton's building.

In "Our Watering Place," a *Household Words* article published at the start of August, Dickens continued to celebrate Broadstairs as a sleepy refuge, where the occasional juggler or ventriloquist might turn up to perform for a "scanty Audience" but even the Wheel of Fortune in the local library was "rusty and dusty, and never turns." By contrast, the town's main attraction was always on the move: the restless jigsaw puzzle of the sea. "Sparkling, heaving, swelling up with life and beauty," for Dickens it offered a happy contrast to the roiling crowds of London. Alongside it there was the "splendid playground" of the beach below his house, which he sometimes used for impromptu pieces of theatre. The artist Eleanor Christian, who met Dickens in Broadstairs in 1840, later recalled that "He pretended to be engaged in a semi-sentimental, semi-jocular, and wholly nonsensical flirtation" with her and a friend, "and we on our side acted mutual jealousy towards each other." It was an improvised drama that ended when one evening he rushed with her to the end of the jetty "and exclaimed in theatrical tones that he intended to hold me there until 'the sad sea waves' should submerge us." She struggled to release herself as the sea rose to her knees, and only after several further declamations from Dickens and a "wrestling match" did she manage to escape back to her friends, "almost crying with vexation, my *only* silk dress clinging clammily round me, and streaming with salt water." He was, she acknowledged, "rather reckless in his fun sometimes," seeming not to realise that in real life, unlike in theatre, there was no magical way for a dress ruined during one performance to reappear as good as new the following night. Dickens also enjoyed gazing at the sea, and "would remain for hours as if entranced; with a rapt, immovable, sphinx-like calm on his face, and that far-off look in his eyes, totally forgetful of everything, and abstracted from us all." Its shifting patterns could also spill over into his conversation—as when he caught a stranger staring at him in the nearby Tivoli Gardens, and asked him "with elaborate politeness" if he was "a native of this place"; when the man stammered that he was not, Dickens apologised and said, "I fancied that I could detect *Broad-stares* on your very face!" The seaside was a place where he could enjoy words behaving like waves, dividing and rejoining in ever-new combinations.

In "How to Spend a Summer Holiday," published in *Household Words* the previous summer, Frederick Knight Hunt had recommended spending a month in a place where a combination of "bracing air," good weather, "cheerful companions," and "increased corporeal exercise" would soon produce improvements in any tourist's physical and mental health. Such advice was fully in line with Dickens's own seaside routines. Already this year the poet Edward FitzGerald had praised those adults who had not yet outgrown the freedom and joy of childhood, the "boy's heart within the man's never ceasing to throb and tremble," and Dickens took a similar approach to his summer holidays. They too were an opportunity to prove that the child was not only the father of the man, as Wordsworth had claimed in his 1802 poem "My Heart Leaps Up," but remained nested inside him like a little Russian doll.

There were long walks across the cliffs, and also activities that were strenuous in a different way, such as "a special memory game which was really hard work by reason of the extra attention and care which is required," and which Dickens played "as if his life depended on the success." For many of these activities he was joined by his extended family, including his widowed mother and brother Fred, as well as assorted friends and colleagues. "Why can't you come down next Saturday (bringing work) and go back with me on Wednesday for the *Copperfield* banquet?" Dickens wrote to Forster in June. The suggestion that his friend should bring work was a reminder that Dickens also expected to spend part of each day sitting at the desk in his small study on the first floor of Fort House, carefully spreading his inky fishing net over articles for *Household Words* and dealing with "the rolling of a sea of correspondence which always flows and never ebbs." It may also have served as a timely warning that a holiday with him didn't always feel like much of a holiday. "Bar-leaping, bowling, and quoits were among the games carried on with the greatest ardour," Forster noted of an earlier summer he had spent with Dickens after the completion of *Nicholas Nickleby*, "and in sustained energy, what is called keeping it up, Dickens certainly distanced every competitor. Even the lighter recreations of battledore and bagatelle were pursued with relentless activity." He made a similar impression on strangers. The Irish writer and politician Justin McCarthy, who first met him in London the following year, remembered that "Dickens rather frightened me . . . His manner was full of energy; there was something physically overpowering about it . . . the very vehemence of his cheery good-humour rather bore one down."

Dickens was somewhat less cheerful about the evidence of other holidaymakers enjoying themselves, especially if they distracted him from his thoughts. "Mr. Dickens was a very nice sort of gentleman," according to the wife of the local coastguard, "but he didn't like a noise," and whenever children played too boisterously near the coastguard station he would ask her husband "to take the children away" or "to keep the people quiet." Occasionally there were also domestic disturbances: when Forster came to visit Fort House, he snored so loudly at night that Dickens could not sleep; after wandering around the house he ended up waking Georgina to keep him company.

Several of the people he met in Broadstairs held on to memories of him like postcards: Dickens trying to avoid being recognised at places of entertainment by "not venturing into the glare of the lights, as his face was too well known"; Dickens escaping the attentions of other tourists by walking to the end of the jetty in the evening, where he took out a pocket comb to accompany Fred's whistling while the rest of the party danced a quadrille. And the longer he lived away from London, the more suspicious he grew of what he had left behind.

Despite his polite public recognition of the Crystal Palace, which he referred to in his speech to the Gardeners' Benevolent Association on 9 June as a "wonderful building" and an "enduring temple to [Paxton's] honour, and to the energy, the talent, and the resources of Englishmen," privately he admitted to Wills the following month that "I have always had an instinctive feeling against the Exhibition, of a faint, inexplicable sort," confidently predicting that the reaction of the public would eventually be one of "boredom and lassitude." By August he was feeling even less tolerant, telling Wills that although he thought an article on "The May Festival at Starnberg" was "very good," the opening paragraph would benefit from being trimmed: "for the Lord's love don't let us have any allusion to the Great Exhibition."

In fact there were several good reasons for his "inexplicable" antagonism. The first is that if Paxton's design "glazed over" a large section of Hyde Park, as Wills had noted in his article "The Private History of the Palace of Glass," it also encouraged his contemporaries to glaze over when it came to more serious issues. The May issue of the *Household Narrative* had already drawn unfavourable comparisons between the "remarkable building" in Hyde Park and the "crowded workshops," "damp cellars" and "stifling garrets" of the workers who built it. Dickens probably also had some doubts about the building itself. While the Crystal Palace undeniably had a certain chilly grandeur, his own preference was always for buildings that could be appreciated on a human scale. In Volume 1 of *The Stones of Venice*, Ruskin had used Dickens's description of the thief who steals Dora's dog in *David Copperfield*, where he is reported to be a man possessing legs like the balustrades of a bridge, to criticise the real balustrades of Renaissance architecture, and this closely echoed Dickens's own pleasure in mixing up buildings and people. At its simplest, this involves scenes in which he briefly jerks buildings into life, producing doorknockers that leer or windows that stare glassily down the street. More elaborately worked examples include the houses that have grown to resemble their owners. In *Nicholas Nickleby*, Arthur Gride lives in a house that is as "yellow and shrivelled" as himself, keeping him from the daylight just as he hoards his money, while Mr. Dombey's house slowly collapses after his son dies: the furniture shrinks, mould covers the walls and mysterious piles of dust appear, as if sympathetically echoing what is happening to Paul's body. In such passages someone's house is much more than just a physical shelter; it is an extension of themselves, like an additional skin or exoskeleton. The Crystal Palace offered no such imaginative opportunities. As Ruskin had already noticed, it was merely a glossy container for material objects rather than a full architectural expression of human life. Compared to the sort of buildings Dickens liked, it was as dead as a doornail.

Nor was Dickens likely to have enjoyed the fact that thousands of different exhibits were on show. Earlier in the year an article in *Household*

Words had expressed some concern that the Exhibition would prove to be overwhelming: "a rich assortment of objects piled about in helpless confusion," like a badly organised bazaar. That would hardly have satisfied Dickens's love of order. He told one correspondent that he kept his ideas "on different shelves of my brain, ready ticketed and labelled, to be brought out when I want them," and when talking about the mysterious workings of memory he referred to "the pigeon-holes of my brain." By the time the Crystal Palace opened its doors, all the exhibits had been sorted into a different set of pigeonholes: the four main classes of Raw Materials, Machinery, Manufactures and Fine Arts, into which everything from lumps of coal to carved cherry stones was expected to fit. Yet even visitors armed with the official catalogue were sometimes baffled by the variety of objects on display, and that is likely to have been a particular cause of concern for Dickens.

In *Martin Chuzzlewit*, one clue that Montague Tigg is not to be trusted can be found in the acquisitive jumble of his "splendid" Pall Mall lodgings, which are decorated with "pictures, copies from the antique in alabaster and marble, china vases, lofty mirrors, crimson hangings of the richest silk, gilded carvings, luxurious couches, glistening cabinets inlaid with precious woods; costly toys of every sort in negligent abundance." Confronted by this sort of list, it is tempting to apply the phrase "negligent abundance" to Dickens's writing as well, but there is an important difference. Novels have characters and plots to organise themselves around, and after Prince Albert's early struggles to get his project off the ground both of these were significantly absent from the Great Exhibition.

"The Catalogue's Account of Itself," contributed by Henry Morley to *Household Words* at the end of August, centres on the catalogue's defence against the accusation that it is "a bore," pointing out that it contains the descriptions of "some fifteen thousand authors; most of them authors for the first time." But these snapshot accounts were chiefly concerned with the materials and function of each item rather than their history. They were new objects for a new age. Such descriptions were very different to Dickens's early sketches like "Meditations in

Monmouth Street," in which he had described the piles of secondhand clothes and other objects that slowly accumulated in junk shops. What particularly fascinated him was the history that such items carried around with them, the slow ticking of an invisible clock that accompanied each threadbare dress or broken chair. When the narrator of *Master Humphrey's Clock* confesses that he has become "attached to the inanimate objects that people my chamber," his sense that they are "old and constant friends" rather than "mere chairs and tables which a little money could replace" might look sentimental to modern eyes, but it is fully in line with Dickens's own views. By contrast, his later distrust of the Veneerings in *Our Mutual Friend* is indicated by the fact that everything they own is "bran-new," from "the hall chairs with the new coat of arms" to the "grand pianoforte with the new action." Just as all their furniture is varnished and highly polished, so "what was observable in the furniture, was observable in the Veneerings—the surface smelt a little too much of the workshop and was a trifle sticky."

Dickens was similarly wary of household items that were presented behind glass, adding a spurious glamour that tried to fool the public into mistaking their true purpose. In *Martin Chuzzlewit*, when Tom Pinch goes window-shopping, he gazes at the "great glowing bottles" in chemists' shops which remind him of both medicines and perfumes, and the tailors' waistcoat patterns "which by some strange transformation always looked amazing there, and never appeared at all like the same thing anywhere else." Such items are a warning to the all-too-trusting Tom not to believe in appearances, but they also suggest another reason for Dickens's suspicion of the Crystal Palace. Even though officially nothing was for sale, walking up and down the building's aisles was like window-shopping on a grand scale. Nor could the catalogue fully capture what some middle-class visitors had come to look at. That is because few of the objects on display were as fascinating as the visitors themselves—an idea neatly captured in one cartoon that depicted crowds of well-dressed men and women preening themselves in "the looking-glass department" of the Exhibition. "The high-paying portion of the public go to look at each other and be looked at," a *Punch* journalist slyly noted, "while the shilling visitors go to gain instruction from what they see."

Dickens also gained instruction from what he saw at the Exhibition, although not from what was officially on display. Visiting Hyde Park again on 11 July, he became far more interested in the sight of a hundred children from one of the schools sponsored by Miss Coutts. After crossing the main road by Kensington Gate, where they wandered between the clattering wheels of coaches perfectly "undisturbed in mind," they entered the Crystal Palace "and went tottering and staring all over the place—the greater part wetting their forefingers, and drawing a wavy pattern over every accessible object." Only after they returned home was it discovered that one child had got lost and ended up in Hammersmith; having passed the night in the local workhouse, he was picked up by his mother, where-upon he asked her when it would all be over. "It was a Great Exhibition, he said, but he thought it long." There is no doubt who the hero of this story is supposed to be. As so often in Dickens's writing, a child innocently sees through the convention and cant that adults have been pretending is the truth.

Looking back on his summer holiday at the end of the year, Dickens rue-fully compared himself to Timon of Athens in his self-imposed exile, reminding the traveller and archaeologist Austen Henry Layard that they had promised "to be more intimate after All Nations should have departed from Hyde Park, and I should be able to emerge from my cave on the sea-shore." Yet although Fort House stood proudly isolated on a headland, over the summer months Dickens had hardly been as cut off as Shakespeare's hero. Broadstairs was indeed "far away from London noise and smoke," as George Eliot would acknowledge the following year, but in practical terms it was much closer than it had been just a few years before. The steamers of the Margate Steam-Boat Company regularly chugged up the Thames to St. Katherine's Dock, and the South Eastern Railway operated trains to London via Canterbury from Margate station, which had opened five years earlier. Such modern transport links meant that whenever Dickens travelled to Wellington Street for the regular editorial meetings that were required to keep the "great humming-top" of *Household Words* going, his journey now took a few hours rather than a day or more.

Like any modern commute, things didn't always run smoothly. On 12 July, Dickens published "A Narrative of Extraordinary Suffering" in *Household Words*, describing in mock epic detail what happens to "Mr. Lost" when he tries to travel to and from London after putting his trust in a recent copy of *Bradshaw's Monthly Railway Guide*. Unfortunately its timetables turn out to be full of misprints and misinformation. After a comedy of errors involving blocked lines and recommended changes of train that are impossible to make, he is last seen sitting in the Euston Square Hotel "continually turning over the leaves of a small, dog's-eared quarto volume with a yellow cover, and babbling in a plaintive voice, 'BRADSHAW, BRADSHAW.'" Yet by comparison with the stagecoaches of Dickens's youth, the very existence of a railway guide provided further evidence of how interconnected the country was becoming.

This did not stop at the country's ports or even at the furthest reaches of the Empire. In "Wings of Wire," published in *Household Words* in December 1850, Frederick Knight Hunt had celebrated the new technology of the telegraph. In an age of "express trains, painless operations, crystal palaces" and every other modern marvel, he enthused, no invention was more exciting than "the strange machine that enables one side of a country to speak with another, regardless of the intervening hundreds of miles of hills, streams, and plains." By the end of this year more than two thousand miles of telegraph had been laid across Britain, much of it running alongside the new railway tracks, and soon this network of humming copper wires would be extended throughout the country. As Hunt explained, "One wire dipped into the earth, and starting from some great, central point, say London, with other wires spreading from it, may run in all directions, as the nerves of the human body run from the brain all over the frame." And it didn't stop there. Shakespeare's Puck had boasted that he could "put a girdle round about the earth in forty minutes," but once telegraph wires were laid around the globe the "Spirit of Electro-Magnetism" would be able to "fill the wires with itself, and make the circuit complete, through the intervening earth, eight times in a second!"

Just a few months after Knight's article was published, this dream appeared to be edging ever closer to reality. No fewer than thirteen telegraph machines were on display in the Crystal Palace, based on a variety of different designs, but all offering the same promise of a world in which people could communicate with each other almost instantaneously, even if physically they were hundreds of miles apart. Not that the new technology made older forms of communication obsolete. Matthew Arnold's poem "Dover Beach" was probably begun on his honeymoon in June this year, shortly before the world's first submarine telegraph cable, armoured with iron and insulated by a gutta-percha casing, was successfully laid between Dover and Calais. Arnold, however, used his verse to create much shorter, tighter lines of communication. "Ah, love, let us be true / To one another!" his speaker cries, as his voice reaches out into the unknown across a line break and stumbles upon a rhyme ("true / To"), like someone who declares their love and is startled to discover their feelings are reciprocated. But the telegraph went much further. As Richard Horne put it in a poem published in *Household Words* in June, this new technology could turn out to be "The Great Peace-Maker," because it allowed "thought-swift messengers" to pass along the ocean bed "Till England whispers India in the ear, / America—north, south—from pole to pole— / And words of friendship may pass round the world"—a vision of the future in which Horne's dashes mimicked both the snaking cables of the telegraph and the speed of the messages they relayed. A few years later Dickens experimented with a handwritten version of the same idea, using his memorandum book to jot down a plan for a story that would bring "two strongly contrasted places and strongly contrasted sets of people" into contact with each other by means of an electric message: "Describe the message—*be* the message—flashing along through space—over the earth, and under the sea." It was Prince Albert's dream of *"the unity of mankind"* being brought to life with a few strokes of the pen.

Dickens was also using the pages of *Household Words* to celebrate some of the other ways in which the world was becoming a smaller place. In two articles on "Short Cuts Across the Globe" published in 1850, Harry Wills had explained how the projected Panama and Suez Canals would speed up trade and improve "the mutual relations of civilised states," because such routes also brought man "in closer communion with his distant brotherhood, and results in concord, prosperity, and peace." By 1851, visitors to London had the option of travelling around the world even more quickly, and without ever having to leave the city. For example, one afternoon this summer Charles and Emma Darwin chose to take a day trip from Southampton to Calcutta by visiting the Gallery of Illustration in Regent Street, where the naval officer Thomas Waghorn's journey to India had been reconstructed in a diorama, a series of scenes painted on a brightly lit backdrop that slowly revolved across the darkened stage like a primitive form of home cinema. An advertisement in the *Athenaeum* outlined the route that audience members would take, vicariously travelling across the Bay of Biscay, and on to Gibraltar, Malta, Algiers, Cairo, Suez, the Red Sea, Ceylon, Madras, and "the magnificent Mausoleum of the Taj Mahal, the exterior by moonlight, the beautiful gateway and the gorgeous interior, lighted by crystal and golden lamps." It was only one of many dioramas and panoramas on show this year that promised to open a window onto distant parts of the world. There were also attempts to cast fresh light on more familiar landscapes: at the Gallery of Illustration, alongside the passage-to-India diorama there was one entitled *Our Native Land* that attempted to depict what an advertisement described as "the amusements and employments of a country life during the several varieties of spring, summer, autumn, and winter," all accompanied by poetic recitations and excerpts from Beethoven's Pastoral Symphony played on the pianoforte.

But in this Great Exhibition year it was the promise of exotic travels at one remove that attracted the largest crowds. At the Egyptian Hall in Piccadilly there was a triple bill: a panorama featuring a trip up the Nile, another depicting the overland route to Oregon and California that had recently been revised to take account of the gold rush, and a diorama of the Holy Land that began with the wandering of the Israelites and ended "among the scenes consecrated by the Saviour's presence." In "Some Account of an Extraordinary Traveller," published in *Household Words* the previous April, Dickens had already described what the customers of such attractions could expect. Here he had some fun at the expense of Mr. Booley, a short, fat, bald resident of Islington who undertakes "immense journies" on his own. Whether he is dodging alligators in the American South, or serenely voyaging past the Egyptian pyramids, he never has to change out of his English clothes or even shrug off his English accent. "When I was a boy, such travelling would have been impossible," Mr. Booley explains, but "It is a delightful characteristic of these times, that new and cheap means are continually being devised, for conveying the results of actual experience, to those who are unable to obtain such experiences for themselves; and to bring them within the reach of the people." His position as Dickens's unofficial spokesman is confirmed by his conclusion:

> Some of the best results of actual travel are suggested by such means
> to those whose lot it is to stay at home. New worlds open out to
> them, beyond their little worlds, and widen their range of reflection,
> information, sympathy, and interest. The more man knows of man,
> the better for the common brotherhood among us all.

The fictitious Mr. Booley was only one of many Londoners who were imagining what it would feel like to go out into the world, just as the world was coming to London. The most bizarre example of this trend in 1851 was Wyld's Great Globe, a brick rotunda topped by a zinc-ribbed dome in London's Leicester Square that opened on 2 June. Built on a scale of ten miles to the inch, it allowed visitors to climb a series of staircases to four viewing platforms, from which they could inspect a giant spherical model of the entire globe, where plaster-moulded continents were surrounded by stationary blue seas, and red-tipped volcanoes belched out plumes of cotton-wool smoke. This new tourist attraction also made its way into *Household Words*. In July, Henry Morley's article "The Globe in a Square"

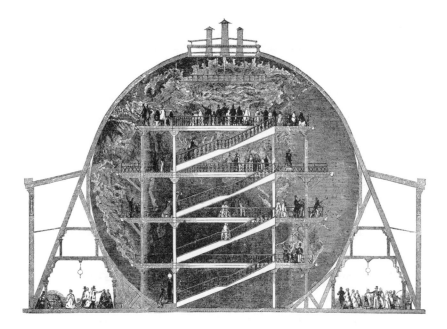

described what it was like to wander around edited highlights of the world "boxed up in a diameter of sixty feet," and Morley also praised the ambition of the scheme, concluding that "Great Globes like this should be erected wherever there exist large populations that have intellects to satisfy."

By contrast, Dickens's movements this summer were far less leisurely, and on occasion were noticeably fraught. "All the Nations of the Earth brought letters of introduction to me in London," he told Augustus Tracey, who was Governor of the Westminster House of Correction and one of the officials who recommended women for Urania Cottage, "and there was nothing for it but Flight." This impulse to flee hadn't been wholly satisfied by his relocation to Broadstairs. Earlier in the summer he had also travelled overnight from London Bridge station to Paris by the South Eastern Railway's new "Double Special Express Service." He later wrote about his experiences in "A Flight," published in *Household Words* in August, where he tried to describe what he referred to in a letter as "that queer sensation born of quick travelling." It wasn't unusual at the time to compare travelling by train to flying. As early as 1830, the actress Fanny Kemble took a train from Liverpool to Manchester, writing that "When I closed my eyes this sensation of flying was quite delightful, and strange beyond description," while several European railway companies would later adopt the symbol of a winged wheel as their trademark. Nor was it uncommon to develop this loose analogy into more extravagant flights of fancy: in 1867 the journalist John Hollingshead celebrated the fact that a train could carry him to his destination "swifter than the genii bore Aladdin from city to city." In fact, according to Dickens's article, one of the most charming features of this cross-Channel journey is how quickly it has become a matter of routine. Whenever one of his fellow passengers becomes flustered he is instantly soothed by an official explaining that there is "Plenty of time . . . No hurry." Meanwhile the patterns of Dickens's prose echo this sense that he and his fellow passengers are human cogs in a different kind of well-oiled machine: "For Paris, Sir? No hurry . . . No hurry, ladies and gentlemen, for Paris. No hurry whatever!"

Whereas some Victorian passengers viewed this surrender of control with alarm (Ruskin complained that the railway "transmutes a man from a traveler into a living parcel"), it is something Dickens welcomes. Not only does it allow him to marvel at how little he has to do ("Something snorts for me, something shrieks for me . . . and away I go"), it also gives him more time to scrutinise his fellow passengers. Yet once the train starts to move, the style of his account becomes far more unsettled. While many railway guides of the period described the famous buildings and other sights that could be glimpsed out of a train window, neatly lining them up on the page like a collection of doll's houses, Dickens recognises that the actual experience of travelling by train dislocates the scenery into a series of blurry snapshots:

> Bang, bang! A double-barrelled Station! Now a wood, now a bridge, now a landscape, now a cutting, now a —Bang! a single-barrelled Station—there was a cricket match somewhere with two white tents, and then four flying cows, then turnips—now, the wires of the electric telegraph are all alive, and spin, and blur their edges, and go up

and down, and make the intervals between each other most irregu-
lar: contracting and expanding in the strangest manner. Now we
slacken. With a screwing, and a grinding, and a smell of water
thrown on ashes, now we stop!

Here fragments of writing pile up on the page, and Dickens switches
between present ("now") and past ("then") tenses in trying to capture the
sensation of things going too fast to be grasped while they are actually
happening. The result is a passage in which his syntax starts to behave like
the telegraph wires he sees out of the train window, as his sentences too
find themselves "contracting and expanding in the strangest manner." Far
from being satisfied with the "formal railway line of sentence" that Virginia
Woolf would later identify as a key feature of Victorian fiction, Dickens
recognises that when it comes to recounting the disorientating experience
of modern travel, some trains of thought might benefit from being
rerouted.

Although Dickens's restlessness this summer reflected his more general dislike of stagnation, such activity also worried him. One of his
literary heroes, Walter Scott, had continued trying to write his way out of
debt even when he was close to death, and Dickens had long been haunted
by the "pathetic description" in John Gibson Lockhart's 1838 biography of
Scott's pen falling from his hand as the tears coursed silently down his
cheeks. This fear took on a specific shape after he had visited Abbotsford
in 1841, where he saw Scott's clothes displayed in "a vile glass case," including "an old white hat, which seemed to be tumbled and bent and broken
by the uneasy, purposeless wandering hither and thither of his heavy
head." But Dickens's description came ten years later, in a letter written in
July 1851, and it seems that Scott was particularly in his thoughts during
these summer months of moving between one temporary home and
another. The copyrights to Scott's novels had been sold in March for
£15,000, considerably less than his publisher had paid for them, and this
would have confirmed Dickens's fears about the fragile nature of literary
success. Even Scott's old white hat may have been an extra cause of anxi-

ety, as a white bowler hat was Dickens's own preferred form of summer headgear, and it would have been fully in keeping with his tendency to project possible futures for himself if he had borrowed Scott's fate and imagined it as his own.

Two weeks before Dickens published "A Flight," he realised why he was feeling so unsettled. "I begin to be pondering afar off, a new book," he told Miss Coutts on 17 August. "Violent restlessness, and vague ideas of going I don't know where, I don't know why, are the present symptoms of the disorder." It was an early sign of his dawning awareness that he wasn't running away from something. In fact he was moving towards it— gradually edging his way closer to the writing of a novel in which he would remind his readers that telegrams and railways weren't the only ways in which they were all connected.

Dickens's restlessness hadn't been helped by his failure to secure a new London home. Earlier this year his search had uncovered several more candidates: No. 1 Cambridge Terrace, which he liked "exceedingly" but thought the ground rent too high; a house in Highgate on which he was outbid by a rival; and Balmoral House, overlooking Regent's Park and close to the canal, which he thought "decidedly good" and wanted to look around again with Henry Austin "to consider how a study of good size could best be built out from the existing villa." All had proven to be dead ends. This would have been annoying for anyone, but it was especially so for a writer like Dickens, who often seemed to invest as much emotional energy in houses as he did in the people who lived in them.

"Most people amuse themselves, at one time or other of their lives, by fancying what sort of house they would like to live in," begins an article by Harriet Martineau published in *Household Words* the following year. Dickens's detailed interest in his own home can be seen in an inventory of Devonshire Terrace that he compiled with Catherine in May 1844, shortly before he let the house for a year while the whole family travelled to Italy; the list for the ground-floor library alone included a "French polished mahogany revolving study table, with drawers," a mahogany bookstand, a rosewood letter box, eleven plaster casts, a Brussels carpet, two sets of white curtains flanked by yellow silk damask curtains ("gilt cornice, fringe and trimmings complete"), and "a spring recumbent reading chair, with desk and candle sconce," in addition to a long list of books. He was equally interested in the homes of other people, as his work for Urania Cottage and his fundraising efforts for the Guild this year had shown.

This also reflected a current trend. One of the Great Exhibition attractions that Prince Albert had paid for personally was a model lodging house, designed by the architect Henry Roberts to provide accommodation for four working-class families. Constructed out of hollow bricks for improved heat and sound insulation, with large windows and a fashionable Gothic roofline, this experimental building was erected in the grounds of the Cavalry Barracks, Hyde Park, by the Society for Improving the Condition of the Labouring Classes, with more than 250,000 visitors coming to inspect a layout that managed to squeeze a living room, kitchen/scullery, three bedrooms and a toilet into each apartment. (The building was later dismantled and rebuilt on the edge of Kennington Park, where it can still be seen today.) Dickens visited these "Model Houses for Families" on 27 May, and a few weeks later he published Henry Morley's article "Mr. Bendigo Buster on the Model Cottages" in *Household Words*, which described the dwellings in approving detail, albeit from the perspective of a blustering landlord who complains that "Their object is to defraud owners of existing cottage property, by offering to tenants a superior article at the same price." For Dickens this was a dream that lingered. In February 1853 he returned to the slum district of Bermondsey to investigate possible sites for a model lodging house, which he planned to advertise in handbills encouraging any local landlord to visit "for the purpose of shewing him at how small an expence he can improve the houses he now lets—of giving him friendly advice—and even of assisting him to do what is right, if he will only do it." But in the summer of 1851 Dickens still had his own house to put in order.

Tavistock House.

Finally, on 25 July, he signed a forty-five-year lease on Tavistock House, a five-storey property that was on the western edge of a grand terrace of three town houses in Bloomsbury. Created by the subdivision of a Regency mansion, these houses had originally been built as part of the Bedford estate on the eastern side of Tavistock Square. Compared to Devonshire Terrace, Dickens's new address was a decided step up the property ladder: a carriage sweep led into a shared front court, and a set of trim iron railings in front of each town house added an extra air of respectability. Tavistock House had formerly been the residence of Dickens's friend, the artist Frank Stone, who told him in April that he was about to relinquish the lease. By mid-July Dickens had asked Austin to visit the house, which

Dickens judged to be "in the dirtiest of all possible conditions," and give a surveyor's opinion on "the likelihood of the roof tumbling into the kitchen, or the walls becoming a sort of brick and mortar minced veal." The house was large and "decidedly cheap," and Dickens thought it "might be made very handsome." Negotiations went on for several days, with Dickens offering successively £1,300 ("which I make without any idea of bargaining for the property"), and then giving "carte blanche" for up to £1,500. Finally, on 23 July, he wrote jubilantly to Stone that he had reached an agreement and instructed his solicitor William Loaden to purchase the lease for £1,542. Tavistock House was his.

Immediately he started to plan a detailed scheme of renovations, after persuading Stone to move to Devonshire Terrace for the next couple of months while Dickens's own family remained in Broadstairs. As soon as the house was empty, Dickens set about bringing it up to his usual high standards, commissioning Austin to oversee the works and installing a servant to deal with day-to-day enquiries. In early September he became concerned that he was running out of time, and sent a long letter to Austin that was punctuated by a refrain worrying that nothing was happening as quickly as he had hoped:

> I am in that state of mind which you may (once) have seen described in the newspapers, as "bordering on distraction"—the house given up to me, the fine weather going on (soon to break, I dare say), the Painting season oozing away, my new book waiting to be born, and
>   NO WORKMEN ON THE PREMISES
> along of my not hearing from you!! I have torn all my hair off, and constantly beat my unoffending family.
>
> Wild notions have occurred to me of sending in my own Plumber to do the Drains. Then I remember that you have probably written to prepare *your* man, and restrain my audacious hand. Then Stone presents himself, with a most exasperatingly mysterious visage, and says that a Rat has appeared in the Kitchen, and it's his opinion (Stone's—not the Rat's) that the Drains "want compo-ing."—for the

use of which explicit language, I could fell him without remorse. In my horrible desire to "compo" everything, the very postman becomes my enemy because he brings no letter from you, and, in short, I don't see what's to become of me unless I hear from you tomorrow. Which I have not the least expectation of doing.

Going over the house again, I have materially altered the plans—abandoned conservatory and front balcony—decided to make Stone's Painting Room the drawing room (it is nearly six inches higher than the room below) to carry the entrance passage right through the house to a back door leading to the garden, and so reduce the once-intended drawing room, now school-room, to a manageable size—making a door of communication between the new drawing room and the study. Curtains and Carpets, on a scale of awful splendor and magnitude are already in preparation, and still—still—

NO WORKMEN ON THE PREMISES

His letter crossed with one from Austin recommending a builder: William Cubitt of Gray's Inn Road, whose brother Thomas had developed the northern side of Tavistock Square in 1825, and who would be given a month to complete the renovations. He was an exclusive choice: having previously been responsible for building the eastern front of Buckingham Palace, his other projects in 1851 included the completion of the Queen's summer residence, Osborne House on the Isle of Wight. Dickens told Austin that Catherine was delighted; after being "in a great state of despair" she was "greatly recovered since the receipt of your note this morning, and begins to think we *shall* have a house after all." Dickens was equally relieved, and before long he was firing off letters in all directions from Fort House: to the carpenters William Smith in Tottenham Court Road, to arrange for the regilding of mirrors and the exact positioning of some glass bookshelves in the drawing room; to Harry Wills, for a gardener to visit Devonshire Terrace and "see whether the greater part of the shrubs &c in the garden, can be transplanted"; and to Austin, repeatedly, whenever he wanted a sounding board for ideas that ranged from where to position bells for summoning servants to his bedroom, to the need for a window in the bathroom that could be fully opened "for the sake of fresh air always pouring in." Soon these plans had taken over his life, or at least he enjoyed pretending that they had. "The gravy at dinner has a taste of glue in it," he wrote to Austin from Broadstairs. "I smell paint in the sea."

His impending arrival in Tavistock House would also be a homecoming of a different sort. Tavistock Square shared its name with Tavistock Street, another part of the Bedford estate, which was situated between the Strand and Covent Garden, and is where the hero lives in Dickens's first published story "A Dinner at Poplar Walk." As we are warned about this character's "love of order" at the start of the story, it is likely that his "first floor flat in Tavistock-street" is far neater than the suburban house of his cousin that he visits, where a dog steals bread and butter from the table and devours it "with the buttered side next to the carpet."

Since then a great deal had changed in Dickens's life—he was now a writer who could purchase splendid carpets as well as joke about them—yet even now his past could ambush him unawares. Something that had particularly unsettled him when he was a boy, during the time when Warren's blacking warehouse moved from Old Hungerford Stairs to Chandos Street, was the demand for him to work alongside another boy, Bob Fagin, in a window overlooking Bedford Street. Here passers-by could admire their dexterity as they covered small earthenware bottles of Warren's product with pieces of oiled paper, tied them round with string, and then pasted on a printed label—a living window display. Over the years Dickens had managed to master this anxiety of being exhibited in public through his theatrical performances, which allowed him to transform his natural shyness into a form of showmanship. This shyness could still take over when he didn't have any footlights to hide behind. The daughter of Lord John Russell remembered that Dickens was "conspicuous" on his visits to their family home, "owing to wearing a pink shirt front embroidered with white," but sometimes "he would be seized with a fit of shyness or modesty" and slip away directly after dinner, so that "people who came in later, having been asked to meet him would all be saying: 'But where is Mr. Charles Dickens?'" But Dickens didn't have to attend formal dinner parties to know what it felt like to be treated as public property. As his experience of being subjected to *Broad-stares* in Broadstairs had shown him, it simply wasn't always possible to control who was looking at him or what they were looking for. "We sit in our new house all day, trying to touch the hearts of the workmen by our melancholy looks, and are patched with oil and lime and haggard with white lead," he told Richard Watson in a letter at the end of October. "All the doors are always open; and there is no repose or privacy, as Irish Labourers stare in through the very slates."

AUTUMN

Home

DESIGN FOR THE CONVERSION OF THE EXHIBITION-BUILDING INTO A TOWER 1000 FEET HIGH.
By Mr. C. BURTON, Architect.

D ickens wasn't the only writer who would attempt a new kind of novel this year. Published in Britain on Saturday 18 October as *The Whale*, and in America three weeks later as *Moby-Dick; or, The Whale*, Herman Melville's latest work would turn out to be as elusive in its meaning as the creature Captain Ahab pursues through its pages. A globetrotting revenge tragedy, an intimate epic, a sailor's yarn that kept turning into an encyclopaedia of seafaring . . . it was a whole library squeezed into just three volumes. The *Britannia*'s reviewer confessed, "we are at a loss to determine in which category of works of amusement to place it," while the *Spectator* was equally baffled, describing it as "a singular medley of naval observation, magazine article writing, satiric reflection upon the conventionalisms of civilised life, and rhapsody run mad."

Not all of this was Melville's fault. *The Whale* was published in London by Richard Bentley, whose periodical *Bentley's Miscellany* had been edited by Dickens between 1837 and 1839, before a protracted series of contract renegotiations led to an acrimonious falling-out between the two men. In Dickens's caustic characterisation Bentley was "the Burlington Street Brigand," a publisher who robbed authors of the income that was rightfully theirs, but in the case of *The Whale* he also deprived Melville of something even more fundamental to a writer: his words. Although the book had been set in type in New York over the summer, and the proof sheets sent to London in September, when the first edition appeared in British bookshops the following month it was substantially different to the version Melville had originally written. Bentley or another editor had cut or reworked dozens of passages, removing jokes, obscenities, Americanisms and examples of blasphemy, and they had also failed to include the epilogue in which the narrator ("Call me Ishmael") explains how he escaped from the wreck of the *Pequod,* so that mysteriously the story now appeared to be narrated by someone who had not survived to tell the tale. Two chapters that avoided the worst of this editorial meddling were Melville's account of how a dead whale was stripped of its flesh by the ship's crew, and his revelation that looking closely at its skin revealed the "numerous rude scratches" that were inflicted on it during a whale's bumpy passage around the world. Both chapters appear to have been read by Bentley and his team as a coded set of instructions. As they worked through the proof sheets of Melville's novel, cutting up some parts and crossing out others, they treated *The Whale* very like a whale.

Three days earlier, on Wednesday 15 October, the Great Exhibition had shut its doors for the final time. During the closing ceremony, a choir sang the first verse of the national anthem, and a list of award-winners was presented by Lord Canning on behalf of the prize juries, before Prince Albert rose from an ivory throne to make a speech in which he expressed his hope that "the interchange of knowledge, resulting from the meeting of enlightened people in friendly rivalry, may be dispersed far and wide over distant lands; and thus, by showing our mutual dependence upon each other, be a happy means of promoting unity among nations, and peace and good-will among the various races of mankind." It was a good speech, although bad weather meant that many in the audience heard little beyond the steady thrumming of rain on the glass roof. Then there was another verse of the national anthem, a prayer of thanksgiving led by the Bishop of London, a burst of the Hallelujah Chorus, and by 12:30 p.m. it was all over. It was a surprisingly downbeat ending to what had been widely celebrated as the greatest festival the world had ever seen. In fact a report in *The Times* the following day referred to the ceremony as a "necessary termination," which was chiefly a reference to the fact that the Great Exhibition had come to its scheduled conclusion, but also made it sound oddly like an old horse being shot to avoid a slower, more painful demise.

Over the previous months, the meaning of the Crystal Palace had become almost as hard to pin down as Melville's whale. It was a temporary structure that had taken up a seemingly permanent place in the public imagination; a container that had become as famous as any of its contents. Nor was its future at all certain. Since its successful opening, what nobody had been able to agree upon was whether it should be retained in its current location, dismantled and rebuilt elsewhere, or simply demolished once the Exhibition came to an end. Paxton had led a campaign to turn the building into an elegant winter garden full of plants and statuary, thereby returning it to its glasshouse origins, and in June he had published *What is to Become of the Crystal Palace?*, a pamphlet in which he sketched out his ideas. He was supported by Henry Cole, writing under the pseudonym "Denarius" (a penny), in another pamphlet, *Shall We Keep the Crystal Palace and have Riding and Walking in all Weathers among Flowers, Fountains, and Sculpture?*, a question that Cole answered enthusiastically in the affirmative. However, both men were opposed by other pamphleteers, such as "Greville" in *An Answer to "What is to Become of the Crystal Palace?,"* who drew attention to the "solemn compact" that had been made between the Treasury and the Commissioners of Woods and Forests concerning the building's removal, a decision that still had Prince Albert's support. Finally, on 29 April 1852, following a parliamentary inquiry, the House of Commons agreed that the building would have to be dismantled, and the following month Paxton and his financial backers launched the Crystal Palace Company to rebuild it on the summit of Sydenham Hill in southeast London.

But as the 25,000 or so people who had attended the closing ceremony on 15 October filed out of the building into a wet and muddy Hyde Park, it was still far from clear whether they would ever be allowed to return, and what sight would greet them if they did. Other suggestions for what to do with the building ranged from the boldly imaginative to the spectacularly eccentric. British architect Charles Burton proposed stacking sections of Paxton's modular design on top of each other to create a tapering "Prospect Tower" fifty storeys high, with "vertical railways" that would transport visitors to an observation deck in the clouds. (A watercolour showed the tower soaring above a pleasure garden containing both

Stonehenge and the Sphinx, which suggested that Burton's scheme was more an architectural fantasy than a serious contribution to town planning.) Sir Titus Salt, the Bradford industrialist, visited Hyde Park with his engineer to see whether he might be able to incorporate parts of the Crystal Palace into the giant textile mill he was constructing in his new model town of Saltaire. *The Times* wondered if the whole building should instead be moved across the Thames to a strip of land in Battersea that attracted boisterous working-class crowds, where it "might be made the medium of elevating the rude and uncivilised tastes of those swarms who, during the summer months especially, betake themselves to the river for amusement."

Meanwhile *Punch* offered several waggish counter-suggestions. As well as picturing John Bull surrounded by tropical vegetation and happily reading a volume of *Paxton's Flower Garden*, a lavishly illustrated work published between 1850 and 1853, it argued that the Crystal Palace should be pulled down because otherwise "it will be a perpetual source of temptation to the little boys to break the windows." Alternatively, according to a spoof letter supposedly sent in by a fashionable young woman who refused to wear a waterproof bonnet, perhaps it should be retained as "a large glass Parasol, under which we can laugh at the rain that is pattering over our heads, and snap our fingers at our wretched English climate." This smuggled in an extra joke, because the roof of the Crystal Palace had never been made perfectly watertight, and during the closing ceremony some of the crowd had to put up ordinary umbrellas to keep themselves dry as the rain hammered down outside.

Earlier in the summer, *Household Words* had added its own voice to the developing controversy. On 19 July, in "What is Not Clear About the Crystal Palace," Henry Morley argued that whatever happened to the Palace would ultimately be a good outcome. If it remained in Hyde Park "London gains one more pleasure," while if it were to be removed "the moral power of the Exhibition" would be strengthened by making it stand out as "a single perfect fact" in a world of messy compromises. Two weeks later, in "Foreign Airs and Native Places," Morley returned

to the same topic, this time in support of Paxton's plans to erect a whole
series of winter gardens attached to hospitals, on the model of the
"Crystal Sanatorium" he had recently proposed for the new City of
London Hospital for Diseases of the Chest at Victoria Park. Paxton's
design, published in the *Illustrated London News* on 5 July, showed
another chunky cylinder built from modular iron and glass, like a fragment of the Crystal Palace that had escaped from Hyde Park and settled
in a different part of London. Here the air would be artificially filtered
and kept at an even temperature throughout the building, producing a
form of air conditioning that would allow invalids to "pass months or
years continuously in a foreign climate, without leaving home." It was
a "bold" idea, Morley admitted, but Paxton's "scheme of the glass
palace" had been equally "bold," and that had turned out to be a master-
stroke. Who was to say that the future would not involve dozens of
miniature Crystal Palaces sprouting up all over the country like mush-
rooms?

Dickens chose not to contribute directly to this debate, instead expressing his gratitude that since the close of the Great Exhibition the country
had "fallen into a pleasant dulness." Yet buildings and moving were still

at the forefront of his mind as he continued to supervise the renovation of Tavistock House. The key difference was that this was a project where he was in charge, and while he continued to fret at the snail-like progress of his builders he also used his writing to bring these feelings safely back under control. A week before confessing that he found the subject of what do to with the Crystal Palace "a horrible nuisance," he considered posting a "COMMIT NO NUISANCE" notice outside his new house, thereby anticipating the trouble he would have some months later with a delivery man who was spotted relieving himself by the gate. (When Dickens threatened to have him arrested, "He was rather urgent to know what I should do 'if I was him,'—which involved a flight of imagination into which I didn't follow him.") At the end of October, Dickens gloom-ily surveyed some of the other things that were still interfering with his domestic plans:

> White lime is to be seen in the kitchens—faint streaks of civilization dawn in the Water Closet—the Bath Room is gradually resolving itself from an abstract idea into a fact—youthful—extremely youthful—but a fact. The drawing-room encourages no hope what-

ever. Nor the Study. Staircase, painted. Irish Laborers howling in the schoolroom, but I don't know why: I see nothing. Gardener vigorously lopping the trees, and really letting in the light and air. Foreman, sweet tempered but uneasy. Inimitable hovering gloomily through the premises all day, with an idea that a little more work is done when he flits, bat-like, through the rooms, than when there is no one looking on.

Exaggerating his helplessness for comic effect, Dickens turns himself into a minor character in his own story, or a bat-like version of an omniscient narrator who can hover in the background without getting personally involved. It is as if he were living out the scene in *Dombey and Son* when Florence returns to her father's house during some renovations:

> There was a labyrinth of scaffolding raised all round the house, from the basement to the roof. Loads of bricks and stones, and heaps of mortar, and piles of wood, blocked up half the width and length of the broad street at the side. Ladders were raised against the walls; labourers were climbing up and down; men were at work upon the steps of the scaffolding; painters and decorators were busy inside; great rolls of ornamental paper were being delivered from a cart at the door; an upholsterer's waggon also stopped the way; no furniture was to be seen through the gaping and broken windows in any of the rooms; nothing but workmen, and the implements of their several trades, swarming from the kitchens to the garrets. Inside and outside alike: bricklayers, painters, carpenters, masons: hammer, hod, brush, pickaxe, saw, and trowel: all at work together, in full chorus!

The main difference is that whereas Florence's surroundings are being made strange to her, Dickens's renovations were designed to make Tavistock House ever more familiar to him. They represented his attempt to make a real house match as closely as possible the "abstract idea" of a perfect family home he already carried around inside his head.

It was an expensive business. By the end of September, he was reporting that after suffering "a severe, spasmodic, house-buying-and-repairing
attack" his wallet had been left "extremely weak and all but exhausted."
And yet Dickens's bank records at Coutts show that he spent a further £25
on 30 October, followed by sums of £28 10s and £26 16s 6d in the first two
weeks of November, all of it on new furniture. (This would have amounted
to two years' salary for a clerk like Bob Cratchit.) But in home renovation,
as in everything else Dickens attempted, only perfection would do; com-
promise was just another word for failure. Nothing was too small to
notice. According to Mamie, he chose every item in the bedroom she was
to share with her sister, from wallpaper that was patterned with wild flowers and a pair of iron bedsteads hung with flowery chintz, to the "two
toilet tables, two writing tables, two easy chairs, &c., &c., all so pretty and
elegant." Even when Dickens was away from London—he spent most of
the first half of October in Broadstairs, punctuated by a visit to the Duke
of Devonshire at Chatsworth, where "a bedstead like a brocaded and
golden Temple" particularly caught his eye—he was consumed with
thoughts of moving into his new house. Sometimes this manifested itself
in a more general desire to keep on the move. In late September he complained to Forster of "an intolerable restlessness," and on 17 October, the
same day he wrote to Austin eagerly looking forward to drinking "a glass
of champagne to the new House, and the Illustrious Architect," he walked
from Broadstairs to Minster and back, a fifteen-mile round trip.

Dickens had also been juggling the renovations to Tavistock House
with two other ongoing projects. The first was his work at Urania Cottage.
In November, he reported to Miss Coutts that one inmate had "given us a
little trouble" by stealing a bonnet and some clothes, and he had arranged
for her to be discreetly convicted by a local magistrate to minimise any bad
publicity. More optimistically, he had been introduced to "a little country
girl of 17—rather pretty—who had been deserted by her father, and had
been tramping and hop-picking and vagabonding generally, all her life";
after impressing Dickens with her quietness and gentleness, he concluded
she would be "decidedly worth the trial," here meaning a spell in Urania

Cottage rather than more courtroom proceedings. Dickens's second project was his continuing work for the Guild. In the first half of November there were further performances at the Assembly Rooms in Bath, where the players were greeted by a large and enthusiastic audience, and then the Victoria Rooms in Bristol, where Dickens expected "another great house." Alongside these theatrical activities he continued to enjoy the small improvised dramas of everyday life. According to one member of the Amateur Company, when they were left to amuse themselves after supper their favourite game was "leap-frog, which we played all round the supper-table," while Dickens wrote admiringly from Bristol about one of the actors who had revealed his hidden talents as a magician by swallowing candles and doing "wonderful things with the Poker." Nor was Tavistock House a complete change of scene. The following year Dickens would turn the ground-floor schoolroom into "The Smallest Theatre in the World," where according to Charley his father "revised and adapted the plays, selected and arranged the music, chose and altered the costumes, wrote the new incidental songs, invented all the stage business, [and] taught everybody his or her part." But even before he moved in Dickens appeared to be treating Tavistock House like a much larger stage set, even fantasising about the kind of play for which this house would serve as a suitable backdrop. His letter to Austin in September complaining that there were "NO WORKMEN ON THE PREMISES" had ended with the postscript "Ha! Ha! Ha! (I am laughing demonically)," as if he had accidentally found himself trapped in a badly written melodrama.

Despite this disruption he continued to plan his new novel, telling Austin on 7 October that he was having to deal with "the whirling of the story through one's mind, escorted by workmen," and five days later sending Bradbury & Evans the "sketch of a Bill-Advertisement" for a "A NEW STORY BY CHARLES DICKENS," as yet untitled but with a promise that "the first Number will appear, early in the New Year." (His publishers wisely chose not to commit to this vague timetable for a work of which Dickens had so far not written a single word.) There were also some last-minute literary inspirations to digest, such as Nathaniel Hawthorne's novel *The Scarlet Letter*, which Dickens had read over the summer shortly after the first British edition was published. He wasn't particularly impressed, telling Forster that the "psychological part of the story is very much overdone, and not truly done I think," although certain parts of it do seem to have inserted their hooks into his memory. These included the lasting shame of bearing an illegitimate child that attaches itself to a character named Hester, and an introduction in which Hawthorne described the world of his story as "a neutral territory, somewhere between the real world and fairy-land, where the Actual and the Imaginary may meet."

Perhaps this is what lay behind Dickens's decision to arrange for a copy of *The Scarlet Letter* to be left on his sister-in-law Georgina's bedroom table when she travelled down to Broadstairs in September, because in his mind she occupied a similar middle ground between the actual and the imaginary. A pencil sketch done by Daniel Maclise in 1843, the year after Georgina came to live in Devonshire Terrace to help her sister manage a rapidly growing household, shows her placed between Dickens and his wife, with her face caught in profile and her eyes cast demurely downwards. The image nicely captures "Aunt Georgy's" main role in the

Dickens family, which was to act as a bridge, and sometimes a buffer, between husband and wife. When she first joined the family she was just fifteen years old, a year younger than her sister Mary had been when she moved in with Dickens and Catherine shortly after their marriage in 1836. That arrangement had ended in tragedy after Mary died in Dickens's arms, although having left his physical household it seems she quickly took up full-time residence in his head. "For a year, I dreamed of her, every night—sometimes as living, sometimes as dead," Dickens told a doctor in February 1851; some years after her death she had appeared to him again in Italy, on a night when the local people were encouraged to pray for the souls of the departed, "Which I have no doubt I had some sense of, in my sleep; and so flew back to the Dead." It is hard to see how Catherine could hope to compete with such a rival as the years ticked by. While she grew older and more solid in appearance, her ghostly sister was in every sense untouchable. Georgina also had the handicap of still being alive, but it seems that in Dickens's eyes her value lay not only in the practical help she could offer—teaching the children to read, serving as his amanuensis, and even accompanying him on some of his punishingly long walks—but also in the idea she represented. For although he routinely bracketed the two women together in his letters this year ("Kate and Georgina send their loves," he writes, or "Kate and Georgina send their fondest regards"), increasingly he appears to have viewed "the gentle Georgina" or "My Dearest Georgy" as everything that Catherine was not: calm, reliable, organised.

How far this reflected the truth or simply his need to turn people into sharply defined characters is hard to say. Much of his writing involves individuals—usually men—encountering someone who turns out to be their unexpected double or secret twin: Charles Darnay and Sydney Carton in *A Tale of Two Cities*, or Pip and Trabb's boy in *Great Expectations*. Perhaps living with two sisters encouraged Dickens to apply the same principle to his own life. In *David Copperfield*, David had first married the adorable but silly Dora, who is incapable of doing anything to help him beyond holding his pens, and had then moved on to the angelic but sexless

Agnes (even her name is a near-anagram of "Angel"), to whom his "heart turned naturally . . . and found its refuge and best friend." That may have given Catherine pause for thought, not least the part of the novel where Dickens removes the obstacle to David and Agnes marrying by quietly killing Dora off. Even Georgina didn't fully escape Dickens's love of a good death scene, because a few years later he added a new character sketch to his memorandum book: "From a child herself, always 'the children' (of somebody else) to engross her. And so it comes to pass that she never has a child herself—is never married—is always devoted 'to the children' (of somebody else) . . . and dies quite happily." Some of Dickens's letters this autumn were equally coiled and complicated in their hidden emotional life. In one he describes how Catherine was in London inspecting the building work: "She is all over paint, and seems to think that it is somehow being immensely useful to get into that condition." Although this may have been part of a long-running joke about his wife's clumsiness, Dickens's smile is rather a thin one. The underlying assumption appears to have been that when it came to practical household matters she was about as useful as Dora holding David's pens.

At different points in *David Copperfield*, both Dora (despairingly) and Agnes (admiringly) are described as a "housekeeper," and this was also to be Georgina's role in Tavistock House. While Catherine would continue to be officially in charge of the household, it was her younger sister whom Dickens admiringly referred to as his "little housekeeper." This was another aspect of life that involved an unpredictable mixture of the actual and the imaginary. Running Dickens's household was a demanding practical role, requiring skills that ranged from a firm hand when dealing with the servants to keeping a sharp eye on the account book. At the same time, when Dickens described a housekeeper's jingling bundle of keys he tended to treat them like a set of talismans or magic charms, as if they had powers that stretched far beyond merely unlocking the pantry or protecting the family silver.

His own family history may have had a part to play in this. His paternal grandmother, Elizabeth Ball, was a domestic servant who had ended up as the housekeeper of Crewe Hall, an estate in Cheshire, and although she died when Dickens was twelve years old, she is reported to have been "an inimitable story-teller" who had "a gift for extemporising fiction for the amusement of others." Dickens knew that the details of running a household were hardly the stuff of most people's fantasies—when he finally met the Queen in 1870, their topics of conversation included the servant problem and "the cost of butcher's meat, and bread"—but he too sometimes found himself making them sound like the raw materials of a fairy tale. "Pleasant little Ruth! Cheerful, tidy, bustling, quiet little Ruth!" he coos over Ruth Pinch in *Martin Chuzzlewit* as he describes how she lives with her brother Tom. "Well might she take the keys out of the little chiffonier which held the tea and sugar; and out of the two little damp cupboards down by the fireplace . . . and jingle them upon a ring before Tom's eyes when he came down to breakfast! Well might she, laughing musically, put them up in that blessed little pocket of hers with a merry pride!" Dickens's writing practically hugs itself with pleasure.

By mid-November Cubitt's workmen had finally left Tavistock House, and Dickens and his family had moved in. "I am beginning to find my papers, and to know where the pen and ink are," he told Miss Coutts. "Order is re-established."

In an unpublished autobiography, the artist Marcus Stone (son of Frank) described the results of Dickens's extensive renovation work. "It was an almost unrecognisable Tavistock House," he wrote. "The dirty, dismal, dilapidated mansion was now in a perfect condition of restoration, [and] the order and completeness of Devonshire Terrace was established on a more important scale." From the top floors there were views of the London skyline: when Hans Christian Andersen stayed with the Dickens family in 1857—and in fact considerably outstayed his welcome—he had "a snug room looking out on the garden," and over the treetops he "saw the London towers and spires appear and disappear as the weather cleared or thickened." The main first-floor living room was also at the rear of the house, and was papered in green damask; here all of Dickens's pictures had been rehung in exactly the same positions they had occupied in Devonshire Terrace, although now with a more generous amount of space between them in a room that was at least twice the size. Dickens's keen eye for interior design was also detectable in every other room, from a concealed toilet in the main bathroom to the mirrors that were placed in the recesses of his mahogany bookcases to highlight their architectural symmetry. "The whole establishment," Stone concluded, was "sumptuously appointed" though "entirely without any suggestion of ostentation."

The bantering tone of some of Dickens's letters this autumn indicates that not everyone saw it that way. A week after he moved in, he wrote to Elizabeth Gaskell describing his new basement kitchen as "an apartment painted in an Arabesque manner, with perfumes burning night and day on tripods of silver—crimson hangings of silk damask concealing the saucepans—and melodious singing-birds of every country, pendant in gilded cages from the fretted roof." The following month he extended this joke, telling her that "We have just bought a neat little dinner service of pure gold for common use. It is very neat & quiet." He was probably responding to the latest buzz of London gossip, as a few days later Mrs. Gaskell wrote to another correspondent that she had heard about "the splendour of Mr. Dickens' house" from an informant who had recently dined there and reported that Dickens had "bought a dinner-service of *gold* plate." That wasn't very likely, although the fact that the story spread as far as it did indicated how ready people were to believe that Dickens would choose the equivalent in tableware of his garish silk waistcoats. Mr. Bounderby's complaint in *Hard Times* that any factory worker who was dissatisfied with their lot expected "to be fed on turtle soup and venison, with a gold spoon" was only a lightly satirical version of the vulgar tastes that many assumed were Dickens's own.

Other guests wondered if he saw any incongruity between his love of home comforts and his vocal championing of the poor. When George Eliot visited Tavistock House a few years later, her sharp eyes immediately noticed the "splendid library, of course, with soft carpet, couches etc, such as became a sympathiser with the suffering classes." Her withering conclusion was "How can we sufficiently pity the needy unless we know fully the blessings of the plenty?" This autumn she had her own domestic situation to worry about, having returned to live at 142 Strand on 29 September, just ten days before John Chapman bought the *Westminster Review* for £300 and installed her as the editor. William Hale White, a fellow lodger in this unpredictably bohemian household, later remembered how she would sit in her "dark room at the back of No. 142" as she worked on the journal. "I can see her now," he wrote in a letter to the *Athenaeum*, "with her hair over her shoulders, the easy chair half sideways to the fire, her feet over the arms, and a proof in her hands." That reminiscence was in response to the publication of a biography written by her husband John Cross, which was so bland White could "hardly recognise her" in its pages. It was a book that had tried to tame the radical intellectual White remembered, and in his view it "made her too 'respectable.'"

Dickens was similarly aware of how easily the demand to be "respectable" could become an excuse for dullness or a shield to hide behind. In *David Copperfield*, Steerforth's personal manservant is a "respectable-looking man" who makes himself out to be equally respectable on the inside. "If his nose had been upside-down, he would have made that respectable. He surrounded himself with an atmosphere of respectability, and walked secure in it. It would have been next to impossible to suspect him of anything wrong, he was so thoroughly respectable." Yet Dickens tended to satirise precisely those things he found most attractive, introducing small elements of them into his writing as a form of literary homeopathy, and some of his own activities this autumn would probably have been met by this servant with a discreetly approving nod.

For example, October had seen the publication of a slim volume entitled *What Shall We Have For Dinner?*, a collection of menus or "Bills of Fare for from Two to Eighteen Persons," together with an appendix containing "Receipts [i.e., recipes] for some dishes, the preparation of which may not be generally understood," all assembled by Catherine Dickens with a preface by her husband in the guise of "Lady Maria Clutterbuck." Priced at one shilling, the same as an instalment of one of Dickens's novels, it came at a time when a growing middle class had led to an increased demand for published guides of many kinds, from recipe books to etiquette manuals, all offering instructions on how to run and feed a household properly. Dickens had already indicated in *David Copperfield* why such books were needed. When David plans his first bachelor dinner party, he has absolutely no idea what food to order, so he consults his landlady Mrs. Crupp:

> Mrs. Crupp then said what she would recommend would be this. A pair of hot roast fowls—from the pastry-cook's; a dish of stewed beef, with vegetables—from the pastry-cook's; two little corner things, as a raised pie and a dish of kidneys—from the pastry-cook's; a tart, and (if I liked) a shape of jelly—from the pastry-cook's. This, Mrs. Crupp said, would leave her at full liberty to concentrate her mind on the potatoes, and to serve up the cheese and celery as she could wish to see it done.

Clearly David's landlady is not much of a cook, but the fact that his own contribution to the menu—other than the impulse purchase of a slab of mock turtle soup from a shop in the Strand—is limited to paying for it indicates just how useful he would have found a copy of *What Shall We Have For Dinner?* if one had been around to consult.

Dickens himself was far more knowledgeable about what to purchase for the dinner table and where to find it. In 1857 he told Wills that he was "going to Newgate-Market with Mrs. Dickens after breakfast to shew her where to buy fowls," and a few months earlier Nathaniel Hawthorne recorded in his diary how "careful" Dickens was of his wife, "taking on himself all possible trouble as regards his domestic affairs, making bargains at butchers and bakers, and doing, as far as he could, whatever duty pertains to an English wife." Dickens also enjoyed entertaining his friends with the results. The inventory for Devonshire Terrace included fifty-four dinner plates, twenty soup plates and two soup tureens, together with three dessert services and a further two dinner services: a blue one and "a common Green dinner-set." Whether or not Dickens later added a set of gold crockery for his move to Tavistock House, clearly his dining habits were very different from the days at Warren's when, if he had no money left to buy food, he would wander across to Covent Garden during his tea break "and [stare] at the pine-apples." If "Every one is to live as he can afford, and the meal of the tradesman ought not to emulate the entertainments of the higher classes," as Maria Rundell had claimed in her popular 1808 book *A New System of Domestic Cookery*, Dickens's publication of "Bills of Fare" that included "Boiled Salmon, Lobster Sauce, Filleted Lobster, Shrimp Sauce, Cucumbers" alongside frugal family dinners of suet dumplings and minced beef with bacon, offered more than a steam-clouded window into what went on in his own kitchen. For an aspirational middle-class family like his own, *What Shall We Have For Dinner?* was also a badge of belonging. It asked a question to which he could now truthfully answer: whatever we like.

There may also have been more altruistic reasons behind the publication of his only literary collaboration with his wife. Dickens often connected food with love—he had already written a long poem called "The Bill of Fare" in the 1830s during his courtship of a young woman named Maria Beadnell, creating a smorgasbord of food-based puns in which he identified himself as a young cabbage who had "lost his heart"— and it is possible that *What Shall We Have For Dinner?* was a project intended to occupy Catherine after Dora's death, a practical form of therapy. Yet the choice of "Lady Maria Clutterbuck" as a literary pseudonym resonates more oddly. It was the role Catherine had played earlier in the year in Boucicault's *Used Up*: a widow whom Charles Coldstream (played by Dickens) asks to marry out of sheer boredom. "If a wife, now, could be had like a dinner, for the ordering," he speculates, and in an attempt to add some spice to his life he promises to ask "the first that comes." Enter a dowdy widow named Lady Maria Clutterbuck. Later in the play he thinks better of this plan, as Maria disappears from the story and a younger woman named Mary takes centre stage. It turns out that she is the one he really wants to marry, and this time out of love rather than convenience. To summarise: someone called Charles propositions a middle-aged matron played by Catherine, but he ends up marrying a fresh-faced innocent named Mary. Whether this echo of his own life was a coincidence, a joke Dickens shared with his wife, or one he enjoyed at her expense, it adds an inscrutable subtext to the publication of a book to which he added a preface explaining that *What Shall We Have for Dinner?* was intended to rescue unfortunate couples from "domestic suffering" and keep "domestic relations" happy.

Readers who are used to the conventions of modern cookery books are likely to find *What Shall We Have For Dinner?* a somewhat puzzling publication. Many of the menus feature the same dishes returning like unwanted leftovers: out of 166 separate Bills of Fare, Water Cresses appears 40 times, Toasted Cheese 42 times and Macaroni a stomach-challenging 56 times. Other awkward details include several misspellings (Croquits, Brocoli), and mysterious references in some of the menus to an unspecified Vegetable, while several of the recipes read more like memories of favourite dishes than detailed instructions on how to prepare them:

LAMB'S HEAD AND MINCE.

Cut a lamb's head in half, boil and then brown in a Dutch oven or with a salamander; mince liver and dish up together.

RICE BLANCMANGE.

Boil rice in milk, put in a mould, and let stand until cold.

BAKED IRISH STEW.

An ordinary Irish stew, with a little gravy added, and baked until nicely browned: about half an hour.

Yet the book ran to four further editions by 1860, and was soon recognisable enough to be used as the reference point for a joke in *Punch*, where under the heading "What Shall We Have For Dinner?" Lady Maria Clutterbuck writes to explain that a boa constrictor who swallowed a blanket "was tired of having nothing but *volaille* [poultry] for dinner, so he thought he would just try a *Blanquette* [white meat in a white sauce]."

Catherine's part in this success shouldn't be underestimated. Several of the recipes were openly borrowed from one of the period's most celebrated chefs, Alexis Soyer, including Cod Rechauffé à la Soyer, Salmon Curry à la Soyer and Steak à la Soyer, which indicates that she had a good understanding of contemporary tastes, while she appears to have used Soyer's cookery book *The Gastronomic Regenerator* (which was written in the voice of an alter ego known as "Hortense" or "Mrs. B") as the unacknowledged source for three other recipes: Maître d'Hôtel Butter, Sauce à la Maître d'Hôtel and Fondue. She also borrowed from at least three further cookery writers, which suggests considerably more knowledge than might be expected from someone who supposedly needed her husband to show her where to buy basic ingredients like a chicken.

Dickens's presence in the book is equally pervasive. Cedric Dickens, the novelist's great-grandson, reported that the inspiration for *What Shall We Have For Dinner?* was a trip that Dickens and his wife took to the Great Exhibition, after which they "visited the fashionable restaurant of M. Alexis Soyer, the famous ex-chef of the Reform Club, established at Gore House, formerly the residence of his friends Lady Blessington and Count d'Orsay." Inspired by the elaborate cuisine available here, "Mrs. Dickens, encouraged by M. Soyer's example, decided to collect and print some of her own bills of fare and recipes." There may be an element of family legend wrapped up in this story, but what is certain is that Dickens already had a keen interest in both menus and recipes.

"I have just ordered dinner in this curious den for five people, cod and oyster sauce, Roast beef, and a pair of ducks, plum pudding, and Mince Pies," he wrote to Catherine while she was still his fiancée in 1835. Much later, when he had moved to Gad's Hill Place following their separation, he waited with his guests for the dinner menu to be placed on the sideboard after lunch and then discussed each item with the professional detachment of a restaurant critic: "Cock-a-leekie? Good, decidedly good; fried soles with shrimp sauce? Good again; croquettes of chicken? Weak, very weak; decided want of imagination here." Mamie recalled how "he would apparently be so taken up with the merits or demerits of a menu that one might imagine he lived for nothing but the coming dinner." Other menus are introduced more surreptitiously into his fiction, from the miserable workhouse fare in *Oliver Twist* ("three meals of thin gruel a day, with an onion twice a week, and half a roll on Sundays") to the great heaps of food that Scrooge sees piled up in *A Christmas Carol*: "turkeys, geese, game, poultry, brawn, great joints of meat, sucking-pigs, long wreaths of sausages, mince-pies, plum-puddings, barrels of oysters, red-hot chestnuts, cherry-cheeked apples, juicy oranges, luscious pears, immense twelfth-cakes, and seething bowls of punch, that made the chamber dim with their delicious steam." It reads less like a piece of narrative than the instructions for a buffet.

There are also some scenes that appear to be on the point of breaking out from the confines of fiction and turning into a cookery lesson. Evidence that "cheerful, tidy, bustling, quiet Ruth Pinch" in *Martin Chuzzlewit* is a worthy housekeeper for her brother Tom comes when she mentions that "I think I could make a beef-steak pudding, if I tried," and Dickens describes in great detail how she goes about her task, rolling pastry and chopping up steak, with this "first experiment of hers in cookery" proving to be so successful that her brother insists "she must have been studying the art in secret for a long time past." This relationship between fiction and cookery extended both ways. One of Dickens's favourite recipes was leg of mutton stuffed with oysters, which appears several times in *What Shall We Have For Dinner?* and also in *Little Dorrit*, where John Chivery, the son of the prison's turnkey, is invited to dinner by a debt collector whose sister "with her own hands stuffed a leg of mutton with oysters on the occasion, and sent it to the baker's." Even Ruth Pinch's beefsteak pudding would later reappear in print in a slightly different form, because in 1845 the bestselling cookery writer Eliza Acton sent Dickens a copy of her new publication, *Modern Cookery in All its Branches*, which included a recipe for "Ruth Pinch's beefsteak puddings, à la Dickens."

Theory and practice do not always work together this smoothly in Dickens's fiction. The dinner party at which David Copperfield's landlady serves up her potatoes rapidly becomes a drunken blur, and when the newly wealthy Pip attempts to host a small dinner in *Great Expectations* the waiter he has hired for the occasion turns out to have "wandering habits," with the result that the bread ends up on the bookshelves, the cheese in the coal scuttle, and a cooked chicken in Pip's bed, "where I found much of its parsley and butter in a state of congelation when I retired for the night." It is like a culinary commentary on Pip's own feelings of being out of place.

Nor were theory and practice always perfectly aligned in Dickens's own household. While Georgina shared the main domestic responsibilities with a number of servants, including a nursery maid, a governess and Catherine's long-serving maid Anne Brown, Dickens took an unusually active role in everyday household matters. "Even the kind of interest in a housewife which is commonly confined to women, he was full of," Forster noted, before gruffly going on to explain that this meant "there was not an additional hook put up wherever he inhabited, without his knowledge," thereby relieving anyone worried about Dickens's masculinity by making it clear that his friend's "home concerns" were chiefly centred on DIY. Yet Dickens's fiction tells a different story, especially in novels like *Our Mutual Friend*, where Eugene instructs Mortimer on the importance of good housekeeping, shows off the narrow room he has "very completely and neatly" fitted out as a kitchen, and lovingly lists the room's contents: "miniature flour-barrel, rolling-pin, spice-box, shelf of brown jars, chopping-board, coffee-mill, dresser elegantly furnished with crockery, saucepans and pans, roasting jack, a charming kettle, an armour of dish-covers." It is the sort of catalogue more commonly found in passages of epic poetry. "The moral influence of these objects, in forming the domestic virtues, may have an immense influence upon me," he tells Mortimer, hopefully. Once again the home is revealed to be a test of personality and a training ground for what Eugene refers to as "habits of punctuality and method."

For all the tongue-in-cheek humour of such passages, they accurately reflected Dickens's belief that good order began inside the home and radiated outwards from it like the ripples in a pond. On 9 October he described himself as someone who was "accustomed to keep everything belonging to him in a place of its own, and to sit in the midst of a system of Order," capitalising the key word "Order" as if it were a personal friend. This is unlikely to have surprised anyone who met him this year through his work for Urania Cottage or the Guild of Literature and Art. Nor would it have come as much of a shock to his own family. Later he would refer to his household at Gad's Hill Place as a "machine" that he expected to work in "perfect order," and according to his children he treated Tavistock House in much the same way. "He was, I think, the most tidy and orderly man ever born," reported Mamie. "He could not bear to see a chair out of its place." The daily routine was organised along strict military lines. "To each boy was appropriated a particular peg for his hats and coats," his son Henry recalled, "a parade was held once a week for overhauling the inevitable fresh stains on our garments; and one of us was deputed in turn to be the general custodian of the implements of the games, whose duty it was to collect them at the end of the day and put them in their appointed places." That quasi-biblical phrase "appointed places" leaves no doubt about how seriously Dickens took such household tasks.

At times, he acknowledged, his "love of order" seemed "almost a *disorder.*" This was especially true of his habits when travelling away from home, when he would rearrange the furniture in hotel rooms to create a more familiar environment. Sometimes he was even more particular, carefully unpacking his inkstand and spreading out his pens "in the usual form" before he could start writing. Meanwhile he hated the thought of anything being moved at home. "Keep things in their places," he warned Catherine in 1844, "I can't bear to picture them otherwise." In *David Copperfield*, similarly, when Agnes visits David's lodgings she rearranges the furniture to re-create the layout of Aunt Betsey's cottage, and puts his books back into "the old order of my schooldays." One aim of housekeeping, it seems, was simply to keep things as they were.

The house of fiction was another matter. Although Dickens did what he could to ensure that his real home was as orderly as the toy mansion he had played with as a boy, the world of stories was one in which he could make as much mess as he liked before deciding whether or not to clear it up. "Before settling down to his day's work," Mamie recalled, "he would go over all the house and all over the garden to see that everything was in its place and in order." And then he would sit down at his desk and find imaginative ways of wrecking it.

Sometimes this took the form of introducing episodes like Silas Wegg's evening routine in *Our Mutual Friend*, during which he walks to the Boffin house so that he can gloat over his power "to strip the roof off the inhabiting family like the roof of a house of cards," or Gabriel Varden's behaviour in *Barnaby Rudge*, throwing his wife's house-shaped collecting box onto the floor and crushing it to pieces under his heel. At other times it could take on the momentum of a plot. *The Cricket on the Hearth* opens with a scene in which the kettle "hum-hum-hums" and the cricket "chirp-chirp-chirps," but their antics have about as much narrative interest as a coal scuttle until Tackleton enters, dismissing home as "Four walls and a ceiling" and threatening to scrunch the merry cricket underfoot. He is the real hero of the story. Without him none of the alternative narrative outcomes that are glimpsed in what follows would be available, including infidelity and murder, and the reappearance of the kettle and cricket on the final page would be merely another performance of the same domestic ritual rather than a celebration of Tackleton's failure to destroy their home. Like all of Dickens's finest home-wreckers, he makes the happy ending possible by putting everything it represents at risk.

The critic John Carey has written well about these figures, arguing that they represent anarchic tendencies that Dickens could neither repress nor allow himself openly to express, revealing that the side of him who once exclaimed "Blow Domestic Hearth!" was present in his fiction all along. There had been an early experiment with this idea in his first published story, "A Dinner at Poplar Walk," where the host coolly watches his dog ruining the curtains, and then locks it outside the door, where it sets up "a most appalling howling" and vigorously scratches the paint off the bottom panels. But Dickens's fascination with the destruction of domestic ideals would later take on far stranger forms, even before he decided to separate from his wife and make his children choose which parent they wanted to live with.

His staging of *The Frozen Deep*, a play he co-authored with Wilkie Collins and staged in the schoolroom of Tavistock House in January 1857, offers a case in point. Theatre was another environment in which everything had to be "in its place and in order," and for this play Dickens took particular trouble over the authenticity of his costumes and props, boasting that there was scarcely anyone in the cast "who might not have gone straight to the North Pole itself, completely furnished for the winter." His greatest *coup de théâtre* involved these imaginary polar explorers opening a door at the rear of the stage (a space that was created by removing the schoolroom's main window) to reveal the howling Arctic outside—actually an enclosed piece of his garden, where the illusion was completed by a white backdrop and flurries of paper snow that stagehands dropped from above. Creating a space that was at once familiar and foreign, Dickens's staging generated a particular emotional charge in the final scene, when Wardour, played by Dickens himself in a wild grey wig, staggered on in search of Clara, the woman for whom he has saved his rival and sacrificed himself. "I must wander, wander, wander," he explains, "restless, sleepless, homeless—till I find her!" His success ("Found!") represents both a triumph of domestic values and their deadly cost, as he wins a kiss from Clara before nobly expiring centre stage. Curtain. Applause. On one level it was nothing more than a routine Victorian melodrama, but on another it was a curiously self-revealing piece of writing. More than five years after he had moved into his new home, Dickens was still conscious of its potential to become a strange and savage place, where strains of the popular song "Home, Sweet Home" drifting across the stage turn out to be a siren call drawing Wardour on to his death.

Dickens's writing also provided more subtle ways of disrupting the domestic security he personally craved. A week before she described *Oliver*

Twist as "excessively interesting," Queen Victoria confessed to her diary that she never felt "quite at ease or at home when reading a Novel." Probably this comment reflected her sense of public duty, but in terms of what she was reading it was also a perceptive piece of literary criticism. For despite a letter he once sent to Forster envisaging a new periodical named *The Cricket* that would turn him into "A cheerful creature that chirrups on the Hearth," nobody was more suspicious of his attempts to work a "vein of glowing, hearty, generous, mirthful, beaming reference in everything to Home and Fireside" than Dickens himself.

Narrative snapshots like the Cratchits' happy family Christmas may linger in the memory, but in Dickens's fictional world they are set against a background where the domestic ideal is far more likely to be flaking around the edges. In the worst cases even the talismanic word "home," described in *Martin Chuzzlewit* as "a name . . . stronger than magician ever spoke," finds its powers evaporating. In *David Copperfield*, when Emily writes to tell Mr. Peggotty she has eloped with Steerforth, she repeats "home" like a moth beating its wings against the window—"When I leave my dear home—my dear home—oh, my dear home!—in the morning . . . it will be never to come back, unless he brings me back a lady"—but the writing snags only briefly before, like Emily herself, it moves on. There is a sad parallel later in the novel when Mr. Peggotty explains how he pursued his niece across Europe—"Ever so fur as I went . . . Ever so fur she run . . . ever so fur in the night"—where even some more echoes of "Home, Sweet Home" ("Be it ever so humble, there's no place like home") seem powerless to tempt her back. Nor is she an isolated case. Dickens's suspicion of his own sentimental rhetoric often makes itself felt in a gap between theories of domestic felicity and the grubby truth of how his characters actually live. His later works, in particular, are far more likely to depict ideal homes as unrealised blueprints rather than real places. In *The Cricket on the Hearth*, Caleb Plummer weaves stories about his "enchanted home" to fool his blind daughter into thinking that their creaky wooden shack is actually as trim and spruce as the dolls' houses he makes, while in *Great Expectations* Mr. Pocket compensates for his chaotic home life by writing tracts on "the management of children and servants" which are "considered the very best text-books on those themes." In seeing through the fictions his characters have created, Dickens glances suspiciously at everything he enthusiastically celebrates elsewhere.

This is a common pattern in his writing, although at the time of his move to Tavistock House it had been given an extra edge by the recent appearance of another work by Nathaniel Hawthorne, the "weird, wild" novel *The House of the Seven Gables*. The story of a gloomy house that is haunted by a history of fraudulent business dealings and sudden death, there is strong circumstantial evidence that Dickens read it soon after the first British edition was published in August. Hawthorne's decision to sprinkle his novel with references to what his preface describes as "the realities of the moment"—galvanic batteries, railways, photography, the telegraph, transatlantic steamships, mesmerism, spiritualism—would certainly have caught Dickens's attention. So would the moral that underpins Hawthorne's plot, which is that "the wrong-doing of one generation lives into the successive ones," an idea that resonates even in small narrative moments, such as Hepzibah Pyncheon's "tread of backward and forward footsteps to and fro across the chamber" shortly before she tearfully gazes on a miniature of her brother, recently released from prison after a thirty-year sentence for a murder he did not commit, as if walking up and down is her own quiet acknowledgement of the fact that both of their lives have stuttered to a halt. Nor is it a coincidence that the novel is named after the building at its heart, because Hawthorne spends considerable time drawing out parallels between the two, such as the fact that the house has many "passages," just as the beginning of his story is described as a "threshold." More particularly, one of the central characters is uncannily like a prototype for the heroine Dickens would shortly put at the heart of his new novel. Just as Dickens's Esther Summerson (summer, sun) brings light and joy to Bleak House, so does Hawthorne's Phoebe Pyncheon—whose name is associated with Phoebus, another name for the sun god Apollo—restore "the quiet glow of natural sunshine" to Hepzibah Pyncheon's gloomy old house.

(When she leaves there is a great storm that is brought by an "east wind," as if stoking the fears of Esther's guardian John Jarndyce, whose enigmatic response to any domestic worry is that the wind must be "in the east.") And throughout his novel, Hawthorne draws attention to how easily the heroic and the ludicrous can swap places, and how often tragedy is spliced by everyday trivialities. Or, as his narrator puts it, "Life is made up of marble and mud."

Of all the rooms in Tavistock House that occupied Dickens's attention in the weeks leading up to his move, one was especially significant. "It really becomes of the most serious importance to me, to get into my Study," he told Austin on 5 October. By the end of the month he was practically gnawing his pen in frustration. "I am perfectly wild to get into my new Study (having a new book in my mind); and all the Trades of the civilised earth seem to be whistling in it, and intending to grow grey in it." His anxiety reflected more than the practical need to have a room where he could work. As the home had become increasingly separated off from the workplace in the minds of many middle-class Victorians, being seen instead as a domestic refuge from the unpredictable currents of commercial life that swirled around outside, male writers often felt the need to cordon off a defined area for themselves within the larger domestic space. (The rise of the modern man cave is merely the latest development of this idea.) Thomas Carlyle famously attempted to construct a soundproofed study for himself at the top of his house in Chelsea. Later in the century, other writers' rooms were poked around in magazine series such as the *Idler*'s "Lions in their Dens," the *Strand Magazine*'s "Illustrated Interviews," and the *World*'s "Celebrities at Home," all of which recognised that the "place" of literature in modern life might include the physical environment in which it was produced alongside the cultural position it tried to uphold.

Interest in Dickens's study became especially pronounced after his death. *The Empty Chair* (1870), Sir Samuel Luke Fildes's watercolour of his study at Gad's Hill Place, depicted the novelist's chair pushed back from his desk, as if he had only just left the room. R. W. Buss's unfinished *Dickens's Dream* (1875) was even more open-ended: here the novelist was fully realised, but many of the characters swarming out of his head were left as incomplete black-and-white sketches, like a collection of ghosts. What is missing from both pictures is any evidence of other people, yet it seems that Dickens sometimes used his study as an intimate social space where he could entertain his friends, a home within the home. In May 1849 he had hosted a party in his Devonshire Terrace study where he introduced his latest literary discovery Elizabeth Gaskell to friends including Forster and the Carlyles, and his newly renovated first-floor study in Tavistock House was intended to be similarly welcoming whenever he opened it up for guests. His instructions to Austin had included a "good sensible study-stove" to create a suitably cosy atmosphere, and a watercolour of the room painted after he had moved in shows a selection of comfortable chairs, one of which is occupied by Dickens reading a book while a friend stretches out for a snooze in front of a glowing fire.

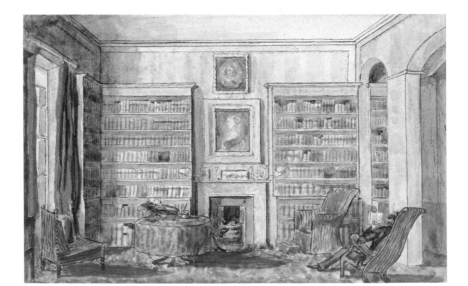

In early December, Henry Morley was invited round to Tavistock House for "a dish of tea," where those assembled in Dickens's "luxurious" new study included Augustus Egg, Richard Horne and his wife, Harry Wills and his wife, and several other guests. Morley noticed that the books on display now included a set of dummy book spines on a cupboard door and also on the sliding door that separated Dickens's study from the living room. These were probably imitations of imitations, based on a similar illusion Dickens had seen at Chatsworth, but the list of titles he produced for his own fake books gave them an edge of distinctly modern satire: *Hansard's Guide to Refreshing Sleep* ("As many volumes as possible"), *Five Minutes in China* (three volumes), and so on. There were also joke titles such as *Paxton's Bloomers* (five volumes), which brought together two of the year's most famous individuals and wrapped them around a complicated pun. Sat alongside other dummy spines that pretended to deal with the history of the nation—*King Henry the Eighth's Evidences of Christianity* (five volumes), or *History of the Middling Ages* (six volumes)—such titles revealed Dickens's understanding that recent events were no less significant. It was just that these books had yet to be written.

Someone else who was a regular guest at Dickens's social gatherings in Tavistock House, the former actress Emmeline Compton, who had played the role of Lucy in *Not So Bad As We Seem*, recalled her "kind, genial, and attentive host" as a man whose "restless disposition" meant that he was "desirous of continually *doing* something," even if this only meant playing with his hair, which was "so abundant that it would sometimes hang over his forehead, often compelling him to throw it back with his hand." It might be thought that sitting down at his desk to start a new novel would be the opposite of *doing* anything, especially when compared to the frantic energy Dickens devoted to everything else. Yet looked at from another angle, the movement of his hand across the page was a concentrated version of all these other activities, just as he told Miss Coutts in October that his "tangible house" was a place where he now looked forward to constructing the "less substantial Edifice" of a new novel out of paper and ink.

The title was key. Harry Stone has drawn attention to the care Dickens took with the titles for *Household Words* articles, often drawing up several alternatives before choosing the one he thought most likely to grab a reader's attention. "The title was the open sesame to all that lay within." Dickens took even more trouble over his fiction. The memorandum book he started in 1855 contained dozens of possible titles for stories, including some that he later used (*Our Mutual Friend* and *Somebody's Luggage*) and many more that he did not, lined up on the page like seeds he would never plant:

SCATTERED LEAVES

FAR APART

DAY AFTER DAY

ROLLING STONES

SOMETHING WANTED

BROKEN CROCKERY

MY NEIGHBOUR

NOW, OR NEVER!

Dickens was also interested in the titles chosen by other writers. In 1862 he read Wilkie Collins's new novel shortly before it began its serialisation in *All the Year Round*, and sent him no fewer than twenty-six possible titles, four of which—including *The Turning Point*—Collins highlighted with one or more ticks. (Given this dizzying range of options, perhaps Collins was enjoying a private joke when he eventually decided that the novel should appear under the title *No Name*.)

Now Dickens started to experiment with trial titles for his new novel. All of them were written on undated "slips" (half-sheets) of off-white paper, and were laid out in a rough imitation of how they would appear on a printed title page. On one slip Dickens tried out "Tom-all-alone's" and "The Ruined House," and on another he weighed up alternatives to "House," adding "Building," "Factory" and "Mill" over this word in thin handwritten layers. Another option read: "Tom-all-alone's. The Solitary House where the grass grew," which was doubly underlined—usually a signal to the printer that some text was to be put in bold. He tried, also, "Tom-All-Alone's. The Ruined Mill. That got into chancery and never got out" and "Tom-all-alone's. The Solitary House where The Wind Howled." Dickens was circling around a number of related ideas, although whether he was doing this to highlight them or avoid them was not yet clear. Finally, on the last sheet that was bundled among the sheaf of papers with the novel's manuscript, Dickens made a decisive move:

> <u>Bleak House</u>
> —<u>and the</u> <u>East Wind</u>.
> ——<u>How they</u> <u>both got</u> <u>into chancery</u>
> ———<u>and never</u> <u>got out</u>.

Then he drew a slanted line across the page and underneath it he wrote:

> Bleak House.

It was a title that combined a place and a mood, but as yet there were few clues about what the novel itself would explore: perhaps a desolate country house like the one outside Chatham that Dickens remembered from his childhood, where a recluse named Tom Clarke had lived alone for twenty-five years; perhaps some other lives that were being strangled by legal red tape. Dickens's indecision reveals that even at this late stage he didn't know what direction his hand would move in when he finally set pen to paper.

In February he had written a long letter to Dr. Thomas Stone, the author of an essay on "Dreams" that was about to be published in *Household Words*, pointing out that in addition to the unconscious mind looping back over certain subjects, as he had dreamed of Mary Hogarth night after night, other dreams played only slight variations on the same basic plots. "We all fall off that Tower—we all skim above the ground at a great pace and can't keep on it." At the same time, Dickens acknowledged, dreams did sometimes rearrange the fragments of waking life, and this could be an extra source of creativity. "I think, on waking, the head is usually full of words." *Bleak House* would work in a similar way. Like some of the plans for the Crystal Palace that were currently being debated by his contemporaries, it would dismantle the materials of the previous year and reassemble them in a surprising new form.

WINTER

Starting Again

After a period of largely bright and clear skies, at the end of November the weather changed. A table published in the London *Daily News* on Saturday 29 November summarised the previous day's reports from around the country. Greenwich: "Foggy." Birmingham: "Foggy." Plymouth: "Foggy." Liverpool: "Foggy."

Inside 142 Strand, a couple of miles away from Tavistock House, George Eliot was helping John Chapman draft the *Westminster Review*'s prospectus, due to be published in December, in which they would announce the "fundamental principle" of their journal as "the recognition of the Law of Progress." It was a law many of their contemporaries were already doing their best to uphold. Gate receipts from the Great Exhibition had produced a surplus of more than £186,000, the equivalent of tens of millions of pounds today; with a matching parliamentary grant this was enough to purchase eighty-seven acres of land in South Kensington, and create a group of new public institutions that would collectively become known as "Albertopolis": the Victoria and Albert, Natural History and Science Museums; the Royal Colleges of Art and Music; Imperial College; and the Central Hall of Arts and Sciences, later renamed the Royal Albert Hall. The future was also starting to reveal itself in other ways. After overcoming some early technical difficulties, the newly laid Submarine Telegraph across the Channel had recently opened to the public; the latest political news was sent from Paris to London on the evening of 13 November, in time to be included in the first editions of the following day's newspapers. On Friday 28 November, Charlotte Brontë wrote to her publisher George Smith from Haworth Parsonage to reassure him that she was still making progress on her latest novel *Villette*, telling him ominously that she would get on with it as fast as she could "If my health is spared." (In fact she died less than four years later, three weeks before her thirty-ninth birthday, the only one of the Brontë children to have survived that long.) The same day, waiting for the editor of the *Athenaeum* was a letter written by the photography pioneer Henry Fox Talbot, explaining the results of an experiment he had conducted earlier that year at the Royal Institution, where he had placed a printed image on a rapidly revolving piece of paper and taken a photograph at the same moment an electric spark lit up the image. "From this experiment the conclusion is inevitable," he wrote, "that it is in our power to obtain the pictures of all moving objects, no matter in how rapid motion they may be, provided we have the means of *sufficiently* illuminating them with a sudden electric flash." It was the first successful experiment in modern flash photography.

But as he sits in his study at Tavistock House, Dickens's attention is focused on just one thing: a sheet of blue-grey paper measuring 8¾ by 7¼ inches. It lies on his desk like an open invitation.

"At the end of November, when he had settled himself in his new London abode, the book was begun," Forster reported, "and as generally happened with the more important incidents of his life, but always accidentally, begun on a Friday." In a *Household Words* article on "Fate Days," published in September 1850, William Blanchard Jerrold had mocked the idea that supposedly enlightened individuals still had lucky or unlucky days. A charity worker who raises funds for a mission to the South Sea Islands will not work on a Monday, because "On a Monday her poodle died, and on a Monday she caught that severe cold at Brighton, from the effects of which she is afraid she will never recover." Someone else who scolds a gypsy for telling fortunes refuses to attend a picnic planned for a Wednesday, because she is convinced that it will rain or a wheel will come off her carriage. "She attaches no importance whatever to the star under which a child is born, does not think there is a pin to choose between Jupiter and Neptune; and she has a positive contempt for ghosts; but she believes in nothing that is

begun, continued, or ended on a Wednesday." But even if Dickens agreed
with Jerrold in public that "Day-fatality" was "the expression of an
undisciplined and extremely weak mind," in private he was equally super-
stitious when it came to the connection between Fridays and beginnings.
He had been born on a Friday, and so had his "favourite child" David
Copperfield, who observes that on this day "the clock began to strike, and
I began to cry, simultaneously." For Dickens to start writing *Bleak House* on
a Friday was merely extending this pattern to include the newest member
of his fictional family.

But how to begin? The opening line of any novel is potentially a turning point in the history of the form, a moment when it is nudged in a
different direction. Some years earlier Dickens had drawn attention to *The
Pickwick Papers* as his first novel by beginning with a reference to sunrise.
"The first ray of light which illumines the gloom, and converts into a dazzling brilliancy that obscurity in which the earlier history of the public
career of the immortal Pickwick would appear to be involved . . ." he
writes, facetiously using the sort of heroic language Mr. Pickwick will
spend the rest of the novel failing to live up to. Gaskell's *Cranford*, which
would start its serialisation in *Household Words* that December, also begins
with a beginning: "In the first place, Cranford is in possession of the
Amazons; all the holders of houses above a certain rent are women." By
contrast, in his late story "George Silverman's Explanation," Dickens
acknowledged how difficult it could be to find a narrative *open sesame*, as
his narrator dithers and backtracks before picking up enough momentum
to carry on:

FIRST CHAPTER

It happened in this wise:— But, sitting with my pen in my hand looking at those words again, without descrying any hint in them of the
words that should follow, it comes into my mind that they have an
abrupt appearance. They may serve, however, if I let them remain,
to suggest how very difficult I find it to begin to explain my explanation. An uncouth phrase: and yet I do not see my way to a better.

SECOND CHAPTER

It happened in *this* wise:— But, looking at those words, and comparing them with my former opening, I find they are the self-same
words repeated . . .

"Make a clear beginning altogether," Mr. Jarndyce will later advise the
dreamy and easily distracted Richard in *Bleak House*, but Dickens knew that
when it came to a new piece of writing this was much easier said than
done. One friend recalled him confessing that he was often slow to begin
a story, being affected by something like despondency when he first put
pen to paper, "or, as he elsewhere humorously puts it, 'going round and
round the idea, as you see a bird in its cage go about and about the sugar
before he touches it.'" This wary approach was compounded by the sheer
difficulty of writing anything at all. As Dickens later explained in a paragraph he added to Henry Morley's 1853 article "H.W.," which described
how an issue of *Household Words* was put together, the kind of would-be
contributor who sent in substandard contributions to the journal "has no
more conception of the necessity of entire devotion" to the craft of writing "than he has of an eternity from the beginning."

> Correction and re-correction in the blotted manuscript, considera-
> tion, new observation, the patient massing of many reflections,
> experiences and imaginings for one minute purpose, and the patient
> separation from the heap of all the fragments that will unite to serve
> it—these would be Unicorns or Griffins to him—fables altogether.

A novel required an even more patient arrangement of "reflections, experiences and imaginings," particularly one that would take threads from the
past year and create a new fictional pattern in which they would be slack-
ened or drawn tight. (Dickens liked the metaphor of writing as a form of
weaving: in a postscript to *Our Mutual Friend* he would later refer to "the
story-weaver at his loom.") So what kind of story would best fit the con-
tours of the world in which he now found himself?

When Macaulay looked back on the past year he was confident that "1851 would long be remembered as a singularly happy year of peace, plenty, good feeling, innocent pleasure and national glory." That was far more optimistic than Dickens's call at the end of 1850 for "another Exhibition—for a great display of England's sins and negligences," but in the subsequent twelve months Dickens hadn't seen much to change his mind. The only difference was that he had decided this display should take the form of a novel, and unlike the high society figures he would later introduce to Sir Leicester Dedlock's country residence of Chesney Wold, who are determined "to put a smooth glaze on the world, and to keep down all its realities," *Bleak House* would deal with the raw stuff of life. Not all of it, of course: the messier elements of sex and death would continue to be delicately hinted at rather than bluntly confronted, and the process of turning real life into a story would iron out some of the more delicate wrinkles of experience. But when *Bleak House*'s mad Miss Flite lists the names of her caged birds—Hope, Joy, Youth, Peace, Rest, Life, Dust, Ashes, Waste, Want, Ruin, Despair, Madness, Death, Cunning, Folly, and so on—she is offering more than just a potted biography of her own life. It is also a quick-fire summary of the novel in which she finds herself.

Dickens's new writing routine at Tavistock House began with breakfast served punctually at 9:30 a.m., always "a rasher of bacon and an egg and a cup of tea." That was followed by regular hours spent working on *Bleak House*, usually from 10 a.m. to 2 p.m., before he stopped for lunch—or at least his hand stopped; often his mind was left behind in the shadowy world of his novel. Mamie later remembered that although the children's lunchtime chatter did not seem to disturb him, "any sudden sound, as the dropping of a spoon, or the clinking of a glass, would send a spasm of pain across his face." After lunch there was usually a long walk, which he needed to calm himself down and also to work up his ideas for the next day's writing. That was followed by his correspondence, editorial work on *Household Words*, and evening social engagements: a routine that unfolded

while he slowly built up his novel sentence by sentence: a mosaic of fragments in which over time the imaginative cement used to stick the
individual pieces together would magically seem to disappear.

He insisted on perfect silence while he wrote. Mamie recalled his
study as "rather a mysterious and awe-inspiring chamber" that nobody
was allowed to enter during working hours. "We little ones had to pass
the door as quietly as possible, and our little tongues left off chattering."
What went on inside was a mystery even to those who witnessed it for
themselves. In 1853–4 Edward Matthew Ward painted Dickens sitting at
his writing desk, and the scene is one of exquisite order: a small vase of
fresh flowers and a candle are arranged just so, Dickens's left hand is seen
resting on a trim, neat beard—an early experiment with the look he
would end up keeping for the rest of his life—and his right hand is holding a quill pen like a surgeon wielding a scalpel. Not pictured are the
bronze ornaments he was later reported to keep on his desk, including
a pair of duelling frogs and a dog seller, or possibly a dog thief, with "lots
of little dogs in his pockets and under his arms." But as a static image
what it can't show is the actual process of writing, during which Dickens
felt himself to be physically surrounded by his characters, and—as we
have already seen in Mamie's account of her father's "facial pantomime"—
sometimes acted out their conversations in a mirror (there is one visible
to his left on page 238) before dashing back to write down what they had
said to him, or through him. At times his characters gave the impression
they had taken on a form of independent life. When Dickens was writing
A Christmas Carol, he admitted that if he went for a walk "Tiny Tim and
Bob Cratchit were ever tugging at his coat-sleeve, as if impatient for him
to get back to his desk and continue with the story of their lives," and
thereafter he resolved to shut his characters in his study after he had
finished with them for the day "and only meet them again when he came
back to resume his task."

In the case of *Bleak House* there were some scrappy working notes written on pale blue paper, often only a handful of key words for each chapter,
which served as the keyholes through which Dickens could glimpse the

main elements of his plot. His notes for the first instalment of four chapters amounted to just sixty words, twenty-three of which were the names
of his central characters, with the rest mostly taking the form of terse
reminders to himself ("work up from this," "Open country house picture,"
"Telescopic Philanthropy") together with a huge plot spoiler he would
need to keep from his readers for many months to come: "Esther
Summerson. Lady Dedlock's child." And once he had a rough idea of
where he was going, he picked up his pen, dipped it in a bottle of black
ink, and began.

LONDON.

The first word thrusts us into the heart of the largest city in the world. It
is also the seed from which everything else springs, as Dickens transforms
the scene outside his study window into an atmosphere that is busy with
crowds and slippery with confusion.

> Michaelmas term lately over, and the Lord Chancellor sitting in
> Lincoln's Inn Hall. Implacable November weather. As much mud in
> the streets as if the waters had but newly retired from the face of the
> earth, and it would not be wonderful to meet a Megalosaurus, forty
> feet long or so, waddling like an elephantine lizard up Holborn Hill.
> Smoke lowering down from chimney-pots, making a soft black driz-
> zle, with flakes of soot in it as big as full-grown snowflakes—gone
> into mourning, one might imagine, for the death of the sun. Dogs,
> indistinguishable in mire. Horses, scarcely better; splashed to their
> very blinkers. Foot passengers, jostling one another's umbrellas in a
> general infection of ill temper, and losing their foot-hold at street-
> corners, where tens of thousands of other foot passengers have been
> slipping and sliding since the day broke (if this day ever broke),
> adding new deposits to the crust upon crust of mud, sticking at those
> points tenaciously to the pavement, and accumulating at compound
> interest.

"Michaelmas term" is not the sort of phrase used by many people outside universities or law courts: there is more than one sense in which it is the term of an insider. Immediately we are asked to consider how far language might divide people as well as bring them together. The appearance of a dinosaur is far more startling, but here it seems to emerge quite naturally from its surroundings on the page. That is because the first sentence isn't a proper sentence. Nor is the second, or third, or fourth, or fifth. In fact a sentence that fulfils the demands of traditional grammar doesn't appear until the start of the fourth paragraph. Main verbs have disappeared, to be replaced by participles that describe people sitting, jostling, slipping and sliding, but without any sense of purpose or direction. Instead we are presented with a form of syntax that keeps making abrupt historical connections and awkward geographical leaps, just as the fog confuses where one thing ends and another begins.

Dickens's prose isn't only interested in breaking things down. It also keeps trying to build them up. For example, at one level the "crust upon crust of mud" on the pavements is simply a messy material fact; earlier this year Mayhew had pointed out that London's "mud" was not one substance but many, an unpredictable physical compound made from the manure produced by horses and other animals at a rate of a thousand tons per week, together with the dust from macadamised or stone-paved roads, all of it "mixed with water and with general refuse, such as the remains of fruit and other things thrown into the street and swept together." Dickens's "crust upon crust" is a figurative version of what happens when one layer of mud is laid on top of another, rather as Christina Rossetti would later dramatise the steady accumulation of snow in her poem "A Christmas Carol," later set to music as the hymn "In the Bleak Midwinter": "Snow had fallen, snow on snow / Snow on snow." But whereas Rossetti's lines beautifully capture the appearance of falling snowflakes as they disappear into a slowly rising mass, in *Bleak House* language is crushed into meaningless fragments that can be swept up and reused: later in this chapter the Lord Chancellor will be addressed as "My Lord," and then as "M'lud," the linguistic equivalent of "mud." It is an idea Dickens will return to throughout *Bleak House*. If old relationships are falling apart, he will use his writing to put them back together again.

Above and below and around everything else there is the fog:

> Fog everywhere. Fog up the river, where it flows among green aits and meadows; fog down the river, where it rolls defiled among the tiers of shipping and the waterside pollutions of a great (and dirty) city. Fog on the Essex marshes, fog on the Kentish heights. Fog creeping into the cabooses of collier-brigs; fog lying out on the yards and hovering in the rigging of great ships; fog drooping on the gunwales of barges and small boats. Fog in the eyes and throats of ancient Greenwich pensioners, wheezing by the firesides of their wards; fog in the stem and bowl of the afternoon pipe of the wrathful skipper, down in his close cabin; fog cruelly pinching the toes and fingers of his shivering little 'prentice boy on deck.

The fog adds a sense of mystery and unexpected romance to events, as if we are seeing them through a theatrical gauze, but it also casts a thick blanket of sameness over everything. Fog . . . fog . . . fog . . . fog . . . fog: it creeps into every sentence, multiplying itself and exhausting synonyms. Occasionally it clears for a few seconds, allowing us to catch a glimpse of ordinary people leading their separate lives, but it soon closes in again. Meanwhile Dickens's use of the present tense—for the only time in his career he will stick with it throughout the main narrative—suggests that the current situation is both ongoing and inescapable; this is simply how it is. The result is prose that reads more like a reporter's shorthand notes than a traditional piece of fiction, as if we are being presented with the raw, unshaped stuff of experience before it has been tidied up and repackaged into a story.

The fact that we move around between so many different locations in the opening paragraphs might make us think that we are accompanying an omniscient narrator, an anonymous storytelling authority who can see through the fog and make sense of everything for us. But as the narrative develops it quickly becomes apparent that even this figure doesn't always seem to be sure what's going on, and is sometimes just as puzzled and surprised as we are. Although we are told what has happened, we rarely learn why it matters, and here the opening paragraphs offer a small lesson in how we will have to read what follows. After this particular fog lifts, the world of *Bleak House* will continue to be a murky one where Dickens's characters have to search for meaningful clues and connections, and so do we. It is a world in which even the smallest details can carry a latent threat, as the metaphor of foot passengers jostling one another "in a general infection of ill temper" will later become a deadly reality when London suffers an outbreak of smallpox. Already Dickens is laying down sentences like traps.

In the fourth paragraph we are told that "the dense fog is densest, and the muddy streets are muddiest" near the "leaden-headed old obstruction" known as Temple Bar, one of the old entrances to the City of London where a narrow stone archway prevented the traffic from flowing freely. It is a physical location that practically demands to be viewed as a metaphor. Next to Temple Bar is the legal Bar in the shape of the Royal Courts of Justice. This is where cases like Jarndyce and Jarndyce slowly grind their way through Chancery, another place that is characterised by obstruction, as growing piles of papers prevent anyone involved from moving on with their lives. And Dickens's prose works in a similar way. When we first hear a lawyer speaking, he squeezes out his words as if they are caught in a personal bottleneck: "Begludship's pardon—victim of rash action— brains." Facts are divulged like secrets. This particular lawyer's name is Mr. Tangle—he will never appear again, which makes him seem like another of the ghosts generated by the fog—but we are introduced to very few other identifiable individuals as yet. Instead the opening chapter deals mostly with anonymous crowds and representative social types, like the jostling foot passengers and shivering cabin boy, all of whom are joined by the same weather no matter how different their lives are in other ways. It is an early example of an idea that the rest of the novel will draw out in much more detail, which is that the "two nations" of rich and poor could be less like opposed armies than the two sides of a spinning coin. Watch them closely and the images start to merge.

As Dickens continues to write, he relies on the same trick of literary perspective developed in his earlier fiction. The world shrinks to the size of a few slips of paper, and these slips expand until they contain the world. At the start of his career he could fill as many as twenty slips in a day, but now his progress is slower, more cautious. "An average day's work with him was 2 or 2½" slips, according to Georgina Hogarth, and "a very, *very* hard day['s] work was 4 of them." In the first handful of slips for *Bleak House* Dickens had already established the basic rules of what was to come. He would capture the world in unsparing detail, while rearranging these details into the shape of a story. He would also follow the same principles he had been championing for over a year in the pages of *Household Words*, by showing his readers that the world they lived in was "not necessarily a moody, brutal fact, excluded from the sympathies and graces of imagination." Instead, by describing the "haggard and unwilling look" of the gas lamps that light up London's shops, or the stubbornness of Chancery lawyers who spend their days running up against "walls of words," he would take the mute facts of ordinary life and lend them a new and unexpected eloquence. Inevitably this process would organise itself along sight lines that brought some facts into the foreground and pushed others out of view. But in showing how his characters interact with each other—their meetings, letters, conversations, kisses—Dickens would not only try to entertain his readers. He would also offer them a fictional miniature of social life, a model of how to behave—and how not to behave—that might "mutually dispose them to a better acquaintance and a kinder understanding."

At the start of his career, Dickens told George Henry Lewes that he didn't know where his stories came from, as they arrived "ready made to the point of the pen," which made them sound as if they weren't really fiction at all. But this isn't what the earliest pages of the *Bleak House* manuscript show. Much of Dickens's writing is foggily indistinct, producing sentences that are full of crossings-out and second thoughts that sit on top of first thoughts or balloon out into the margins. Some of this may be down to the fact that he was returning to novel-writing after an extended break, and was finding it hard to "grind sparks out of this dull blade," as he told Forster a few months later. But in fact all of Dickens's manuscripts after this one are similar in appearance. Compared to the drafts of earlier works like *Oliver Twist*, where the handwriting flows so easily it looks as if Dickens is remembering a story rather than making one up, the manuscript of a novel like *Bleak House* reveals a creative process more like the one Bulwer Lytton had described in his 1838 essay "On Art in Fiction." This is the novelist having to "grope his way," tentatively turning over new ideas and reaching out for meaningful patterns. In these first pages Dickens is not so much writing down a set of finished thoughts as he is thinking aloud, letting his pen travel across the page and seeing where it goes.

When H. F. Chorley reviewed the first instalment of *Bleak House* in the *Athenaeum*, he welcomed it as Dickens's "pledge" that he had restored his relationship with the novel-reading public, but he admitted that it was unusually difficult to anticipate what would happen next. If *Bleak House* was a mystery novel, at this stage the greatest mystery was what kind of novel it would turn out to be. One clue was provided by the publication in *Heath's Keepsake* at the end of November of Dickens's short story "To Be Read At Dusk," in which a recently married Englishwoman is disturbed by a face in a dream; later she vanishes from a palace in Genoa and is finally seen crouching in the corner of a carriage alongside the man whose face had previously haunted her. (An extra layer of irony lies in the fact that Dickens's story closely resembled one he had earlier been told by Mrs. Gaskell, forcing him into an embarrassed apology when she read his printed version.) It was just the latest example of Dickens's interest in psychological phenomena such as second sight and déjà vu. Already he had written about an experience of "imaginary recollection" in *Pictures from Italy*, and had included a long description in *David Copperfield* of something that had very little to do with his plot but everything to do with its importance to Dickens himself. "We have all some experience of a feeling, that comes over us occasionally, of what we are saying and doing having been said and done before, in a remote time," David tells us, "of our having been surrounded, dim ages ago, by the same faces, objects and circumstances—of our knowing perhaps well what will be said next, as if we suddenly remembered it!" Esther will later have a similar experience in *Bleak House*, when she sees Lady Dedlock in her parish church and is flustered by the appearance of a face that is "like a broken glass to me, in which I saw scraps of old remembrances." It is an early indication that she knows far more than she is aware of, or at least more than she is willing to disclose just yet. But although she is surprised by this realisation, the reader probably is not, because by this stage it has already become clear that Dickens's novel is going to work in a similar way. Almost every page is a broken glass in which we are encouraged to see scraps of old remembrances; almost every sentence demonstrates what Dickens meant when he wrote in his preface to the finished novel: "In *Bleak House*, I have purposely dwelt upon the romantic side of familiar things."

The plot of the first two chapters is quite hard to follow; as can happen when moving around in the fog, it is easy to get lost. After the opening paragraphs we continue to be shunted between different locations. The rest of Chapter 1 ("In Chancery") takes us into a courtroom where the case of Jarndyce and Jarndyce "drones on," and then with Chapter 2 ("In Fashion") we are thrust into the lifeless life of Chesney Wold, where the rain falls on a stagnant landscape and even the sounds of everyday life are soaked and muted. (Dickens later admitted that he had borrowed "many bits" of Rockingham Castle in his descriptions of Chesney Wold, and it is possible that he also drew on Bulwer Lytton's Knebworth for extra details of architecture and atmosphere.) The description of Lincolnshire is followed by a quick trip back to Sir Leicester's London residence, where he and Lady Dedlock are shown the latest set of legal papers by their lawyer Mr. Tulkinghorn, including a mysterious handwritten document that makes Lady Dedlock feel a sensation that is "like the faintness of death." Later we will learn that this document was written by Lady Dedlock's former lover "Nemo," a man whose name means "Nobody" but whose life will turn out to be one of the main threads connecting everybody.

The fact that "In Fashion" follows "In Chancery" initially makes it seem as if Dickens is setting up a series of contrasts: the country versus the city; social refinement versus legal cunning. In fact these worlds are revealed to be mirror images of each other. Both are "things of precedent and usage," Dickens's narrator tells us, meaning that both thoughtlessly repeat the patterns of the past, and there are frequent verbal parallels to remind us that what happens in one cannot easily be separated from what happens in the other. Mr. Tulkinghorn is "surrounded by a mysterious halo of family confidences," just as the Chancellor sits in the High Court "with a foggy glory round his head," while both high society and the law are described as "sleeping beauties" that are waiting to be woken up by the hero, like fairy tales that have lost their way. They are just a few of the characters who keep trying to bring things shuddering to a halt. And here the opening chapters of *Bleak House* provide a perfect introduction to this world of checks and blockages, because although Dickens's writing is restless with narrative details, very little appears to be actually happening.

The wider context for this lack of action was Dickens's suspicion of anything that threatened to stall the free circulation of goods and ideas. In his *Household Words* article on "Valentine's Day at the Post Office," published in June 1850, he pointed out that "the stoppage of Monday's Post Delivery in London would stop, for many precious hours the natural flow of the blood from every vein and artery in the world, and its return from the heart through all those tributary channels." Just as the world kept turning, so the age should keep moving. And in *Bleak House* this is more than just an abstract idea. As Robert Newsom has pointed out, the first instalment is full of Dickens's attempts to reproduce the clogged routines and snagging habits of modern life. There are straightforward repetitions, as in the courtroom, where "Eighteen of Mr. Tangle's learned friends, each armed with a little summary of eighteen hundred sheets, bob up like eighteen hammers in a pianoforte, make eighteen bows, and drop into their eighteen places of obscurity." There are also moments when Dickens's writing clenches itself into alliterative pairings like "slipping and sliding," or "shirking and sharking," or "sapped and sopped," or when he uses his description of the lawyers in Chancery, who are "mistily engaged in one of the ten thousand stages of an endless cause, tripping one another up on slippery precedents," to disclose little bits of internal stitching that writers usually try to keep hidden away: "engaged . . . stages . . . tripping . . . slippery." Even perfectly ordinary words return unexpectedly: Dickens's description of the smoke making "a soft black drizzle" is echoed a few paragraphs later in the appearance of Chancery solicitors Chizzle, Mizzle and Drizzle, just as it will later take on a horrific new form when Krook spontaneously combusts. "See how the soot's falling," Mr. Guppy observes, unaware that what is really floating around in the air is fatty flakes of Krook's body. The world of *Bleak House* is one in which apparently nothing can escape, not even individual words.

That is partly because in these opening pages Dickens's language is several steps ahead of his plot. Although we do not yet know how everything will fit together, his writing is already reaching for connections. At times this produces a form of narrative that verges on poetry in disguise. When we learn that Chancery "gives to monied might the means abundantly of wearing out the right," or Esther remembers sitting beside her "godmother" (actually her aunt) as "the clock ticked, the fire clicked," Dickens makes the world sound as if it is full of rhymes that are just waiting to be disclosed. Other connections take the form of literary allusions. For example, we are told that Chesney Wold has been "extremely dreary," like the moated grange in Tennyson's poem "Mariana" where another unhappy woman is trapped ("She only said 'My life is dreary,'" Tennyson writes. "Then, said she, 'I am very dreary'"), a connection that is strengthened by the same lines appearing alongside Millais's painting *Mariana* when it was exhibited at the Royal Academy in the summer, and also by the fact that the Dedlocks' country residence is located in Tennyson's birthplace of Lincolnshire. Similarly, Lady Dedlock's decision to return to London "With all her perfections on her head" turns her into a modern version of the Ghost in *Hamlet*, who finds himself trapped in Purgatory after dying "with all my imperfections on my head." Both allusions make it sound as if she is living a life that has already been written.

Yet unexpected connections are also central to comedy, as can be seen in everything from puns to the meetings of long-lost twins in dramas like Shakespeare's *The Comedy of Errors*, and this is another idea that the first instalment of *Bleak House* plays with. Clive James points out that "Common sense and a sense of humour are the same things, moving at different speeds." Similarly, a plot and a narrative are the same story moving at different speeds, and Dickens's style allows him alternately to accelerate and dawdle as he takes his readers through the novel's opening chapters. Certain phrases are packed with latent comedy, such as the "interminable briefs" that simultaneously hold up the Court of Chancery and keep it going. Others look purely factual but turn out to be satirical swipes in disguise, such as "This is the Court of Chancery," which has lurking within it a memory of "This is the house that Jack built," a nursery rhyme in which every time it seems that the story has come to an end there is another detail to add, another delay to put up with. Even the pedestrians slipping over in London's muddy streets resemble extras in a piece of narrative slapstick.

Suddenly the narrative focus switches with a jolt to another location and, without any warning, to another narrator. Chapter 3 is entitled "A Progress," which recalls moral fables like Bunyan's *The Pilgrim's Progress* (1678), or artistic sequences like Hogarth's *A Harlot's Progress* (1731–2) and *A Rake's Progress* (1733–5), not to mention the subtitle to Dickens's own novel *Oliver Twist; or, The Parish Boy's Progress*. Such overlapping echoes give the impression that Dickens is writing several novels at once, and this is reinforced by the second narrator's decision to launch into a set of recollections about her unhappy childhood. From a sprawling social problem novel we now appear to have entered the more focused world of a *Bildungsroman*, although at times that focus is hard to distinguish from the feeling that the new narrator is keeping far more from us than she is willing to disclose. (It is only indirectly that we learn her name is Esther.)

"I have a great deal of difficulty in beginning to write my portion of these pages," she tells us. One trace of this difficulty can be detected in that little word "great," which has already been used several times in the first two chapters, and which Esther keeps returning to in her own narrative. Her doll sits in a "great chair," just as Sir Leicester Dedlock does in the previous chapter, and she also wonders if the London fog is caused by a "great fire," echoing the narrator's earlier conclusion that it would be better for everyone if the misery caused by Chancery cases could be "burnt away in a great funeral pyre." Presumably one reason for this overlap between the vocabulary of Dickens's two narrators is that a word like "great" hovers between objective measurements and subjective values, and so asks us to think carefully about how far we agree on various features of the world we share. (As we have already seen, Dickens was not the only visitor who thought the Great Exhibition was "Great" only in the sense that it was very big.) This idea is further developed in the rest of the chapter, as Esther tells us how she has suffered personally from some of the problems already identified at the start of the novel. Her aunt has a stroke, and finally dies after more than a week spent lying motionless in bed with her old frown "carved upon her face"—another twisted parody of the story of Sleeping Beauty, and a personal attack of the paralysis affecting the whole nation. Later Esther moves to London and notices many of the same things the first narrator has already identified, such as the clattering confusion of city crowds and streets that are "so full of dense brown smoke that scarcely anything was to be seen." Evidently this is a novel in which people will have to find things out for themselves. Yet the difficulty Esther has in writing down her recollections is nothing compared to the difficulty many readers have experienced in reading them.

Dickens's choice of name recalls Hester in Hawthorne's *The Scarlet Letter*, just as his decision to turn Esther into a narrator may have been influenced by the women whose hidden backstories he had recently been transcribing into his Urania Cottage case book. In addition, he would have been aware of the biblical figure of Esther, who famously refuses her husband's demand to reveal her beauty to the world: a latent irony Dickens's plot will later twitch into life when his own Esther catches smallpox and becomes horribly scarred. Her character also reveals the far longer recoil of Dickens's memory, because from 1843 onwards he had taken a particular interest in an orphaned girl named Esther Elton, who had earlier been her father's housekeeper and had impressed Dickens greatly with her "quiet, unpretending domestic heroism; of a most affecting and interesting kind."

Unfortunately, when the first instalment of *Bleak House* was published, not everyone who read Esther's narrative was much affected by it or particularly interested in it. An early review in the *Spectator* expressed the "wicked wish" that "she would either do something 'spicy' or confine herself to superintending the jam-pots of Bleak House," while Charlotte Brontë was even more dismissive of Esther's narrative as "too often weak and twaddling." That criticism suggests Esther talks too much and says too little (the dictionary defines "twaddle" as "empty verbosity"), but as *Bleak House* develops we learn that what she doesn't tell us can be just as important.

She spends most of the opening instalment on the move, and her voice is equally hard to pin down. A week after the death of his baby daughter Dora, Dickens wrote to his old friend Thomas Mitton to tell him that "I am quite happy again, but I have undergone a good deal." Something similar can be heard in Esther's narrative: it is the bright, brittle voice of someone who is determined to move forward but repeatedly finds her mind drifting back to an unhappy past. It means that although her account pretends to be perfectly frank and open, it also contains several puzzles that are never solved, such as her decision to bury her doll in the garden after her aunt's death, which could signify anything from a reenactment of the funeral to a renunciation of her own childhood. Like the man she meets on a coach who "looked very large in a quantity of wrappings" and later turns out to be her new guardian John Jarndyce, much of what goes on inside her head remains hidden away. "My disposition is very affectionate," she tells us after recalling that her birthdays at school were especially miserable, "and perhaps I might still feel such a wound, if a wound could be received more than once." That repetition of "wound" pokes through the surface of her account like a shark's fin.

Esther's school appears to run on much the same lines as Dickens's Urania Cottage. "Nothing could be more precise, exact, and orderly than Greenleaf," she tells us proudly. "There was a time for everything all round the dial of the clock, and everything was done at its appointed moment." The effectiveness of her training is revealed in the next chapter, when she is sent to stay overnight with the philanthropist Mrs. Jellyby before travelling on to her guardian's home. Dickens published a generous tribute to her real-life inspiration, Caroline Chisholm, in the issue of *Household Words* that coincided with the first instalment of *Bleak House*, where the "mission" of Chisholm's Family Colonisation Loan Society is praised and her name is described as "in very many humble homes a household word." Knowing what else was coming that week, perhaps Dickens was trying to balance his own books. But his genuine admiration of Mrs. Chisholm's charity work could not erase his memory of her children's dirty faces, and in Chapter 4 he makes Mrs. Jellyby's home a vivid example of domestic chaos. Here everything reflects Mrs. Jellyby's own mistaken priorities. From the "tarnished brass plate on the door" to her daughter Caddy's "frayed and satin slippers trodden down at heel," nothing seems to be "in its proper condition or its right place." This includes the paper and ink Mrs. Jellyby uses to send out dozens of letters every day; when Esther first sees Caddy resentfully biting down on her pen she thinks prob-

ably "nobody ever was in such a state of ink," while Mrs. Jellyby herself spends the evening drinking coffee and "sitting in quite a nest of waste paper." Both are like distorted images of Dickens himself, as he sat at his desk filling in slip after slip, just as the ever-growing piles of paper in Chancery are like grotesque parodies of a serialised novel.

"The whole house is disgraceful. The children are disgraceful. *I'm* disgraceful," Caddy complains, but Esther has already done what she can to bring a little order to the Jellyby household by "making our room a little tidy, and in coaxing a very cross fire that had been lighted, to burn; which at last it did, quite brightly." In effect, her work is a rehearsal for the housekeeping role she will shortly take up in Bleak House, rather as the inmates of Urania Cottage were expected to take their newly acquired cleaning and darning skills and put them into practice in Australia. During the next instalment Esther will celebrate the "quaint variety" and "perfect neatness" of everything in John Jarndyce's home, and will end the chapter by giving "my little basket of housekeeping keys such a shake, that they sounded like little bells." (It is particularly moments like this that have made some readers want to give her a good shake too.) Soon she is running Bleak House like the well-oiled machine Dickens aspired to create in his own home. "When I see you, my dear Miss Summerson, intent upon the perfect working of the whole little orderly system of which you are the centre," Skimpole tells her, "I feel inclined to say to myself—in fact I do say to myself very often—THAT'S responsibility!" The fact that this compliment is thickly laced with irony, coming as it does from a man who is happy to eat hothouse peaches while his family goes hungry, does not cancel out the fact that we are also supposed to be impressed by her neat hands and tidy mind.

That is partly because she is Dickens's appointed representative in the novel. (We recall that in October this year he described himself as "accustomed . . . to sit in the midst of a system of Order.") As early as Chapter 3 an old gardener at her school presents her with a nosegay of geraniums, Dickens's favourite flower, and as *Bleak House* develops the roles of novelist and character blur even further. "Don't tell stories, Miss Summerson," says Caddy crossly, meaning that she shouldn't exaggerate or fib, but by then Esther has already told the young Jellyby children several stories, beginning with "Little Red Riding Hood" and moving on to "Puss in Boots and I don't know what else." It is Dickens's way of reminding us that as a storyteller she too has enough imagination to see "the romantic side of familiar things."

This aspect of the novel has also attracted criticism. "I had always rather a noticing way," Esther tells us at the start of her narrative, but there are many occasions when this sounds suspiciously like Dickens's own way of looking at things, much as some viewers were convinced in 1847 that Maclise's portrait of Catherine represented Dickens himself "in some female character." Vladimir Nabokov once pointed out that when Esther receives a frosty parting kiss from her aunt that feels like "a thaw-drop from the stone porch," or another character fiddles with his glasses case, "softly turning the case about and about, as if he were petting something," her narrative "reverts to a general Dickensian style." The same is true of Esther's talent for rapid comic sketches, describing Mrs. Jellyby's "lame invalid of a sofa," or noticing that a stuffed trout in a glass case at Bleak House is "as brown and shining as if it had been served with gravy." None of these are the sort of details one would expect a character like Esther to mention unless she had previously read a lot of Dickens—and that is impossible, because *Bleak House* is a fictional world where apparently his writing does not exist. (It is one of the least believable things about Dickens's novels of contemporary life that nobody in them has read anything by Dickens.) The result is like watching a ventriloquist abandoning the pretence that his dummy has a distinct personality, even as its mouth continues to clatter up and down.

Yet Esther is needed in *Bleak House* for the same reason she is needed in Bleak House. She is there to organise the potentially overwhelming nature of experience, to clean up narrative clutter. One word Forster returns to when discussing this novel is "muddle"—his view of Mrs. Jellyby is that she lives in "a household muddle outmuddling Chancery itself"— and the fictional world Dickens creates is indeed one of muddle.

Repeatedly, his writing appears to be on the verge of disintegrating into lists; repeatedly, he reminds us of how easily things and people can fall apart, with references to the "cracked walls" of Bleak House in the days when it was a ruin, Miss Flite as a "cracked old woman," and ultimately the "cracking of the framework of society." Throughout all of this, Esther's voice works to repair and restore the world around her.

Putting these two voices together—an anonymous narrator and a named individual, a bird's-eye view that is spliced with a ground-level perspective—Dickens gradually builds up a whole fictional world and teaches us how to read it. Not that we don't sometimes need a little help. Slightly further on in the novel the callow young lawyer Mr. Guppy and his friend take a tour of Chesney Wold, where they "straggle about in the wrong places, look at the wrong things, don't care for the right things, gape when more rooms are opened, [and] exhibit profound depression of spirits." If this is a good summary of the feelings many people have when visiting a stately home, it is also a timely warning about how we might approach a novel like *Bleak House* unless we have some sort of guide.

Several chapters later Dickens will introduce Inspector Bucket, a police officer who takes on many of the narrator's responsibilities as he mounts "a high tower in his mind" and points out significant details with his "fat forefinger." A "stoutly built, steady-looking, sharp-eyed man in black, of about the middle-age," the shrewd and relentless Bucket is closely modelled on Inspector Field; even his "fat forefinger" echoes Field's "corpulent forefinger." There may also have been a more personal connection: Bucket's investigation of Lady Dedlock has curious echoes of Inspector Field being used earlier in the year to manage the threat of Rosina Bulwer Lytton, another wife with the potential to embarrass an aristocratic husband.

Bucket's emergence as a central figure has led to *Bleak House* being viewed as one of the earliest detective novels: a whodunnit that includes a murder mystery and ends with the revelation that almost every character is part of a tangled web of secrets and lies. Actually this is a novel that turns everyone into a detective—even minor characters like Mrs. Snagsby, who is so obsessed with the idea her husband is keeping a dreadful secret from her that she dedicates her life "to nocturnal examinations of Mr. Snagsby's pockets; to secret perusals of Mr. Snagsby's letters; . . . to watchings at windows, listenings behind doors, and a general putting of this and that together by the wrong end." It turns out that her fears are wholly unfounded, but her amateur sleuthing is just one example of another general pattern. If *Bleak House* is a crash course in reading, it is also a useful introduction to the dangers of misreading.

The idea that we cannot always trust our eyes is introduced very early in the novel. The first mention of Lady Dedlock comes in a passage that tells us one thing while hinting at something else entirely:

> My Lady Dedlock (who is childless), looking out in the early twilight from her boudoir at a keeper's lodge, and seeing the light of a fire upon the latticed panes, and smoke rising from the chimney, and a child, chased by a woman, running out into the rain to meet the shining figure of a wrapped-up man coming through the gate, has been put quite out of temper. My Lady Dedlock says she has been "bored to death."

Hundreds of pages later this scene will be rearranged and replayed when Esther discovers Lady Dedlock lying beside the gate of a burial ground, wrapped up in another woman's clothes and "drenched in the fearful wet of such a place, which oozed and splashed down everywhere." Esther stoops down, pushes aside the woman's long dank hair, turns her face, and discovers that "it was my mother, cold and dead." It is the moment when the final piece of the plot clicks into place, and suddenly Lady Dedlock's change of mood on seeing a happy family reunion makes perfect sense. But at the time what puts us off this scent is the narrator's bracketed aside "(who is childless)." The same thing happens a few pages later, when the lawyer Conversation Kenge refers to Esther's aunt as "your sole relation (in fact, that is; for I am bound to observe that in law you had none), being deceased . . ." In both instances we are told something that is not true, as Dickens uses his brackets like the props for one of his conjuring tricks, by pretending to share confidential information with us while actually engaging in a piece of narrative misdirection.

According to George Orwell, "The outstanding, unmistakable mark of Dickens's writing is the unnecessary detail," the verbal traces of an overflowing imagination that piled ideas on top of each other with a generosity that could be overwhelming. But one of the challenges posed by *Bleak House* is knowing which details *are* unnecessary in a world where everything is potentially significant. Usually a long narrative is put together in a deliberately uneven way: some parts stand out while others recede into the background, producing an unpredictable rhythm of skipping and lingering when we read. What details like "(who is childless)" or "(in fact . . . you had none)" reveal is that this is a novel that is forever lighting fuses under tiny pieces of information. Most of these fuses will quickly fizzle out, but some may quietly smoulder away for many pages before bursting back into life. At this stage we just don't know which. In Dickens's previous novel, the conclusion reached by David Copperfield after thinking back over "every little trifle" involved in his marriage to Dora was that "trifles make the sum of life." After reading *Bleak House* we might be tempted to add: and of novels too.

For Dickens's earliest readers, the words on the page were only part of the story. After paying their shilling for the opening instalment, the first thing they would have seen was a familiar blue-green wrapper with a complicated illustration by Hablot Browne ("Phiz"). Here lawyers create havoc by playing a game of blind man's buff; a couple face in opposite directions and ignore the distressed cupid standing between them; a group of philanthropists smile benevolently (one is holding a sign that reads "HUMBUG") while a man pursued by the lawyers dangles precariously overhead. Inside there were also the first of Browne's illustrations (two plates were included with each instalment), depicting Esther's first encounter with Miss Flite in the foggy London street, and her night-time conversation with the frustrated, furious Caddy Jellyby. Over the course of serialisation, ten of

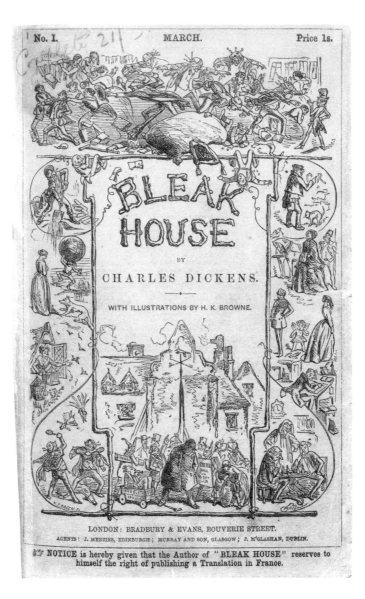

Browne's illustrations would form a series of so-called "dark plates," which he created by taking his usual engraved metal plates and etching them with an additional set of fine parallel lines. Each of these dark plates made it appear as if the novel's characters were emerging from the shadows, or perhaps retreating back into them—an appropriate set of images to accompany Dickens's response to his own call a year earlier for a "dark Exhibition of the bad results of our doings."

At the same time it was impossible to escape lingering echoes of the other Exhibition. Starting with the first number in March 1852, each month the latest instalment of Dickens's novel was accompanied by a twenty-four-page supplement, the *Bleak House Advertiser*. Alongside advertisements for items such as Milton's Hair Lubricant (guaranteed to restore the hair "and speedily render it vigorous, abundant, and beautiful") and Parr's Life Pills ("especially efficacious in all the ailments incident to the Fair Sex"), the first issue included several more with explicit commercial links to the summer's great event, including "Rimmel's Toilet Vinegar (as exhibited in the Fountain of the Crystal Palace)" and jewellery made by Watherston & Brogden Goldsmiths, who were offering special discounts in response to "the numerous calls made upon them since the Great Exhibition." If *Bleak House* was to be a "dark Exhibition," that is partly because from the start it presented itself as the other Exhibition's shadowy twin.

The first instalment, comprising Chapters 1–4 of the novel, ends with Esther falling into a fitful sleep. "At first I was painfully awake, and vainly tried to lose myself, with my eyes closed, among the scenes of the day," she recalls. "At length, by slow degrees, they became indistinct and mingled." As an ending it is more of a bridge than a cliffhanger, because over the following months Dickens would do something similar with his novel. *Bleak House* too would continue to offer indistinct and mingled memories of his life, and the lives of his readers, selected from the previous year.

Later it is revealed that the London town house of the Dedlocks has a conservatory, like a scaled-down miniature of the Crystal Palace, where blooming peach blossom can be seen "turning itself exotically to the great hall fire from the nipping weather out of doors." The idea that peach blossom could exist just a pane's thickness from snow was another example of Dickens's theory about the smallness of the world, in which different people and ideas "were continually knocking up against each other." Further echoes of the Great Exhibition in the novel take human form. A character like the dancing master Turveydrop, introduced to us as "a fat old gentleman with a false complexion, false teeth, false whiskers, and a wig," is a relic of the Regency age, but he also "exhibits" himself like the men and women who ambled fashionably up and down the aisles of the Crystal Palace. Set against his example is the frank young industrialist Watt Rouncewell, who has managed to escape the stultifying atmosphere of Chesney Wold, where his mother is the housekeeper, and is offered to us as a model of energy and patient enterprise. He also has just enough of a radical edge to make him interesting, because his first name recalls Wat Tyler, the leader of the Peasants' Revolt, as well as the steam engine pioneer James Watt. And all around them lies the dirty, frustrating, irresistible city that had been written about in so many different ways over the previous year.

A third of the way through the novel, trooper George wanders through the city's night-time streets. After a visit to Astley's Theatre he "makes his way to that curious region lying about the Haymarket and Leicester Square, which is a centre of attraction to indifferent foreign hotels and indifferent foreigners, racket-courts, fighting-men, swordsmen, foot-guards, old china, gaming houses, exhibitions, and a large medley of shabbiness and shrinking out of sight." This is the seamy underside of the Great Exhibition, and if it attracts a ramshackle group of businesses, including George's own shooting gallery, clearly it attracts Dickens too. Shabby it may be, but it is also full of variety and pulsing with life. If there is an alternative to the decaying traditions embodied in Sir Leicester, perhaps it is to be found in a place like Leicester Square, where at the time Dickens wrote this episode Wyld's Great Globe was still showing Great Britain as a tiny patch of moulded plaster on a giant painted sea.

Alongside these cultural echoes, Dickens can be observed working through more personal recollections of the past year. Some of these are like the figures one might expect to hear softly pacing up and down the Ghost's Walk at Chesney Wold. For example, the blithely irresponsible Skimpole, based on Leigh Hunt, caricatures the sort of gentlemanly amateur writer that the Guild of Literature and Art had sought to replace, but he is also another of the older men who drift through the pages of

Dickens's fiction begging and borrowing their way out of trouble, and is therefore also modelled partly on Dickens's father. Similarly, the death of Dora Dickens seems to lie behind the unusual number of children in this novel who are damaged or threatened in some way, a figure that is high even when compared to Dickens's earlier fiction. When Esther wakes up after her night at Mrs. Jellyby's, the first thing she sees is the eyes of "a dirty-faced little spectre fixed upon me." It is Peepy Jellyby, a child who is covered in bruises as well as dirt, and the way this morning scene is described makes it sound as if Peepy is already halfway to becoming a character like the nameless baby who dies quietly on a shelf during Esther's later visit to a poor brickmaker's cottage. It is a shocking event but not an unexpected one. "An't my place dirty?" scowls the brickmaker. "Yes, it is dirty—it's nat'rally dirty, and it's nat'rally onwholesome; and we've had five dirty and onwholesome children, as is all dead infants, and so much the better for them, and for us besides." As the critic John O. Jordan has written, "Images of dead and dying infants are everywhere in the novel." They are the saddest evidence yet of a world in which potential is forever being thwarted, the future shelved.

The aftermath of the Great Exhibition, the creaky machinery of the law, the desperate need for sanitation reform, the wraith-like appearance of abused and neglected children, the disgrace of a broken political system, the fleeting solace of popular entertainment—the world of *Bleak House* is one in which, as Dickens would write about Christmas in this year's special holiday issue of *Household Words*, he had decided to "shut out Nothing." Instead, as he sat at his desk in Tavistock House, his hand inching across the page, he found himself embarking on a novel that until the final double number was published in September 1853 would keep crossing back and forth between fact and fiction, the actual and the possible.

By the first week in December he had finished all of the opening instalment except Chapter 2, which was inserted later in revision. And then came Christmas, "always a time which in our home was looked forward to with eagerness and delight," according to Mamie. On Christmas Eve,

Dickens took his children to a toy shop in Holborn to choose their presents, although the main celebrations took place a few days later. The
family tradition was that on New Year's Eve Dickens would stand with his
pocket watch in his hand and wait for the midnight chimes. "A few minutes
of breathless silence," his daughter remembered, "and all eyes fixed upon
him as he stood by the open door—whatever the weather might be—then
a beautiful voice saying, 'a Happy New Year. God bless us all!'" After that
his guests would shake hands and make merry; or as Dickens described a
previous Christmas holiday to Cornelius Felton, "Such dinings, such danc-
ings, such conjurings, such blindmans-buffings, such theatre-goings, such
kissings-out of old years and kissings-in of new ones . . ."

The climax of these celebrations came on Twelfth Night, Charley
Dickens's birthday, when Miss Coutts would send him an elaborate cake
decorated with coloured sugar paste and white icing. After that was cut up
and shared around, in the evening there was usually some form of organised entertainment for the family and their guests. In previous years
Dickens had exhibited magic lantern slides, or dressed up as a conjuror
with the stage name the Unparalleled Necromancer Rhia Rhama Rhoos
to perform tricks like the Pudding Wonder, in which he would pour flour
and eggs into a volunteer's hat and then reach into it to produce—
ta-dah—a plum pudding; or the Travelling Doll Wonder, in which a
wooden doll would be made to disappear and then reappear bearing messages from various far-flung parts of the globe, having travelled "enormous
distances in half a minute" according to a playbill Dickens printed in 1849.
(There are echoes of this trick in *Bleak House*, because after Esther buries
her doll it also returns in a number of surprising ways, whether this takes
the form of the brickmaker with a sick baby who growls that "If you was
to leave me a doll, I wouldn't nuss it," or the French maid Hortense going
into Lady Dedlock's service and being treated as "this doll, this puppet,
caressed—absolutely caressed—by my Lady.") In 1852, now that Dickens's
children were a little older, it was their turn to take the lead in this year's
Twelfth Night entertainment, joining Mark Lemon's children in a performance of the 1847 burlesque *Guy Fawkes; or, a Match for a King*, written by

Albert Smith, whose previous works had included theatrical adaptations of Dickens's Christmas stories *The Cricket on the Hearth* and *The Battle of Life*. That was followed by a family outing to Drury Lane on 13 January to see *Harlequin Hogarth; or, the Two London 'Prentices*, a pantomime version of the moral fable that had been made famous by William Hogarth's series of twelve engravings *Industry and Idleness* (1747).

For the Christmas issue of *Household Words* this year, George Sala had written an article on "Getting Up a Pantomime" in which he celebrated pantomime's comforting annual traditions. "Goodness! though we know them all by heart, how we love those same Pantomimes still! Though we have seen the same Clowns steal the same sausages, and have been asked by the Pantaloon 'how we were to-morrow?' for years and years, how we delight in the same Clown and Pantaloon still!" If a reassuring lack of surprises was one reason for the form's enduring popularity, another was its topicality. Victorian pantomimes typically burlesqued the previous year's events, and *Harlequin Hogarth* was no exception. As the title page of the published text punningly explained, "This DISH is partly served up on Hogarth's 'PLATES,' with EXTRA SEASONING to suit the TIMES." In one scene designed to show "The World turned upside down" the characters included "Mrs. Bloomer, Tailor!," while the climax of the whole pantomime was an "elaborate and extensive" scene celebrating the "Triumph of INDUSTRY!!!"—a suitable end to the year of the Great Exhibition of the Works of All Industry.

And while all this was happening, Dickens was busy preparing for the publication of the first monthly instalment of *Bleak House* on 28 February. It was almost exactly halfway through his writing career, and it would prove to be a central hinge in his life.

AFTERWORD

The World's Story

Although officially the Great Exhibition was open for less than six months, it lasted much longer in the public imagination. More than forty years later, Thomas Hardy published a short story in which an old man still vividly remembers seeing visitors arriving at Waterloo station on one of the special excursion trains that had brought thousands of factory workers and agricultural labourers to London. The cheapest seats were located in open carriages that offered no protection from the wind and rain, and some passengers arrived in "a pitiable condition from their long journey; blue-faced, stiff-necked, sneezing, rain-beaten, chilled to the marrow." In many cases they were leaving for the first time the place where they had been born—which until now was also where they might have been expected to work, marry, raise children and die, all within the same few square miles. According to Hardy's narrator, the arrival of these visitors in the "bustle and crush" of a modern railway terminus created an unprecedented collision of the old and the new, or what he describes as "a precipice in Time": "As in a geological 'fault' we had presented to us a sudden bringing of ancient and modern into absolute contact, such as probably in no other year since the Conquest was ever witnessed in this part of the country."

Hardy had long enjoyed playing with this sort of idea. In his early novel *A Pair of Blue Eyes* the hero is a geologist, and when he tumbles over a cliff edge he finds himself staring into the empty eyes of a fossil embedded in the rock: "Time closed up like a fan before him." What had made the year of the Great Exhibition different was that it had involved an entire nation looking at itself and—at first tentatively, and then more confidently—celebrating the arrival of a new, self-consciously modern age. Nor was Britain thought to be the only country in which such remarkable changes were taking place. Contemplating the number of foreign visitors who had come to London, and saluting the Great Exhibition's promotion of "bloodless strife—the war of industry," a journalist in *The Art-Journal* summed up a complicated set of events in a single phrase. The year had been "a turning-point in the world's story."

It still wasn't entirely clear what kind of story this would be. Within months of the closing ceremony there were already signs that the new era of peace and harmony Prince Albert had anticipated might need to be postponed for a while longer. On 2 December Prince Louis Napoleon Bonaparte staged a bloody *coup d'état* in France, followed in November the following year by his election as Emperor, and in December his assumption of the title of Napoleon III. He was an old friend of Miss Coutts, and Dickens had often met—and disliked—him when he had lived in England. His rise to power represented the death of any radical political hopes still lingering from 1848, and when Dickens met him again in 1854, riding with Prince Albert and a cavalry bodyguard outside Boulogne and "talking extremely loudly about the view," his response was polite but chilly. "I took off my wide-awake without stopping to stare, whereupon the Emperor pulled off his cocked hat; and Albert (seeing, I suppose, that it was an Englishman) pulled off his. Then we went our several ways."

There were also sceptics who wondered if the Great Exhibition really had made much difference to most people's lives. In August 1851, the journalist William Henry Smith imagined another French visitor arriving by train, this time the ghost of clear-sighted Enlightenment thinker Voltaire. He is met by a professor of mechanics who is bubbling with enthusiasm for the "enormous progress that this age has made beyond all others" and the "glorious prospects" that seem to be opening up for Britain in particular. Voltaire is not convinced. What about the slums still swarming with life, some of them just a few hundred yards from the Crystal Palace? "And oh, heaven! what life it is! They are heaped like vermin. They prey upon each other. How they suffer! how they hate!" Or the fact that the train bringing him to London is an "iron slave" that requires "many other slaves, unfortunately not of iron, to attend to it," from the man who greases its wheels to an invisible army of engineers, signalmen, porters and lamp-trimmers? "The railroad train runs, it seems, not only upon those hundred wheels of iron which we see and count," Voltaire observes, "but on a hundred other wheels forged out of human flesh and blood." Somewhat chastened, the professor admits "we are at present in a state of transition."

Yet in the decades to come the professor's optimism would increasingly drown out Voltaire's scepticism, and 1851 would be widely acclaimed as the year that ushered in a new era of progress. Inevitably there was an element of wish fulfilment in this version of events, but that did not pre-vent it from being endlessly repeated by politicians, economists and plenty of ordinary people like Hardy's narrator. No matter how much the coun-try's prosperity was accompanied by—or even built on—lives of grinding poverty, the Crystal Palace became famous as a structure that had allowed Britain to transform itself into the leading industrial economy in the world. It was the national equivalent of Clark Kent entering a phone booth and exiting as Superman.

The building itself was an important part of this story. After Joseph Paxton's main structure was removed from Hyde Park, all that was left behind to remind visitors of what had previously soared above their heads was a set of ornate cast-iron gates made by the Coalbrookdale Company. In 1871 they were moved to their current location at the south end of West Carriage Drive during the construction of the Albert Memorial, where anyone who remembered the Great Exhibition more fondly than Dickens could look at them as a suitable emblem of what the Exhibition had come to represent: a gateway to the future. Meanwhile Paxton busied himself designing even more ambitious constructions in glass, including the Great Victorian Way: a ten-mile-long glittering girdle around London that, if it had been built to Paxton's specifications, would have included a street, a railway and an arcade, all enclosed in a glass-and-iron structure seventy-two feet wide, like a transept of the Crystal Palace that had been stretched into a giant architectural hoop. Paxton's commitment to architectural innovation did not extend to his domestic life; in 1851 he celebrated his success with the Crystal Palace by adding another wing to Barbrook, his grand villa on the Duke of Devonshire's Chatsworth estate, which included a four-storey Italianate tower built from local sandstone. But the influence of the Exhibition continued to extend itself elsewhere, starting with the "New York Crystal Palace Exhibition" of 1853–4, held in an enormous glass-and-iron structure in Bryant Park, and continuing with the development of glass-fronted department stores in Paris, Vienna, New York, London, Sydney and many other cities worldwide.

None of this would have greatly impressed Dickens. After an enlarged version of the Crystal Palace was rebuilt at Sydenham, where the gardens were filled with scale models of dinosaurs designed by the sculptor Benjamin Waterhouse Hawkins, including a scaly Megalosaurus caught in mid-waddle, Dickens continued to dislike the building's grandiose architecture and disagree with those who admired it. In 1854 he refused to print a "very well done" article on the building that had been sent in to *Household Words*, telling Wills that the "flatulent botheration" of official guidebooks was bad enough. Three years after the Great Exhibition, having "so very large a building continually rammed down one's throat" was driving him to distraction, and although the new Crystal Palace was "a very remarkable thing in itself" he still regarded it as "the most gigantic Humbug ever mounted on a long-suffering-people's shoulders." Rarely had he been so out of step with his contemporaries.

In other ways, too, 1851 had revealed the shape of things to come. "No great thing was ever done by looking back," Dickens told Henry Austin on 21 January 1852. That remark came just four days after George Sala's article "Things Departed" had appeared in *Household Words*, borrowing the character of a mournful Conservative speaker to observe "how curiously we adapt ourselves to the changes that are daily taking place around us; how, one by one, old habits and old customs die away, and we go about our business as unconcernedly as though they never had been." Spring-mounted hackney coaches, voluminous greatcoats, tinderboxes instead of matches . . . everywhere the speaker looks there are absences where once-familiar objects and ideas have "departed with the leaves and the melting snow." Evidence as to what was replacing them could be seen in the new words and phrases that were being added to the English language; according to the Merriam-Webster dictionary, those first widely used from 1851 included *art form, blood test, busker, cack-handed, carbohydrate, chic, crybaby, day-tripper, decolonize, factory farm, flying start, free fall, headlamp, hold up, kindergarten, manhandle, missing link, mooch, national park, nugget, overindulge, paper clip, police state, resourceful, science fiction, senile dementia, small-scale, stocktaking* and *wet dream.*

Other clues about the future dating from 1851 are hard to read now without the mental accompaniment of a warning siren. For example, during the July meeting of the British Association for the Advancement of Science (an organisation that had been mercilessly parodied by Dickens as the Mudfog Society at the start of his career), a paper had been delivered on the destruction of the tropical rainforests. The trees were being chopped down to feed the world's growing appetite for raw materials, and the authors warned that such actions were storing up "calamities for future generations." Nobody outside the room seems to have paid much attention, but it was an early sign that the industrial processes celebrated in Hyde Park might end up contributing to a rather different "precipice in Time." Already the clock was ticking.

On 7 February 1852, three weeks before the publication of the first instalment of *Bleak House*, Dickens celebrated his fortieth birthday at home with a dinner party for his closest friends. For some people the only real surprise was that he wasn't much older. George Sala finally met Dickens this year at the *Household Words* offices, and realised that he was actually a decade younger than he looked. "The silky locks had thinned, and were grizzling," he later wrote, and while Dickens's eyes were still bright and restless, "the brows and cheeks were deeply lined [with] premature furrows and wrinkles." A daguerreotype probably taken in 1855 by John E. Mayall, who had a portrait gallery at 443 West Strand and then 224 Regent Street, showed Dickens in profile, and even a stiff upright collar and experimental moustache couldn't hide the fact that his face was becoming creased and worn.

Soon he would start wearing a broad flannel belt around his waist to protect his weak kidneys, and he was fully aware that in his case the ageing
process appeared to be speeding up. "Whether we look as we used to look,
I can't quite determine," he had written the previous July to George
Putnam, who had been Dickens's secretary on his tour of America in 1842,
before going on to admit that he was "much redder and browner, I believe,
than I was in those times—more robust—less interesting—shorter
haired—a more solid-looking personage—and not younger." That may
have been a flattering version of the truth. The mother of *Household Words*
contributor Edmund Yates hadn't seen Dickens for more than a decade,
and when she met him a couple of years later she reported that "she
should not have recognised him, for, save for his eyes, there was no trace
of the original Dickens about him."

He was still robust enough to go for walks of up to twenty miles a
day, his ear permanently cocked for oddities he could use in his fiction,
like the fact that a shabby Charing Cross omnibus tout whose services
he used this January—"one of those melancholy, faded, red-nosed, gin-
and-watery, whelk-and-periwinkly men, always 'half muddled' yet never
drunk"—was known as Sloppy, a name Dickens would later borrow for
the letter-box-mouthed youth in *Our Mutual Friend* who "do the Police
in different voices" when he reads a newspaper aloud to Betty Higden.
But in other respects he was fast approaching the thoughtful, serious-
looking figure who would later appear on the Bank of England £10 note.
In 1859 he would be painted by his friend William Powell Frith, adopting
a pose that deliberately echoed the famous 1839 portrait by Daniel
Maclise. Once again Dickens was viewed sitting at a desk with his legs
nonchalantly crossed, looking over his right shoulder as if interrupted
by something or searching for inspiration somewhere. And once again
he wrote about the portrait as if it depicted someone else, telling Frith
that he was willing for "the gifted Individual whom you will transmit to
posterity" to be photographed in the same velvet coat if it would help
to achieve a better likeness.

As he sat in his Tavistock House study in February 1852, working on the next instalment of *Bleak House*, Dickens could reflect that much else in his life had changed since Maclise had painted him as a fresh-faced young writer with shrewd, laughing eyes. His popularity was still growing: whereas *David Copperfield*'s average monthly circulation had been around 22,000 copies, that of *Bleak House* never fell below 34,000 copies. (By comparison each number of Thackeray's *Vanity Fair* had sold around 5,000 copies.) "I have never had so many readers," Dickens boasted to Mrs. Richard Watson the following year. His income was also increasing: his share of the profits of *Bleak House* would eventually amount to £11,000, more than seven times the cost of the lease of Tavistock House. Yet in many ways it was his choice of this address that was the clearest sign of his success. The wide streets and grand squares of northern Bloomsbury were the result of a "systematic transformation" of the area into "a restricted upper-middle-class suburb," and although geographically it was less than four miles away from the Marshalsea Prison he still vividly remembered from his childhood, psychologically it might as well have been on a different planet. It meant that each time he entered the grand carriage sweep that led to his new front door, he could reassure himself that he had not only reached home. In more than one sense he had *arrived*.

His move to Bloomsbury and the first instalment of *Bleak House* came shortly before another new arrival. "I am happy to say that Mrs. Dickens is just confined with a brilliant boy of unheard-of dimensions, and is wonderfully well," he wrote to Wills on 13 March. The new baby was christened Edward Bulwer Lytton Dickens, nicknamed "The Plornishghenter" by his father, a tag that could be lengthened to "Plornishmaroontigoonter" or shortened to "Plorn" or "Plornish"—the final choice being a name Dickens would later give to a family in *Little Dorrit*, whose children include a four-year-old boy. "He *is* a fine little fellow, ain't he, sir," his proud mother tells Clennam in an instalment published shortly after Plornish Dickens had celebrated his own fourth birthday, allowing Dickens to smuggle a family joke into an otherwise superfluous narrative detail. He was the tenth child born to his parents and would prove to be the last.

The birth of Plorn provided Dickens with another visible reminder that he was now a respectable family man, although that did not prevent him from keeping in touch with the more raffish world of professional theatre. The former actress Emmeline Compton, who had noticed how Dickens always needed to be "*doing* something," was married to Henry Compton, the leading Shakespearean clown of his generation, and in the memoir of his life written by his sons Compton recalled Dickens's "brilliance and animation" whenever guests were invited to dine at Tavistock

House. Like everything Dickens took seriously, these dinners were carefully stage-managed. "The dining-tables were purposely made very narrow, to facilitate opposite guests talking with one another," Compton's sons explained, and sometimes "the end of the table touched a mirror, which reflected the whole scene, and increased the brilliance of its appearance." Like his work with the Guild of Literature and Art over the previous year, Dickens's dinner parties revealed the important role that theatre would continue to play in his life.

So what did he see when he looked in the mirror in his study where he acted out characters from *Bleak House*? A curious, confident narrator who is perfectly at ease in the world, or another version of Esther, the formerly unwanted child who is aware that her new loving home could be taken away from her at any moment? It is a threat that animates the whole novel. Even the name of the character who will later be revealed as Esther's father, the poor law-writer known as Nemo, is echoed in dozens of repetitions of "nobody," as Dickens sets him up as the narrative equivalent of the Invisible Man, a character who is absent for large stretches of the story but continues to exert a powerful grip on its language. In the first instalment "Nobody can see" the small lawyer with a big voice who intervenes in the court that is debating Jarndyce and Jarndyce, and later Esther notices that "Nobody had appeared" to help young Peepy Jellyby when his head is caught in some railings. Such echoes represent the danger of an interconnected world breaking down—a danger that is most clearly embodied in the figure of Nemo himself, who passes through the world largely unnoticed and alone. For Dickens, who had started his career as a legal clerk, it was another warning of how different his life might have been, and how vulnerable he remained as a writer whose social position depended on his remaining popular with the reading public. On 3 February 1852, he sent one reader an "autobiographical shake of the hand" (i.e., a signed letter), but he already knew from the fate of writers like Harrison Ainsworth how quickly such correspondence could dry up. Perhaps that was another reason why Frith's painting later depicted him looking over his shoulder.

His personal life was equally vulnerable. One entry he added to his memorandum book a few years later was "A misplaced and mis-married man. Always, as it were, playing hide and seek with the world and never finding what Fortune seems to have hidden when he was born." Read with the knowledge that he and Catherine would shortly undergo a messy public separation, it now sounds less like the plot for a possible story than a sad private confession. Another entry removed the fig leaf of fiction entirely. "The man who is incapable of his own happiness. One who is always in pursuit of happiness. Result. Where is happiness to be found then. Surely not everywhere? Can that be so, after all? Is *this* my experience?" The past year had given a dreadful warning of how a failing marriage could turn out, with Dickens having to enlist Inspector Field in an attempt to prevent Rosina Bulwer Lytton from sabotaging the opening night of *Not So Bad As We Seem*, and soon the parallels between Bulwer Lytton's situation and his own would draw closer.

A cache of recently discovered letters reveals that during the period leading up to his separation from Catherine in 1858, Dickens tried to have her declared insane. The fact that Forster was Secretary to the Commissioners of Lunacy added ominous weight to his chances of success, as did the fact that Dr. John Conolly, one of the country's leading experts in mental illness, was a close friend. In the end Dickens failed, according to a writer Catherine confided in towards the end of her life, because "bad as the law is in regard to proof of insanity he could not quite wrest it to his purpose." A month after this episode Bulwer Lytton got far closer to achieving the same goal for himself. After Rosina had again tried to embarrass him, this time during a by-election campaign where she appeared at a husting to denounce him as "a monster who should have been transported to the colonies long ago," he arranged for her to be seized and declared insane by Dr. Conolly. She was then incarcerated in a private lunatic asylum, where she remained for several weeks until a public outcry forced her release. It was as if both writers were hoping to solve their personal problems with the sort of plot they might once have reserved for one of their novels.

Fortunately there were already the first glimpses of a future in which marriage would not be the only option for a writer who wanted to share their life with someone else. In October 1851, George Eliot's work on the *Westminster Review* had led to her meeting the philosopher and critic George Henry Lewes. Described as a "witty, French, flippant sort of man" by the American feminist Margaret Fuller, he would soon join Eliot in a display of genuine personal courage by choosing to live together openly as a couple, despite the fact that Lewes was already married to someone else. But that was not the sort of future Dickens could ever imagine for himself. Although he tolerated Wilkie Collins's equally unconventional personal life, while he and Collins were travelling together in Italy in 1853 he was quick to write to Catherine announcing that his friend had revealed a "code of morals" which "I instantly and with becoming gravity Smash." At such moments he revealed more than a touch of Mr. Podsnap in his own character; he too was suspicious of anything that might bring a blush into the cheek of a young person. In public, anyway. After his separation from Catherine he would later construct an elaborate double life for himself with the young actress Ellen Ternan, involving a second household, secret payments, and possibly even an illegitimate son who died young—a male version of Esther who never made it as far as telling his story. Much about this relationship remains unknown, despite decades of biographical detective work, but looked at from the perspective of a year that had ended with a novel centred on another illegitimate child yearning to know more about her father, it starts to look as if fiction for Dickens was far more than just a reflection of life. It was a way of sounding out its possibilities.

Other decisions taken in 1851 would continue to influence Dickens's day-to-day life. There were further theatrical performances in support of the Guild of Literature and Art: in February the Amateur Company was in Manchester and Liverpool, and in May it was in Shrewsbury and Birmingham, followed by an ambitious summer tour that took it from Nottingham to Derby, Newcastle, Sunderland, Sheffield and finally back to Manchester in September. Yet Dickens's charitable scheme would never satisfy his own ambitions for it. Although £3,615 was generated in the first year of fundraising, and three almshouses did eventually open at Knebworth in 1865 (although no writers or artists ever moved into them), the Guild continued to be sneered at as a "literary Soup-Kitchen," and the parliamentary bill incorporating the organisation did not allow it to award any pensions for seven years, by which time public interest in the scheme had quietly melted away. Dickens did dedicate *Bleak House* to the Guild when it was published in volume form in 1853, but already his choice of words—"DEDICATED AS A REMEMBRANCE OF OUR FRIENDLY UNION TO MY COMPANIONS IN THE GUILD OF LITERATURE AND ART"—had the appearance of an epitaph.

Some of his most important friendships from this year were also starting to fade. Despite the arrival of the magnificently named Edward Bulwer Lytton Dickens, his older namesake became increasingly jealous of the critical acclaim and popular success enjoyed by Plorn's father, a rival who was "destined to eclipse me." Later his jealousy spilled over into displays of open resentment, telling his own son that Dickens was not what the public thought him to be. "Dickens is *not* a great fellow," he announced. "He wants heart and is a great humbug." This could produce moments of exquisite torture, such as having to take the chair at a dinner held in 1869 in Dickens's honour. "It was not a pleasant position for me to go into the hornet's nest of my enemies his special friends are," he grumbled. "They think to ignore or deny me advances him, and I suspect that he sanctions that policy."

Luckily he seemed not to have noticed that *Bleak House*'s Jo, who is forced to keep moving on while Skimpole sings a plaintive ballad about a boy "Thrown on the wide world, doomed to wander and roam, / Bereft of his parents, bereft of a home," was more than just a fictional hybrid assembled from real individuals. These included the crossing sweeper George Ruby and probably another boy who had been "turned adrift on the world friendless and unprotected" by his relatives in July 1851, according to the *Annual Register*, and had been found "cold, stiff, and dead" the next morning. But Jo was also a descendant of the illiterate street sweeper

Beck who appears in Bulwer Lytton's 1846 novel *Lucretia*: "a lonesome, squalid, bloodless thing, which the great Monster, London, seemed to have spewed forth of its own self—one of its sickly, miserable, rickety offspring . . . this living reproach, rising up from the stones of London against our social indifference to the souls which wither and rot under the hard eyes of science and the deaf ears of wealth." Very little separates this piece of writing from Dickens's description of "very muddy, very hoarse, very ragged" Jo. Very little apart from talent.

The events of 1851 would produce more delayed aftershocks in the lives of Dickens's children. For example, the idea that Australia offered a fresh start continued to intrigue Dickens, and some years later he managed to persuade two of his sons to take up the challenge. Alfred and Plorn were not fallen, unlike most of the girls in Urania Cottage, but in their father's eyes they were very likely to become failures if they stayed in Britain—in fact Dickens would later discover that Alfred had left behind several unpaid tailor's bills, like a younger version of the spendthrift uncle after whom he had been named. The results of Dickens's attempt to prevent history from repeating itself were mixed. After arriving in New South Wales in 1865, Alfred found a job managing a far-off sheep station, where he declared himself "as happy as a king." Perhaps encouraged by this news, two years later Dickens withdrew the fifteen-year-old Plorn from school, telling the headmaster that he intended "an active life" for his youngest child—one that would later involve Plorn being elected a member of the Legislative Assembly of New South Wales. Yet ultimately neither son was as successful as fictional characters like Micawber or Magwitch. Plorn lost his seat in 1894, and eight years later he died alone in a hotel during a summer heat wave. Alfred was financially broken by an economic depression in the 1890s and spent the last years of his life touring Britain and America, offering reminiscences of his father and reading extracts from his books. If he made the connection back to his brother Charley's observation that "the children of my father's brain were much more real to him at times than we were" he tactfully avoided mentioning this in public. Anyone who knew Dickens probably wouldn't have been surprised to learn that his way of dealing with his own trouble-some children had been to treat them like the characters in a story he didn't have time to write.

On 16 March, with publication of the second number of *Bleak House* just a fortnight away, Dickens wrote to Miss Coutts, telling her that although he had recently been in "an unsettled and anxious condition" he was now ready to "shut myself up in Bleak House again." However, the completed novel would repeatedly remind its readers that for most people such self-isolation was neither possible nor desirable. As the previous year had shown, from headline-grabbing events like the Great Exhibition to the collaborative effort of putting on a play, human life was also social life, and *Bleak House* was Dickens's most ambitious attempt yet to show what this meant in practice.

"Why, Esther," says her guardian John Jarndyce after Sir Leicester Dedlock unexpectedly pays them a visit, "our visitor and you are the two last persons on earth I should have thought of connecting together!" By this stage of the story we are likely to be considerably less surprised than Jarndyce, and his reference to "connecting" reminds us why. Words like "connect" and "connexion" form some of Dickens's most self-conscious pieces of internal architecture in *Bleak House*, where they refer both to complicated social links like Esther's parentage and to the sparks of thought that might light up such links in someone's mind. Although these words are repeated dozens of times, they remain an understated presence in the novel, reminding us that connections to other people are often shad-owy, their discovery uncertain. That is why we sometimes see the process breaking down, as it does when Miss Flite's face softens into a smile as she silently looks at Esther and seems "to lose the connexion in her mind." Attempts to make new connections are as much the business of the novel as discovering old ones, at once an urgent social need and a powerful motor driving the story on. Recall the question Dickens's narrator asks roughly a third of the way through *Bleak House*: "What connexion can there have been between many people in the innumerable histories of this world who from opposite sides of great gulfs, have, nevertheless, been very curiously brought together!" What the events of the previous year had shown Dickens was that there were many possible answers to this question, including commerce, disease, language, friendship, family and love. His own contribution was to suggest an answer that embraced all these and more: stories. For the central idea that animates *Bleak House*, its narrative heartbeat, is not just that our individual stories have points of connection. It is that we are all parts of the same story.

"Literature cannot be too faithful to the people," Dickens announced in a speech given in Birmingham at the start of 1853, "cannot too ardently advocate the cause of their advancement, happiness and prosperity"—a claim that generated "[*Loud applause*]" in the room where he had just been presented with an award celebrating his status as "a national writer." It came at a time when he was increasingly being recognised as an international writer too. A year after the final double number of *Bleak House* appeared, the American periodical *Peterson's Magazine* published Alice Gray's "The Turning Point," a moral fable about a fateful encounter between a virtuous citizen and a criminal on the run, which included a satirical reference to the members of a local missionary society who do not help because their eyes are fixed on the other side of the world—"Barrioboola [*sic*] Gha, perhaps"—like a local chapter of Mrs. Jellyby's colonisation society. The following year an anonymous eighty-line poem titled "Borroboola [*sic*] Gha: A Poem for the Times" appeared in another American periodical, in which a preacher appeals for charity to assist "some heathens, / Thousands of miles afar, / Who live in a land of darkness," shortly before the poem's speaker stumbles across a starving child and his dying mother nearby. "Alas for the cold and hungry / That met me every day, / While all my tears were given / To the suffering far away!" he exclaims. Already a set of ideas that had been shaped by one time and place were picking up enough momentum to escape their gravitational pull.

Dickens's novel was on the move in other ways too. Popular echoes of its famous opening included a parody published in 1863 ("Fog. So dense you could cut it with a knife") and the description of November in *A Tale of Two Cities*, "with its fogs atmospheric and fogs legal," which sounds more like an offcut from *Bleak House* that Dickens's printers had inserted by mistake. More significantly, from April 1852 to December 1853, *Bleak House* was reprinted in its entirety by *Frederick Douglass's Paper* in Rochester, New York—a decision based on the fact that Dickens's novel, despite the clear British focus of its plot, had a broader social mission that was no respecter of national boundaries. Even the scene in which we are told that children like Jo are "dying thus around us every day" was enlisted in the "Literary Notices" section of the paper to remind Douglass's readers that "us" included them. While young Americans might not be dying from poverty in quite the same numbers as youths were on the streets of London, the section's editor Julia Griffiths pointed out, her readers should still be moved by Dickens's writing. "He who can stand by the death-bed of the poor idiot 'Jo,' without having the kindly sympathies of his nature called forth," she wrote, "must be callous to the wants and miseries of his kind." Douglass's own sympathy with the novel eventually went further still. Twenty-five years later, he erected a small one-room structure behind his

home in Washington DC—a forerunner of the modern garden office—and dubbed it "The Growlery" in tribute to the end of *Bleak House*, when Esther explains that "with the first money we saved at home, we added to our pretty house by throwing out a little Growlery expressly for my guardian."

Nor did the international influence of *Bleak House* end there. In 2002, the literary scholar Henry Louis Gates, Jr reported his discovery of a previously unknown antebellum manuscript, the title page of which read "The Bondwoman's Narrative by Hannah Crafts, a Fugitive Slave Recently Escaped from North Carolina." Widely thought to be the earliest surviving novel by a Black woman, it ripples with echoes of *Bleak House* from the start. "Gloom everywhere. Gloom up the Potomac; where it rolls among meadows no longer green," writes Crafts, in a tight imitation of Dickens's "Fog everywhere. Fog up the river, where it flows among green aits and meadows." Similarly, while Esther opens her account with the admission that "I have a great difficulty in beginning to write my portion of these pages, for I know I am not clever," Crafts's escaped slave is even more apologetic. "It may be that I assume to[o] much responsibility in attempting to write these pages," she confesses. "I am neither clever, nor learned, nor talented." There are flashes of all three qualities in the rest of the novel, as Crafts returns to and reworks numerous scenes from Dickens's original. Sometimes these parallels are so close that reading *The Bondwoman's Narrative* is like coming across a translation written in the same language: just as Esther resolves "to be industrious, contented, and kind-hearted, and so do some good to some one, and win some love to myself if I could," so Hannah plans "to be industrious, cheerful, and true-hearted, to do some good though in an humble way, and to win some love if I could." Inevitably such parallels have led to accusations of plagiarism, but a better way of thinking about them might be as a form of imaginative solidarity. If Hannah's voice echoes Esther's, perhaps that is because Crafts wanted to demonstrate a more loyal and loving relationship than that of a slave and her master. "I won't be a slave all my life," declares Caddy Jellyby in *Bleak House*, having decided to follow her own heart rather than continue to submit to her mother's demands. Although Dickens's presence behind

Esther's voice undoubtedly complicates this process, *The Bondwoman's Narrative* generously attempts a literary version of the same idea.

"The house of fiction," Henry James would later famously claim, has "not one window, but a million." No single aperture gives access to what James called "the need of the individual vision" and "the pressure of the individual will." Yet by the time Dickens completed *Bleak House* the novel provided far more than just a window onto his own world. With not one but two unreliable narrators, and a tone that is as hard to pin down as a blob of mercury, it also offered a set of windows onto the future of the novel as a whole. It was a favourite of Joseph Conrad: "a work from the master for which I have such an admiration, or rather such an intense and unreasoning affection . . . I have read it innumerable times both in Polish and in English; I have read it only the other day . . ." Agatha Christie also learned from it as an experimental piece of detective fiction: "such a good plot . . . !" she exclaimed after trying to write a film adaptation. One fragment even found a new home for itself in James Joyce's *Finnegans Wake* (1939) with his reference to "derryjellybies," a dizzyingly complex portmanteau word that squashes together elements of a place (Derry), a sweet (jelly babies), an Arabic cloak (djellaba), an airship (dirigible) and the Jellybys. As one modern critic has put it, "After *Bleak House* the novel was never quite the same again."

When Dickens died he left his final novel *The Mystery of Edwin Drood* unfinished, but after 1851 he would increasingly be seen as a writer who couldn't ever be finished. Mamie tried to sum up what the world had lost with his death. "Yes, yes, you are his daughter of course. But just think what he is to *me* in my life," she recalled readers saying to her, noticing that "it is always the present tense. 'I *love* your Father.' And this is what I mean by his being so much *in* this world." Always the present tense: as if he had just stepped out of the room and could return at any moment.

Perhaps nobody has ever got closer to capturing Dickens's elusive personality than Eleanor Christian, the young author whose silk dress he had ruined during that awkward summer flirtation in Broadstairs. The last time she saw him was in 1858, when he gave a reading of *A Christmas Carol* in Southampton. She was shocked by how much older he looked. "He seemed to have withered and dwindled into a smaller man," she wrote, "and his former 'flashy' style of dress had faded into shabbiness." But his performance was as gripping as ever, entering fully into each character and "seeming to enjoy the fun and sympathise with the pathos as if all were quite new to him." Her heart went out to him:

> I longed for a touch of his hand, and a kindly word, and I lingered in the entrance of the assembly room, nearly frozen with cold, to wait his coming out; but discovered he had left by means of a window near his platform.

Acknowledgements

Some parts of this book draw on earlier research I have published on Dickens and his contemporaries, rather as the Crystal Palace was assembled in Hyde Park from sections made elsewhere. However my interest in this topic was first sparked into life by John Butt's article "'Bleak House' in the Context of 1851," originally published in the journal *Nineteenth-Century Fiction* Vol. 10 No. 1 (June 1955). Since then I've learned a great deal from other critics and scholars, and although specific debts are recorded in my notes I am grateful to all those whose writing has influenced this book in other ways. For reading and commenting on early drafts I would particularly like to thank John Bowen, Mac Castro, Ushashi Dasgupta, Hugo Murphy, Francis O'Gorman, Sam Plumb, Adrian Poole, Sophie Ratcliffe, Luc Rosenberg and Helen Small. For helping with specific research questions I am indebted to Lee Ault (Dickens Museum Broadstairs), Mark Dickens, Traccy Earl (Coutts), Aidan Haley (Chatsworth), Richard Hilton, Leon Litvack, the Morgan Library, Louisa Price (Dickens House Museum), David Shipton and Katie Callaghan (Rockingham Castle), and Michael Slater and Alex Werner (Museum of London), while Archie Cornish expertly sorted out my tangled notes. Most of this book was written while I was recovering from a haematopoietic stem cell transplant, a procedure I underwent in 2018 to try to halt the progression of an aggressive form of multiple sclerosis, and I could not have done any of it without the support of my colleagues and friends at Magdalen College, Oxford. Finally, I would like to thank Michal Shavit, Daisy Watt, Katherine Fry, John Garrett, and the rest of the editorial team at Jonathan Cape for their sharp eyes and great kindness at all stages of this book, and my agent Peter Straus for giving me a chance in the first place.

Notes

Wherever possible I have quoted from Oxford University Press's Clarendon editions of Dickens's works or the paperback editions published by Oxford World's Classics. However, given the number of alternative editions that are available, I have supplied chapter numbers rather than page references to help readers who would like to track down specific quotations. I follow the usual practice of using abbreviated titles for novels such as *The Posthumous Papers of the Pickwick Club* and *The Life and Adventures of Nicholas Nickleby*. Articles originally published in *Household Words* and *All the Year Round* are quoted from the original magazines: digital copies can be viewed at djo.org.uk. Other works referred to frequently are abbreviated as follows:

Interviews and Recollections	*Dickens: Interviews and Recollections*, ed. Philip Collins, 2 vols. (London: Macmillan Press, 1981)
Letters	*The Letters of Charles Dickens*, ed. Madeline House, Graham Storey et al., 12 vols. (Oxford: Clarendon Press, 1965–2002)
Life	John Forster, *The Life of Charles Dickens*, 3 vols. (London: Chapman & Hall, 1872–4)
Memoranda	*Charles Dickens' Book of Memoranda*, ed. Fred Kaplan (New York: New York Public Library, 1981)
Speeches	*The Speeches of Charles Dickens*, ed. K. J. Fielding (Oxford: Clarendon Press, 1960)

PROLOGUE: SUPPOSING

3   **"shattered in all directions":** *Household Narrative of Current Events* (1850), p. 273.

3   **rapidly being assembled:** See illustration. "Crystal Palace" was used six times in the same issue of *Punch* (13 July 1850) that also contained a contribution by Douglas Jerrold in which he referred to "a palace of very crystal"; when an early version of Paxton's design was published a week earlier in the *Illustrated London News* it was referred to merely as a "building" and a "structure" (p. 13).

4   **"nearly Two Feet in Length":** *Illustrated London News*, 2 November 1850, p. 16.

4 **under the tropical sun:** *Household Narrative* (1850), p. 266.

4 **"most perfect living skeleton":** Ibid., p. 271.

4 **"to recruit his health":** Ibid., p. 273.

5 **an Italian beach in 1822:** The disputed question of exactly which part of Shelley was plucked from the embers of his funeral pyre is discussed by Hermione Lee in *Body Parts: Essays on Life-Writing* (London: Chatto & Windus, 2005).

5 **"proud to possess":** Leigh Hunt, *The Autobiography of Leigh Hunt*, 3 vols. (London: Smith, Elder & Co., 1850), i. 68; in his second volume Hunt also celebrates the "child-like simplicity of the poet" (ii. 20).

5 **" 'Very kind, but very German' ":** See Christopher Ricks, *Tennyson* (London and Basingstoke: Macmillan, 1972), pp. 231–2.

5 **"Let me count the ways":** Elizabeth Barrett Browning, *Poems*, 2 vols. (London: Chapman & Hall, 1850), ii. 479.

5 **"The old order changeth":** Alfred Tennyson, *Poems*, 2 vols. (London: Edward Moxon, 1842), ii. 15.

5 **"digs at it with his pencil":** To the Hon. Mrs. Richard Watson, 30 December 1850, *Letters*, vi. 251.

6 **"any more sittings from me":** F. G. Kitton (ed.), *Charles Dickens by Pen and Pencil* (London: Sabin and Dexter, 1889), p. 60.

6 **"suppose myself to be the original":** To John Forster, 6 January 1856, *Letters*, viii. 9.

6 **"but not my own":** To Richard Lane, 26 November 1861, *Letters*, ix. 523.

7 **"pumped out of him":** *Pen Photographs of Charles Dickens's Readings* (1871), repr. in Kitton (ed.), *Dickens by Pen and Pencil*, p. 87.

7 **Antoine Claudet:** See illustration.

7 **neat shelves of books:** See illustration; Kitton (ed.), *Dickens by Pen and Pencil*, p. 58.

8 **"fifty human beings":** *Life*, i. 97.

8 **"told *his own father a lie!*":** *Interviews and Recollections*, pp. 192, 337, 271.

9 **"Fancy Dress":** To F. C. Beard, 5 April 1870, *Letters*, xii. 505 (see illustration).

9 **chains and padlocks:** "The British Lion in America" and "Charles Dickens and the Honest Little Boy" (see illustration), repr. in B. W. Matz (ed.), *Dickens in Cartoon and Caricature* (Boston: privately printed for the Bibliophile Society, 1924), plates XX and XXI.

9 **"a wonderfully embroidered shirt":** John Coleman, *Fifty Years of an Actor's Life*, 2 vols. (London: Hutchinson, 1904), ii. 544.

9 **"about the shirt-front":** Ibid., ii. 23–4.

9 **"yellow kid gloves":** Ibid., ii. 544.

9 **"muddy combination of them all":** Mamie Dickens quoting "one who knew him intimately"; however she confesses that she finds it hard to be sure, as "I never saw eyes so constantly changing in colour and expression as his did," Kitton (ed.), *A Supplement to Charles Dickens By Pen and Pencil* (London: Sabin and Dexter, 1890), p. 46.

10   **repertoire of alter egos:** Charles and Mary Cowden Clarke, *Recollections of Writers* (London: Samson Low, Marston, Searle, & Rivington, 1878), p. 326n.

10   **distinct style of handwriting:** To Mrs. Cowden Clarke and Miss Novello, 19 September 1848, *Letters*, v. 409.

10   **"All social evils":** To Mrs. Howitt, 22 February 1850, *Letters*, vi. 41.

10   **"Brighten it":** To W. H. Wills, 5 August 1853, *Letters*, vii. 126.

11   **"Dickensy":** The *OED* doesn't always include the earliest citations for new words, but its examples for these coinages accurately indicate the growing desire to find a word to characterise something new in fiction: this sense of *Dickensian* is traced back to 1853, *Dickensish* to 1849, *Dickensy* to 1855 and *Dickensesque* to 1856.

11   **"imitations of myself":** To Miss Burdett Coutts, 14 August 1850, *Letters*, vi. 147.

11   **"a miserable November evening":** "Hints to Novelists, for 1846," *The Comic Almanack for 1846* (London: David Bogue, 1845), pp. 71–2.

11   **"excessively interesting":** She would later praise the Crystal Palace in exactly the same terms; see journal entries for 30 December 1838 and 8 January 1839 (*Oliver Twist*), and 7 June 1851 (Great Exhibition); the journals are available online at queenvictoriasjournals.org.

11   **"put together *Dombey!*":** *Life*, ii. 336.

12   **"set him up in life for ever":** "The Begging-Letter Writer," *Household Words*, 18 May 1850, pp. 169–72.

12   **"the most remarkable invention":** To Edmund B. Green, 14 February 1842, *Letters*, iii. 61.

12   **"fast fading away":** Thomas Powell, *The Living Authors of England* (New York: D. Appleton & Co., 1849), pp. 158, 169, 178, 160.

12   **"raving mad":** "Extraordinary Case," *The Times*, 10 January 1849, p. 4.

12   **socially committed Dickens:** For an early example of this argument, see "Boz Versus Dickens" in *Parker's London Magazine* 2 (February 1845), pp. 122–8.

13   **"*Boz has written himself out*":** *The Period*, 13 November 1869, repr. in Matz (ed.), *Dickens in Cartoon and Caricature*, pp. 154–5. Emphasis original.

13   **"perhaps he was not far wrong":** *Life*, iii. 37–8.

13   **"What next? what next?":** "Morna," *The Battle of London Life; or, Boz and his Secretary* (London: George Peirce, 1849), pp. 1, 5.

14   **"Mr. Punch" and "Pugnose":** Mark Hovell, *The Chartist Movement*, ed. T. F. Tout, 3rd edn. (Manchester: Manchester University Press, 1970), p. 292.

14   **nearly half a million people:** *Household Narrative* (1850), p. 274.

14   ***net-work*:** "Any netlike or complex system or collection of interrelated things, as topographical features, lines of transportation, or telecommunications routes (*esp.* telephone lines)" (*OED*, "network," 4a). The first example given is from 1839 (a "net-work of islands") and the first recorded use of the word being used in a technological sense is "The three kingdoms would be intersected by a net-work of railroad measuring twelve thousand miles" (W. H.

Wills, "The Railway Wonders of the Last Year," *Household Words*, 17 August 1850, p. 482). See also Jonathan H. Grossman, *Charles Dickens's Networks: Public Transport and the Novel* (Oxford: Oxford University Press, 2012).

15 **"essential to social advancement"**: Dionysius Lardner, *A Treatise on the New Art of Transport, or Management, Prospects, and Relations, Commercial, Financial, and Social* (London: Taylor, Walton, and Maberly, 1850), p. 1.

15 **"got my steam up"**: To Miss Catherine Hogarth, 25 November 1835, *Letters*, i. 97.

15 **"powerful Locomotive"**: To Miss Palfrey, 4 April 1868, *Letters*, xii. 91.

15 **"what I want is, Facts"**: *Hard Times* (1854), ch. 1.

15 **through London four abreast**: Edward Cheshire, "The Results of the Census of Great Britain in 1851," *Journal of the Statistical Society of London* 17:1 (March 1854), p. 46.

15 **to ward off cramps**: Thomas Sternberg, *The Dialect and Folk-Lore of Northamptonshire* (London: John Russell Smith, 1851), quoted in Nigel Pennick, *Witchcraft and Secret Societies of Rural England: The Magic of Toadmen, Plough Witches, Mummers, and Bonesmen* (Rochester, Vermont: Destiny Books, 2011), p. 152.

16 **"A perfect and absolute blank"**: Lewis Carroll, *The Hunting of the Snark: An Agony, in Eight Fits* (London: Macmillan, 1876), p. 16.

16 **"four miles. Bah!"**: To Charles Knight, 30 December 1854, *Letters*, vii. 492–3.

16 **"habit of snorting"**: *David Copperfield* (1849–50), ch. 11.

17 **measure up to its name**: Most people were aware that the "Great" half of Great Britain referred to its geography rather than its status, but that did not prevent them from happily confusing the two; an article published in *All the Year Round* in 1859 would boast of "something in our blood that fitted us for the sea," with all that followed in terms of trade and naval power, but conclude that "this would not have produced our greatness alone," James Hannay, "Ships and Crews," *All the Year Round*, 20 August 1859, p. 389.

17 **"genuine mode of fraternisation"**: *Punch*, vol. 20 (1851), pp. 11, 188.

17 **"the Land of Promise"**: John Heraud, "The Old Year and the New Year," *Illustrated London News*, 21 December 1850, p. 499.

18 **"her excellent conduct"**: "Supposing," *Household Words*, 20 April 1850, p. 96; 10 August 1850, p. 480; 7 June 1851, p. 264; 6 September 1851, p. 576. A fifth and final "Supposing" article appeared in *Household Words* on 10 February 1855, p. 48.

19 **"Barnum will ever be President"**: To Dr. Elisha Bartlett, 26 December 1850, *Letters*, vi. 248.

19 **"all on whom it looked"**: "A December Vision," *Household Words*, 14 December 1850, pp. 265–7.

20 **"all hearts and hands, set right"**: "The Last Words of the Old Year," *Household Words*, 4 January 1851, pp. 337–9.

20 **set of blue crockery**: "A Christmas Tree," *Household Words*, 21 December 1850, p. 290.

20 **"a pendant":** Rosemary Ashton, *Thomas and Jane Carlyle: Portrait of a Marriage* (London: Chatto & Windus, 2002), Introduction n. 26.

20 **"some female character":** William Powell Frith, *My Autobiography and Reminiscences*, 3 vols. (London: Richard Bentley & Son, 1888), i. 30–1.

21 **"back to that time of my life":** *Life*, i. 33.

21 **"stale tarts so temptingly exposed":** "The Streets—Morning," originally published in the *Evening Chronicle*, 21 July 1835, repr. in *Sketches by Boz* (1836).

22 **"kept for my dinner":** *Life*, i. 36.

22 **"stale pastry put out for sale":** *David Copperfield*, ch. 11.

22 **"wandering fancy":** *Martin Chuzzlewit* (1842–4), ch. 33.

22 **"beyond that place and time":** *David Copperfield*, ch. 4.

22 **honorary family members:** See Michael Allen and David Parker, "Inside Devonshire Terrace," *Dickensian* 75 (1979).

22 **"children—real and imaginary":** To Miss Burdett Coutts, 23 August 1850, *Letters*, vi. 154.

22 **"more real to him at times":** *Interviews and Recollections*, p. 120.

22 **"hallooing 'Dickens!' ":** To the Hon. Mrs. Richard Watson, 28 January 1851, *Letters*, vi. 272.

23 **"one memorable day":** *Great Expectations* (1860–1), ch. 9.

23 **"of my own free will I wore it":** *A Christmas Carol* (1843), Stave One.

23 **"Whether I shall turn out":** *David Copperfield*, ch. 1.

23 **"the product of his age":** R. H. Horne, *A New Spirit of the Age*, 2 vols. (London: Smith, Elder & Co., 1844), i. 50.

24 **"retard its tendencies":** Harriet Martineau, *A History of England During the Thirty Years' Peace*, 2 vols. (London: Charles Knight & Co., 1849–50), ii. 704–5. Although Martineau regretted that Dickens did not have "a sounder social philosophy" and a loftier moral tone, she applauded him for "showing forth what was doing in the regions of darkness, and in odd places where nobody ever thought of going to look."

24 **"beginning to write . . . these pages":** *Bleak House* (1852–3), ch. 3.

24 **"going to pieces":** Ibid., ch. 28.

25 **"gloves, coffee-grounds, umbrellas":** Ibid., chs. 4, 30.

25 **"one of Mrs. Jellyby's closets":** Robert Newsom, *Dickens on the Romantic Side of Familiar Things: Bleak House and the Novel Tradition* (New York: Columbia University Press, 1977), p. 97.

25 **"a vast glass, vibrating":** *Bleak House*, ch. 48.

26 **"blooming, buzzing confusion":** *The Principles of Psychology*, 2 vols. (New York: Henry Holt & Co., 1890), i. 488, describing the assault on a baby's senses (in other accounts "blooming" is sometimes misquoted as "booming").

26 **"the usual sense":** "turning-point, n. 2. (*fig*)" (*OED*).

27 **"the ends which He designed":** Frederick Arnold, *Turning-Points in Life*, 2 vols. (New York: Harper and Brothers, 1873), pp. 1–3. Modern assessments include Marshall Brown, *Turning Points: Essays in the History of Cultural Expressions* (Stanford, CA: Stanford University Press, 1997), Andrew Abbott, "On the

Concept of Turning Point," repr. in *Time Matters: On Theory and Method* (Chicago: University of Chicago Press, 2001), and *Turning Points: Concepts and Narratives of Change in Literature and Other Media*, ed. Ansgar Nünning and Kai Marcel Sicks (Berlin: De Gruyter, 2012).

27   **"the turning point in Adam's life?":** Hugh McSorley, *The Temptation: Six Sermons* (London: J. F. Shaw, 1858), p. 18.

27   **"foundation of his future character":** Samuel Smiles, *Self-Help; With Illustrations of Character and Conduct* (London: John Murray, 1859), p. 228.

28   **"we shouldn't say it":** Mark Twain, "The Turning-Point of My Life," *Harper's Bazaar* 44 (February 1910), pp. 118– 19, repr. in *What is Man? and Other Essays* (New York and London, 1917).

28   **career as a professional writer:** William M. Thayer, *Turning Points in Successful Careers* (New York: T. Y. Crowell & Company, 1895), pp. 356–63: "The Choice that made Him a Great Writer."

28   **a single moment in 1833:** 1867 preface to *The Pickwick Papers*.

28   **"the turning-point of my existence":** *David Copperfield*, ch. 17: "Somebody Turns Up."

28   **"A great event in my life":** *Great Expectations*, ch. 37.

28   **a path that bristled with fingerposts:** Compare the thoughts of Stevens, the narrator of Kazuo Ishiguro's novel *The Remains of the Day*, as he looks back at a life of impeccable service and ruthless self-denial: "Indeed, it might even be said that this small decision of mine constituted something of a key turning point; that the decision set things on an inevitable course towards what actually happened [. . . yet] when with the benefit of hindsight one begins to search one's past for such 'turning points,' one is apt to start seeing them everywhere" (London: Faber and Faber, 1989), pp. 184–5.

29   **"he rose steadily":** "Douglas Jerrold," *Household Words*, 5 February 1859, p. 220.

29   **"the great turning-point in English History":** "How King Charles's Head Was Loosened," *All the Year Round*, 23 April 1864, p. 256.

29   **"very curiously brought together!":** *Bleak House*, ch. 16.

30   **"web of very different lives":** Ibid., ch. 47.

30   **"a novel quite unlike any":** Paul Schlicke's entry on *Bleak House* in *The Oxford Companion to Charles Dickens: Anniversary Edition*, ed. Paul Schlicke (Oxford: Oxford University Press, 2011), p. 48.

30   **"inky fishing-net":** To John Forster, 22 June 1856, *Letters*, viii. 139.

30   **"a collection of holes tied together with string":** Julian Barnes, *Flaubert's Parrot* (London: Jonathan Cape, 1984), p. 38.

30   **"record the atoms as they fall":** "Let us record the atoms as they fall upon the mind in the order in which they fall, let us trace the pattern, however disconnected and incoherent in appearance, which each sight or incident scores upon the consciousness," "Modern Fiction," *The Common Reader* (1925, repr. New York: Harcourt, Brace & World, Inc., 1953), p. 155.

31   **"on the tip toe of expectation":** To Percival Leigh, 10 March 1850, *Letters*, vi. 61.

WINTER: STAGES

35   **another mild day:** On 3 March 1851 Dickens explained that he rarely left his
      house before breakfast: "Busy or idle, I have found it such a comfort always to
      have the first few hours of the morning to myself" (to Eliot Warburton,
      Letters, vi. 303).

35   **a gentle breeze:** "Daily Weather Table," *London Daily News* (27 January 1851),
      reporting "The State of the Weather: at Nine o'clock on Saturday morning" in
      Greenwich.

35   **"light step and jaunty air":** Arthur Locker, in Kitton (ed.), *Charles Dickens by
      Pen and Pencil*, p. 173.

35   **"a turning point in all men's careers":** *Morning Post*, 4 January 1851.

35   **comical determination in a foot race:** Matz (ed.), *Dickens in Cartoon and
      Caricature*, plate XIX (see illustration).

35   **"his lips slightly working":** Charley Dickens, in *Interviews and Recollections*,
      p. 121.

35   **"I wonder what on earth I do there":** 10 February 1851, *Letters*, vi. 287.

36   **"without crowds about them":** To John Forster, 30 August 1846, *Letters*, iv.
      612–13; less than a month later he was still conscious of the lack of busy
      streets, especially at night, telling Forster "I don't seem able to get rid of my
      spectres unless I can lose them in crowds" (*Letters*, iv. 622).

36   **"to let nothing escape him":** Kitton (ed.), *Dickens by Pen and Pencil*, p. 64.

36   **"behind a dictionary":** *David Copperfield*, ch. 27.

37   **"of all its millions":** *Interviews and Recollections*, p. 326.

37   **smudges representing London's buildings:** See illustration; *A Balloon View of
      London* (London: Bank and Co., 1851).

37   **"ascending platform":** See illustration; Richard D. Altick, *The Shows of London*
      (Cambridge, Mass.: Belknap Press, 1978), ch. 11.

37   **"marriageable daughters in scores":** *Morning Chronicle*, 10 July 1835, repr. in
      The Dent Uniform Edition of Dickens' Journalism, ed. Michael Slater and John
      Drew, 4 vols. (London: J. M. Dent, 1994–2000), ii. 14–17.

37   **liable to get in their way:** *Pictorial Half-Hours of London Topography* (London:
      Charles Knight, 1851).

38   **"at the corner of every street":** "Gin-Shops," *Sketches by Boz*, ch. 22.

39   **three members of the same family:** *The Annual Register, or a View of the
      History and Politics of the Year 1851* (London: F. & J. Rivington, 1852), p. 5.

39   **drowning two workmen:** *Household Narrative* (1850), p. 293.

39   **"the stirring world about us":** "A Preliminary Word," *Household Words*, 30
      March 1850, p. 1.

39   **"The voice of Time . . . cries to man":** *The Chimes* (1844), ch. 3.

39   **the earth revolves around the sun:** "Old Lamps for New Ones," *Household
      Words*, 15 June 1850, pp. 266–7.

39   **a cloud of choking dust:** This was more than just narrative licence: thanks to
      poor regulations and patchy standards in the construction industry, the news
      was full of buildings that had fallen down; Dickens would later falsely be

accused of basing this instalment of the novel on the collapse of four houses
that made up Maple's shop on Tottenham Court Road. See James Fitzjames
Stephen's long unsigned review, "The Licence of Modern Novelists," *Edinburgh
Review* 106 (July 1857), pp. 124–56, in which Stephen argued that Dickens
selected "one or two of the popular cries of the day" to spice up each novel,
and "even the catastrophe in *Little Dorrit* is evidently borrowed from the recent
fall of houses in Tottenham Court Road." Dickens pointed out the chronologi-
cal inconsistency of this claim in a rapidly written rebuttal, "Curious Misprint
in the Edinburgh Review," *Household Words*, 1 August 1857, pp. 97–100.

40   **"never heeding, never asking":** "On Duty With Inspector Field," *Household
      Words*, 14 June 1851, p. 267.

40   **all living in just one room:** I owe this story to Judith Flanders, *The Victorian
      City: Everyday Life in Dickens's London* (London: Atlantic Books, 2012),
      pp. 195–6.

40   **"all placed carefully under glass":** *Interviews and Recollections*, p. 242.

40   **"but speaking to no one":** "The Streets—Morning" (1835), repr. in *Sketches by
      Boz*, ch. 1.

41   **"I'll give up snuff":** *Memoranda*, pp. 2, 25. This memorandum book was
      begun in 1855; Forster argued that "Never before had his teeming fancy
      seemed to want such help; the need being less to contribute to its fullness than
      to check its overflowing."

41   **"any historic doubts":** "In Memoriam," repr. in *Lives of Great Victorian Literary
      Figures I: Charles Dickens*, ed. Corinna Russell (London: Routledge, 2003),
      p. 507.

42   **"exploring the city":** The timeline is sketched out in G. S. Haight (ed.), *George
      Eliot and John Chapman: with Chapman's Diaries*, 2nd edn. (Hamden, Conn.:
      Archon Books, 1969).

43   **"My Dear Sir":** To George Eliot, 18 January 1858, *Letters*, viii. 506.

43   **"neither tall nor short":** *Interviews and Recollections*, p. 100.

43   **"half so much as to yesterday":** *Life*, i. 91.

43   **"on putting it to the nose":** Cyrus Redding, *Fifty Years' Recollections, Literary
      and Personal, with Observations on Men and Things*, 3 vols. (London: Charles J.
      Skeet, 1858), ii. 138.

43   **"lived a lot by his nose":** William Edrupt, in *Interviews and Recollections*,
      p. 193—although Edrupt also claimed that "When we walked down by the
      Thames he would sniff and sniff—'I love the very smell of this,' he used to
      say" (p. 195).

43   **"in the house half a dozen times":** To E. W. Banks, 11 November 1839,
      Letters, i. 599–600.

44   **"shall be himself again":** [R. H. Horne], "Father Thames," *Household Words*, 1
      February 1851, pp. 445–50. Just north of the *Household Words* offices, Long
      Acre "was well known for its coach manufactures and overlooked by the
      smoking chimneys of several breweries and foundries," Mary L. Shannon,
      *Dickens, Reynolds, and Mayhew on Wellington Street: The Print Culture of a
      Victorian Street* (London: Routledge, 2015), p. 93.

44   **"Charles Dickens Street":** Matz (ed.), *Dickens in Cartoon and Caricature*,
      pp. 233–4 (see illustration).

44   **London was becoming Dickensian:** For some readers this sensation of déjà
      vu included people as well as places. "When I got to London," wrote the
      American visitor Francis Parkman in 1843, "I thought I had been there before:
      The hackney coachmen and cabmen: the walking advertisements: and a
      hundred others seemed so many incarnations of Dickens's characters," quoted
      in Philip Collins, "Dickens and London," in *The Victorian City: Images and
      Realities*, ed. Jim Dyer and Michael Wolff, 2 vols. (London: Routledge and
      Kegan Paul, 1973), ii. 551.

44   **re-create in later works:** Rosemarie Bodenheimer points out that the
      walking routes taken by Dickens as a child often overlap with the places in
      his fiction ("Dickens's London keeps his history close at hand"), just as at the
      end of *Bleak House* Lady Dedlock walks towards "the landmarks of her past
      shame," *Knowing Dickens* (Ithaca, NY: Cornell University Press, 2007),
      pp. 172, 197.

44   **"last night's gentlemanly frolics":** *Nicholas Nickleby*, ch. 26.

45   **"pick and choose from":** *Oliver Twist*, ch. 19.

45   **"barrenness and frigidity":** *Nicholas Nickleby*, ch. 37.

45   **"chopping-block":** *Household Words*, 27 April 1850, p. 105.

45   **"Press on!":** "Press On. A Rivulet's Song," *Household Words*, 22 June 1850,
      p. 301.

46   **"squalor, and misery":** These descriptions are taken from an 1846 letter to
      Forster in which Dickens described a valley in Switzerland "where, at the
      border of two cantons, you might separate two perfectly distinct and different
      conditions of humanity by drawing a line with your stick in the dust on the
      ground" (*Letters*, iv. 611).

46   **a further seventeen years for his release:** "The Martyrs of Chancery [i],"
      Household Words, 7 December 1850, pp. 250–2.

47   **secretly developed:** "The Martyrs of Chancery [ii]," *Household Words*, 15
      February 1851, pp. 493–6.

47   **"attraction of repulsion":** *Life*, i. 19.

47   **"obtained his release at last":** *The Pickwick Papers*, chs. 42, 44.

47   **"squelched and utterly undone":** To John Forster, 18 January 1844, *Letters*,
      iv. 24.

47   **"the robber instead of the robbed":** Ibid., [?October–November 1846], *Letters*,
      iv. 651.

48   **"damaged, weak and unpopular":** Charles C. F . Greville, *The Greville
      Memoirs: A Journal of the Reigns of King George IV, King William IV and Queen
      Victoria*, ed. Henry Reeve, 8 vols. (Cambridge: Cambridge University Press,
      1888), v. 397.

48   **"great Dust Heap down at Westminster":** To the Hon. Mrs. Richard Watson,
      3 July 1850, *Letters*, vi. 123.

48   **"I wallow in words":** *David Copperfield*, ch. 43.

48   **"contempt at every part of his life":** *Life*, i. 83.

48   **"Don't talk about it—do it!":** See, e.g., Dickens's article "Home for Homeless
      Women" on Urania Cottage: "'Don't talk about it—do it!' is the motto of the
      place," *Household Words*, 23 April 1853, p. 172.

48   **"sacrifice to abridge or end it":** *Life*, i. 102.

49   **"What it needs is stronger leaders":** All quotations are taken from *Latter-Day
      Pamphlets*, "edited by" Thomas Carlyle (London: Chapman & Hall, 1850),
      pp. 5, 287, 34, 32.

49   **distant, long-suffering stare:** By Robert Scott Tait; the photograph is now in
      the National Portrait Gallery.

49   **"his friends rather sorry for him":** Hallam Tennyson (ed.), *Tennyson and his
      Friends* (London, Macmillan and Co., 1911), p. 132.

49   **"Ring in the thousand years of peace":** *In Memoriam* (London: Edward
      Moxon, 1850), p. 163.

50   **"modern history failed to turn":** G. M. Trevelyan, *British History in the
      Nineteenth Century* (New York: Longman's Green, 1922), p. 292.

50   **"little bag in his hand":** Percy Fitzgerald, "Some Memories of Dickens and
      'Household Words,'" in *The Dickens Souvenir of 1912*, ed. Dion Clayton
      Calthrop and Max Pemberton (London: Chapman & Hall, 1912), p. 23.

50   **"rarely departed from":** J. C. Hotten, *Charles Dickens: The Story of his Life*
      (London: J. C. Hotten, 1872), p. 352.

50   **"on entering the office":** Garret Dumas, reported in Thomas Wright, *The Life
      of Charles Dickens* (London: Herbert Jenkins, 1935), p. 207.

50   **"to stay overnight":** Percy Fitzgerald, *Memories of Charles Dickens* (Bristol and
      London: J. W. Arrowsmith &c, 1913), p. 125.

51   **"lying dead in her coffin":** Frederic G. Kitton, *Charles Dickens: His Life,
      Writings, and Personality* (London: T. C. & E. C. Jack, 1902), p. 182.

51   **"The men in it":** *Memoranda*, p. 1.

51   **"red-faced and ireful":** "H. W.," *Household Words*, April 16 1853, p. 161.

52   **"a man of action and business":** To J. P. Hullah, [11 December 1836], *Letters*,
      i. 210; *Life*, i. 65–6.

52   **last considerably longer:** To John Forster, 24 and 26 April 1842, *Letters*, iii. 211.

53   **"interpreting him and explaining him":** Quoted in Ian Hamilton, *Keepers of
      the Flame: Literary Estates and the Rise of Biography* (London: Hutchinson, 1992),
      p. 153.

53   **"should not be called the Life of Dickens":** Ibid., p. 156.

53   **the occasional verbal cull:** On Forster's revisions, see James A. Davies, *John
      Forster: A Literary Life* (Leicester: Leicester University Press, 1983), pp. 158–83;
      much of the information in this section is drawn from Davies's fine and
      fair-minded book.

53   **"Don't fail to erase anything":** To John Forster, [5 April 1841], *Letters*, ii. 253.

53   **writers in modern culture:** "Remarks on Two of the Annuals," *Newcastle
      Magazine* (1829), pp. 27–38.

54   **"fly to him for critical refuge":** *The Letters and Private Papers of William
      Makepeace Thackeray*, ed. Gordon N. Ray, 4 vols. (London: Oxford University
      Press, 1945–6), ii. 252.

54 **"law, divinity and diplomacy":** *Examiner*, 5 January 1850, p. 2; the context was Forster's dispute with Thackeray over his representation of the literary profession in *Pendennis*.

54 **together with royal coachmen:** *Examiner*, 19 January 1850, p. 35.

54 **"fit audience find, though few":** *Paradise Lost*, vii. 37.

54 **"low scribbler":** R. H. Barham's comment opposite Forster's name on the members' list of the Garrick Club, quoted in Davies, *John Forster*, p. 82.

54 **"often uneasy, shrinking":** *Life*, i. 52.

55 **foghorn attempts at whispering:** See Peter Ackroyd, *Dickens* (London: Sinclair-Stevenson, 1990), p. 207.

55 **"Monstrous!," "Incredible!," "In-tol-erable!":** To Clarkson Stanfield, 14 May 1856, *Letters*, viii. 119.

55 **"the cheek of the young person":** *Our Mutual Friend*, ch. 11.

55 **"a young English female":** "Remarks on Two of the Annuals," pp. 33–4.

55 **"quite an ordinary habit":** *Life*, i. 180.

55 **"divided up among the publishers":** See *Letters*, vi. 14n.

56 **A humorous drawing:** Reproduced as Plate XI in Matz (ed.), *Dickens in Cartoon and Caricature* (see illustration).

56 **thickly intertwined:** This paragraph draws on Mary L. Shannon's fine investigative work in *Dickens, Reynolds, and Mayhew on Wellington Street*.

57 **"smoke of innumerable candles":** G. A. Sala's description of some of the smaller offices in 1859, in *Twice Round the Clock; or The Hours of the Day and Night in London* (London: J. and R. Maxwell, 1859), p. 327.

57 **"the people who inhabit it":** *Sketches by Boz*, ch. 7.

57 **"beautiful fairies":** "Where We Stopped Growing," *Household Words*, 1 January 1853, p. 362.

59 **"use of the pruning-knife":** Harry Stone describes Dickens's editorial practices—which extended to suggesting new articles and giving alternative titles to those already submitted—in "Dickens 'Conducts' *Household Words*," *Dickensian* 64 (May 1968), pp. 71–85.

59 **"Familiar in his mouth":** *Henry V*, IV, iii.

59 **"more desirous to avoid than imitation":** To W. H. Wills, 11 February 1850, *Letters*, vi. 35.

59 **"in which Ironmongers keep Nails":** To Mrs. S. C. Hall, 23 April 1844, *Letters*, iv. 110; this comparison is discussed by John M. Drew in *Dickens the Journalist* (Basingstoke: Palgrave Macmillan, 2003), p. 110, and Sabine Clemm, *Dickens, Journalism, and Nationhood: Mapping the World in Household Words* (New York and London: Routledge, 2009), p. 11.

60 **"there is Romance enough":** *Household Words*, 30 March 1850, p. 1.

60 **"made of sticking-plaister":** Ibid., p. 14.

60 **"rapidly cut their throats":** Ibid., p. 7.

61 **"persons now in requisition":** This poster, printed in 1839 and headlined "EMIGRATION to SOUTH AUSTRALIA," targeted Cornish emigrants (State Library of South Australia Digital Collections).

61 **about to change for the better:** See illustration. It is worth noting that the destination of around 80 per cent of emigrants in 1851 was not Australia but America; in an analysis of the ship lists from this year, William E. Van Vugt observes that "fully two-thirds of the British arriving in 1851 travelled alone: and they came from a wide variety of backgrounds. Along with farmers and artisans came many unskilled laborers, selected members of the modern industrial labor force, as well as tertiary workers and professionals," "Prosperity and Industrial Emigration from Britain during the Early 1850s," *Journal of Social History*, vol. 22, no. 2 (Winter, 1988), pp. 339–54 (p. 349).

62 **"can ever know want":** *Household Words*, 30 March 1850, p. 20.

62 **"no words could convey":** This short article or "Chip" was a follow-up to "The Power of Small Beginnings," published in the 20 July 1850 issue.

62 **"as *they* arrived safe":** *Household Words*, 30 March 1850, pp. 20–2.

63 **"the first shadows of a new story":** 21 February 1851, *Letters*, vi. 298.

63 **"tremendous pile of transparency":** This became a standard way of referring to the Crystal Palace; e.g., J. C. Whish, the winner of an essay competition to consider the Exhibition's economic and moral impact, wrote shortly before the official opening that it would become "the greatest wonder of the world" (*The Great Exhibition Prize Essay*, 4th edn. (1852), p. 1), and a poem written later to mark the removal of the building referred to it simply as "The gleaming wonder of the world" (Samuel Warren, *The Lily and the Bee: An Apologue of the Crystal Palace* [Edinburgh and London: William Blackwood and Son, 1851], p. 24). Wills's article was later reprinted as an appendix to the official catalogue of the Exhibition.

63 **"exposing his private parts":** Joseph Paxton, letter quoted in Kate Colquhoun, *A Thing in Disguise: The Visionary Life of Joseph Paxton* (London: Fourth Estate, 2003), p. 205.

64 **"if the Crystal Palace don't begin to fall down":** To Charles Manby, 20 February 1851, *Letters*, vi. 296.

64 **"the wind has got into some little notoriety":** "The Wind and the Rain," *Household Words*, 31 May 1851, p. 217.

64 **"it refused to do so":** Speech to the Gardeners' Benevolent Association, *Speeches*, p. 134.

64 **like one of his own novels:** See Robert Tracy, "Lighthousekeeping: *Bleak House* and the Crystal Palace," *Dickens Studies Annual* 33 (2003), p. 46.

65 **a few days before his death:** Mamie Dickens, *Charles Dickens by his Eldest Daughter* (London: Cassell & Co., 1885), pp. 120–1.

65 **"Fairy palaces":** *Hard Times*, ch. 10.

65 **smelly business it usually was:** See, e.g., "A Paper-Mill," *Household Words*, 31 August 1850, and "Pottery and Porcelain," *Household Words*, 4 October 1851.

66 **"the back windows of life!":** To the Hon. Mrs. Richard Watson, 24 January 1851, *Letters*, vi. 266.

66 **"so radiant and so strong":** "Plate Glass," *Household Words*, 1 February 1851, pp. 433–7.

66   **"The Working Men of England":** See Audrey Short, "Working Under Glass In 1851," *Victorian Studies,* vol. 10, no. 2 (December 1966), pp. 194–5.

67   **"to advance its objects":** To the Bishop of Oxford, 7 March 1859, *Letters,* vi. 57.

68   **"let us be Therewith Content":** See illustration; the source is St. Paul's First Epistle to Timothy 6:8–10.

68   **"I sweeps a crossing":** *Household Narrative* (1850), p. 5. This exchange was also reported in the *Examiner* (possibly by Dickens), *Times, Punch,* and the *Ragged School Union Magazine.*

69   **"in his very cradle":** 3 May 1843, *Letters,* iii. 482.

69   **"the Protestant religion was established":** *A Child's History of England* (1851–3), ch. 36.

69   **"Still, the Britons *would not* yield":** Ibid., ch. 1.

69   **"the most conceited man on earth":** Ibid., ch. 32.

70   **"to do their duty":** Ibid., ch. 35.

70   **"divided into certain portions":** Ibid., ch. 3.

70   **"bed of straw and rushes":** Ibid., ch. 12.

70   **" 'No?' cried the King":** Ibid., ch. 4. Percy Fitzgerald noticed the "oddity" in Dickens's book that certain passages "fell into rhythmical shape"; cutting up Dickens's prose to make it more closely resemble lines of verse, he gives as an example:
>   "The English broke and fled.
>   The Normans rallied and the day was lost.
>   O what a sight beneath the moon and stars!
>   The lights were shining in the victors' tents,
>   Pitched near the spot where blinded Harold fell.
>   Etc., etc." (*Memories of Charles Dickens,* p. 154)

71   **the celebrated dandy Count d'Orsay:** To Miss Burdett Coutts, 10 February 1851, *Letters,* vi. 285; Dickens reported on his findings in "A Monument of French Folly," *Household Words,* 8 March 1851.

71   **"which all Paris ran to see":** D'Orsay quoted in Willard Connely, *Count d'Orsay: The Dandy of Dandies* (London: Cassell & Company, 1952), p. 528; for this and other details of d'Orsay's life in Paris, I am grateful to the editors of the Pilgrim Edition of Dickens's letters.

71   **"wit and humour":** Earl of Ilchester, *Chronicles of Holland House, 1820–1900* (London: John Murray, 1937), p. 381.

71   **nonchalantly upon his hip:** Reproduced in *Dickensian* 47 (March 1951); the famous 1834 caricature of d'Orsay adopting this pose would later be reinterpreted by cartoonist Rea Irvin as Eustace Tilley, the original cover illustration of the *New Yorker* magazine.

71   **"expressing defiance melodramatically":** *Sketches by Boz,* ch. 12.

72   **"another sort of life":** *Life,* ii. 206.

72   **" 'Toss up for it' ":** *Great Expectations,* ch. 31.

72   **"rapidly in a low voice":** Mamie Dickens, *My Father As I Recall Him* (London: The Roxburghe Press, 1896), pp. 49–50.

73   **"I say, what is man?":** *Sketches by Boz*, ch. 5.

73   **"I speak to you, as I would to myself":** To W. C. Macready, 1 April 1842, *Letters*, iii. 173, 176.

74   **"until the journey is worked out!":** To John Forster, 13 April 1856, *Letters*, viii. 89; their relationship is also discussed by Rosemarie Bodenheimer in *Knowing Dickens*, pp. 98–100.

74   **"from my bodily eyes last night":** To W. C. Macready, 26 February 1851, *Letters*, vi. 301.

74   **"improved and charmed us":** *Speeches*, p. 115.

74   **a four-panel dressing-room screen:** The Macready–Dickens screen has recently been restored and can be seen at Sherborne House.

75   **"I fear you may be shipwrecked":** To Miss Fanny M. Lomax, *Letters*, vi. 253–4; it seems that she heeded his warning, as no publication by her has been identified.

75   **"he might as well be dead":** To Mrs. Charles Dickens, 24 June 1850, *Letters*, vi. 116; to Lord John Russell, 18 December 1851, *Letters*, vi. 239–40.

75   **"great services he has rendered":** *Globe* (16 April 1851), quoted in *Letters*, vi. 284n.

76   **"Good heavens! Is he still alive":** S. M. Ellis, *William Harrison Ainsworth and his Friends*, 2 vols. (London and New York: John Lane, 1911), ii. 264.

76   **"about a dozen":** To Frank Stone, 23 April 1850, *Letters*, vi. 89.

76   **"rasping my very heart":** To J. A. Widger, 3 January 1851, *Letters*, vi. 255–6.

76   **"trading on my name":** To Miss Burdett Coutts, 18 January 1851, *Letters*, vi. 263.

76   **"mainly gin":** Sala to Yates, n.d. [?22 Oct 1868], *Letters of George Augustus Sala to Edmund Yates, in the Edmund Yates Papers, University of Queensland Library*, ed. Judy McKenzie (St. Lucia, Qld: University of Queensland, 1993), p. 116.

77   **"the triumph of fiction":** Edmund Gosse, "The Tyranny of the Novel," repr. in *Questions at Issue* (London: William Heinemann, 1893), p. 7.

77   **"those lighter productions":** [Archibald Alison], "The Influence of the Press," *Blackwood's Edinburgh Magazine* 36 (September 1834), pp. 373–91 (p. 373).

77   **"they have accomplished that":** Thomas Carlyle, *On Heroes, Hero-Worship, and the Heroic in History* (London: Chapman & Hall, 1841), pp. 144, 153, 155.

77   **"more independent than I found it":** To W. M. Thackeray, 9 January 1848, *Letters*, iv. 227.

77   **"Literary Man in England":** To Sir Edward Bulwer Lytton, 5 January 1851, *Letters*, vi. 259.

78   **working on a prospectus:** "The Guild of Literature and Art," *Household Words*, 10 May 1851, pp. 145–7.

79   **"a quick and considerable popularity":** *The History of Pendennis* (1849–50), ch. 42.

79   **"disparaging his literary fellow-labourers":** "Encouragement of Literature by the State," *Examiner*, 5 January 1850.

79   **"fairly achieved by their genius":** "The Dignity of Literature," *Morning Chronicle*, 12 January 1851; *Examiner*, 19 January 1850, p. 35. The dispute is

analysed with great insight by Michael J. Flynn in *"Pendennis, Copperfield*, and the Debate on the 'Dignity of Literature,'" *Dickens Studies Annual* 41 (2010), pp. 151–89; see also Daniel Hack, "Literary Paupers and Professional Authors: The Guild of Literature and Art," *Studies in English Literature, 1500–1900* 39.4 (Autumn 1999), pp. 691–713.

79   **"vulgarizing each other":** To W. M. Thackeray, 9 January 1848, *Letters,* v. 227–8.

80   **"a great fight up there with Dickens":** *The Letters and Private Papers of William Makepeace Thackeray,* ed. Gordon N. Ray, 4 vols. (Cambridge, Mass.: Harvard University Press, 1945–6), ii. 333.

80   **"THACKERAY and DICKENS":** [David Masson], *"Pendennis* and *Copperfield*: Thackeray and Dickens," *North British Review* (May 1851), p. 578.

80   **"someone he wanted to see":** D. J. Taylor, *Thackeray* (London: Chatto & Windus, 1999), p. 403.

80   **"at best, middling writers":** Quoted in Gordon N. Ray, *Thackeray: The Age of Wisdom, 1847–1863* (London: Oxford University Press, 1958), pp. 151–2.

81   **"of any government":** Leigh Hunt, "Case of the Royal Society of Literature," *Tatler* 237 (7 June 1831), p. 946.

81   **"the calling to which he belongs":** "The Guild of Literature and Art," *Household Words,* 10 May 1851, p. 147.

81   **"necessary comforts of gentlemen":** Ibid., p. 145.

81   **"all writers, of either sex":** *Prospectus for the Guild of Literature and Art* (pamphlet printed by Bradbury & Evans) dated 12 April 1851, repr. as Appendix D in *Letters,* vi. 852. This was a revision to the proof sent to the Duke of Devonshire on 4 March 1851 that he bound into his leather scrapbook.

82   **"the company of gentlemen":** Lady Emily Lutyens, *A Blessed Girl: Memoirs of a Victorian Childhood* (London: R. Hart-Davis, 1953), pp. 58–9.

82   **regardless of the accident of birth:** Compare Samuel Smiles: "Riches and rank have no necessary connexion with genuine gentlemanly qualities. The poor man may be a true gentleman,—in spirit and in daily life. He may be honest, truthful, upright, polite, temperate, courageous, self-respecting, and self- helping,—that is, be a true gentleman," *Self-Help,* pp. 327–8. Robin Gilmour discusses the period's changing definitions of "gentleman" in *The Idea of the Gentleman in the Victorian Novel* (London: Allen & Unwin, 1981).

83   **"good old Toryism":** Edward Bulwer Lytton to C. d'Eyncourt, 31 March 1851, quoted in Leslie Mitchell, *Bulwer Lytton: The Rise and Fall of a Victorian Man of Letters* (London and New York: Hambledon and London, 2003), p. 187.

83   **"sore all over":** *Oxford Dictionary of National Biography,* quoted in Michael Sadleir, *Bulwer and his Wife: A Panorama, 1803–1836* (London: Constable, 1933), p. 358.

84   **"wretched and isolated, *but alone*":** Quoted in Mitchell, *Bulwer Lytton,* p. 27.

85   **"*marred* as the Irish pronounce it":** 1851 annotation to letter from Edward Bulwer Lytton to Rosina Lytton, 29 August 1827; quoted in Mitchell, *Bulwer Lytton,* p. 37.

85   **"It was a dark and stormy night":** Lady Bulwer Lytton, *Miriam Sedley; or, The Tares and the Wheat: A Tale of Real Life*, 3 vols. (London: W. Shoburl, 1851), i. 2. The narrator also warns gloomily that "in my onward journey through the world, as I grew up, I could not but remark that bad husbands, like confluent small-pox, even when they die away leave indelible traces for life upon their victims," i. 50.

85   **"the only check I have on him":** Edward Bulwer Lytton to A. E. Chalon, 26 February 1856, *Unpublished Letters of Lady Bulwer Lytton to A. E. Chalon, R. A.* (London: Eveleigh Nash, 1914), p. 249.

85   **"fettered together":** *Memoranda*, p. 18.

85   **"fettered yet forsaken":** 28 September 1854, *Unpublished Letters*, p. 112; her letter goes on to claim that she is "riveted to a man who has left no vice unexhausted or virtue unassumed, or who, more properly speaking, has worn every known sin threadbare, and invented many others not yet patent in the infernal regions."

85   **"I despair of my release":** Quoted in Sadleir, *Bulwer and his Wife*, p. 403.

85   **"Low birth and iron fortune":** *Speeches*, p. 117; in Bulwer Lytton's romantic melodrama *The Lady of Lyons* (1838) the line is actually "those twin gaolers of the daring heart" (III, ii).

85   **"refined and polished":** Horne, *A New Spirit of the Age*, i. 309.

86   **"good-natured, pleasant, conversable":** Ibid., i. 310.

86   **"called in aid to rejuvenate it":** Quoted in W. Teignmouth Shore, *Charles Dickens and his Friends* (London: Cassell and Company, 1909), pp. 185–6.

86   **"Where are my whiskers":** Quoted in Mitchell, *Bulwer Lytton*, p. 90.

86   **"the romantic passions of the stage":** *Speeches*, p. 117.

86   **"Society of Literary Men":** *Eugene Aram* (1832).

86   **"the vast debt which the world owes to authors":** *Ernest Maltravers* (1837).

86   **"the most heart-sickening object":** Quoted in Mitchell, *Bulwer Lytton*, p. 123.

87   **"a means of getting it":** To John Forster, [?30–31 December 1844], *Letters*, iv. 245.

87   **another begging letter:** Both letters were sent on 13 October 1848; *Letters*, v. 423–44.

87   **"absolutely under my command":** Charles Foster Kent, *Charles Dickens as a Reader* (London: Chapman & Hall, 1872), pp. 263– 4.

88   **other possible identities:** William J. Carlton, " 'Old Nick' at Devonshire Terrace: Dickens Through French Eyes in 1843," *Dickensian* 59 (1963), p. 142.

88   **"one hurrah of applause":** Charles and Mary Cowden Clarke, *Recollections of Writers*, p. 324.

88   **"a whirl of triumph":** To the Hon. Mrs. Richard Watson, 23 November 1850, *Letters*, vi. 216.

89   **"A very *Household Word*":** J. B. Van Amerongen, *The Actor in Dickens* (London: Cecil Palmer, 1926), p. 16.

89   **"theatrical entertainment, properly conducted":** *Nicholas Nickleby*, ch. 22.

89   **"the position it should occupy"**: Kitton, *Dickens by Pen and Pencil*, p. 110;
      Kitton adds that Dickens's other roles included costume and playbill designer,
      prompter and stage manager.

89   **"serious earnest work"**: Charles and Mary Cowden Clarke, *Recollections of
      Writers*, p. 300.

89   **two selves, the serious and the playful:** "It was an excellent saying of the first
      Lord Shaftesbury, that, seeing every man of any capacity holds within himself
      two men, the wise and the foolish, each of them ought freely to be allowed his
      turn; and it was one of the secrets of Dickens's social charm that he could, in
      strict accordance with this saying, allow each part of him its turn; could afford
      thoroughly to give rest and relief to what was serious in him, and, when the
      time came to play his gambols, could surrender himself wholly to the
      enjoyment of the time, and become the very genius and embodiment of one
      of his own most whimsical fancies," *Life*, i. 194.

90   **"the most appalling duration"**: To Miss Fanny M. Lomax, 1 January 1851,
      Letters, vi. 254.

90   **"spirited and enlightened"**: To John Forster, 30 November 1849, *Letters*, v.
      663.

90   **"on my back on the floor"**: *Letters*, vi. 254.

90   **"beautiful and complete little Theatre"**: To Frederick Dickens, 12 January
      1851, *Letters*, vi. 261. On 12 November 1851, *The Times* carried an advertise-
      ment by L. & H. Nathan announcing that "they have just finally decorated
      their PORTABLE THEATRE for the approaching festive season, the same that
      they made expressly for Rockingham Castle last season for the performances
      of Charles Dickens, Esq., and friends" (*Letters*, vi. 538n.).

90   **optimism over just how much space:** "Thirteen feet and a half of depth,
      diminished by stage fittings and furniture, is a small space . . . ," Dickens to the
      Hon. Mrs. Richard Watson, 14 December 1850, *Letters*, vi. 235.

90   **characteristically thorough preparation:** "It cannot possibly be a success, if
      the smallest pepper-corn of arrangement be omitted," ibid. Having seen this
      aspect of Dickens's character up close, Mrs. Watson later recalled "his
      extraordinary love of order, in all arrangements to be made,—into every
      particular did he go, with the strongest *will*, as being the only thing to be
      done,—and no one could resist the wonderful (so to call it) tyranny he exerted,
      not for himself, but for the carrying out of the object in hand!" Kitton (ed.),
      Dickens by Pen and Pencil, p. 145.

90   **"The Theatre will be opened"**: The poster is on display in Rockingham
      Castle.

90   **"the glory of Letters"**: Edward Bulwer Lytton, *Not So Bad As We Seem; or,
      Many Sides to a Character* (London: Chapman & Hall, 1851), p. 56.

91   **"*certain to go nobly*"**: To Sir Edward Bulwer Lytton, 5 January 1851, *Letters*, vi.
      256.

91   **"his form on the top"**: *Speeches*, pp. 120, 134.

91   **"With every apology"**: *Letters*, vi. 304–5.

92   **"I worship him"**: Devonshire Collections, Chatsworth.

92   **a scrapbook compiled by the Duke**: Ibid.

92   **"stage architect"**: R. H. Horne, "Bygone Celebrities I," *Gentleman's Magazine* (February 1871), p. 248.

SPRING: DISAPPEARANCES

95   **advertisements jostling for attention**: See illustration.

95   **article on "Disappearances"**: *Household Words*, 7 June 1851, pp. 246–50; the Metropolitan Police set up a plain-clothes detective branch in 1842; see Haia Shpayer-Makov, *The Ascent of the Detective: Police Sleuths in Victorian and Edwardian England* (Oxford: Oxford University Press, 2012).

96   **"placards and advertisements"**: *The Mystery of Edwin Drood* (1870), ch. 15.

96   **nostalgic essay "Gone Astray"**: *Household Words*, 13 August 1853, pp. 553–7.

97   **a sad trail of objects**: See Andrew Lambert, *Franklin: Tragic Hero of Polar Exploration* (London: Faber and Faber, 2009).

97   *The Arctic Council: Franklin*: See illustration.

97   **"coal bags, empty canisters"**: *Annual Register* (1851), p. 483.

98   **handkerchief formed into a bundle**: *Household Words*, 28 December 1850, pp. 319–22.

99   **"Brokers' and Marine-store Shops"**: Repr. in *Sketches by Boz*.

99   **"rusty weapons of various kinds"**: *The Old Curiosity Shop*, ch. 1.

100   **"Spitalfields silk manufactures"**: "Great Industrial Exhibition of 1851," *Illustrated London News*, 1 March 1851, p. 179.

100   **"the turning point"**: *The Dublin Review*, vol. 31 (September–December 1851), p. 550.

100   **Two poems:** *Household Words*, 8 March 1851, pp. 565, 572.

101   **"Look upon it reverently"**: "Three May-Days in London. III. The May Palace (1851)," *Household Words*, 3 May 1851, p. 124.

101   *"Wot is to Be"*: "Vates Secundus," *The Great Exhibition "Wot is to Be"; or Probable Results of the Industry of All Nations in the Year '51, Showing What is to be Exhibited, Who is to be Exhibited: In Short, How it is All Going to be Done* (London: Committee of the Society for Keeping Things in Their Places, 1850).

101   **biblical echo:** Ecclesiastes 3:1.

102   **"A Voice from the Factory"**: *Household Words*, 5 April 1851, pp. 35–6.

102   **"a kinder understanding"**: "A Preliminary Word," *Household Words*, 30 March 1850, p. 1.

103   **"my diamond ring"**: To Miss Burdett Coutts, 1 August 1850, *Letters*, vi. 141.

103   **"You have lost sight of your true position"**: To John Overs, 23 November 1841, *Letters*, ii. 427.

103   **"an extremely dense crowd"**: "Greenwich Fair," first published in the *Evening Chronicle* (16 April 1835), repr. in *Sketches by Boz*.

103   **"struggling current of angry faces"**: *Oliver Twist*, ch. 50.

104   **"pressing the end of her nose"**: *David Copperfield*, ch. 1.

104   **"Great Unwashed"**: *The History of Pendennis*, ch. 30.

104 **noses against the glass:** "London During the Great Exhibition," *Illustrated London News*, 17 May 1851, p. 423; these fears are discussed in Clemm, *Dickens, Journalism, and Nationhood*, p. 18.

104 **"red-hot proletarians":** See Bill Bryson, *At Home: A Short History of Private Life* (London: Doubleday, 2010), p. 50.

104 **"Glass is damned thin stuff":** See John Lucas, "Past and Present: *Bleak House* and *A Child's History of England*," in John Schad (ed.), *Dickens Refigured: Bodies, Desires and Other Histories* (Manchester: Manchester University Press, 1996), p. 147.

104 **"THE RICH AND THE POOR":** Benjamin Disraeli, *Sybil; or, The Two Nations*, 3 vols. (London: Henry Colburn, 1845), ii. 149–50.

105 **"as he went along":** *Dombey and Son*, ch. 3.

105 **"poor throughout England":** All references to *London Labour and the London Poor* (hereafter abbreviated in footnotes to *LLLP*) are to the four-volume edition published in 1861–2, repr. with an introduction by John D. Rosenberg (New York: Dover Publications, 1968).

106 **"the scramble for a living":** *The Great World of London*, 1 (March 1856), p. 63.

106 **"very persecuted harp-player":** See E. P. Thompson and Eileen Yeo (eds), *The Unknown Mayhew* (New York: Pantheon, 1971), p. 47.

106 **"if they ain't aggravated":** *LLLP*, iii. 73.

106 **"buy anoder monkey":** Ibid., iii. 180.

106 **"it's a calling":** Ibid., iii. 33.

106 **"I'm past eight, I am":** Ibid., i. 152.

107 **"profound rubbish":** Henry Mayhew, *Young Benjamin Franklin; or, The right road through life* (London: David Byrce, 1861), p. 250n.

107 **close relations in Mayhew:** *LLLP*, ii. 110; ii. 145; i. 272; ii. 226. These parallels are discussed in Anne Humpherys, *Travels into the Poor Man's Country: The Work of Henry Mayhew* (Athens: University of Georgia Press, 1977), pp. 178–94, and Richard J. Dunn, "Dickens and Mayhew Once More," *Nineteenth-Century Fiction* 25 (1970), pp. 348–53.

107 **"which is which, or what is what":** *Little Dorrit*, ch. 15.

108 **"Total quantity of rain":** *LLLP*, ii. 203, 401.

108 **"Bill-Sticking":** *Household Words*, 22 March 1851, pp. 602–6.

108 **"a beautiful and delicate complexion":** Dickens had already noticed the ubiquitous advertisements for Kalydor (they also featured in his own publications); in *Nicholas Nickleby*, when the mad old gentleman woos Miss La Creevy, his extravagant rhetoric includes "Where are grace, beauty and blandishments like those? In the Empress of Madagascar? No. In the Queen of Diamonds? No. In Mrs. Rowland, who every morning bathes in Kalydor for nothing?" (ch. 49).

109 **"Halloa old girl!":** To Daniel Maclise, 12 March 1841, *Letters*, ii. 231; see illustration.

109 **a cartoon by John Tenniel:** 19 July 1851, repr. in Jeffrey A. Auerbach, *The Great Exhibition: A Nation on Display* (New Haven and London: Yale University Press, 1999), p. 160. Some of the items displayed alongside each other at the Great

Exhibition, such as medical equipment and pistols, also suggested an element of muddled thinking; Henry Sutherland Edwards spotted the contradiction, writing a lengthy piece of doggerel that pointed out "to go into one single case, / In her surgical instruments France had rewards, / While she also gained prizes for muskets and swords. / To promoters of death the same medals they give / As to those who enable sick mortals to live," *An Authentic Account of the Chinese Commission, which was sent to report on the Great Exhibition; wherein the opinion of China is shown as not corresponding at all with our own* (London: H. Vizitelly, n.d.), p. 29.

110 **"Ravens every one of 'em":** "From the Raven in the Happy Family [i]," *Household Words*, 11 May 1850, pp. 156–8.

110 **slices of his time this spring:** For an impressively detailed history of Urania Cottage, see Jenny Hartley, *Charles Dickens and the House of Fallen Women* (London: Methuen, 2008); in this section I draw on Hartley's research, and also that of Philip Collins in *Dickens and Crime*, 2nd edn. (London: Macmillan, 1964), ch. 4. As most of the inmates were under the age of eighteen, I follow Hartley and Dickens himself in referring to them as "girls" while they were resident in Urania Cottage and "women" after they left.

110 **"nothing in London that is *not* curious":** To Jonathan Jones, 22 March 1851, *Letters*, vi. 327.

111 **"in solitude and peace":** *Oliver Twist*, ch. 47.

111 **"Theer's mighty countries" "Wives is very scarce theer":** *David Copperfield*, chs. 51, 63.

111 **"in the course of a day or two":** Arnold, *Turning-Points in Life*, i. 83.

111 **"those who help themselves":** *Speeches*, p. 122.

112 **"trusted to her own keeping":** To Miss Burdett Coutts, 26 May 1846, *Letters*, iv. 553.

112 **"but a kind of Nunnery":** Ibid., 17 May 1849, *Letters*, v. 541.

112 **"innocently Cheerful family":** Ibid., 28 October 1847, *Letters*, v. 179.

112 **"*tempted* to virtue":** Ibid., 3 November 1847, *Letters*, v. 183.

112 **"about a year":** "Home for Homeless Women," *Household Words*, 23 April 1853, pp. 169–75.

113 **"playing our parts":** "In Memoriam," *Macmillan's Magazine* (July 1870), quoted in Malcolm Andrews, *Charles Dickens and his Performing Selves: Dickens and the Public Readings* (Oxford: Oxford University Press, 2006), p. 260.

113 **"very neat and modest":** To Miss Burdett Coutts, 3 November 1847, *Letters*, v. 185.

113 **"Don't talk about it—do it!":** "Home for Homeless Women," *Household Words*, 23 April 1853, p. 172.

113 **"order, punctuality, and good temper":** To Miss Burdett Coutts, 3 November 1847, *Letters*, v. 186.

114 **"active management":** To Harriet Martineau, 19 April 1853, *Letters*, vii. 68.

114 **"every half-hour of the day":** *Charles Dickens and the House of Fallen Women*, p. 57.

114 **prostitutes:** To Miss Burdett Coutts, 31 August 1850, *Letters*, vi. 159.

114 "about the streets for a year": Ibid., p. 160.

114 "tastes like a sweetmeat": Ibid., 22 June 1854, *Letters*, vii. 359; see *Charles Dickens and the House of Fallen Women*, p. 235.

115 "spoke very low": To Miss Burdett Coutts, 4 June 1851, *Letters*, vi. 407.

115 "Committee of One": Ibid., 27 May 1856, *Letters*, viii. 125.

115 "from the Magdalen": Ibid., [April 1850—7 March 1851], *Letters*, vi. 308.

115 "penitent prostitutes": To William Brown, 16 January 1848, v. 235n.

115 "afflict me already": To Henry Austin, 28 March 1849, *Letters*, v. 516.

116 "soft watery pint [*sic*] of view": Ibid., [23] January 1851, *Letters*, vi. 265.

116 "well adapted to my young people": to Miss Burdett Coutts, 28 January 1851, *Letters*, vi. 269.

116 "fear and trembling": To Henry Austin, 30 January 1851, *Letters*, vi. 272.

116 "some houseless wretches": *Oliver Twist*, ch. 5.

116 "motherless child!": *The Old Curiosity Shop*, ch. 44.

116 "forget the houseless": *David Copperfield*, ch. 13. Dickens's likely source is *King Lear*; after Lear has been expelled from his daughter's castle he finds himself sympathising with "houseless poverty" and the "houseless heads and unfed sides" of other "Poor naked wretches" like himself; see Adrian Poole, "The Shadow of Lear's 'Houseless' in Dickens," in *Shakespeare Survey* 53 (2000).

116 *The Outcast*: See illustration.

117 "though never so comely": Christopher Ricks (ed.), *The Poems of Tennyson*, 2nd edn., 3 vols. (Harlow: Longman, 1987), iii. 9.

117 Ellen Glyn or Emma Spencer: I follow here Philip Collins's argument in *Dickens and Crime*, ch. 4.

117 " 'Oh, lady! lady!' ": *Oliver Twist*, ch. 40.

117 "shunned of all our dainty clay": *Dombey and Son*, ch. 58.

118 "it seems too bold": *David Copperfield*, ch. 47.

118 "You shall go tomorrow morning": To Miss Burdett Coutts, 19 November 1852, *Letters*, vi. 804.

118 "rolled into one": Hartley, *Charles Dickens and the House of Fallen Women*, p. 25.

119 "touching in the extreme": To Miss Burdett Coutts, 28 October 1847, *Letters*, v. 178.

119 "wiping her face with her shawl": To William Brown, 6 November 1849, *Letters*, v. 639.

119 "weeping aloud": *David Copperfield*, ch. 22.

119 "from them, abroad": To Miss Burdett Coutts, 3 November 1847, *Letters*, v. 186.

119 "what their children may be": Ibid., 21 March 1851, *Letters*, vi. 323.

120 "narrowly investigated everything": Ibid., 8 November 1850, *Letters*, vi. 207.

120 "narrowly and secretly examined": Ibid.

120 "never tired of questioning them": George Augustus Sala, *Things I Have Seen and People I Have Known*, 2 vols. (London: Cassell and Company, 1894), i. 95.

120 for the presiding magistrate: "The Ruffian: By the Uncommercial Traveller," *All the Year Round*, 10 October 1868.

120 "DRUNK WHEN HE CAME IN": To John Forster, [?12 February 1847], *Letters*, v. 26–7. I borrow these two examples from John Carey, *The Violent*

Effigy: A Study of Dickens's Imagination (London: Faber and Faber, 1973), pp. 38–9.

121   **"which bring unto me":** To Thomas Beard, 8 September 1847, *Letters*, v. 161.

121   **"she cannot go wrong":** To Georgina Hogarth, 24 January 1867, *Letters*, xi. 304.

121   **"a clever Detective Policeman":** W. H. Wills, "The Modern Science of Thief-Taking," *Household Words*, 13 July 1850, pp. 368–72.

121   **"Disappearances":** To Mrs. Gaskell, 27 May 1851, *Letters*, vi. 401.

122   **"the edification of visitors":** Repr. in *Sketches by Boz*.

122   **"in everybody's footsteps":** To John Forster, 7 October 1849, *Letters*, v. 622.

122   **"sketch of the editorial presence":** "A Detective Police Party," *Household Words*, 27 July 1850, p. 410.

122   **"at a passing glance":** *Interviews and Recollections*, p. 82.

123   **"and stood mute":** *Our Mutual Friend*, ch. 15.

123   **another of his alter egos:** "A Memoir of Inspector Field," *Illustrated Times*, 2 February 1856, p. 70.

123   **"On Duty with Inspector Field":** *Household Words*, 14 June 1851, pp. 265–70.

124   **"corpulent forefinger":** "A Detective Police Party," *Household Words*, 27 July 1850, p. 409.

124   **"very glad to know him":** To Augustus Egg, 8 March 1851, *Letters*, vi. 310.

125   **"Genius of Disorder":** To Wilkie Collins, 13 July 1856, *Letters*, viii. 161.

125   **"most disheartening preliminaries":** To the Duke of Devonshire, 20 March 1851, *Letters*, vi. 321.

125   **"get a meaning into it":** To Sir Edward Bulwer Lytton, 23 March 1851, *Letters*, vi. 330.

126   **"in energetic restlessness":** To the Duke of Devonshire, 28 March 1851, *Letters*, vi. 337.

126   **"assiduous and unwearying":** "Bygone Celebrities I: The Guild of Literature and Art at Chatsworth," *Gentleman's Magazine* (February 1871), p. 249.

126   **correspondence from 25 April:** *Letters*, vi. 361–7.

127   **"ingenious Mechanism":** Advertisement for sale of the theatre in the *Athenaeum* (11 September 1852); see *Letters*, vi. 777n.

127   **"long list":** To Sir Edward Bulwer Lytton, 28 March 1851, *Letters*, vi. 338.

127   **"gold double chain":** To C. A. Barry [?March 1851], *Letters*, vi. 344.

128   **"covered in sawdust":** To Wilkie Collins, 12 May 1851, *Letters*, vi. 385.

128   **The 1851 census:** Details from https://ukcensusonline.com/census/1851.

128   **"sometimes stayed to dinner":** *Letters*, vi. 333n.

128   **"swollen and disfigured":** Robert Wade, *Stricture of the Urethra: Its Complications and Effects. A Practical Treatise on the Nature and Treatment of those Affections*, 4th edn. (London: John Churchill, 1860), p. 269; see also Jonathan Charles Goddard and Nicholas Cambridge, "What the Dickens?," *Urology News*, vol. 23, no. 1 (November/December 2018).

129   **"a slaughter house of blood":** To Mrs. Charles Dickens, 25 March 1851, *Letters*, vi. 333.

129   **"a little occasional smarting":** Wade, *Stricture of the Urethra*, p. 270.

129 **"very weak and low"**: *Letters*, vi. 334–5.

129 **"the death of him"**: Ibid., pp. 341, 336.

129 **"a picture of dreariness"**: To Mrs. Charles Dickens, 26 March 1851, *Letters*, vi. 334.

130 **"rely upon him for the future"**: E. Davey, "The Parents of Charles Dickens," *Lippincott's Magazine* 13 (June 1874), pp. 772– 3.

130 **"memory of our dear father"**: MS letter from Alfred Dickens to Elizabeth Dickens, 7 April 1851 (Dickens Museum).

130 **"thorough business habits"**: *Gentleman's Magazine* (June 1851), quoted in *Letters*, vi. 343n.

130 **"my poor father"**: For example, letters to Thomas Beard, John Forster, and George Hogarth on 31 March (*Letters*, vi. 342–4).

130 **"turn up"**: *David Copperfield*, ch. 52.

131 **"the better man I think him"**: *Life*, iii. 32.

131 **"rhetorical exuberance"**: *Life*, iii. 30.

131 **"so worried and worn"**: To Mrs. Charles Dickens, 4 April 1851, *Letters*, vi. 347.

131 **"Lying Awake"**: *Household Words*, 30 October 1852, pp. 145–8.

132 **"mentally-measured route"**: George Augustus Sala, *Charles Dickens* (London: Routledge, 1870), p. 132.

132 **"Night Walks"**: *All the Year Round*, 21 July 1860, pp. 348–52, repr. in *The Uncommercial Traveller*.

132 **the city's usual rhythms**: The context for Dickens's essay is brilliantly explored in Matthew Beaumont's *Nightwalking: A Nocturnal History of London* (London: Verso, 2015).

133 **"my part was very difficult"**: *Life*, ii. 492.

133 **"in a moment"**: To Henry Austin, 15 April 1851, *Letters*, vi. 352.

133 **"suddenly gave way completely"**: "Charles Dickens At Home, By His Eldest Daughter," *Cornhill Magazine* NS, 4 (January 1885), p. 38.

133 **"So shall we know the angels"**: *The Old Curiosity Shop*, ch. 71.

133 **"bears us to the ocean!"**: *Dombey and Son*, ch. 16.

134 **"which they had fought"**: Ricks (ed.), *The Poems of Tennyson*, ii. 465.

134 **"in her joyousness"**: Appendix II of *Correspondence*, v. 540–3; see Rebecca Stott, *Darwin and the Barnacle* (London: Faber & Faber, 2004), p. 170, and for the impact of her death on Darwin's faith and thought, Randal Keynes, *Annie's Box: Charles Darwin, his Daughter and Human Evolution* (London: Fourth Estate, 2001).

135 **one of the strangest letters**: To Mrs. Charles Dickens, 15 April 1851, *Letters*, vi. 353–6; Dickens also used "if" to reassure himself that Dora's death was for the best, writing that "if, with a wish, I could cancel what has happened and bring the little creature back to life, I would not do it. God be thanked!" (to F. M. Evans, 17 April 1851, *Letters*, vi. 355).

135 **"exercise, and cold water"**: To Henry Austin, 12 March 1851, *Letters*, vi. 314.

135 **"confusion and nervousness at times"**: To the Hon. Mrs. Richard Watson, 9 March 1851, *Letters*, vi. 31.

135 **"3 or 4 years":** To Henry Austin, 12 March 1851, *Letters*, vi. 314.

135 **"violent headaches":** To Dr. James Wilson, 8 March 1851, *Letters*, vi. 309n.

136 **following the birth of Dora:** This diagnosis is disputed by Lillian Nayder in *The Other Dickens: A Life of Catherine Hogarth* (Ithaca, NY: Cornell University Press, 2011), drawing on the popular vascular theory of nervous disorders to note that "the application of cold water to Catherine's extremities would draw blood away from her head and thereby equalize her circulation, reducing if not altogether eliminating her headaches and the 'fulness' that caused them" (p. 178).

136 **"for her health":** To W. Booth, 13 March 1851, *Letters*, vi. 314.

136 **suicidal feelings and many more:** These are among the "authenticated cases treated by the water cure" outlined by Catherine Dickens's Malvern practitioner Dr. James Wilson in *The Practice of the Water Cure, with Authenticated Evidence of its Efficacy and Safety* (London: H. Bailliere and A. H. Baily, 1844).

136 **"useful to them beyond doubt":** Quoted in Stott, *Darwin and the Barnacle*, p. 120.

136 **"wine-cured Lady B":** Quoted in Mitchell, *Bulwer Lytton*, p. 92; Mitchell notes that Bulwer Lytton's other medical fads included "an India rubber machine" to treat his deafness, and "Frictionless Gloves" to assist with his mesmeric experiments.

136 **"in your neighbourhood":** To Dr. James Wilson, 8 March 1851, *Letters*, vi. 309.

137 **"twenty-four or thirty-six hours":** James Wilson and James M. Gully, *The Dangers of the Water Cure and its Efficacy Examined and Compared with those of the Drug Treatment of Diseases, and an Explanation of its Principles and Practice; with an Account of Cases Treated at Malvern, and a Prospectus of the Water Cure Establishment at that Place* (London: Cunningham and Mortimer, 1843), p. 165.

137 **"healthy husbands!":** Wilson, *The Practice of the Water Cure*, pp. 79, 26.

137 **Harriet Martineau's article:** "Malvern Water," *Household Words*, 11 October 1851, pp. 67–71.

138 **"to catch the morning air":** To John Forster, 15 March 1851, *Letters*, vi. 316.

139 **"in terror and rapture":** Joseph Leech, *Three Weeks in Wet Sheets; Being the Diary and Doings of a Moist Visitor to Malvern* (London: Hamilton, Adams & Co; Bristol: John Ridler; Malvern: Lamb and Son, 1856), pp. 75–6. Rebecca Stott offers a full account of this treatment in *Darwin and the Barnacle*.

139 **"a—SHOWER BATH":** To Thomas Beard, 18 July 1849, *Letters*, v. 574.

139 **"drawn close for shower":** To Henry Austin, 14 October 1851, *Letters*, vi. 520 (see illustration).

140 **"that charming mystery of mysteries":** "A Few Facts About Matrimony," *Household Words*, 13 July 1851, p. 374.

140 **"whatever I do must be right":** To Miss Catherine Hogarth, [?June 1835], *Letters*, i. 63.

140 **"on acquaintance":** Leslie Staples, "New Letters of Mary Hogarth and Her Sister Catherine," *Dickensian* 63 (1967), p. 76.

140 **"one part of your disposition":** To Miss Catherine Hogarth, [?12 October 1835], [?August 1835], 9 July 1835, 18 December 1835, *Letters*, i. 76, 73, 69, 110.

141 *"overbearings"*: *Life of Lord Jeffrey, with a Selection from his Correspondence*, ed. Lord Cockburn, 2 vols. (Edinburgh: Adam and Charles Black, 1852), ii. 465–6; this letter is discussed in Nayder, *The Other Dickens*, pp. 153–4.

141 **"to the Fondling"**: To W. C. Macready, 14 April 1846, *Letters*, iv. 532.

141 **"towards my country's population"**: To Mrs. Gore, 7 September 1852, *Letters*, vi. 756.

141 **"her own good-natured footing"**: Henry Shaen Solly, *The Life of Henry Morley, L.L D.* (London: Edward Arnold, 1898), p. 201.

141 **"Bully and Meek"**: To David C. Colden, 31 July 1842, *Letters*, iii. 291.

141 **"a very wicked man"**: To W. C. Macready, 2 February 1849, *Letters*, v. 484; Gladys Storey, *Dickens and Daughter* (London: Frederick Muller, 1939), pp. 94, 219.

142 **"do her good"**: To F. M. Evans, 17 April 1851, *Letters*, vi. 355. "Firmness" was a quality Dickens prided himself on possessing; on New Year's Day 1850 he used the language of phrenology to inform Rev. James White of his resolution not to sit for any more portrait painters, although "I confess that my organ of firmness: feels rather flabby" (*Letters*, vi. 1).

142 **she wrote to the Duke again:** *Letters*, vi. 379–80n.

143 *"a dead father in the other"*: Chatsworth scrapbook. Bulwer Lytton included a copy of this playbill in the file he later assembled in a doomed attempt to prove Rosina's lunacy in 1858: see Michael J. Flynn, "Dickens, Rosina Bulwer Lytton, and the 'Guilt' of Literature and Art," *Dickens Quarterly*, vol. 29, no. 1 (March 2012), pp. 68–80.

143 **"not cool at all, oh no"**: *Letters*, vi. 389n.

143 **"out of all hearing"**: To Sir Edward Bulwer Lytton, 9 May 1851, *Letters*, vi. 380.

144 **communicating with the dead:** The rest of Louis Alphonse Cahagnet's rambling subtitle provides a good summary of his argument: *Wherein the Existence, the Form, the Occupations, of the Soul after its Separation from the Body are Proved by Many Years' Experiments, by the means of Eight Ecstatic Somnambulists, who had Eighty Perceptions of Thirty-Six Deceased Persons of Various Conditions. A Description of them, their Conversation, etc., with Proofs of their Existence in the Spiritual World.* (London: Geo. Peirce, 1851).

144 **"between man and man"**: *Interviews and Recollections*, p. 319.

144 **"whatever you are!"**: *A Christmas Carol*, Stave One.

144 **a hazy "middle state"**: *Examiner*, 26 February 1848, p. 132.

144 **"humbug"**: *Interviews and Recollections*, p. 318.

145 **"choked up with too much burying"**: *A Christmas Carol*, Stave Four.

145 **"Like a football, on the stones"**: "City Graves," *Household Words*, 14 December 1850, p. 277. Judith Flanders discusses these issues in *The Victorian City*, pp. 221–2.

145 **"and pull him in"**: *Great Expectations*, ch. 1.

146 **"towards 12 o'Clock"**: To Sir Edward Bulwer Lytton, 1 May 1851, *Letters*, vi. 372.

146 **"Mr. Nightingale's Diary"**: Ibid.

146   **"scarcely to merit the name":** "Bygone Celebrities II: *Mr. Nightingale's Diary*,"
       Gentleman's Magazine, 6 (May 1871), p. 660.

147   **"tormenting remembrance":** Quotations are taken from Charles Dickens, *Mr.
       Nightingale's Diary: A Farce in One Act* (1851, repr. Boston: James R. Osgood and
       Company, 1871).

147   **"our said client":** Ralph Straus, *Dickens: A Portrait in Pencil* (London: Gollancz,
       1928), p. 110.

147   **"the greatest reluctance possible":** See Arthur Waugh, *A Hundred Years of
       Publishing* (London: Chapman & Hall, 1930), p. 42.

SUMMER: MAKING AN EXHIBITION

151   **"the class to which they belong":** See Julia Petrov, "'A Strong-Minded
       American Lady': Bloomerism in Texts and Images, 1851," *Fashion Theory* 20:4
       (2015), pp. 394–5.

152   **"into the public arena":** Gayle V. Fischer, *Pantaloons and Power: A Nineteenth-
       Century Dress Reform in the United States* (Kent, Ohio and London: The Kent
       State University Press, 2001), p. 6.

152   **"brought to her name":** D. C. Bloomer, *Life and Writings of Amelia Bloomer*
       (Boston: Arena Publishing Company, 1895), p. 65.

152   **"ball and chain":** "Our Costume," *The Lily*, 4 (April 1851), p. 31.

152   **"half-serious, half-playful":** Bloomer, *Life and Writings of Amelia Bloomer*,
       p. 66.

152   **"very good":** To J. H. Nightingale, 14 December 1852, *Letters*, vi. 820. J. H.
       Nightingale and C. Millward's farce was first performed at the Theatre Royal,
       Adelphi on 2 October. The closing scene includes an explicit reference to
       Dickens, as Mr. Green asks his wife "how could you desert your offspring—
       your smiling babes, your knitting, crochet, and your other household works,
       for fooleries like this [i.e., her costume]?," and she replies "Don't bother me
       with your *household words,* what *the dickens* do I care for such stuff?"
       Nightingale sent Dickens a copy in December 1852.

153   **"most daringly manifested":** "Bloomerism in Edinburgh," *The Times*, 28
       August 1851.

153   **to wear the trousers:** *Punch*, vol. 21 (1851), pp. 184, 189 (see also pp. 196, 200,
       202, 208–9, 210, 217–19, 232).

153   **"crippling and *confining sheath!*":** Ibid., p. 128.

153   **"more than they did in those days":** [J. E. Panton], *Leaves from a Life* (London:
       Eveleigh Nash, 1908), pp. 17–18.

154   **"trousers of the brightest patterns":** "A Curious Disease," *New York Times*,
       27 May 1876, quoted in Becky Munford, "Medical Bloomers and Irrational
       Rationalists: Pathologising the Woman in Trousers," *Women's History Review*,
       vol. 28, no. 6 (2018), pp. 988–9.

154   **"wherever I appeared":** Bloomer, *Life and Writings of Amelia Bloomer*, p. 69.

154   **"several outbreaks of laughter":** "Lecture on Bloomerism," *The Times*, 8
       October 1851, p. 7.

154 **"unusually violent"**: "A Bloomer No Martyr," *Illustrated London News*, 4 October 1851, p. 403. See Munford, "Medical Bloomers and Irrational Rationalists," pp. 994–5.

154 **"Sucking Pigs"**: *Household Words*, 8 November 1851, pp. 145–7.

155 **"Bloomeriana"**: *Punch*, vol. 21 (1851), pp. 204–5.

155 **"to go out speechifying"**: "From the Raven in the Happy Family," *Household Words*, 11 May 1850, p. 158.

156 **"as bold as Joan d'Arc"**: "Turkish Costume," *Harper's New Monthly Magazine*, July 1851, p. 288.

156 **"the voices of little children!"**: *A Child's History of England*, ch. 22.

156 **"the door was always on the swing"**: Eneas Mackenzie, *What Has Mrs. Caroline Chisholm Done for the Colony of New South Wales?* (1862), quoted in Hartley, *Charles Dickens and the House of Fallen Women*, p. 198.

157 **"my continual companions"**: To Miss Burdett Coutts, 4 March 1850, *Letters*, vi. 53.

157 **"immediately before him"**: "Full Report of the Second Meeting of the Mudfog Association for the Advancement of Everything," *Bentley's Miscellany*, vol. 4 (1838), p. 223.

157 **"the apostle of Bloomerism"**: "Bloomerism in Finsbury," *The Times*, 30 September 1851, quoted in Petrov, "A Strong- Minded American Lady," p. 398.

157 **"art and industry around them"**: "The Great Exhibition," *Morning Chronicle*, 4 October 1851, quoted in Petrov, "A Strong- Minded American Lady," p. 398.

158 **"home to his own country"**: *Little Dorrit*, ch. 25.

158 **"wooden shoes!"**: "The Foreign Invasion," *Household Words*, 11 October 1851, p. 60.

158 **"any other season"**: *Punch*, vol. 20 (1851), p. 207.

158 a half-page cartoon: Ibid., p. 197 (see illustration).

160 **"busy hum"**: *The Times*, 2 May 1851; *Illustrated London News*, 3 May 1851.

160 **"very monotonous"**: Benjamin Disraeli, *Tancred: or, The New Crusade*, 3 vols. (London: Henry Colburn, 1847), i. 233.

161 **"Crystal Parliament"**: Discussed in Bryson, *At Home*, p. 15.

161 **"inventions of the human mind"**: John Ruskin, *The Stones of Venice. Volume the First. The Foundations* (London: Smith, Elder & Co., 1851), p. 32.

161 **"stately and unaccusable whole"**: John Ruskin, *The Stones of Venice. Volume the Second. The Sea-Stories*, 2nd edn. (London: Smith, Elder & Co., 1867), pp. 159–60.

162 **"magnified a conservatory!"**: John Ruskin, *The Opening of the Crystal Palace Considered in Some of its Relations to the Prospects of Art* (London: Smith, Elder & Co., 1854), p. 5.

162 **"To meet the sun"**: "A May Ode," *The Times*, 1 May 1851.

162 **"marvellous power of effect"**: To the Rev. P. Brontë, 7 June 1851, repr. in *The Brontës: Life and Letters*, ed. Clement Shorter, 2 vols. (London: Hodder and Stoughton, 1908), ii. 216.

162 **"as if it was choking"**: Stuart Dodgson Collingwood, *The Life and Letters of Lewis Carroll (Rev. C. L. Dodgson)* (London: T. Fisher Unwin, 1899), p. 52.

162 **"the Kingdom of God":** Sermon for the Westminster Hospital, quoted in Frances Eliza Kingsley (ed.), *Charles Kingsley: His Letters and Memories of his Life*, 2 vols. (London: K. Paul, Trench, 1883), i. 280.

162 **sick in the bushes:** Bryson, *At Home*, p. 49.

162 **"who didn't see it":** To G. W. Curtis, [?April 1851], *Letters*, vi. 371.

163 **"has not decreased it":** To the Hon. Mrs. Richard Watson, 11 July 1851, *Letters*, vi. 428.

163 **image of the novelist:** "Catalogue of the Portraits of Charles Dickens," Kitton (ed.), *Dickens by Pen and Pencil*, p. xiv.

163 **"coldness and gentility":** *The Old Curiosity Shop*, ch. 27.

163 **familiar to him:** My information about the exhibits is chiefly drawn from the *Official Descriptive and Illustrated Catalogue of the Great Exhibition of the Works of Industry of All Nations*, 5 vols. (London: Spicer Brothers, 1851).

163 **"mashed rags":** "The Pasha's New Boat," *Household Words*, 22 November 1851, p. 209.

163 **"under a glass cover":** "An Immortal Idea," *Punch*, vol. 20 (1851), p. 63.

164 **"to stare our fill":** 13 October 1851; this idea is discussed in Andrew H. Miller, *Novels Behind Glass: Commodity Culture and Victorian Narrative* (Cambridge: Cambridge University Press, 1995), p. 52.

164 **"crystal palace":** See Lee Jackson, *Palaces of Pleasure* (New Haven: Yale University Press, 2019), p. 275; Jackson quotes a review in *The Odd Fellow* (28 December 1839): "Up goes the curtain, discovering a crystal palace, inhabited by a queen and several ladies of honour."

164 ***an exhibition of yourself:*** I am grateful to Sophie Ratcliffe for drawing my attention to the history of this phrase.

164 **"curious exhibition of himself":** *A Child's History of England*, ch. 12.

165 **"repulsive exhibition of herself":** To Miss Burdett Coutts, 17 April 1850, *Letters*, vi. 84.

165 **"gin and oranges":** *The Times*, 24 May 1851; 5 July 1851; quoted in Jackson, *Palaces of Pleasure*, p. 148.

165 **cartoon of the forthcoming Exhibition:** "Specimens from Mr. Punch's Industrial Exhibition of 1850," *Punch*, vol. 18 (1850), p. 145.

165 **loose term "labour":** See Clemm, *Dickens, Journalism and Nationhood*, p. 21.

166 **"return with any change":** To G. S. Herbert, 23 June 1851, *Letters*, vi. 415.

166 **"the verge of starvation":** "A Biography of a Bad Shilling," *Household Words*, 25 January 1851, p. 425.

166 **"dissemination of cheap pleasures":** "Cheap Pleasures—a Gossip," *Household Words*, 24 May 1851, p. 202.

166 **"talent strangely applied":** "Chronicle," *Annual Register* (1851), p. 59.

167 **"a professed riding master":** *The Bachelors Pocket Book for 1851* (London: W. Ward, 1851), n.p. This book is extremely rare, and I am grateful to Michael Slater for sharing this information from his own copy. It is also mentioned by Judith Flanders in *The Victorian City*, p. 404, and discussed by Michael Slater in *Sexuality in Victorian Literature* (Tennessee Studies in Victorian Literature, vol.

27), ed. Don Richard Cox (Knoxville: University of Tennessee Press, 1984), pp. 128–40.

167 **"a dexterity unapproachable":** *Interviews and Recollections*, p. 312.

167 **article by Harry Wills:** "Epsom," *Household Words*, 7 June 1851, pp. 244–5.

167 **"the happiest terms":** Blanchard Jerrold and Gustave Doré, *London: A Pilgrimage* (1872, repr. London: Anthem Press, 2005), p. 78.

168 **"dependent on the other":** To the Editor of the *Morning Chronicle*, 25 July 1842, *Letters*, iii. 285.

168 **"the robber of St. James":** This example is discussed in Shannon, *Dickens, Reynolds, and Mayhew on Wellington Street*, pp. 150–1.

168 **"Easterly, into Mayfair":** *Speeches*, p. 128.

168 **"crystal palace of the sea":** "The World of Water," *Household Words*, 24 May 1851, pp. 205–6.

169 **"an exhibition of themselves":** *The Adventures of Mr. and Mrs. Sandboys and Family, who came up to London to "enjoy themselves," and to see the Great Exhibition* (London: David Bogue, 1851), p. 160.

170 **"further exertions":** Repr. in Jonathon Shears (ed.), *The Great Exhibition, 1851: A Sourcebook* (Manchester: Manchester University Press, 2017), pp. 32–3.

170 **"foreign countries and our own":** Charles Babbage, *The Exposition of 1851; or, Views of the Industry, the Science, and the Government*, 2nd edn. (London: John Murray, 1851), p. 134.

170 **"collection of intellectual treasures":** Michael Leapman, *The World for a Shilling: How the Great Exhibition of 1851 Shaped a Nation* (London: Headline, 2001), p. 206.

170 **"foreign wanderings":** *The Parlour Magazine of the Literature of All Nations* (London: Houlston & Stoneman, 1851), pp. 1–2.

171 **"suspended from her neck":** *The Comic Almanack and Diary*, ed. Henry Mayhew (London: David Bogue, 1851), p. 13.

171 **the other diners:** Jokes about dirty Frenchmen were a staple of *Punch*, while in Thomas Onwhyn's *Mr. and Mrs. Brown's Visit to the Great Exhibition*, one of the illustrations "depicts three cannibals at a restaurant making an offer for a toothsome English child sitting opposite" (Leapman, *The World for a Shilling*, p. 216).

171 **"kept that at home":** W. Wells Brown ("A Fugitive Slave"), *Three Years in Europe; or Places I Have Seen and People I Have Met* (London: Charles Gilpin, 1852), p. 211.

171 **a poem by Elizabeth Barrett Browning:** "Hiram Power's [*sic*] Greek Slave," *Household Words*, 26 October 1850, p. 99.

171 **"American manufacture":** *Punch*, vol. 20 (1851), p. 236; further responses to the statue are discussed in Auerbach, *The Great Exhibition*, p. 168.

172 **"but as a *man*":** *The Frederick Douglass Papers, Series Three: Correspondence, Volume 1: 1842–1852*, ed. John R. McKivigan (New Haven: Yale University Press, 2009), p. 54.

172 **"abominable portrait":** To Macready, 17 March 1848, *Letters*, v. 263.

172   **"sweetest, and yet boldest, writing":** "North American Slavery," *Household Words*, 18 September 1852, p. 1.

172   **fierce opposition to slavery:** In March 1848 he sent Macready a copy of Frederick Douglass's autobiography to prepare him for his own trip to America later that year.

172   **"expound King Lear to me":** To the Earl of Carlisle, 15 April 1857, *Letters*, viii. 313. See Laura Korobkin, "Avoiding 'Aunt Tomasina': Charles Dickens Responds to Harriet Beecher Stowe's Black American Reader, Mary Webb," *English Literary History*, vol. 82, no. 1 (March 2015), pp. 115–40.

173   **" 'prejudice against white people' ":** *Interviews and Recollections*, p. 236.

173   **tangle of attitudes towards foreigners:** See Clemm, *Dickens, Journalism, and Nationhood*, pp. 30–47.

173   **"long-faced, and lantern-jawed":** "A Monument of French Folly," *Household Words*, 8 March 1851, p. 553.

173   **"ridiculous or wrong":** "Insularities," *Household Words*, 19 January 1856, p. 1.

174   **"stoppage":** "The Great Exhibition and the Little One," *Household Words*, 5 July 1851, pp. 356–60.

174   **"commit suicide":** "The Foreign Invasion," *Household Words*, 11 October 1851, p. 64.

174   **"assemble in one character":** "Foreigners' Portraits of Englishmen," *Household Words*, 21 September 1850, p. 601.

175   **"sense of national greatness":** "A Pilgrimage to the Great Exhibition from Abroad," *Household Words*, 28 June 1850, pp. 321–4.

175   **"little moveable theatre":** Charles Knight, *Passages of a Working Life*, 3 vols. (London: Bradbury & Evans, 1865), iii. 115.

175   **"her foreign Ambassadors":** *Illustrated London News* (24 May 1851), quoted in *Letters*, vi. 392n.

176   **"fiendish lineaments":** I draw these examples from Flynn, "Dickens, Rosina Bulwer Lytton, and the 'Guilt' of Literature and Art," pp. 73–4.

176   **incidents of other kinds:** "Bygone Celebrities I: The Guild of Literature and Art at Chatsworth," pp. 253–4.

176   **"rather too long":** Friday 16 May 1851, www.queenvictoriasjournals.org.

177   **"more in point than in wit":** Reviews are quoted from the Duke of Devonshire's scrapbook at Chatsworth.

177   **"below mediocrity":** Quoted in *Letters*, vi. 392n.

177   **"it is tribute!":** *Not So Bad As We Seem*, p. 88.

177   **"SUCCESS TO THE SCHEME!":** Ibid., p. 139.

177   **aristocratic patronage:** This ambiguity is discussed in Hack, "Literary Paupers and Professional Authors," pp. 705– 8.

177   **"most unfortunate and most degraded":** See Ray, *Thackeray: The Age of Wisdom*, pp. 152–3.

178   **"men who live for others":** *Not So Bad As We Seem*, p. 15.

178   **"a traitor and a sneak":** Quoted in Ray, *Thackeray: The Age of Wisdom*, pp. 152–3.

178 "even madder than usual": "Je ne puis soutenir le bruit, et la foule, de
     Londres—où tout le monde est meme plus fou que l'ordinairement, apropos
     de l'Exposition," *Letters*, vi. 392.

178 "to save myself": To William Phillips, 16 December 1850, *Letters*, vi. 237.

179 "remarkably drunk": To John Forster, 9 September 1839, *Letters*, i. 578.

179 "their Curiosity-Shop wanderings": To Thomas Beard, 1 June 1840, *Letters*,
     ii. 77.

179 "The house is excellent": To Mrs. Charles Dickens, 17 August 1850, *Letters*, vi.
     150.

180 "sea views and comfort": To Thomas Beard, 27 June 1847, *Letters*, v. 102.

180 "airy nest": To the Duke of Devonshire, 1 June 1851, *Letters*, vi. 405

180 a "Hermitage": To Mrs. Gore, 4 July 1851, *Letters*, vi. 420.

180 "the Broadstairs people": To W. H. Wills, 7 April 1851, *Letters*, vi. 349.

180 "O it is wonderful!": To John Forster, [1 June] 1851, *Letters*, vi. 406.

180 "bleakly situated": Thomas Wright, *The Life of Charles Dickens*, pp. 207–8.

180 historical "piety": Elizabeth Bowen, *Eva Trout, or Changing Scenes* (London:
     Jonathan Cape, 1969), p. 129.

181 "enlivened in the summer months": G. W. Bonner, *The Picturesque Pocket
     Companion to Margate, Ramsgate, Broadstairs, and the parts adjacent* (London:
     William Kidd, 1831), p. 183.

181 the people he had spotted: To C. C. Felton, 1 September 1843, *Letters*, iii. 548.

181 "The invaders from all nations": To Miss Geraldine Jewsbury, 25 June 1851,
     Letters, vi. 417.

181 The biblical allusion: Acts 17:24.

182 "rusty and dusty": "Our Watering Place," *Household Words*, 2 August 1851,
     pp. 433–4.

182 "swelling up with life and beauty": Ibid., p. 436.

182 "splendid playground": Taken from Edmund Yates's later description of Fort
     House's surroundings: "The sands immediately below afford a splendid
     playground; there is an abundant supply of never-failing ozone; there is a good
     lawn, surrounded by borders well-stocked with delicious-smelling common
     English flowers, and there is, or was in those days, I imagine, ample opportu-
     nity for necessary seclusion," quoted in Frederic G. Kitton, *The Dickens Country*
     (London: A. & C. Black, 1911), p. 194.

182 "wholly nonsensical flirtation": Eleanor E. Christian, "Recollections of
     Charles Dickens," *Temple Bar* (April 1888), pp. 490–1.

182 "abstracted from us all": Ibid., p. 489.

182 "*Broad-stares* on your very face!": Ibid., p. 488.

182 "How to Spend a Summer Holiday": *Household Words*, 6 July 1850, pp. 556–8.

183 "throb and tremble": *Euphranor, A Dialogue on Youth* (London: William
     Pickering, 1851), p. 18.

183 "a special memory game": Mary Boyle, quoted in Hilary Macaskill, *Charles
     Dickens at Home* (London: Frances Lincoln, 2011), p. 127.

183 "the *Copperfield* banquet": To John Forster, [1 June 1851], *Letters*, vi. 406.

183 **"always flows and never ebbs":** To the Rev. George M. Musgrave, 15 October 1851, *Letters*, vi. 521.

183 **"relentless activity":** *Life*, i. 160.

184 **"Dickens rather frightened me":** *Interviews and Recollections*, p. 295.

184 **"keep the people quiet":** Quoted in Ackroyd, *Dickens*, p. 602.

184 **a pocket comb:** *Interviews and Recollections*, pp. xvii, 37.

184 **"the resources of Englishmen":** *Speeches*, p. 134.

184 **"boredom and lassitude":** To W. H. Wills, 27 July 1851, *Letters*, vi. 448–9.

184 **"allusion to the Great Exhibition":** Ibid., 10 August 1851, *Letters*, vi. 457.

185 **"glazed over":** "The Private History of the Palace of Glass," *Household Words*, 18 January 1851, p. 390.

185 **the workers who built it:** *Household Narrative* (1851), pp. 97, 115.

185 **balustrades of Renaissance architecture:** *The Stones of Venice*, i. 159.

185 **"yellow and shrivelled":** *Nicholas Nickleby*, ch. 51.

185 **happening to Paul's body:** *Dombey and Son*, ch. 23.

186 **"in helpless confusion":** "The Queen's Bazaar," *Household Words*, 22 February 1851, p. 522.

186 **"different shelves of my brain":** To the Editor of the *Knickerbocker Magazine*, [?June or July 1851], *Letters*, i. 558.

186 **"pigeon-holes of my brain":** *Interviews and Recollections*, p. 146.

186 **"negligent abundance":** *Martin Chuzzlewit*, ch. 28.

186 **"authors for the first time":** "The Catalogue's Account of Itself," *Household Words*, 23 August 1851, p. 522.

187 **"old and constant friends":** *Master Humphrey's Clock*, ch. 1.

187 **"a trifle sticky":** *Our Mutual Friend*, ch. 2.

187 **"the same thing anywhere else":** *Martin Chuzzlewit*, ch. 5.

187 **"looking-glass department":** "Memorials of the Great Exhibition—1851, No. IX.—The Looking-Glass Department," *Punch's Almanac for 1851*, p. ix.

188 **"the shilling visitors":** "The Shilling days at the Crystal Palace," *Punch*, vol. 20 (1851), p. 240.

188 **"he thought it long":** To the Hon. Mrs. Richard Watson, 11 July 1851, *Letters*, vi. 429.

188 **"my cave on the seashore":** To A. H. Layard, 16 December 1851, *Letters*, vi. 555.

188 **"London noise and smoke":** To Mrs. Peter Taylor, 19 August 1852, repr. in *George Eliot's Life as Related in her Letters and Journals*, ed. J. W. Cross, 3 vols. (Boston: Harper & Brothers, 1885), i. 207, describing Broadstairs as a "pretty, quiet place, which 'David Copperfield' has made classic."

189 **"great humming-top":** To Leigh Hunt, 31 January 1855, *Letters*, vii. 518.

189 **" 'BRADSHAW, BRADSHAW' ":** "A Narrative of Extraordinary Suffering," *Household Words*, 12 July 1851, pp. 361–3.

190 **"eight times in a second!":** "Wings of Wire," *Household Words*, 7 December 1850, pp. 241–5.

190 **"true / To one another!":** "Dover Beach" (1867), repr. in *Arnold: Poems*, ed. Kenneth Allott (Harmondsworth: Penguin, 1954, repr. 1985), p. 181.

190 **"pass round the world"**: "The Great Peace-Maker. A Sub-Marine Dialogue," *Household Words*, 14 June 1851, pp. 275–7.

190 **"under the sea"**: *Memoranda*, p. 19.

190 *"the unity of mankind"*: Elsewhere the development of the telegraph stimulated even more ambitious fantasies; in 1850 the American writer Joseph Brady argued that "This noble invention is to be the means of extending civilization, republicanism, and Christianity over the earth: Then will wrong and injustice be forever banished. Every yoke shall be broken, and the oppressed go free. Wars will cease from the earth," "The Magnetic Telegraph," *Ladies Repository* 10 (1850), pp. 61– 2. I am grateful to Dan O'Hara for this example.

191 **"concord, prosperity and peace"**: "Short Cuts Across the Globe [i]," *Household Words*, 13 April 1850, pp. 67–8.

191 **"crystal and golden lamps"**: See Stott, *Darwin and the Barnacle*, pp. 188–9.

191 *Our Native Land*: Altick, *The Shows of London*, p. 460.

192 **"the Saviour's presence"**: Ibid.

192 **"brotherhood among us all"**: "Some Account of an Extraordinary Traveller," *Household Words*, 20 April 1850, pp. 73–7.

193 **"Great Globes"**: "The Globe in a Square," *Household Words*, 12 July 1851, p. 372.

193 **"All the Nations"**: To Augustus Tracey, 10 October 1851, *Letters*, vi. 517.

193 **"A Flight"**: *Household Words*, 30 August 1851, pp. 529–33.

193 **"born of quick travelling"**: To Albert Smith, 12 November 1854, *Letters*, vii. 464.

194 **"strange beyond description"**: Wolfgang Schivelbusch, *The Railway Journey: The Industrialization of Time and Space in the 19th Century* (Berkeley, CA: University of California Press, 1986), pp. 129, 78.

194 **"from city to city"**: Quoted in Alison Byerly, *Are We There Yet?: Virtual Travel and Victorian Realism* (Ann Arbor: University of Michigan Press, 2013), p. 151.

194 **"a living parcel"**: *The Seven Lamps of Architecture* (1849), in *The Library Edition of the Works of John Ruskin*, 39 vols., ed. E. T. Cook and Alexander Wedderburn (London: George Allen, 1903–12), viii. 159.

195 **"railway line of sentence"**: *The Letters of Virginia Woolf*, ed. N. Nicolson and J. Trautmann, 6 vols. (London: Hogarth Press, 1975–80), iii. 135.

195 **"pathetic description"**: To the Hon. Mrs. Richard Watson, 11 July 1851, *Letters*, vi. 427.

195 **"his heavy head"**: Ibid.

195 **his publisher had paid for them**: *Annual Register* (1851), "Chronicle," pp. 35–6.

196 **possible futures for himself**: *Interviews and Recollections*, p. 272.

196 **"symptoms of the disorder"**: To Miss Burdett Coutts, 17 August 1851, *Letters*, vi. 463.

196 **"exceedingly"**: To Messrs Holland and Sons, 7 February 1851, *Letters*, vi. 283.

196 **"the existing villa"**: To W. Booth, 13 March 1851, *Letters*, vi. 314.

196 **"they would like to live in"**: "Household Scenery," *Household Words*, 14 August 1852, p. 513.

197   **a long list of books:** "Inventory of Contents of 1 Devonshire Terrace, May 1844," *Letters*, iv. 705.

197   **"at the same price":** "Mr. Bendigo Buster on the Model Cottages," *Household Words*, 5 July 1851, p. 337.

197   **"if he will only do it":** To Miss Burdett Coutts, 1 February 1851, *Letters*, vii. 20.

198   **extra air of respectability:** See Macaskill, *Charles Dickens at Home*, pp. 79–83.

199   **"made very handsome":** To Henry Austin, 14 July 1851, *Letters*, vi. 431.

199   **"bargaining for the property":** To Frank Stone, 16 July 1851, *Letters*, vi. 435.

199   **"carte blanche":** Ibid., 20 July 1851, *Letters*, vi. 438.

199   **£1,542:** Ibid., 23 July 1851, *Letters*, vi. 440.

200   **"ON THE PREMISES":** To Henry Austin, 7 September 1851, *Letters*, vi. 479.

200   **"a house after all":** Ibid.

200   **"can be transplanted":** To W. H. Wills, 9 September 1851, *Letters*, vi. 480.

201   **"always pouring in":** To Henry Austin, 1 October 1851, *Letters*, vi. 501–2.

201   **"paint in the sea":** Ibid., 19 September 1851, *Letters*, vi. 485.

201   **"next to the carpet":** Repr. in *Sketches by Boz* as "Mr. Minns and his Cousin."

202   **" 'where is Mr. Charles Dickens?' ":** *Interviews and Recollections*, p. 111.

202   **"through the very slates":** To the Hon. Richard Watson, 31 October 1851, *Letters*, vi. 533.

AUTUMN: HOME

205   **"rhapsody run mad":** *The Critical Response to Herman Melville's Moby-Dick*, cd. Kevin J. Hayes (Westport, Conn. and London: Greenwood Press, 1994), pp. xvi, 3.

205   **"Burlington Street Brigand":** To Thomas Beard, [17 December 1839], *Letters*, i. 619.

206   **"numerous rude scratches":** Ch. 67 ("Cutting In") and ch. 68 ("The Blanket") in Herman Melville, *The Whale* (London: Richard Bentley, 1851), 3 vols.

206   **"various races of mankind":** *The Times*, 16 October 1851.

206   **"necessary termination":** Ibid.

207   **the Exhibition came to an end:** See *Letters*, vi. 525 n. 4.

207   **the Crystal Palace Company:** Ibid.

207   **"Prospect Tower":** Burton's plans were published in *The Builder* in 1852 (see illustration).

208   **"to the river for amusement":** Leapman, *The World for a Shilling*, pp. 273–6.

208   **"wretched English climate":** *Punch*, vol. 21 (1851), pp. 71–3, 97.

208   **"a single perfect fact":** *Household Words*, 19 July 1851, pp. 400–2.

209   **"without leaving home":** See illustration; escalating costs meant that this part of the hospital was never built.

209   **"scheme of the glass palace":** *Household Words*, 2 August 1851, pp. 446–50.

209   **"into a pleasant dulness":** To Miss Burdett Coutts, 17 November 1851, *Letters*, vi. 542.

210   **"a horrible nuisance":** To Henry Austin, 17 October 1851, *Letters*, vi. 523.

210 **"COMMIT NO NUISANCE":** To Eliot Warburton, 23 October 1851, *Letters*, vi. 525 (see illustration).

210 **"into which I didn't follow him":** To J. B. Cardale, 22 January 1853, *Letters*, vii.14.

211 **"no one looking on":** To Henry Austin, 25 October 1851, *Letters*, vi. 526.

211 **"in full chorus!":** *Dombey and Son*, ch. 28.

212 **"all but exhausted":** To the Hon. Miss Emily Eden, 28 September 1851, *Letters*, vi. 499.

212 **"pretty and elegant":** "Charles Dickens At Home, By His Eldest Daughter," p. 39.

212 **"brocaded and golden Temple":** To Mrs. Charles Dickens, 2 October 1851, *Letters*, vi. 504.

212 **"an intolerable restlessness":** To John Forster, [?late September 1851], *Letters*, vi. 501.

212 **"the Illustrious Architect":** To Henry Austin, 17 October 1851, *Letters*, vi. 523.

212 **reported to Miss Coutts:** To Miss Burdett Coutts, 17 November 1851, *Letters*, vi. 541.

213 **"another great house":** To Henry Austin, 13 November 1851, *Letters*, vi. 536.

213 **"round the supper-table":** Frederic G. Kitton, *Dickensiana* (London: George Redway, 1886), p. 46.

213 **"things with the Poker":** To Mrs. Charles Dickens, 13 November 1851, *Letters*, vi. 539.

213 **"his or her Part":** Quoted in Ackroyd, *Dickens*, p. 648.

213 **"ON THE PREMISES":** To Henry Austin, 7 September 1851, *Letters*, vi. 479.

213 **"escorted by workmen":** Ibid., 7 October 1851, *Letters*, vi. 510.

213 **"in the New Year":** To F. M. Evans, 12 October 1851, *Letters*, vi. 518.

214 **"not truly done I think":** To John Forster, [summer 1851], *Letters*, vi. 453.

214 **"a neutral territory":** Nathaniel Hawthorne, *The Scarlet Letter: A Romance* (Boston: Ticknor, Reed, and Fields, 1850), p. 42.

214 **to Broadstairs in September:** To Mrs. Charles Dickens, 11 September 1851, *Letters*, vi. 482.

215 **"back to the Dead":** To Dr. Thomas Stone, 2 February 1851, *Letters*, vi. 277.

215 **"send their loves":** To Mrs. John Leech, 3 February 1851, *Letters*, vi. 280.

215 **"send their fondest regards":** To Sir Edward Bulwer Lytton, 4 July 1851, *Letters*, vi. 421.

215 **"the gentle Georgina":** To the Rev. Edward Tagart, 20 January 1850, *Letters*, v. 478.

215 **"My Dearest Georgy":** To Miss Georgina Hogarth, 31 August 1850, *Letters*, vi. 160.

215 **unexpected double:** This is discussed by Rosemarie Bodenheimer in *Knowing Dickens*, ch. 4: "Another Man."

216 **"refuge and best friend":** *David Copperfield*, ch. 34.

216 **"dies quite happily":** *Memoranda*, p. 10.

216 **"all over paint":** To the Hon. Richard Watson, 31 October 1851, *Letters*, vi. 533.

216   **"housekeeper"**: *David Copperfield*, chs. 15, 44.

216   **"little housekeeper"**: To W. H. Wills, 29 August 1850, *Letters*, vi. 158.

217   **"the amusement of others"**: Quoted in Ackroyd, *Dickens*, p. 5.

217   **"butcher's meat, and bread"**: George Dolby, *Charles Dickens As I Knew Him*
      (London: T. Fisher Unwin, 1885), pp. 45–8; Dickens's chequebook payments
      after he opened a bank account at Coutts & Co. in November 1837 are
      analysed by Lillian Nayder in *The Other Dickens*, pp. 65–6.

217   **"a merry pride!"**: *Martin Chuzzlewit*, ch. 39.

217   **"Order is re-established"**: To Miss Burdett Coutts, 17 November 1851, *Letters*,
      vi. 542.

217   **"cleared or thickened"**: Kitton, *Charles Dickens*, p. 209.

218   **"suggestion of ostentation"**: Quoted in *Letters*, vi. 481n.

218   **"the fretted roof"**: To Mrs. Gaskell, 25 November 1851, *Letters*, vi. 545.

218   **"very neat & quiet"**: Ibid., 21 December 1851, *Letters*, vi. 558.

218   **"dinner service of *gold* plate"**: [?] and 30 December 1851, Mrs. Gaskell to
      Emily [?]Tagart, *The Letters of Mrs. Gaskell*, ed. J. A. V. Chapple and Arthur
      Pollard (Manchester: Manchester University Press, 1966), p. 175.

219   **"blessings of the plenty"**: Quoted in Macaskill, *Charles Dickens at Home*, p. 84.

219   **"too 'respectable' "**: *Athenaeum*, 28 November 1885, p. 702.

219   **"so thoroughly respectable"**: *David Copperfield*, ch. 21.

219   *What Shall We Have For Dinner?*: Quotations from *What Shall We Have for
      Dinner?* are taken from the transcript reproduced in Susan M. Rossi-Wilcox,
      Dinner for Dickens: The Culinary History of Mrs. Charles Dickens's Menu Books
      (Totnes: Prospect Books, 2005).

220   **"wish to see it done"**: *David Copperfield*, ch. 24.

220   **"where to buy fowls"**: To W. H. Wills, 4 January 1857, *Letters*, viii. 253;
      Michael Slater offers a more generous interpretation in *Dickens and Women*
      (Stanford: Stanford University Press, 1983), p. 128.

220   **"an English wife"**: Nathaniel Hawthorne, *The English Notebooks*, ed. Randall
      Stewart (New York: Modern Language Association of America; London:
      Oxford University Press, 1941), p. 379.

220   **"common Green dinner-set"**: The inventory is repr. as Appendix C in *Letters*,
      iv. 704–26.

221   **"the pine-apples"**: *Life*, i. 36.

221   ***"entertainments of the higher classes"***: "A Lady" [Maria Rundell], *A New System
      of Domestic Cookery; Formed Upon Principles of Economy* (London and Edinburgh,
      1808), p. v.

221   **"lost his heart"**: The manuscript of "The Bill of Fare" (1831) is in the Dickens
      Museum London.

221   **"the first that comes"**: Dion Boucicault, *Used Up; A Petite Comedy, in Two Acts*
      (London: National Drama Acting Office, 1844), Act 1.

223   *"Blanquette"*: *Punch*, vol. 21 (1851), p. 237.

223   **ingredients like a chicken:** For more details on Catherine Dickens's recipes
      (including the sources of her sauces), see Rossi-Wilcox's wide-ranging
      discussion in *Dinner for Dickens*, pp. 96–9.

223 **"bills of fare and recipes"**: Cedric Dickens, *Dining with Dickens* (Oxford: Alden Press, 1984), p. 12.

223 **"Mince Pies"**: To Miss Catherine Hogarth, [18 December 1835], *Letters*, i. 109.

224 **"nothing but the coming dinner"**: *My Father As I Recall Him*, p. 19.

224 **"dim with their delicious steam"**: *Oliver Twist*, ch. 2; *A Christmas Carol*, Stave 3.

224 **"for a long time past"**: *Martin Chuzzlewit*, ch. 39.

224 **"sent it to the baker's"**: *Little Dorrit*, ch. 25.

224 **"à la Dickens"**: Rossi-Wilcox points out these connections in *Dinner for Dickens*, pp. 98–103.

225 **"wandering habits"**: *Great Expectations*, ch. 22.

225 **"home concerns"**: *Life*, iii. 513.

225 **"habits of punctuality and method"**: *Our Mutual Friend*, ch. 6.

226 **"a system of Order"**: To the Hon. Spencer Lyttelton, 9 October 1851, *Letters*, vi. 514.

226 **"perfect order"**: To Mamie Dickens, 15 September 1858, *Letters*, viii. 659.

226 **"a chair out of its place"**: *Charles Dickens, by his Eldest Daughter*, p. 102.

226 **"their appointed places"**: Henry Dickens, *Memories of My Father* (London: V. Gollancz, 1928), p. 25.

226 **"almost a *disorder*"**: To the Hon. Mrs. Richard Watson, 6 April 1852, *Letters*, vi. 635.

226 **"in the usual form"**: To John Forster, [?10–11 August 1844], *Letters*, iv. 174.

226 **"Keep things in their places"**: To Mrs. Charles Dickens, 8 November 1844, *Letters*, iv. 216.

227 **"in its place and in order"**: *Charles Dickens, by his Eldest Daughter*, pp. 102–3.

227 **under his heel**: See *The Violent Effigy*, pp. 16–17.

227 **"Four walls and a ceiling"**: *The Cricket on the Hearth*, ch. 1.

227 **"Blow Domestic Hearth!"**: Reported in Charles and Mary Cowden Clarke, *Recollections of Writers*, 2nd edn. (London: Sampson Low, Marston, Searle & Rivington, 1878), p. 324.

228 **off the bottom panels**: Repr. in *Sketches by Boz* as "Mr. Minns and his Cousin."

228 **"In its place and in order"**: To W. W. F. De Cerjat, [19] January 1857, *Letters*, viii. 265.

228 **"furnished for the winter"**: On Dickens's staging of the play see Robert Louis Brannan (ed.), *Under the Management of Mr. Charles Dickens: His Production of "The Frozen Deep"* (Ithaca, NY: Cornell University Press, 1966); all quotations from the play are taken from this edition.

229 **"when reading a Novel"**: *The Girlhood of Queen Victoria: a Selection from her Diaries 1832–40*, ed. Viscount Esher, 2 vols. (London: John Murray, 1912), ii. 83.

229 **"to Home and Fireside"**: To John Forster, [?early July 1845], *Letters*, iv. 328.

229 **"magician ever spoke"**: *Martin Chuzzlewit*, ch. 35.

229 **"Be it ever so humble"**: The same line is echoed more craftily by Uriah Heep, whose ambition to wheedle his way into the Wickfield house is foreshadowed in sly references to his "umble dwelling" and "numble abode," *David Copperfield*, chs. 17, 16.

229 **"enchanted home"**: *The Cricket on the Hearth*, ch. 2.

230 **"text-books on those themes":** *Great Expectations*, ch. 33.

230 **"weird, wild":** Longfellow, quoted in Brenda Wineapple, *Hawthorne: A Life* (New York: Random House, 2004), p. 238.

231 **throughout his novel:** Nathaniel Hawthorne, *The House of the Seven Gables, A Romance* (Boston: Ticknor, Reed, and Fields, 1851), pp. v, iv, 37, 19, 40, 319, 239, 48.

231 **"into my Study":** To Henry Austin, 5 October 1851, *Letters*, vi. 505.

231 **"to grow grey in it":** To the Hon. Mrs. Richard Watson, 31 October 1851, *Letters*, vi. 532.

231 **defined area for themselves:** This is discussed in John Tosh, *A Man's Place: Masculinity and the Middle-Class Home in Victorian England* (New Haven and London: Yale University Press, 1999, repr. 2007), p. 17.

231 **magazine series:** See Nicola J. Watson (ed.), *Literary Tourism and Nineteenth-Century Culture* (Basingstoke: Palgrave Macmillan, 2009).

232 **"sensible study-stove":** To Henry Austin, 5 October 1851, *Letters*, vi. 505.

232 **a watercolour:** *Residence of Charles Dickens*, watercolour given to the Museum of London by J. Trude Fripp in 1912 (see illustration).

233 **"a dish of tea":** *The Life of Henry Morley*, p. 200.

233 **dummy book spines:** The full list of dummy book titles is reprinted as Appendix C in *Letters*, vi. 851.

233 **"throw it back with his hand":** *Interviews and Recollections*, p. 191.

233 **"less substantial Edifice":** To Miss Burdett Coutts, 9 October 1851, *Letters*, vi. 513.

234 **"the open sesame":** Stone, "Dickens 'Conducts' *Household Words*," p. 84.

234 **dozens of possible titles:** *Memoranda*, pp. 5–6; several of Dickens's aborted titles in these lists (e.g., "MEMORY CARTON") eventually fed their way into the plot of *A Tale of Two Cities*.

234 **twenty-six possible titles:** To Wilkie Collins, 24 January 1862, *Letters*, x. 21.

234 **undated "slips":** They are reproduced in Harry Stone (ed.), *Dickens' Working Notes for His Novels* (Chicago and London: University of Chicago Press, 1987), pp. 183–204, and discussed by George H. Ford in "The Titles for *Bleak House*," *Dickensian* 65 (1969), pp. 84–9.

236 **"usually full of words":** To Dr. Thomas Stone, 2 February 1851, *Letters*, vi. 278.

236 **surprising new form:** Internal evidence suggests that Dickens had more than one historical setting in mind; although he includes references to such modern phenomena as the telegraph and a journey to Lincolnshire by train, he also has Esther observe that "in those coach days" it takes nine hours to travel from London to the coastal town of Deal; see John Sutherland, *Inside Bleak House: A Guide for the Modern Dickensian* (London: Duckworth, 2005), pp. 185–6.

WINTER: STARTING AGAIN

239 **"the Law of Progress":** Published in the *Athenaeum*, 27 December 1851, p. 1386. Rosemary Ashton has argued from internal evidence that Chapman

had the leading hand in this document: "The prose has his flabbiness of style, not Marian's sharpness," *142 Strand: A Radical Address in Victorian London* (London: Chatto & Windus, 2006), p. 107.

240 **"If my health is spared":** Elizabeth Gaskell, *The Life of Charlotte Brontë*, 2 vols. (London: Smith, Elder & Co., 1857), ii. 237.

240 **"a sudden electric flash":** See Larry J. Schaaf, "Sparks, Spinning Wheels & Whites of Egg," *The Talbot Catalogue Raisonée*, https://talbot.bodleian.ox.ac.uk/2016/06/17/sparks-spinning-wheels-whites-of-egg/. I stress the *modern* nature of this technique to distinguish it from earlier attempts that used chemicals to shorten photographic exposure times. In 1839–40, for example, the London-based geologist Captain Levett Ibbetson experimented with limelight to create bursts of intense brightness, allowing him to capture images in five minutes that would have taken five times as long if relying on sunlight alone; one daguerreotype of a cross-section of coral that was published in the *Westminster Review* 34 (September 1840) "has a strong claim to be considered the first flash photograph," notes Kate Flint in *Flash! Photography, Writing, and Surprising Illumination* (Oxford: Oxford University Press, 2017), p. 20.

240 **"on a Friday":** *Life*, ii. 441.

241 **"extremely weak mind":** *Household Words*, 14 September 1850, pp. 596–8.

241 **"simultaneously":** *David Copperfield*, ch. 1.

241 **"how to begin?":** Matthew Beaumont discusses Dickens's strategy in "Beginnings, Endings, Births, Deaths: Sterne, Dickens, and *Bleak House*," *Textual Practice* 26 (2012), pp. 807–27.

241 **"The first ray of light":** *The Pickwick Papers*, ch. 1.

241 **"In the first place":** "Our Society at Cranford," *Household Words*, 13 December 1851, p. 90.

242 **"the self-same words repeated":** "George Silverman's Explanation" (1868), chs. 1–2.

242 **"a clear beginning altogether":** *Bleak House*, ch. 29.

242 **" 'before he touches it' ":** Kitton (ed.), *Dickens by Pen and Pencil*, p. 59.

242 **"fables altogether":** *Household Words*, 16 April 1853, p. 160.

242 **"story-weaver at his loom":** "Postscript, in Lieu of Preface," *Our Mutual Friend*.

243 **"national glory":** Quoted in Asa Briggs, *Victorian People: A Reassessment of Persons and Themes, 1851–67* (Chicago and London: University of Chicago Press, 1955, rev. edn. 1972), p. 49.

243 **take the form of a novel:** Robert Tracy in "Lighthousekeeping: *Bleak House* and the Crystal Palace," argues that Dickens's novel is "an alternate Exhibition to the one in the Crystal Palace" (p. 46).

243 **"keep down all its realities":** *Bleak House*, ch. 12.

243 **biography of her own life:** Ibid., ch. 14.

243 **the next day's writing:** Information on Dickens's breakfast is drawn from Annie Field's diary entry for 8 January 1868, in *Interviews and Recollections*, p. 317.

243 **"any sudden sound":** *My Father As I Recall Him*, p. 65.

244 **"left off chattering":** "Charles Dickens At Home, By His Eldest Daughter," p. 33.

244 **Edward Matthew Ward:** See illustration.

244 **"lots of little dogs":** Charles Collins, "Charles Dickens's Study," *The Graphic*, Christmas number 1870.

244 **"to resume his task":** James Fields, in *Interviews and Recollections*, p. 311.

245 **"Lady Dedlock's child":** Stone (ed.), *Dickens' Working Notes for His Novels*, p. 207.

245 **"compound interest":** *Bleak House*, ch. 1; further references are given only where it is not already clear from the context which chapter is being referred to.

246 **The appearance of a dinosaur:** in the *Household Words* article "Our Phantom Ship on an Antediluvian Cruise," published in the issue of 16 August 1851, Henry Morley had imagined boarding a ship at London Bridge and sailing back into the primeval past, where among the creatures he spots is "A sort of crocodile, thirty feet long, with a big body, mounted on high thick legs: Megalosaurus is his name, and, doubtless, greedy is his nature" (p. 494).

246 **"swept together":** "Of the Street-Dust in London, and the Loss and Injury Occasioned by it," *London Labour and the London Poor*, ii. 187–8.

246 **"Snow on snow":** First published in *Scribner's Monthly* (January 1872); the poem appeared as a hymn in the 1906 edition of the *English Hymnal* set to music by Gustav Holst.

249 **Georgina Hogarth:** Letter to George Harvey, 15 December 1880 (Morgan Library).

249 **"graces of imagination":** "A Preliminary Word," *Household Words*, 30 March 1850, p. 1.

249 **new and unexpected eloquence:** Francis Spufford brilliantly discusses the fictional recalibration of reality in *True Stories: and Other Essays* (New Haven: Yale University Press, 2017), pp. xii–xiii.

249 **"to the point of the pen":** To G. H. Lewes, [?9 June 1838], *Letters*, i. 403.

249 **earliest pages:** The manuscript forms part of the Forster collection at the V&A, reference number MSL/1876/Forster/162 (see illustration).

250 **"this dull blade":** To John Forster, [?10–16 March 1852], *Letters*, vi. 627.

250 **"grope his way":** *The Critical and Miscellaneous Writings of Sir Edward Bulwer Lytton*, 2 vols. (Philadelphia: Lea & Blanchard, 1841), i. 73.

251 **Dickens's "pledge":** *Athenaeum*, 6 March 1852, p. 270.

251 **an embarrassed apology:** To Mrs. Gaskell, 25 November 1851, *Letters*, vi. 545–6.

251 **"imaginary recollection":** "Through Bologna and Ferrara," *Pictures from Italy* (1846).

251 **"suddenly remembered it!":** *David Copperfield*, ch. 39.

251 **"scraps of old remembrances":** *Bleak House*, ch. 18.

252 **"many bits" of Rockingham Castle:** To the Hon. Mrs. Richard Watson, 27 August 1853, *Letters*, vii. 135.

252 **mirror images of each other:** I am drawing here on Robert Newsom's argument in *Dickens on the Romantic Side of Familiar Things*, p. 26; this chapter is

especially indebted to Newsom's sharp-eyed reading of the opening chapters of *Bleak House*.

253 **"tributary channels":** *Household Words*, 22 June 1850, co-written with W. H. Wills; the passage is discussed by David Trotter in *Circulation: Defoe, Dickens, and the Economies of the Novel* (Basingstoke: Macmillan, 1988), p. 103.

253 **Newsom has pointed out:** *Dickens on the Romantic Side of Familiar Things*, pp. 18–45.

253 **"the soot's falling":** *Bleak House*, ch. 32.

254 **" 'I am very dreary' ":** Tennyson, *Poems*, i. 10–14.

254 **"imperfections on my head":** *Hamlet*, I, iv.

254 **"moving at different speeds":** "Exploring the Medium," *Observer*, 4 February 1979.

255 **her name is Esther:** There were some recent precedents for this switching between wide-angle and close-up modes of narrative. The same tactic had been deployed four years earlier in Emily Brontë's *Wuthering Heights*, just as Dickens's story of a girl who grows up and goes to school under the impression she is an orphan had been anticipated by another novel published in 1847, Charlotte Brontë's *Jane Eyre*, although Dickens claimed that he hadn't read it and "disapproved of the whole school," *Interviews and Recollections*, pp. 289–90.

256 **"affecting and interesting kind":** To Miss Burdett Coutts, 10 September 1845, *Letters*, iv. 374–5.

256 **"jam-pots of Bleak House":** Quoted in Jeremy Hawthorn, *Bleak House* (Basingstoke: Macmillan, 1987), p. 26.

256 **"weak and twaddling":** To George Smith, 11 March 1852, *The Letters of Charlotte Brontë, Vol. 3: 1852–1855*, ed. Margaret Smith (Oxford: Oxford University Press, 2004), p. 27.

257 **"empty verbosity":** The full definition is "Senseless, silly, or trifling talk or writing; empty verbosity; dull and trashy statement or discourse; empty commonplace; prosy nonsense" (*OED* "twaddle," n. and adj. 1a).

257 **"a household word":** "Better Ties Than Red Tape," *Household Words*, 28 February 1852, p. 529.

259 **Dickens's appointed representative:** This is discussed by Tracy in "Lighthousekeeping: *Bleak House* and the Crystal Palace," pp. 48–9.

259 **"a system of Order":** To the Hon. Spencer Lyttelton, 9 October 1851, *Letters*, vi. 514.

259 **Dickens's favourite flower:** "He loved all flowers," Mamie Dickens wrote of her father, "but especially bright flowers, and scarlet geraniums were his favourite of all," "Charles Dickens At Home, By His Eldest Daughter," p. 43.

260 **"general Dickensian style":** Vladimir Nabokov, *Lectures on Literature*, ed. Fredson Bowers (Orlando, FL: Harcourt Brace, 1980), pp. 100–1.

260 **"outmuddling Chancery itself":** *Life*, iii. 45.

261 **"cracked walls":** *Bleak House*, chs. 8, 29, 28.

261 **"depression of spirits":** Ibid., ch. 7.

261 **"corpulent forefinger":** Ibid., ch. 22; Philip Collins points out further parallels in *Dickens and Crime*, pp. 207–8.

262 **"by the wrong end":** *Bleak House*, ch. 25.

261 **"my mother, cold and dead":** Ibid., ch. 59.

263 **"unnecessary detail":** George Orwell, "Charles Dickens," *Inside the Whale* (1940), repr. in *Charles Dickens: A Critical Anthology*, ed. Stephen Wall (Harmondsworth: Penguin, 1970), p. 308.

263 **"trifles make the sum of life":** *David Copperfield*, ch. 53.

265 **"since the Great Exhibition":** Emily Steinlight points out that the full-page advertisements for E. Moses and Son (a small chain of tailors and clothiers) that appeared on the inside of the jacket followed the seasons and playfully echoed the language of Dickens's serialisation, starting with an advertisement for overcoats in the first instalment under the headline "ANTI-BLEAK HOUSE"; see "'Anti-Bleak House': Advertising and the Victorian Novel," *Narrative*, vol. 14, no. 2 (May 2006), pp. 132–62.

265 **"nipping weather out of doors":** *Bleak House*, ch. 58.

265 **"knocking up against each other":** This connection is made by John Carey in *The Violent Effigy*, p. 113.

266 **"false whiskers, and a wig":** *Bleak House*, ch. 14.

266 **"shrinking out of sight":** Ibid., ch. 21.

267 **"and for us besides":** Ibid., ch. 8.

267 **"dead and dying infants":** *Supposing Bleak House* (Charlottesville and London: University of Virginia Press, 2011), p. 119.

267 **"shut out Nothing":** "What Christmas Is, As We Grow Older," *Household Words*, 25 December 1851, p. 2; further possible connections are suggested by John Butt in "'Bleak House' and the Context of 1851," *Nineteenth-Century Fiction*, vol. 10, no. 1 (June 1955), pp. 1–21, and Susan Shatto, *The Companion to Bleak House* (London: Unwin Hyman, 1988).

268 **"'God bless us all!'":** *Charles Dickens, by his Eldest Daughter*, p. 110, describing New Year's Eve at Gad's Hill Place.

268 **"kissings-in of new ones":** To C. C. Felton, 2 January 1844, *Letters*, iv. 2–3.

268 **"in half a minute":** *Life*, iii. 111.

268 **"caressed—by my lady":** *Bleak House*, chs. 8, 12. For more on this parallel, see Christopher Pittard, "The Travelling Doll Wonder: Dickens, Secular Magic, and *Bleak House*," *Studies in the Novel*, vol. 48, no. 3 (Fall 2016), pp. 279–300.

269 **"same Clown and Pantaloon still!":** *Household Words*, 20 December 1851, p. 289.

269 **Works of All Industry:** *Harlequin Hogarth; or, The Two London 'Prentices* (London: Thomas Hailes Lacy, n.d.), pp. 21–2.

AFTERWORD: THE WORLD'S STORY

273 **"a precipice in Time":** "The Fiddler of the Reels," originally commissioned for a special "Exhibition Number" of *Scribner's Magazine* (May 1893) to celebrate the Chicago World's Fair, repr. in *Life's Little Ironies* (New York: Harper & Brothers, 1894), pp. 157, 162.

273 **"like a fan before him":** Thomas Hardy, *A Pair of Blue Eyes* (London: Tinsley Brothers, 1873), p. 184.

274 **"turning-point in the world's story":** "Our Industries in the Crystal Palace," *The Art-Journal* 6 (1 June 1851), p. 181.

274 **"went our several ways":** To John Forster, [10 September 1854], *Letters*, vii. 412.

275 **"in a state of transition":** [William Henry Smith], "Voltaire in the Crystal Palace," *Blackwood's Edinburgh Magazine* 70 (August 1851), pp. 143–5.

275 **widely acclaimed:** See Sylvi Johansen, "The Great Exhibition of 1851: A Precipice in Time?," *Victorian Review*, vol. 22, no. 1 (Summer 1996), pp. 59–64. Historical surveys that choose this year as their starting point include Geoffrey Best's *Mid-Victorian Britain 1851–1875* (1972) and Asa Briggs's *Victorian People: A Reassessment of Persons and Themes 1851–1867* (1973).

275 **Great Victorian Way:** Paxton's other schemes included a glass roof over the Royal Exchange in London, hotels linked by a glass walkway, "Hothouses for the Millions," and a "diamond palace" in Paris with a giant Moorish dome. Of these plans only Paxton's mass-produced domestic greenhouses ever got beyond the blueprint stage; see Colquhoun, *A Thing in Disguise*, pp. 188–249.

276 **other cities worldwide:** See Miller, *Novels Behind Glass*, p. 57.

276 **"flatulent botheration":** To W. H. Wills, [15] July 1854, *Letters*, vii. 370.

276 **"long-suffering-people's shoulders":** To the Hon. Mrs. Richard Watson, 1 November 1854, *Letters*, vii. 453.

276 **"by looking back":** To Henry Austin, 21 January 1852, *Letters*, vi. 581.

276 **"the melting snow":** *Household Words*, 17 January 1852, p. 401.

277 **"for future generations":** *Report of the Twenty-First Meeting of the British Association for the Advancement of Science held at Ipswich in July 1851* (London: John Murray, 1852), p. 78.

277 **"furrows and wrinkles":** Sala, *Things I have Seen and People I have Known*, i. 74.

277 **A daguerreotype:** See Andrew Xavier, "A Newly-discovered Daguerreotype of Charles Dickens," *Dickensian* 97 (2001), p. 406. The daguerreotype (see illustration), in a Morocco leather case stamped with Mayall's trademark, was sold to a private collector at Christie's on 11 May 2001 for £39,950. Dickens was impressed by Mayall's skill, telling Miss Burdett Coutts after an earlier sitting at the end of 1852 that he was "quite a Genius," although having to remain still for several minutes inevitably produced a "slight rigidity and desperate grimness" in the sitter's features (*Letters*, vi. 834).

278 **"not younger":** To George W. Putnam, 24 July 1851, *Letters*, vi. 442.

278 **"the original Dickens about him":** *Interviews and Recollections*, pp. 205–6.

278 **known as Sloppy:** Leonardo Cattermole, in Kitton (ed.), *Dickens by Pen and Pencil*, p. 181; the editors of Dickens's letters note that Sloppy was "the subject of long-running jokes by CD, Forster and their friends who talked to him and 'learned various Sloppy-isms' when travelling to visit Cattermole" (*Letters*, vi. 576n.).

278 **"do the Police in different voices":** *Our Mutual Friend*, ch. 16.

278 **"transmit to posterity":** To W. P. Frith, 12 January 1859, *Letters*, ix. 9 (see illustration).

279   **"so many readers":** To the Hon. Mrs. Richard Watson, 27 August 1853,
       Letters, vii. 134.

280   **"upper-middle-class suburb":** Donald J. Olsen, *Town Planning in London: The
       Eighteenth and Nineteenth Centuries* (New Haven: Yale University Press, 1964),
       p. 44.

280   **he had *arrived*:** "arrive 11. *intransitive*. Of a person: to achieve success or
       recognition; to establish one's position or reputation. Frequently used with
       depreciative connotations of pretentiousness or affectation" (*OED*).

280   **"wonderfully well":** *Letters*, vi. 624; three days later some of the novelty had
       worn off, and Dickens told Miss Burdett Coutts that "on the whole I could
       have dispensed with him" (*Letters*, vi. 627).

280   **an instalment:** *Little Dorrit*, ch. 12.

281   **"talking with one another":** *Memoir of Henry Compton*, ed. Charles and
       Edward Compton (1879), repr. in *Interviews and Recollections*, p. 191.

281   **"Nobody can see":** *Bleak House*, ch. 1.

281   **"Nobody had appeared":** *Bleak House*, ch. 4.

281   **"autobiographical shake of the hand":** To A. H. Forrester, 3 February 1852,
       Letters, vi. 589.

282   **"hidden when he was born":** *Memoranda*, p. 6.

282   **"Is *this* my experience?":** Ibid., p. 10.

282   **declared insane:** This followed on from a public letter in which Dickens
       claimed that his wife had "a mental disorder under which she sometimes
       labours," and a further private letter to Miss Burdett Coutts in which he said of
       Catherine that "her mind has, at times, been certainly confused"; see John
       Bowen, "Madness and the Dickens Marriage: A New Source," *Dickensian* 115
       (2019), pp. 5–20.

282   **"to his purpose":** Edward Dutton Cook to William Thomas (7 January 1879),
       quoted in Bowen, "Madness and the Dickens Marriage," p. 9. Thomas knew
       Dickens well, having joined the *Household Words* office in 1851. In *Inconvenient
       People: Lunacy, Liberty and the Mad Doctors in Victorian England* (London: Bodley
       Head, 2012), Sarah Wise notes that "Descendants of Dr. Thomas Harrington
       Tuke, superintendent of Manor House Asylum in Chiswick between 1849 and
       1888, are believed to have seen correspondence in which the novelist asked
       Tuke to investigate the possibility of having his wife committed to Manor
       House. Allegedly, Tuke, in reply, refused, on the grounds that there was no
       evidence that Catherine was of unsound mind. The original letters were
       handed to a researcher in the 1970s and have been missing ever since; as no
       copies were ever made, this story cannot be verified" (pp. 247–8).

282   **"to the colonies long ago":** See Andrew Brown's entry on Edward Bulwer
       Lytton in the *DNB*.

282   **one of their novels:** In *Victorian Fiction: Writers, Publishers, Readers*
       (Basingstoke: Macmillan, 1995), John Sutherland points out that such
       well-publicised cases influenced later novels such as Wilkie Collins's *The
       Woman in White* (1859), which centres on the wrongful placing of a sane
       woman in an asylum, and was originally serialised in *All the Year Round*.

283 **"flippant sort of man":** See David Brooks, *The Road to Character* (New York: Random House, 2015), p. 164.

283 **"gravity Smash":** To Mrs. Charles Dickens, 21 November 1853, *Letters*, vii. 204.

284 **quietly melted away:** See Hack, "Literary Paupers and Professional Authors," p. 708.

284 **"to eclipse me":** Edward Bulwer Lytton to Robert Lytton, 21 November 1862, quoted in Mitchell, *Bulwer Lytton*, p. 120.

284 **"sanctions that policy":** Ibid., 3 November 1869, quoted ibid.

284 **"bereft of a home":** *Bleak House*, ch. 31.

284 **"cold, stiff, and dead":** "Chronicle," *The Annual Register, or a View of the History and Politics of the Year 1851*, pp. 105–6.

285 **"deaf ears of wealth":** *Lucretia: or, The Children of Night* (1846), quoted in Mitchell, *Bulwer Lytton*, p. 176. John Sutherland points out that Beck "turns out, preposterously, to be the villainous heroine's long lost son," which is also a possible link to the story of Esther's illegitimacy in *Bleak House*; see *Inside Bleak House*, p. 121.

285 **"very ragged":** *Bleak House*, ch. 11.

285 **persuade two of his sons:** He also dispatched Frank to join the Bengal Mounted Police, while Sydney joined the Royal Navy and Walter became an officer cadet in the East India Company's Presidency armies just before the Indian Rebellion of 1857.

285 **"as happy as a king":** Quoted in Thomas Keneally, "Travel: Dickens Down Under," *Guardian*, 7 November 2010.

285 **"an active life":** To the Rev. John Taylor, 14 January 1867, *Letters*, xi. 298; in a diary entry, Annie Field noted that Dickens was "often troubled by the lack of energy his children show" and also revealed "how deep his unhappiness is in having so many children by a wife who was totally uncongenial," quoted in *Letters*, xi. xiv.

286 **"in Bleak House again":** *Letters*, vi. 627.

286 **"connecting together!":** *Bleak House*, ch. 43.

286 **"the connexion in her mind":** Ibid., ch. 35.

287 **many possible answers:** Caroline Levine offers a more extended list in discussing how the characters in *Bleak House* are "linked through the law, disease, economics, class, gossip, the family tree, city streets, rural roads, and even global print and philanthropic networks," *Forms: Whole, Rhythm, Hierarchy, Network* (Princeton: Princeton University Press, 2015), p. 125.

287 **"a national writer":** *Speeches*, pp. 154–7.

287 **"Mrs. Jellyby's colonisation society":** *Peterson's Magazine*, vol. 26, no. 4 (October 1854), p. 216.

287 **"the suffering far away!":** "Borroboola Gha: A Poem for the Times," *Frederick Douglass's Paper* (2 February 1855); I am indebted for this example (and others in this section) to Daniel Hack's article "Close Reading at a Distance: The African Americanization of *Bleak House*," *Critical Inquiry*, vol. 34, no. 4 (Summer 2008), pp. 729–53 (p. 741).

288 **"fogs atmospheric and fogs legal"**: Matz (ed.), *Dickens in Cartoon and Caricature*, p. 84.

288 **"miseries of his kind"**: J. G. [Julia Griffiths], "Literary Notices," *Frederick Douglass's Paper* (3 June 1853), quoted in Hack, "Close Reading at a Distance," p. 740.

289 **"The Growlery"**: Ibid., p. 743 (see illustration).

289 **"expressly for my guardian"**: *Bleak House*, ch. 67.

289 **"Gloom everywhere"**: Hannah Crafts, *The Bondwoman's Narrative*, ed. Henry Louis Gates, Jr. (London: Virago Press, 2002), p. 157.

289 **"Fog everywhere"**: *Bleak House*, ch. 1.

289 **"I am not clever"**: *Bleak House*, ch. 3.

289 **"nor learned, nor talented"**: *The Bondwoman's Narrative*, p. 5.

289 **"love to myself if I could"**: *Bleak House*, ch. 3.

289 **"some love if I could"**: *The Bondwoman's Narrative*, p. 11.

289 **"a slave all my life"**: *Bleak House*, ch. 14.

290 **"the individual will"**: Preface to *The Portrait of a Lady* (London: Macmillan and Co., 1921), p. xi.

290 **"only the other day"**: Quoted in Hugh Epstein, "*Bleak House* and Conrad: the Presence of Dickens in Conrad's Writing," *Conrad: Essays in Contexts and Appropriations: Essays in Memory of Yves Hervouet*, ed. Gene M. Moore, Owen Knowles, and J. H. Stape (Amsterdam and Atlanta, GA: Rodopi, 1997), p. 119.

290 **"such a good plot"**: Quoted in Andrew Sanders, *Charles Dickens Resurrectionist* (London: Macmillan, 1982), p. 141.

290 **"derryjellybies"**: James Joyce, *Finnegans Wake* (New York: The Viking Press, 1939), p. 6.

290 **"never quite the same again"**: Norman Page, *Bleak House: A Novel of Connections* (Woodbridge, CT: Twayne Publishers, 1990), p. 17.

290 **"so much *in* this world"**: Kitton (ed.), *Dickens by Pen and Pencil, Supplement*, p. 52.

291 **"a window near his platform"**: *Interviews and Recollections*, p. 41.

Index

List of Illustrations

A Note About the Author

ROBERT DOUGLAS-FAIRHURST is a professor of English literature at the University of Oxford, and a fellow of Magdalen College. His books include *Becoming Dickens: The Invention of a Novelist,* which won the Duff Cooper Prize, and *The Story of Alice: Lewis Carroll and the Secret History of Wonderland,* which was shortlisted for the Costa Biography Award and was a BBC Radio 4 Book of the Week. He writes regularly for publications including *The Times, The Guardian, The Times Literary Supplement* and *The Spectator.* Radio and television appearances include *Start the Week* and *The Culture Show.* He has also acted as the historical consultant on TV adaptations of *Jane Eyre, Emma* and *Great Expectations;* the BBC drama series *Dickensian* and the feature film *Enola Holmes.* In 2015, he was elected a fellow of the Royal Society of Literature. He lives in Oxford, England.